THE HERO WITH A THOUSAND FACES

The Collected Works of Joseph Campbell

Thou Art That:
Transforming Religious Metaphor

The Inner Reaches of Outer Space:
Metaphor as Myth and as Religion

Flight of the Wild Gander: Selected Essays 1944–1968

Sake & Satori: Asian Journals—Japan

Baksheesh & Brahman: Asian Journals—India

The Hero's Journey:
Joseph Campbell on His Life and Work

Myths of Light:
Eastern Metaphors of the Eternal

Mythic Worlds, Modern Words:
Joseph Campbell on the Art of James Joyce

Pathways to Bliss:
Mythology and Personal Transformation

A Skeleton Key to Finnegans Wake:
Unlocking James Joyce's Masterwork

The Mythic Dimension: Selected Essays 1959–1987

The Hero with a Thousand Faces

Mythic Imagination: Collected Short Fiction

Goddesses: Mysteries of the Feminine Divine

Romance of the Grail: The Magic and Mystery of Arthurian Myth

More titles forthcoming

THE HERO WITH A THOUSAND FACES

BOLLINGEN SERIES XVII

THIRD EDITION

Joseph Campbell

JOSEPH CAMPBELL™
FOUNDATION

YogiImpressions®

YogiImpressions®
Yogi Impressions LLP
1711, Centre 1, World Trade Centre,
Cuffe Parade, Mumbai 400 005, India.
Website: www.yogiimpressions.com

Originally published in the United States by
New World Library, 2008

First India Printing: December 2017
Ninth reprint: November 2022
ISBN 978-93-82742-87-6

Printed at: Manipal Technologies Limited

TO MY FATHER AND MOTHER

Since its release in 1949, *The Hero with a Thousand Faces* has influenced millions of readers by combining the insights of modern psychology with Joseph Campbell's revolutionary understanding of comparative mythology. In these pages, Campbell outlines the Hero's Journey, a universal motif of adventure and transformation that runs through virtually all of the world's mythic traditions. He also explores the Cosmogonic Cycle, the mythic pattern of world creation and destruction.

As part of the Joseph Campbell Foundation's Collected Works of Joseph Campbell, this third edition features expanded illustrations, a comprehensive bibliography, and more accessible sidebars.

As relevant today as when it was first published, *The Hero with a Thousand Faces* continues to find new audiences in fields ranging from religion and anthropology to literature and film studies. The book has also profoundly influenced creative artists – including authors, songwriters, game designers, and filmmakers – and continues to inspire all those interested in the inherent human need to tell stories.

CONTENTS

ABOUT THE COLLECTED WORKS OF JOSEPH CAMPBELL

AT HIS DEATH in 1987, Joseph Campbell left a significant body of published work that explored his lifelong passion, the complex of universal myths and symbols that he called "Mankind's one great story." He also left, however, a large volume of unreleased work: uncollected articles, notes, letters, and diaries, as well as audio- and videotape-recorded lectures.

The Joseph Campbell Foundation—founded in 1990 to preserve, protect, and perpetuate Campbell's work—has undertaken to create a digital archive of his papers and recordings and to publish *The Collected Works of Joseph Campbell.*

THE COLLECTED WORKS OF JOSEPH CAMPBELL
Robert Walter, Executive Editor
David Kudler, Managing Editor

PREFACE TO THE 1949 EDITION

"THE TRUTHS CONTAINED in religious doctrines are after all so distorted and systematically disguised," writes Sigmund Freud,

> that the mass of humanity cannot recognize them as truth. The case is similar to what happens when we tell a child that newborn babies are brought by the stork. Here, too, we are telling the truth in symbolic clothing, for we know what the large bird signifies. But the child does not know it. He hears only the distorted part of what we say, and feels that he has been deceived; and we know how often his distrust of the grown-ups and his refractoriness actually take their start from this impression. We have become convinced that it is better to avoid such symbolic disguisings of the truth in what we tell children and not to withhold from them a knowledge of the true state of affairs commensurate with their intellectual level.[1]

It is the purpose of the present book to uncover some of the truths disguised for us under the figures of religion and mythology by bringing together a multitude of not-too-difficult examples and letting the ancient meaning become apparent of itself. The old teachers knew what they were saying. Once we have learned to read again their symbolic language, it requires no more than the talent of an anthologist to let their teaching be heard. But first we must learn the grammar of the symbols, and as a key to this mystery I know of no better modern tool than psychoanalysis. Without regarding this as the last word on the subject, one can nevertheless permit it to serve as an approach. The second step will be then to bring together a host of myths and folktales from every corner of the world, and to let the symbols speak for themselves. The parallels will be immediately apparent; and these will develop a vast and amazingly constant statement of the basic truths by which man has lived throughout the millennia of his residence on the planet.

Perhaps it will be objected that in bringing out the correspondences I have overlooked the differences between the various Oriental and Occidental, modern, ancient, and primitive traditions. The same objection might be brought, however, against any textbook or chart of anatomy, where the physiological variations of race are disregarded in the interest of a basic general understanding of the human physique. There are of course differences between the numerous mythologies and religions of mankind, but this is a book about the similarities; and once these are understood the differences will be found to be much less great than is popularly (and politically) supposed. My hope is that a comparative elucidation may contribute to the perhaps not-quite-desperate cause of those forces that are working in the present world for unification, not in the name of some ecclesiastical or political empire, but in the sense of human mutual understanding. As we are told in the Vedas: "Truth is one, the sages speak of it by many names."[2]

For help in the long task of bringing my materials into readable form, I wish to thank Mr. Henry Morton Robinson, whose advice greatly assisted me in the first and final stages of the work, Mrs. Peter Geiger, Mrs. Margaret Wing, and Mrs. Helen McMaster, who went over the manuscripts many times and offered invaluable suggestions, and my wife, who has worked with me from first to last, listening, reading, and revising.

—J. C.

NEW YORK CITY | JUNE 10, 1948

FIGURE 1. *Medusa* (carved marble, Roman, Italy, date uncertain)

PROLOGUE

The Monomyth

1. *Myth and Dream*

WHETHER WE LISTEN with aloof amusement to the dreamlike mumbo jumbo of some red-eyed witch doctor of the Congo, or read with cultivated rapture thin translations from the sonnets of the mystic Lao-tse; now and again crack the hard nutshell of an argument of Aquinas, or catch suddenly the shining meaning of a bizarre Eskimo fairy tale: it will always be the one, shape-shifting yet marvelously constant story that we find, together with a challengingly persistent suggestion of more remaining to be experienced than will ever be known or told.

Throughout the inhabited world, in all times and under every circumstance, myths of man have flourished; and they have been the living inspiration of whatever else may have appeared out of the activities of the human body and mind. It would not be too much to say that myth is the secret opening through which the inexhaustible energies of the cosmos pour into the human cultural manifestation. Religions, philosophies, arts, the social forms of primitive and historic man, prime discoveries in science and technology, the very dreams that blister sleep, boil up from the basic, magic ring of myth.

The wonder is that characteristic efficacy to touch and inspire deep creative centers dwells in the smallest nursery fairy tale—as the flavor of the ocean is contained in a droplet or the whole mystery of life within the egg of a flea. For the symbols of mythology are not manufactured; they cannot be ordered, invented, or permanently suppressed. They are spontaneous productions of the psyche, and each bears within it, undamaged, the germ power of its source.

What is the secret of the timeless vision? From what profundity of the mind does it derive? Why is mythology everywhere the same, beneath its varieties of costume? And what does it teach?

Today many scientists are contributing to the analysis of the riddle. Archeologists are probing the ruins of Iraq, Honan, Crete, and Yucatan. Ethnologists are questioning the Ostiaks of the river Ob, the Boobies of Fernando Po. A generation of orientalists has recently thrown open to us the sacred writings of the East, as well as the pre-Hebrew sources of our own Holy Writ. And meanwhile another host of scholars, pressing researches begun last century in the field of folk psychology, has been seeking to establish the psychological bases of language, myth, religion, art development, and moral codes.

Most remarkable of all, however, are the revelations that have emerged from the mental clinic. The bold and truly epoch-making writings of the psychoanalysts are indispensable to the student of mythology; for, whatever may be thought of the detailed and sometimes contradictory interpretations of specific cases and problems, Freud, Jung, and their followers have demonstrated irrefutably that the logic, the heroes, and the deeds of myth survive into modern times. In the absence of an effective general mythology, each of us has his private, unrecognized, rudimentary, yet secretly potent pantheon of dream. The latest incarnation of Oedipus, the continued romance of Beauty and the Beast, stand this afternoon on the corner of Forty-second Street and Fifth Avenue, waiting for the traffic light to change.

"I dreamed," wrote an American youth to the author of a syndicated newspaper feature,

> that I was reshingling our roof. Suddenly I heard my father's voice on the ground below, calling to me. I turned suddenly to hear him better, and, as I did so, the hammer slipped out of my hands, and slid down the sloping roof, and disappeared over the edge. I heard a heavy thud, as of a body falling.
>
> Terribly frightened, I climbed down the ladder to the ground. There was my father lying dead on the ground, with blood all over his head. I was brokenhearted, and began calling my mother, in the midst of my sobs. She came out of the house, and put her arms around me. "Never mind, son, it was all an accident," she said. "I know you will take care of me, even if he is gone." As she was kissing me, I woke up.

FIGURE 2. *Viṣṇu Dreaming the Universe* (carved stone, India, c. A.D. 400–700)

> I am the eldest child in our family and am twenty-three years old. I have been separated from my wife for a year; somehow, we could not get along together. I love both my parents dearly, and have never had any trouble with my father, except that he insisted that I go back and live with my wife, and I couldn't be happy with her. And I never will.[1]

The unsuccessful husband here reveals, with a really wonderful innocence, that instead of bringing his spiritual energies forward to the love and problems of his marriage, he has been resting, in the secret recesses of his imagination, with the now ridiculously anachronistic dramatic situation of his first and only emotional involvement, that of the tragicomic triangle of the nursery—the son against the father for the love of the mother. Apparently the most permanent of the dispositions of the human psyche are those that derive from the fact that, of all animals, we remain the longest at the mother breast. Human beings are born too soon; they are unfinished, unready as yet to meet the world. Consequently their whole defense from a universe of dangers is the mother, under whose protection the intra-uterine period is prolonged.[2] Hence the dependent child and its mother constitute for months after the catastrophe of birth a dual unit, not only physically but also psychologically.[3] Any prolonged absence of the parent causes tension in the infant and consequent impulses of aggression; also, when the mother is obliged to hamper the child, aggressive responses are aroused. Thus the first object of the child's hostility is identical with the first object of its love, and its first ideal (which thereafter is retained as the unconscious basis of all images of bliss, truth, beauty, and perfection) is that of the dual unity of the Madonna and Bambino.[4]

The unfortunate father is the first radical intrusion of another order of reality into the beatitude of this earthly restatement of the excellence of the situation within the womb; he, therefore, is experienced primarily as an enemy. To him is transferred the charge of aggression that was originally attached to the "bad," or absent mother, while the desire attaching to the "good," or present, nourishing, and protecting mother, she herself (normally) retains. This fateful infantile distribution of death (*thanatos: destrudo*) and love (*eros: libido*) impulses builds the foundation of the now celebrated Oedipus complex, which Sigmund Freud pointed out some fifty years ago as the great cause of our adult failure to behave like rational beings. As Dr. Freud has stated it: "King Oedipus, who slew his father Laïus and married his mother Jocasta, merely shows us the fulfilment of our own childhood wishes. But, more fortunate than he, we have meanwhile succeeded, in so far as we have not become psychoneurotics, in detaching our sexual impulses from our mothers and in forgetting our jealousy of our fathers."[5]* Or, as he writes again: "Every pathological disorder of sexual life is rightly to be regarded as an inhibition in development."[6]

For many a man hath seen himself in dreams
His mother's mate, but he who gives no heed
To such like matters bears the easier fate.[7]

---

* It has been pointed out that the father also can be experienced as a protector and the mother, then, as a temptress. This is the way from Oedipus to Hamlet. "O God, I could be bounded in a nutshell and count myself a king of infinite space, were it not that I have bad dreams" (*Hamlet* II.ii). "All neurotics," writes Dr. Freud, "are either Oedipus or Hamlet."

And as for the case of the daughter (which is one degree more complicated), the following passage will suffice for the present thumbnail exposition. "I dreamed last night that my father stabbed my mother in the heart. She died. I knew no one blamed him for what he did, although I was crying bitterly. The dream seemed to change, and he and I seemed to be going on a trip together, and I was very happy." This is the dream of an unmarried young woman of twenty-four (Wood, *Dreams*, p. 130).

The sorry plight of the wife of the lover whose sentiments instead of maturing remain locked in the romance of the nursery may be judged from the apparent nonsense of another modern dream; and here we begin to feel indeed that we are entering the realm of ancient myth, but with a curious turn.

"I dreamed," wrote a troubled woman,

> that a big white horse kept following me wherever I went. I was afraid of him, and pushed him away. I looked back to see if he was still following me, and he appeared to have become a man. I told him to go inside a barbershop and shave off his mane, which he did. When he came out he looked just like a man, except that he had horse's hoofs and face, and followed me wherever I went. He came closer to me, and I woke up.
>
> I am a married woman of thirty-five with two children. I have been married for fourteen years now, and I am sure my husband is faithful to me.[8]

The unconscious sends all sorts of vapors, odd beings, terrors, and deluding images up into the mind—whether in dream, broad daylight, or insanity; for the human kingdom, beneath the floor of the comparatively neat little dwelling that we call our consciousness, goes down into unsuspected Aladdin caves. There not only jewels but also dangerous jinn abide: the inconvenient or resisted psychological powers that we have not thought or dared to integrate into our lives. And they may remain unsuspected, or, on the other hand, some chance word, the smell of a landscape, the taste of a cup of tea, or the glance of an eye may touch a magic spring, and then dangerous messengers begin to appear in the brain. These are dangerous because they threaten the fabric of the security into which we have built ourselves and our family. But they are fiendishly fascinating too, for they carry keys that open the whole realm of the desired and feared adventure of the discovery of the self. Destruction of the world that we have built and in which we live, and of ourselves within it; but then a wonderful reconstruction, of the bolder, cleaner, more spacious, and fully human life—that is the lure, the promise and terror, of these disturbing night visitants from the mythological realm that we carry within.

Psychoanalysis, the modern science of reading dreams, has taught us to take heed of these unsubstantial images. Also it has found a way to let them do their work. The dangerous crises of self-development are permitted to come to pass under the protecting eye of an experienced initiate in the lore and language of dreams, who then enacts the role and character of the ancient mystagogue, or guide of souls, the initiating medicine man of the primitive forest sanctuaries of trial and initiation. The doctor is the modern master of the mythological realm, the knower of all the secret ways and words of potency. His role is precisely that of the Wise Old Man of the myths and fairy-tales whose words assist the hero through the trials and terrors of the weird adventure. He is the one who appears and points to the magic shining sword that will kill the dragon-terror, tells of the waiting bride and the castle of many treasures, applies healing balm to the almost fatal wounds, and finally dismisses the conqueror, back into the world of normal life, following the great adventure into the enchanted night.

When we turn now, with this image in mind, to consider the numerous strange rituals that have been reported from the primitive tribes and great civilizations of the past, it becomes apparent that the purpose and actual effect of these was to conduct people across those difficult thresholds of transformation that demand a change in the patterns not only of conscious but also of unconscious life. The so-called rites of passage, which occupy such a prominent place in the life of a primitive society (ceremonials of birth, naming, puberty, marriage, burial, etc.), are distinguished by formal, and usually very severe, exercises of severance, whereby the mind is radically cut away from the attitudes, attachments, and life patterns of the stage being left behind.* Then follows an interval of more or less extended retirement, during which are enacted rituals designed to introduce the life adventurer to the forms and proper feelings of his new estate, so that when, at last, the time has ripened for the return to the normal world, the initiate will be as good as reborn.[9]

Most amazing is the fact that a great number of the ritual trials and images correspond to those that appear automatically in dream the moment the psychoanalyzed patient begins to abandon his infantile fixations and to progress into the future. Among the aborigines of Australia, for example, one of the principal features of the ordeal of initiation (by which the boy at puberty is cut away from the mother and inducted into the society and secret lore of the men) is the rite of circumcision.

---

* In such ceremonials as those of birth and burial, the significant effects are, of course, those experienced by the parents and relatives. All rites of passage are intended to touch not only the candidate but also every member of his circle.

> When a little boy of the Murngin tribe is about to be circumcised, he is told by his fathers and by the old men, "The Great Father Snake smells your foreskin; he is calling for it." The boys believe this to be literally true, and become extremely frightened. Usually they take refuge with their mother, mother's mother, or some other favorite female relative, for they know that the men are organized to see that they are taken to the men's ground, where the great snake is bellowing. The women wail over the boys ceremonially; this is to keep the great snake from swallowing them.[10]

Now regard the counterpart from the unconscious. "One of my patients," writes Dr. C. G. Jung, "dreamt that a snake shot out of a cave and bit him in the genital region. This dream occurred at the moment when the patient was convinced of the truth of the analysis and was beginning to free himself from the bonds of his mother-complex."[11]

It has always been the prime function of mythology and rite to supply the symbols that carry the human spirit forward, in counteraction to those constant human fantasies that tend to tie it back. In fact, it may well be that the very high incidence of neuroticism among ourselves follows from the decline among us of such effective spiritual aid. We remain fixated to the unexercised images of our infancy, and hence disinclined to the necessary passages of our adulthood. In the United States there is even a pathos of inverted emphasis: the goal is not to grow old, but to remain young; not to mature away from Mother, but to cleave to her. And so, while husbands are worshiping at their boyhood shrines, being the lawyers, merchants, or masterminds their parents wanted them to be, their wives, even after fourteen years of marriage and two fine children produced and raised, are still on the search for love—which can come to them only from the centaurs, sileni, satyrs, and other concupiscent incubi of the rout of Pan, either as in the second of the above-recited dreams, or as in our popular, vanilla-frosted temples of the venereal goddess, under the make-up of the latest heroes of the screen.

The psychoanalyst has to come along, at last, to assert again the tried wisdom of the older, forward-looking teachings of the masked medicine dancers and the witch-doctor-circumcisers; whereupon we find, as in the dream of the serpent bite, that the ageless initiation symbolism is produced spontaneously by the patient himself at the moment of the release. Apparently, there is something in these initiatory images so necessary to the psyche that if they are not supplied from without, through myth and ritual, they will have to be announced again, through dream, from within—lest our energies should remain locked in a banal, long-outmoded toy-room, at the bottom of the sea.

Sigmund Freud stresses in his writings the passages and difficulties of the first half of the human cycle of life—those of our infancy and adolescence, when our sun is mounting toward its zenith. C. G. Jung, on the other hand, has emphasized the crises of the second portion—when, in order to advance, the shining sphere must submit to descend and disappear, at last, into the night-womb of the grave. The normal symbols of our desires and fears become converted, in this afternoon of the biography, into their opposites; for it is then no longer life but death that is the challenge. What is difficult to leave, then, is not the womb but the phallus—unless, indeed, the life-weariness has already seized the heart, when it will be death that calls with the promise of bliss that formerly was the lure of love. Full circle, from the tomb of the womb to the womb of the tomb, we come: an ambiguous, enigmatical incursion into a world of solid matter that is soon to melt from us, like the substance of a dream. And, looking back at what had promised to be our own unique, unpredictable, and dangerous adventure, all we find in the end is such a series of standard metamorphoses as men and women have undergone in every quarter of the world, in all recorded centuries, and under every odd disguise of civilization.

The story is told, for example, of the great Minos, king of the island empire of Crete in the period of its commercial supremacy: how he hired the celebrated artist-craftsman Daedalus to invent and construct for him a labyrinth, in which to hide something of which the palace was at once ashamed and afraid. For there was a monster on the premises—which had been born to Pasiphaë, the queen. Minos, the king, had been busy, it is said, with important wars to protect the trade routes; and meanwhile Pasiphaë had been seduced by a magnificent, snow-white, seaborn bull. It had been nothing worse, really, than what Minos' own mother had allowed to happen: Minos' mother was Europa, and it is well known that she was carried by a bull to Crete. The bull had been the god Zeus, and the honored son of that sacred union was Minos himself—now everywhere respected and gladly served. How then could Pasiphaë have known that the fruit of her own indiscretion would be a monster: this little son with human body but the head and tail of a bull?

Society has blamed the queen greatly; but the king was not unconscious of his own share of guilt. The bull in question had been sent by the god Poseidon, long ago, when Minos was contending with his brothers for the throne. Minos had asserted that the throne was his, by divine right, and had prayed the god to send up a bull out of the sea, as a sign; and he had sealed the prayer with a vow to sacrifice the animal immediately, as an offering and symbol of service. The bull had appeared, and Minos took the throne; but when he beheld the majesty of the beast that had been sent and thought what an advantage it would be to possess such a specimen, he determined to risk a merchant's substitution—of which he supposed the god would take no great account. Offering on Poseidon's altar the finest white bull that he owned, he added the other to his herd.

FIGURE 3. *Sileni and Maenads* (black-figure amphora, Hellenic, Sicily, c. 500–450 B.C.)

The Cretan empire had greatly prospered under the sensible jurisdiction of this celebrated lawgiver and model of public virtue. Knossos, the capital city, became the luxurious, elegant center of the leading commercial power of the civilized world. The Cretan fleets went out to every isle and harbor of the Mediterranean; Cretan ware was prized in Babylonia and Egypt. The bold little ships even broke through the Gates of Hercules to the open ocean, coasting then northward to take the gold of Ireland and the tin of Cornwall,[12] as well as southward, around the bulge of Senegal, to remote Yorubaland and the distant marts of ivory, gold, and slaves.[13]

But at home, the queen had been inspired by Poseidon with an ungovernable passion for the bull. And she had prevailed upon her husband's artist-craftsman, the peerless Daedalus, to frame for her a wooden cow that would deceive the bull—into which she eagerly entered; and the bull was deceived. She bore her monster, which, in due time, began to become a danger. And so Daedalus again was summoned, this time by the king, to construct a tremendous labyrinthine enclosure, with blind passages, in which to hide the thing away. So deceptive was the invention, that Daedalus himself, when he had finished it, was scarcely able to find his way back to the entrance. Therein the Minotaur was settled; and he was fed, thereafter, on groups of living youths and maidens, carried as tribute from the conquered nations within the Cretan domain.[14]

Thus according to the ancient legend, the primary fault was not the queen's but the king's; and he could not really blame her, for he knew what he had done. He had converted a public event to personal gain, whereas the whole sense of his investiture as king had been that he was no longer a mere private person. The return of the bull should have symbolized his absolutely selfless submission to the functions of his role. The retaining of it represented, on the other hand, an impulse to egocentric self-aggrandizement. And so the king "by the grace of God" became the dangerous tyrant Holdfast—out for himself. Just as the traditional rites of passage used to teach the individual to die to the past and be reborn to the future, so the great ceremonials of investiture divested him of his private character and clothed him in the mantle of his vocation. Such was the ideal, whether the man was a craftsman or a king. By the sacrilege of the refusal of the rite, however, the individual cut himself as a unit off from the larger unit of the whole community: and so the One was broken into the many, and these then battled each other—each out for himself—and could be governed only by force.

The figure of the tyrant-monster is known to the mythologies, folk traditions, legends, and even nightmares of the world; and his characteristics are everywhere essentially the same. He is the hoarder of the general benefit. He is the monster avid for the greedy rights of "my and mine." The havoc wrought by him is described in mythology and fairy tale as being universal throughout his domain. This may be no more than his household, his own tortured psyche, or the lives that he blights with the touch of his friendship and assistance; or it may amount to the extent of his civilization. The inflated ego of the tyrant is a curse to himself and his world—no matter how his affairs may seem to prosper. Self-terrorized, fear-haunted, alert at every hand to meet and battle back the anticipated aggressions of his environment, which are primarily the reflections of the uncontrollable impulses to acquisition within himself, the giant of self-achieved independence is the world's messenger of disaster, even though, in his mind, he may entertain himself with humane intentions. Wherever he sets his hand there is a cry (if not from the housetops, then—more miserably—within every heart): a cry for the redeeming hero, the carrier of the shining blade, whose blow, whose touch, whose existence, will liberate the land.

Here one can neither stand nor lie nor sit
There is not even silence in the mountains
But dry sterile thunder without rain
There is not even solitude in the mountains
But red sullen faces sneer and snarl
From doors of mudcracked houses[15]

The hero is the man of self-achieved submission. But submission to what? That precisely is the riddle that today we have to ask ourselves and that it is everywhere the primary virtue and historic deed of the hero to have solved. As Professor Arnold J. Toynbee indicates in his six-volume study of the laws of the rise and disintegration of civilizations,[16] schism in the soul, schism in the body social, will not be resolved by any scheme of return to the good old days (archaism), or by programs guaranteed to render an ideal projected future (futurism), or even by the most realistic, hardheaded work to weld together again the deteriorating elements. Only birth can conquer death—the birth, not of the old thing again, but of something new. Within the soul, within the body social, there must be—if we are to experience long survival—a continuous "recurrence of birth" (*palingenesia*) to nullify the unremitting recurrences of death. For it is by means of our own victories, if we are not regenerated, that the work of Nemesis is wrought: doom breaks from the shell of our very virtue. Peace then is a snare; war is a snare; change is a snare; permanence a snare. When our day is come for the victory of death, death closes in; there is nothing we can do, except be crucified—and resurrected; dismembered totally, and then reborn.

Theseus, the hero-slayer of the Minotaur, entered Crete from without, as the symbol and arm of the rising civilization of the Greeks. That was the new and living thing. But it is possible also for the principle of regeneration to be sought and found within the very walls of the tyrant's empire itself. Professor Toynbee uses the terms "detachment" and "transfiguration" to describe the crisis by which the higher spiritual dimension is attained that makes possible the resumption of the work of creation. The first step, detachment or withdrawal, consists in a radical transfer of emphasis from the external to the internal world, macro- to microcosm, a retreat from the desperations of the waste land to the peace of the everlasting realm that is within. But this realm, as we know from psychoanalysis, is precisely the infantile unconscious. It is the realm that we enter in sleep. We carry it within ourselves forever. All the ogres and secret helpers of our nursery are there, all the magic of childhood. And more important, all the life-potentialities that we never managed to bring to adult realization, those other portions of ourself, are there; for such golden seeds do not die. If only a portion of that lost totality could be dredged up into the light of day, we should experience a marvelous expansion of our powers, a vivid renewal of life. We should tower in stature. Moreover, if we could dredge up something forgotten not only by ourselves but by our whole generation or our entire civilization, we should become indeed the boon-bringer, the culture hero of the day—a personage of not only local but world historical moment. In a word: the first work of the hero is to retreat from the world scene of secondary effects to those causal zones of the psyche where the difficulties really reside, and there to clarify the difficulties, eradicate them in his own case (i.e., give battle to the nursery demons of his local culture) and break through to the undistorted, direct experience and assimilation of what C. G. Jung has called "the archetypal images."[17] This is the process known to Hindu and Buddhist philosophy as *viveka,* "discrimination."

As Dr. Jung points out, the theory of the archetypes is by no means his own invention.[18]

Compare Nietzsche: "In our sleep and in our dreams we pass through the whole thought of earlier humanity. I mean, in the same way that man reasons in his dreams, he reasoned when in the waking state many thousands of years.... The dream carries us back into earlier states of human culture, and affords us a means of understanding it better."[19]

Compare Adolf Bastian's theory of the ethnic "Elementary Ideas" (*Elementargedanken*), which, in their primal psychic character (corresponding to the Stoic *Logoi spermatikoi*), should be regarded as "the spiritual (or psychic) germinal dispositions out of which the whole social structure has been developed organically," and, as such, should serve as bases of inductive research.[20]

Compare Franz Boas: "Since Waitz's thorough discussion of the question of the unity of the human species, there can be no doubt that in the main the mental characteristics of man are the same all over the world.... Bastian was led to speak of the appalling monotony of the fundamental ideas of mankind all over the globe.... Certain patterns of associated ideas may be recognized in all types of culture."[21]

Compare Sir James G. Frazer: "We need not, with some enquirers in ancient and modern times, suppose that the Western peoples borrowed from the older civilization of the Orient the conception of the Dying and Reviving God, together with the solemn ritual, in which that conception was dramatically set forth before the eyes of the worshippers. More probably the resemblance which may be traced in this respect between the religions of the East and West is no more than what we commonly, though incorrectly, call a fortuitous coincidence, the effect of similar causes acting alike on the similar constitution of the human mind in different countries and under different skies."[22]

Compare Sigmund Freud: "I recognized the presence of symbolism in dreams from the very beginning. But it was only by degrees and as my experience increased that I arrived at a full appreciation of its extent and significance, and I did so under the influence of... Wilhelm Stekel.... Stekel arrived at his interpretations of symbols by way of intuition, thanks to a peculiar gift for the direct understanding of them.... Advances in psycho-analytic experience have brought to our notice patients who have shown a direct understanding of dream-symbolism of this kind to a surprising extent.... This symbolism is not peculiar to dreams, but is characteristic of unconscious ideation, in particular among the people, and it is to be found in folklore, and in popular myths, legends, linguistic idioms, proverbial wisdom and current jokes, to a more complete extent than in dreams."[23]

Dr. Jung points out that he has borrowed his term *archetype* from classic sources: Cicero, Pliny, the *Corpus Hermeticum,* Augustine, etc.[24] Bastian notes the correspondence of his own theory of "Elementary Ideas" with the Stoic concept of the *Logoi spermatikoi.* The tradition of the "subjectively known forms" (Sanskrit: *antarjñeya-rūpa*) is, in fact, coextensive with the tradition of myth, and is the key to the understanding and use of mythological images—as will appear abundantly in the following chapters.

The archetypes to be discovered and assimilated are precisely those that have inspired, throughout the annals of human culture, the basic images of ritual, mythology, and vision. These "Eternal Ones of the Dream"[25] are not to be confused with the personally modified symbolic figures that appear in nightmare and madness to the still tormented individual. Dream is the personalized myth, myth the depersonalized dream; both myth and dream are symbolic in the same general way of the dynamics of the psyche. But in the dream the forms are quirked by the peculiar troubles of the dreamer, whereas in myth the problems and solutions shown are directly valid for all mankind.

FIGURE 4. *Minotauromachy* (red-figure krater, Greece, c. 470 B.C.)

The hero, therefore, is the man or woman who has been able to battle past his personal and local historical limitations to the generally valid, normally human forms. Such a one's visions, ideas, and inspirations come pristine from the primary springs of human life and thought. Hence they are eloquent, not of the present, disintegrating society and psyche, but of the unquenched source through which society is reborn. The hero has died as a modern man; but as eternal man—perfected, unspecific, universal man—he has been reborn. His second solemn task and deed therefore (as Toynbee declares and as all the mythologies of mankind indicate) is to return then to us, transfigured, and teach the lesson he has learned of life renewed.

It must be noted against Professor Toynbee, however, that he seriously misrepresents the mythological scene when he advertises Christianity as the only religion teaching this second task. *All* religions teach it, as do all mythologies and folk traditions everywhere. Professor Toynbee arrives at his misconstruction by way of a trite and incorrect interpretation of the Oriental ideas of *nirvāṇa*, Buddha, and Bodhisattva; then contrasting these ideals, as he misinterprets them, with a very sophisticated rereading of the Christian idea of the City of God. This is what leads him to the error of supposing that the salvation of the present world-situation might lie in a return to the arms of the Roman Catholic church.

"I was walking alone around the upper end of a large city, through slummy, muddy streets lined with hard little houses," writes a modern woman, describing a dream that she has had.

> I did not know where I was, but liked the exploring. I chose one street which was terribly muddy and led across what must have been an open sewer. I followed along between rows of shanties and then discovered a little river flowing between me and some high, firm ground where there was a paved street. This was a nice, perfectly clear river, flowing over grass. I could see the grass moving under the water. There was no way to cross, so I went to a little house and asked for a boat. A man there said of course he could help me cross. He brought out a small wooden box which he put on the edge of the river and I saw at once that with this box I could easily jump across. I knew all danger was over and I wanted to reward the man richly.
>
> In thinking of this dream I have a distinct feeling that I did not have to go where I was at all but could have chosen a comfortable walk along paved streets. I had gone to the squalid and muddy district because I preferred adventure, and, having begun, I had to go on. . . . When I think of how persistently I kept going straight ahead in the dream, it seems as though I must have known there was something fine ahead, like that lovely, grassy river and the secure, high, paved road beyond. Thinking of it in those terms, it is like a determination to be born—or rather to be born again—in a sort of spiritual sense. Perhaps some of us have to go through dark and devious ways before we can find the river of peace or the highroad to the soul's destination.[26]

The dreamer is a distinguished operatic artist, and, like all who have elected to follow, not the safely marked general highways of the day, but the adventure of the special, dimly audible call that comes to those whose ears are open within as well as without, she has had to make her way alone, through difficulties not commonly encountered, "through slummy, muddy streets"; she has known the dark night of the soul, Dante's "dark wood, midway in the journey of our life," and the sorrows of the pits of hell:

Through me is the way into the woeful city,
Through me is the way into eternal woe,
Through me is the way among the Lost People.[27]

It is remarkable that in this dream the basic outline of the universal mythological formula of the adventure of the hero is reproduced, to the detail. These deeply significant motifs of the perils, obstacles, and good fortunes of the way, we shall find inflected through the following pages in a hundred forms. The crossing first of the open sewer,* then of the perfectly clear river flowing over grass,† the appearance of the willing helper at the critical moment,‡ and the high, firm ground beyond the final stream (the Earthly Paradise, the Land over Jordan):§ these are the everlastingly recurrent themes of the wonderful song of the soul's high adventure. And each who has dared to harken to and follow the secret call has known the perils of the dangerous, solitary transit:

A sharpened edge of a razor, hard to traverse,
A difficult path is this—poets declare![28]

The dreamer is assisted across the water by the gift of a small wooden box, which takes the place, in this dream, of the more usual skiff or bridge. This is a symbol of her own special talent and virtue, by which she has been ferried across the waters of the world. The

---

* Compare Dante, "Inferno," XIV, 76–84 (Dante Alighieri, *The Divine Comedy,* vol. I, p. 89): "a little brook, the redness of which still makes me shudder . . . which the sinful women share among them."

† Compare Dante, "Purgatorio," XXVIII, 22–30 (*op. cit.,* vol. II, p. 214): "A stream . . . which with its little waves was bending toward the left the grass that sprang upon its bank. All the waters that are purest here on earth would seem to have some mixture in them, compared with that which hides nothing."

‡ Dante's Virgil.

§ "Those who in old time sang of the Golden Age, and of its happy state, perchance, upon Parnassus, dreamed of this place: here was the root of mankind innocent; here is always spring, and every fruit; this is the nectar of which each of them tells" ("Purgatorio," XXVIII, 139–144; *op. cit.,* vol. II, p. 219).

dreamer has supplied us with no account of her associations, so that we do not know what special contents the box would have revealed; but it is certainly a variety of Pandora's box—that divine gift of the gods to beautiful woman, filled with the seeds of all the trouble and blessings of existence, but also provided with the sustaining virtue, hope. By this, the dreamer crosses to the other shore. And by a like miracle, so will each whose work is the difficult, dangerous task of self-discovery and self-development be portered across the ocean of life.

The multitude of men and women choose the less adventurous way of the comparatively unconscious civic and tribal routines. But these seekers, too, are saved—by virtue of the inherited symbolic aids of society, the rites of passage, the grace-yielding sacraments, given to mankind of old by the redeemers and handed down through millennia. It is only those who know neither an inner call nor an outer doctrine whose plight truly is desperate; that is to say, most of us today, in this labyrinth without and within the heart. Alas, where is the guide, that fond virgin, Ariadne, to supply the simple clue that will give us courage to face the Minotaur, and the means then to find our way to freedom when the monster has been met and slain?

FIGURE 5. *Shintō Fire Ritual* (photograph by Joseph Campbell, Japan, A.D. 1956)

Ariadne, the daughter of King Minos, fell in love with the handsome Theseus the moment she saw him disembark from the boat that had brought the pitiful group of Athenian youths and maidens for the Minotaur. She found a way to talk with him, and declared that she would supply a means to help him back out of the labyrinth if he would promise to take her away from Crete with him and make her his wife. The pledge was given. Ariadne turned for help, then, to the crafty Daedalus, by whose art the labyrinth had been constructed and Ariadne's mother enabled to give birth to its inhabitant. Daedalus simply presented her with a skein of linen thread, which the visiting hero might fix to the entrance and unwind as he went into the maze. It is, indeed, very little that we need! But lacking that, the adventure into the labyrinth is without hope.

The little is close at hand. Most curiously, the very scientist who, in the service of the sinful king, was the brain behind the horror of the labyrinth, quite as readily can serve the purposes of freedom. But the hero-heart must be at hand. For centuries Daedalus has represented the type of the artist-scientist: that curiously disinterested, almost diabolic human phenomenon, beyond the normal bounds of social judgment, dedicated to the morals not of his time but of his art. He is the hero of the way of thought—singlehearted, courageous, and full of faith that the truth, as he finds it, shall make us free.

And so now we may turn to him, as did Ariadne. The flax for the linen of his thread he has gathered from the fields of the human imagination. Centuries of husbandry, decades of diligent culling, the work of numerous hearts and hands, have gone into the hackling, sorting, and spinning of this tightly twisted yarn. Furthermore, we have not even to risk the adventure alone; for the heroes of all time have gone before us; the labyrinth is thoroughly known; we have only to follow the thread of the hero-path. And where we had thought to find an abomination, we shall find a god; where we had thought to slay another, we shall slay ourselves; where we had thought to travel outward, we shall come to the center of our own existence; where we had thought to be alone, we shall be with all the world.

2. *Tragedy and Comedy*

"HAPPY FAMILIES ARE ALL ALIKE; every unhappy family is unhappy in its own way." With these fateful words, Count Leo Tolstoy opened the novel of the spiritual dismemberment of his modern heroine, Anna Karenina. During the seven decades that have elapsed since that distracted wife, mother, and blindly impassioned mistress threw herself beneath the wheels of the train—thus terminating, with a gesture symbolic of what already had happened to her soul, her tragedy of disorientation—a tumultuous and unremitting dithyramb of romances, news reports, and unrecorded cries of anguish has been going up to the honor of the bull-demon of the labyrinth: the wrathful, destructive, maddening aspect of the same god who, when benign, is the vivifying principle of the world. Modern romance, like Greek tragedy, celebrates the mystery of dismemberment, which is life in time. The happy ending is justly scorned as a misrepresentation; for the world, as we know it, as we have seen it, yields but one ending: death, disintegration, dismemberment, and the crucifixion of our heart with the passing of the forms that we have loved.

"Pity is the feeling which arrests the mind in the presence of whatever is grave and constant in human sufferings and unites it with the human sufferer. Terror is the feeling which arrests the mind in the presence of whatsoever is grave and constant in human sufferings and unites it with the secret cause."[29] As Gilbert Murray has pointed out in his preface to Ingram Bywater's translation of the *Poetics* of Aristotle,[30] tragic *katharsis* (i.e., the "purification" or "purgation" of the emotions of the spectator of tragedy through his experience of pity and terror) corresponds to an earlier ritual *katharsis* ("a purification of the community from the taints and poisons of the past year, the old contagion of sin and death"), which was the function of the festival and mystery play of the dismembered bull god, Dionysos. The meditating mind is united, in the mystery play, not with the body that is shown to die, but with the principle of continuous life that for a time inhabited it, and for that time was the reality clothed in the apparition (at once the sufferer and the secret cause), the substratum into which our selves dissolve when the "tragedy that breaks man's face"[31] has split, shattered, and dissolved our mortal frame.

Appear, appear, whatso thy shape or name,
O Mountain Bull, Snake of the Hundred Heads,
Lion of the Burning Flame!
O God, Beast, Mystery, come![32]

This death to the logic and the emotional commitments of our chance moment in the world of space and time, this recognition of, and shift of our emphasis to, the universal life that throbs and celebrates its victory in the very kiss of our own annihilation, this *amor fati,* "love of fate," love of the fate that is inevitably death, constitutes the experience of the tragic art: therein the joy of it, the redeeming ecstasy:

My days have run, the servant I,
Initiate, of Idaean Jove;
Where midnight Zagreus roves, I rove;
I have endured his thunder-cry;
Fulfilled his red and bleeding feasts;
Held the Great Mother's mountain flame;
I am Set Free and named by name
A Bacchos of the Mailed Priests.[33]

Modern literature is devoted, in great measure, to a courageous, open-eyed observation of the sickeningly broken figurations that abound before us, around us, and within. Where the natural impulse to complain against the holocaust has been suppressed—to cry out blame, or to announce panaceas—the magnitude of an art of tragedy more potent (for us) than the Greek finds realization: the realistic, intimate, and variously interesting tragedy of democracy, where the god is beheld crucified in the catastrophes not of the great houses only but of every common home, every scourged and lacerated face. And there is no make-believe about heaven, future bliss, and compensation to alleviate the bitter majesty, but only utter darkness, the void of unfulfillment, to receive and eat back the lives that have been tossed forth from the womb only to fail.

In comparison with all this, our little stories of achievement seem pitiful; too well we know what bitterness of failure, loss, disillusionment, and ironic unfulfillment galls the blood of even the envied of the world! Hence we are not disposed to assign to comedy the high rank of tragedy. Comedy as satire is acceptable, as fun it is a pleasant haven of escape, but the fairy tale of happiness ever after cannot be taken seriously; it belongs to the never-never land of childhood, which is protected from the realities that will become terribly known soon enough; just as the myth of heaven ever after is for the old, whose lives are behind them and whose hearts have to be readied for the last portal of the transit into night—which sober, modern Occidental judgment is founded on a total misunderstanding of the realities depicted in the fairy tale, the myth, and the divine comedies of redemption. These, in the ancient world, were regarded as of a higher rank than tragedy, of a deeper truth, of a more difficult realization, of a sounder structure, and of a revelation more complete.

The happy ending of the fairy tale, the myth, and the divine comedy of the soul is to be read, not as a contradiction, but as a transcendence of the universal tragedy of man. The objective world remains what it was, but, because of a shift of emphasis within the subject, is beheld as though transformed. Where formerly life and death contended, now enduring being is made manifest—as indifferent to the accidents of time as water boiling in a pot is to the destiny of a bubble, or as the cosmos to the appearance and disappearance of a galaxy of stars. Tragedy is the shattering of the forms and of our attachment to the forms; comedy, the wild and careless, inexhaustible joy of life invincible. Thus the two are the terms of a single mythological theme and experience which includes them both and which they bound: the down-going and the up-coming (*kathodos* and *anodos*), which together constitute the totality of the revelation that is life, and which the individual must know and love if he is to be purged (*katharsis* = *purgatorio*) of the contagion of sin (disobedience to the divine will) and death (identification with the mortal form).

"All things are changing; nothing dies. The spirit wanders, comes now here, now there, and occupies whatever frame it pleases.... For that which once existed is no more, and that which was not has come to be; and so the whole round of motion is gone through again."[34]

"Only the bodies, of which this eternal, imperishable, incomprehensible Self is the indweller, are said to have an end."[35]

It is the business of mythology proper, and of the fairy tale, to reveal the specific dangers and techniques of the dark interior way from tragedy to comedy. Hence the incidents are fantastic and "unreal": they represent psychological, not physical, triumphs. Even when the legend is of an actual historical personage, the deeds of victory are rendered, not in lifelike, but in dreamlike figurations; for the point is not that such-and-such was done on earth; the point is that, before such-and-such could be done on earth, this other, more important, primary thing had to be brought to pass within the labyrinth that we all know and visit in our dreams. The passage of the mythological hero may be over-ground, incidentally; fundamentally it is inward—into depths where obscure resistances are overcome, and long lost, forgotten powers are revivified, to be made available for the transfiguration of the world. This deed accomplished, life no longer suffers hopelessly under the terrible mutilations of ubiquitous disaster, battered by time, hideous throughout space; but with its horror visible still, its cries of anguish still tumultuous, it becomes penetrated by an all-suffusing, all-sustaining love, and a knowledge of its own unconquered power. Something of the light that blazes invisible within the abysses of its normally opaque materiality breaks forth, with an increasing uproar. The dreadful mutilations are then seen as shadows, only, of an immanent, imperishable eternity; time yields to glory; and the world sings with the prodigious, angelic, but perhaps finally monotonous, siren music of the spheres. Like happy families, the myths and the worlds redeemed are all alike.

FIGURE 6. *The Monster Tamer* (inlaid shell and lapis lazuli, Sumerian, Iraq, c. 2650–2400 B.C.)

3. *The Hero and the God*

THE STANDARD PATH of the mythological adventure of the hero is a magnification of the formula represented in the rites of passage: *separation—initiation—return:* which might be named the nuclear unit of the monomyth.[36]

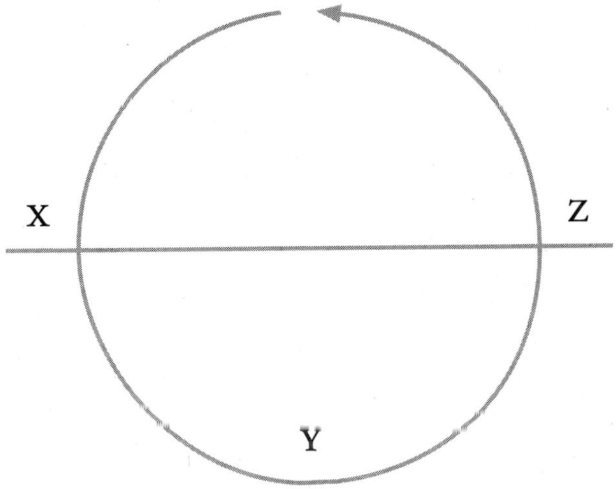

A hero ventures forth from the world of common day into a region of supernatural wonder (*x*): fabulous forces are there encountered and a decisive victory is won (*y*): the hero comes back from this mysterious adventure with the power to bestow boons on his fellow man (*z*).

Prometheus ascended to the heavens, stole fire from the gods, and descended. Jason sailed through the Clashing Rocks into a sea of marvels, circumvented the dragon that guarded the Golden Fleece, and returned with the fleece and the power to wrest his rightful throne from a usurper. Aeneas went down into the underworld, crossed the dreadful river of the dead, threw a sop to the three-headed watchdog Cerberus, and conversed, at last, with the shade of his dead father. All things were unfolded to him: the destiny of souls, the destiny of

Rome, which he was about to found, "and in what wise he might avoid or endure every burden."[37] He returned through the ivory gate to his work in the world.

A majestic representation of the difficulties of the hero-task, and of its sublime import when it is profoundly conceived and solemnly undertaken, is presented in the traditional legend of the Great Struggle of the Buddha. The young prince Gautama Śākyamūni set forth secretly from his father's palace on the princely steed Kanthaka, passed miraculously through the guarded gate, rode through the night attended by the torches of four times sixty thousand divinities, lightly hurdled a majestic river eleven hundred and twenty-eight cubits wide, and then with a single sword-stroke sheared his own royal locks—whereupon the remaining hair, two finger-breadths in length, curled to the right and lay close to his head. Assuming the garments of a monk, he moved as a beggar through the world, and during these years of apparently aimless wandering acquired and transcended the eight stages of meditation. He retired to a hermitage, bent his powers six more years to the great struggle, carried austerity to the uttermost, and collapsed in seeming death, but presently recovered. Then he returned to the less rigorous life of the ascetic wanderer.

One day he sat beneath a tree, contemplating the eastern quarter of the world, and the tree was illuminated with his radiance. A young girl named Sujata came and presented milk-rice to him in a golden bowl, and when he tossed the empty bowl into a river it floated upstream. This was the signal that the moment of his triumph was at hand. He arose and proceeded along a road which the gods had decked and which was eleven hundred and twenty-eight cubits wide. The snakes and birds and the divinities of the woods and fields did him homage with flowers and celestial perfumes, heavenly choirs poured forth music, the ten thousand worlds were filled with perfumes, garlands, harmonies, and shouts of acclaim; for he was on his way to the great Tree of Enlightenment, the Bo Tree, under which he was to redeem the universe. He placed himself, with a firm resolve, beneath the Bo Tree, on the Immovable Spot, and straightway was approached by Kāma-Māra, the god of love and death.

The dangerous god appeared mounted on an elephant and carrying weapons in his thousand hands. He was surrounded by his army, which extended twelve leagues before him, twelve to the right, twelve to the left, and in the rear as far as to the confines of the world; it was

FIGURE 7. *Śakyamūni Buddha Beneath the Bodhi Tree* (carved schist, India, c. late ninth–early tenth century A.D.)

The Buddha's enlightenment is the most important single moment in Oriental mythology, a counterpart of the Crucifixion of the West. The Buddha beneath the Tree of Enlightenment (the Bo Tree) and Christ on Holy Rood (the Tree of Redemption) are analogous figures, incorporating an archetypal World Savior, World Tree motif, which is of immemorial antiquity. Many other variants of the theme will be found among the episodes to come. The Immovable Spot and Mount Calvary are images of the World Navel, or World Axis (see page 32).

The calling of the Earth to witness is represented in traditional Buddhist art by images of the Buddha, sitting in the classic Buddha posture, with the right hand resting on the right knee and its fingers lightly touching the ground.

The point is that Buddhahood, Enlightenment, cannot be communicated, but only the *way* to Enlightenment. This doctrine of the incommunicability of the Truth which is beyond names and forms is basic to the great Oriental, as well as to the Platonic, traditions. Whereas the truths of science are communicable, being demonstrable hypotheses rationally founded on observable facts, ritual, mythology, and metaphysics are but guides to the brink of a transcendent illumination, the final step to which must be taken by each in his own silent experience. Hence one of the Sanskrit terms for sage is *mūni*, "the silent one." *Śākyamūni* (one of the titles of Gautama Buddha) means "the silent one or sage (*mūni*) of the Śakya clan." Though he is the founder of a widely taught world religion, the ultimate core of his doctrine remains concealed, necessarily, in silence.

nine leagues high. The protecting deities of the universe took flight, but the Future Buddha remained unmoved beneath the Tree. And the god then assailed him, seeking to break his concentration.

Whirlwind, rocks, thunder and flame, smoking weapons with keen edges, burning coals, hot ashes, boiling mud, blistering sands and fourfold darkness, the Antagonist hurled against the Savior, but the missiles were all transformed into celestial flowers and ointments by the power of Gautama's ten perfections. Kāma-Māra then deployed his daughters, Desire, Pining, and Lust, surrounded by voluptuous attendants, but the mind of the Great Being was not distracted. The god finally challenged his right to be sitting on the Immovable Spot, flung his razor-sharp discus angrily, and bid the towering host of the army to let fly at him with mountain crags. But the Future Buddha only moved his hand to touch the ground with his fingertips, and thus bid the goddess Earth bear witness to his right to be sitting where he was. She did so with a hundred, a thousand, a hundred thousand roars, so that the elephant of the Antagonist fell upon its knees in obeisance to the Future Buddha. The army was immediately dispersed, and the gods of all the worlds scattered garlands.

Having won that preliminary victory before sunset, the conqueror acquired in the first watch of the night knowledge of his previous existences, in the second watch the divine eye of omniscient vision, and in the last watch understanding of the chain of causation. He experienced perfect enlightenment at the break of day.

Then for seven days, Gautama—now the Buddha, the Enlightened—sat motionless in bliss; for seven days he stood apart and regarded the spot on which he had received enlightenment; for seven days he paced between the place of the sitting and the place of the standing; for seven days he abode in a pavilion furnished by the gods and reviewed the whole doctrine of causality and release; for seven days he sat beneath the tree where the girl Sujata had brought him milk-rice in a golden bowl, and there meditated on the doctrine of the sweetness of *nirvāṇa;* he removed to another tree and a great storm raged for seven days, but the King of Serpents emerged from the roots and protected the Buddha with his expanded hood; finally, the Buddha sat for seven days beneath a fourth tree enjoying still the sweetness of liberation. Then he doubted whether his message could be communicated, and he thought to retain the wisdom for himself; but the god Brahmā descended from the zenith to implore that he should become the teacher of gods and men. The Buddha was thus persuaded to proclaim the path. And he went back into the cities of men where he moved among the citizens of the world, bestowing the inestimable boon of the knowledge of the Way.[38]

The Old Testament records a comparable deed in its legend of Moses, who, in the third month of the departure of Israel out of the land of Egypt, came with his people into the wilderness of Sinai; and there Israel pitched their tents over against the mountain. And Moses went up to God, and the Lord called unto him from the mountain. The Lord gave to him the Tables of the Law and commanded Moses to return with these to Israel, the people of the Lord.[39]

Jewish folk legend declares that during the day of the revelation diverse rumblings sounded from Mount Sinai.

> Flashes of lightning, accompanied by an ever swelling peal of horns, moved the people with mighty fear and trembling. God bent the heavens, moved the earth, and shook the bounds of the world, so that the depths trembled, and the heavens grew frightened. His splendor passed through the four portals of fire, earthquake, storm, and hail. The kings of the earth trembled in their palaces. The earth herself thought the resurrection of the dead was about to take place, and that she would have to account for the blood of the slain she had absorbed, and for the bodies of the murdered whom she covered. The earth was not calmed until she heard the first words of the Decalogue.
>
> The heavens opened and Mount Sinai, freed from the earth, rose into the air, so that its summit towered into the heavens, while a thick cloud covered the sides of it, and touched the feet of the Divine Throne. Accompanying God on one side, appeared twenty-two thousand angels with crowns for the Levites, the only tribe that remained true to God while the rest worshiped the Golden Calf. On the second side were sixty myriads, three thousand five hundred and fifty angels, each bearing a crown of fire for each individual Israelite. Double this number of angels was on the third side; whereas on the fourth side they were simply innumerable. For God did not appear from one direction, but from all simultaneously, which, however, did not prevent His glory from filling the heaven as well as the earth. In spite of these innumerable hosts there was no crowding on Mount Sinai, no mob, there was room for all.[40]

As we soon shall see, whether presented in the vast, almost oceanic images of the Orient, in the vigorous narratives of the Greeks, or in the majestic legends of the Bible, the adventure of the hero normally follows the pattern of the nuclear unit above described: a separation from the world, a penetration to some source of power, and a life-enhancing return. The whole of the Orient has been blessed by the boon brought back by Gautama Buddha—his wonderful teaching of the Good Law—just as the Occident has been by the Decalogue of Moses. The Greeks referred fire, the first support of all human culture, to the world-transcending deed of their Prometheus, and the Romans the founding of their world-supporting city to Aeneas, following his departure from fallen Troy and his visit to the eerie underworld of the dead. Everywhere, no matter what the sphere of interest (whether religious, political, or personal), the really creative acts are represented as those deriving from some sort of dying to the world; and what happens in the interval of the hero's nonentity, so that he comes back as one reborn, made great and filled with creative power, mankind is also unanimous in declaring. We shall have only to follow, therefore, a multitude of heroic figures through the classic stages of the universal adventure in order to see again what has always been revealed. This will help us to understand not only the meaning of those images for contemporary life, but also the singleness of the human spirit in its aspirations, powers, vicissitudes, and wisdom.

The following pages will present in the form of one composite adventure the tales of a number of the world's symbolic carriers of the destiny of Everyman. The first great stage, that of the *separation* or *departure,* will be shown in Part I, Chapter I, in five subsections:

1 "The Call to Adventure," or the signs of the vocation of the hero
2 "Refusal of the Call," or the folly of the flight from the god
3 "Supernatural Aid," the unsuspected assistance that comes to one who has undertaken his proper adventure
4 "The Crossing of the First Threshold"
5 "The Belly of the Whale," or the passage into the realm of night

The stage of *the trials and victories of initiation* will appear in Chapter II in six subsections:

1 "The Road of Trials," or the dangerous aspect of the gods
2 "The Meeting with the Goddess" (*Magna Mater*), or the bliss of infancy regained
3 "Woman as the Temptress," the realization and agony of Oedipus
4 "Atonement with the Father"

5 "Apotheosis"
6 "The Ultimate Boon"

The return and reintegration with society, which is indispensable to the continuous circulation of spiritual energy into the world, and which, from the standpoint of the community, is the justification of the long retreat, the hero himself may find the most difficult requirement of all. For if he has won through, like the Buddha, to the profound repose of complete enlightenment, there is danger that the bliss of this experience may annihilate all recollection of, interest in, or hope for, the sorrows of the world; or else the problem of making known the way of illumination to people wrapped in economic problems may seem too great to solve. And on the other hand, if the hero, instead of submitting to all of the initiatory tests, has, like Prometheus, simply darted to his goal (by violence, quick device, or luck) and plucked the boon for the world that he intended, then the powers that he has unbalanced may react so sharply that he will be blasted from within and without—crucified, like Prometheus, on the rock of his own violated unconscious. Or if the hero, in the third place, makes his safe and willing return, he may meet with such a blank misunderstanding and disregard from those whom he has come to help that his career will collapse. The third of the following chapters will conclude the discussion of these prospects under six subheadings:

1 "Refusal of the Return," or the world denied
2 "The Magic Flight," or the escape of Prometheus
3 "Rescue from Without"
4 "The Crossing of the Return Threshold," or the return
to the world of common day
5 "Master of the Two Worlds"
6 "Freedom to Live," the nature and function of the ultimate boon

---

This circular adventure of the hero appears in a negative form in stories of the deluge type, where it is not the hero who goes to the power, but the power that rises against the hero, and again subsides. Deluge stories occur in every quarter of the earth. They form an integral portion of the archetypal myth of the history of the world, and so belong properly to Part II of the present discussion: "The Cosmogonic Cycle." The deluge hero is a symbol of the germinal vitality of man surviving even the worst tides of catastrophe and sin.

The composite hero of the monomyth is a personage of exceptional gifts. Frequently he is honored by his society, frequently unrecognized or disdained. He and/or the world in which he finds himself suffers from a symbolical deficiency. In fairy tales this may be as slight as the lack of a certain golden ring, whereas in apocalyptic vision the physical and spiritual life of the whole earth can be represented as fallen, or on the point of falling into ruin.

Typically, the hero of the fairy tale achieves a domestic, microcosmic triumph, and the hero of myth a world-historical, macrocosmic triumph. Whereas the former—the youngest or despised child who becomes the master of extraordinary powers—prevails over his personal oppressors, the latter brings back from his adventure the means for the regeneration of his society as a whole. Tribal or local heroes, such as the emperor Huang Ti, Moses, or the Aztec Tezcatlipoca, commit their boons to a single folk; universal heroes—Mohammed, Jesus, Gautama Buddha—bring a message for the entire world.

Whether the hero be ridiculous or sublime, Greek or barbarian, gentile or Jew, his journey varies little in essential plan. Popular tales represent the heroic action as physical; the higher religions show the deed to be moral; nevertheless, there will be found astonishingly little variation in the morphology of the adventure, the character roles involved, the victories gained. If one or another of the basic elements of the archetypal pattern is omitted from a given fairy tale, legend, ritual, or myth, it is bound to be somehow or other implied—and the omission itself can speak volumes for the history and pathology of the example, as we shall presently see.

Part II, "The Cosmogonic Cycle," unrolls the great vision of the creation and destruction of the world which is vouchsafed as revelation to the successful hero. Chapter I, *Emanations,* treats of the coming of the forms of the universe out of the void. Chapter II, *The Virgin Birth,* is a review of the creative and redemptive roles of the female power, first on a cosmic scale as the Mother of the Universe, then again on the human plane as the Mother of the Hero. Chapter III, *Transformations of the Hero,* traces the course of the legendary history of the human race through its typical stages, the hero appearing on the scene in various forms according to the changing needs of the race. And Chapter IV, *Dissolutions,* tells of the foretold end, first of the hero, then of the manifested world.

The cosmogonic cycle is presented with astonishing consistency in the sacred writings of all the continents,[41] and it gives to the adventure of the hero a new and interesting turn; for now it appears that the perilous journey was a labor not of attainment but of reattainment, not discovery but rediscovery. The godly powers sought and dangerously won are revealed to have been within the heart of the hero all the time. He is "the king's son" who has come to know who he is and therewith has entered into the exercise of his proper power—"God's son," who has learned to know how much that title means. From this point of view the hero is symbolical of that divine creative and redemptive image which is hidden within us all, only waiting to be known and rendered into life.

"For the One who has become many, remains the One undivided, but each part is all of Christ," we read in the writings of Saint Symeon the younger (A.D. 949–1022). "I saw Him in my house," the saint goes on.

> Among all those everyday things He appeared unexpectedly and became unutterably united and merged with me, and leaped over to me without anything in between, as fire to iron, as the light to glass. And He made me like fire and like light. And I became that which I saw before and beheld from afar. I do not know how to relate this miracle to you. . . . I am man by nature, and God by the grace of God.[42]

A comparable vision is described in the apocryphal Gospel of Eve.

> I stood on a loftly mountain and saw a gigantic man and another a dwarf; and I heard as it were a voice of thunder, and drew nigh for to hear; and He spake unto me and said: I am thou, and thou art I; and wheresoever thou mayest be I am there. In all am I scattered, and whensoever thou willest, thou gatherest Me; and gathering Me, thou gatherest Thyself.[43]

The two—the hero and his ultimate god, the seeker and the found—are thus understood as the outside and inside of a single, self-mirrored mystery, which is identical with the mystery of the manifest world. The great deed of the supreme hero is to come to the knowledge of this unity in multiplicity and then to make it known.

4. *The World Navel*

THE EFFECT of the successful adventure of the hero is the unlocking and release again of the flow of life into the body of the world. The miracle of this flow may be represented in physical terms as a circulation of food substance, dynamically as a streaming of energy, or spiritually as a manifestation of grace. Such varieties of image alternate easily, representing three degrees of condensation of the one life force. An abundant harvest is the sign of God's grace; God's grace is the food of the soul; the lightning bolt is the harbinger of fertilizing rain, and at the same time the manifestation of the released energy of God. Grace, food substance, energy: these pour into the living world, and wherever they fail, life decomposes into death.

The torrent pours from an invisible source, the point of entry being the center of the symbolic circle of the universe, the Immovable Spot of the Buddha legend,[44] around which the world may be said to revolve. Beneath this spot is the earth-supporting head of the cosmic serpent, the dragon, symbolical of the waters of the abyss, which are the divine life-creative energy and substance of the demiurge, the world-generative aspect of immortal being.[45] The tree of life, i.e., the universe itself, grows from this point. It is rooted in the supporting darkness; the golden sun bird perches on its peak; a spring, the inexhaustible well, bubbles at its foot. Or the figure may be that of a cosmic mountain, with the city of the gods, like a lotus of light, upon its summit, and in its hollow the cities of the demons, illuminated by precious stones. Again, the figure may be that of the cosmic man or woman (for example the Buddha himself, or the dancing Hindu goddess Kālī) seated or standing on this spot, or even fixed to the tree (Attis, Jesus, Wotan); for the hero as the incarnation of God is himself the navel of the world, the umbilical point through which the energies of eternity break into time. Thus the World Navel is the symbol of the continuous creation: the mystery of the maintenance of the world through that continuous miracle of vivification which wells within all things.

FIGURE 8. *Yggdrasil, the World Tree* (etching, Scandinavia, early nineteenth century A.D.)

Among the Pawnees of northern Kansas and southern Nebraska, the priest, during the ceremonial of the Hako, draws a circle with his toe. "The circle represents a nest," such a priest is reported to have said,

> and it is drawn by the toe because the eagle builds its nest with its claws. Although we are imitating the bird making its nest, there is another meaning to the action; we are thinking of Tirawa making the world for the people to live in. If you go on a high hill and look around, you will see the sky touching the earth on every side, and within this circular enclosure the people live. So the circles we have made are not only nests, but they also represent the circle Tirawa-atius has made for the dwelling place of all the people. The circles also stand for the kinship group, the clan, and the tribe.[46]

The dome of heaven rests on the quarters of the earth, sometimes supported by four caryatidal kings, dwarfs, giants, elephants, or turtles. Hence, the traditional importance of the mathematical problem of the quadrature of the circle: it contains the secret of the transformation of heavenly into earthly forms. The hearth in the home, the altar in the temple, is the hub of the wheel of the earth, the womb of the Universal Mother whose fire is the fire of life. And the opening at the top of the lodge—or the crown, pinnacle, or lantern of the dome—is the hub or midpoint of the sky: the sun door, through which souls pass back from time to eternity, like the savor of the offerings, burned in the fire of life, and lifted on the axis of ascending smoke from the hub of the earthly to that of the celestial wheel.[47]

Thus filled, the sun is the eating bowl of God, an inexhaustible grail, abundant with the substance of the sacrifice, whose flesh is meat indeed and whose blood is drink indeed.[48] At the same time it is the nourisher of mankind. The solar ray igniting the hearth symbolizes the communication of divine energy to the womb of the world—and is again the axis uniting and turning the two wheels. Through the sun door the circulation of energy is continuous. God descends and man ascends through it. "I am the door: by me if any man enter in, he shall be saved, and shall go in and out, and find pasture."[49] "He that eateth my flesh, and drinketh my blood, dwelleth in me, and I in him."[50]

For a culture still nurtured in mythology the landscape, as well as every phase of human existence, is made alive with symbolical suggestion. The hills and groves have their supernatural protectors and are associated with popularly known episodes in the local history of the creation of the world. Here and there, furthermore, are special shrines. Wherever a hero has been born, has wrought, or has passed back into the void, the place is marked and sanctified. A temple is erected there to signify and inspire the miracle of perfect centeredness; for this is the place of the breakthrough into abundance. Someone at this point discovered eternity. The site can serve, therefore, as a support for fruitful meditation. Such temples are designed, as a rule, to simulate the four directions of the world horizon, the shrine or altar at the center being symbolical of the Inexhaustible Point. The one who enters the temple compound and proceeds to the sanctuary is imitating the deed of the original hero. His aim is to rehearse the universal pattern as a means of evoking within himself the recollection of the life-centering, life-renewing form.

Ancient cities are built like temples, having their portals to the four directions, while in the central place stands the major shrine of the divine city founder. The citizens live and work within the confines of this symbol. And in the same spirit, the domains of the national and world religions are centered around the hub of some mother city: Western Christendom around Rome, Islam around Mecca. The concerted bowing, three times a day, of the Mohammedan community throughout the world, all pointing like the spokes of a world-extensive wheel to the centering Kaaba, constructs a vast, living symbol of the "submission" (*islam*) of each and all to Allah's will. "For it is He," we read in the Koran, "that will show you the truth of all that ye do."[51] Or again: a great temple can be established anywhere. Because, finally, the All is everywhere, and anywhere may become the seat of power. Any blade of grass may assume, in myth, the figure of the savior and conduct the questing wanderer into the sanctum sanctorum of his own heart.

The World Navel, then, is ubiquitous. And since it is the source of all existence, it yields the world's plenitude of both good and evil. Ugliness and beauty, sin and virtue, pleasure and pain, are equally its production. "To God all things are fair and good and right," declares Heraclitus; "but men hold some things wrong and some right."[52] Hence the figures worshiped in the temples of the world are by no means always beautiful, always benign, or even necessarily virtuous. Like the deity of the Book of Job, they far transcend the scales of human value. And likewise, mythology does not hold as its greatest hero the merely virtuous man. Virtue is but the pedagogical prelude to the culminating insight, which goes beyond all pairs of opposites. Virtue quells the self-centered ego and

FIGURE 9. *Omphalos* (gold phial, Thracian, Bulgaria, fourth–third century B.C.)

makes the transpersonal centeredness possible; but when that has been achieved, what then of the pain or pleasure, vice or virtue, either of our own ego or of any other? Through all, the transcendent force is then perceived which lives in all, in all is wonderful, and is worthy, in all, of our profound obeisance.

For as Heraclitus has declared: "The unlike is joined together, and from differences results the most beautiful harmony, and all things take place by strife."[53] Or again, as we have it from the poet Blake: "The roaring of lions, the howling of wolves, the raging of the stormy sea, and the destructive sword, are portions of eternity too great for the eye of man."[54]

The difficult point is made vivid in an anecdote from Yorubaland (West Africa), which is told of the trickster-divinity Edshu. One day, this odd god came walking along a path between two fields.

> He beheld in either field a farmer at work and proposed to play the two a turn. He donned a hat that was on the one side red but on the other white, green before and black behind [these being the colors of the four World Directions: i.e., Edshu was a personification of the Center, the *axis mundi,* or the World Navel]; so that when the two friendly farmers had gone home to their village and the one had said to the other, "Did you see that old fellow go by today in the white hat?" the other replied, "Why, the hat was red." To which the first retorted, "It was not; it was white." "But it was red," insisted the friend, "I saw it with my own two eyes." "Well, you must be blind," declared the first. "You must be drunk," rejoined the other. And so the argument developed and the two came to blows. When they began to knife each other, they were brought by neighbors before the headman for judgment. Edshu was among the crowd at the trial, and when the headman sat at a loss to know where justice lay, the old trickster revealed himself, made known his prank, and showed the hat. "The two could not help but quarrel," he said. "I wanted it that way. Spreading strife is my greatest joy."[55]

Where the moralist would be filled with indignation and the tragic poet with pity and terror, mythology breaks the whole of life into a vast, horrendous Divine Comedy. Its Olympian laugh is not escapist in the least, but hard, with the hardness of life itself—which, we may take it, is the hardness of God, the Creator. Mythology, in this respect, makes the tragic attitude seem somewhat hysterical, and the merely moral judgment shortsighted. Yet the hardness is balanced by an assurance that all that we see is but the reflex of a power that endures, untouched by the pain. Thus the tales are both pitiless and terrorless—suffused with the joy of a transcendent anonymity regarding itself in all of the self-centered, battling egos that are born and die in time.

PART I

THE ADVENTURE OF THE HERO

FIGURE 10. *Psyche Entering Cupid's Garden* (oil on canvas, England, A.D. 1903)

CHAPTER I

Departure

1. *The Call to Adventure*

LONG LONG AGO, when wishing still could lead to something, there lived a king whose daughters all were beautiful, but the youngest was so beautiful that the sun itself, who had seen so many things, simply marveled every time it shone on her face. Now close to the castle of this king was a great dark forest, and in the forest under an old lime tree a spring, and when the day was very hot, the king's child would go out into the wood and sit on the edge of the cool spring. And to pass the time she would take a golden ball, toss it up and catch it; and this was her favorite plaything.

Now it so happened one day that the golden ball of the princess did not fall into the little hand lifted into the air, but passed it, bounced on the ground, and rolled directly into the water. The princess followed it with her eyes, but the ball disappeared; and the spring was deep, so deep that the bottom could not be seen. Thereupon she began to cry, and her crying became louder and louder, and she was unable to find consolation. And while she was lamenting in this way, she heard someone call to her: "What is the matter, Princess? You are crying so hard, a stone would be forced to pity you." She looked around to see where the voice had come from, and there she beheld a frog, holding its fat, ugly head out of the water. "Oh, it's you, old Water Plopper," she said. "I am crying over my golden ball, which has fallen into the spring." "Be calm; don't cry," answered the frog. "I can surely be of assistance. But what will you give me if I fetch your toy for you?" "Whatever you would like to have, dear frog," she said; "my clothes, my pearls and jewels, even the golden crown that I wear." The frog replied, "Your clothes, your pearls and jewels, and your golden crown, I do not want; but if you will care for me and let me be your companion and playmate, let me sit beside you at your little table, eat from your little golden plate, drink from your little cup, sleep in your little bed: if you will promise me that, I will go straight down and fetch your golden ball." "All right," she said. "I promise you anything you want, if you will only bring me back the ball." But she thought: "How that simple frog chatters! There he sits in the water with his own kind, and could never be the companion of a human being."

As soon as the frog had obtained her promise, he ducked his head and sank, and after a little while came swimming up again; he had the ball in his mouth, and tossed it on the grass. The princess was elated when she saw her pretty toy. She picked it up and scampered away. "Wait, wait," called the frog, "take me along; I can't run like you." But what good did it do, though he croaked after her as loudly as he could? She paid not the slightest heed, but hurried home, and soon had completely forgotten the poor frog—who must have hopped back again into his spring.[1]

This is an example of one of the ways in which the adventure can begin. A blunder—apparently the merest chance—reveals an unsuspected world, and the individual is drawn into a relationship with forces that are not rightly understood. As Freud has shown,[2] blunders are not the merest chance. They are the result of suppressed desires and conflicts. They are ripples on the surface of life, produced by unsuspected springs. And these may be very deep—as deep as the soul itself. The blunder may amount to the opening of a destiny. Thus it happens, in this fairy tale, that the disappearance of the ball is the first sign of something coming for the princess, the frog is the second, and the unconsidered promise is the third.

As a preliminary manifestation of the powers that are breaking into play, the frog, coming up as it were by miracle, can be termed the "herald"; the crisis of his appearance is the "call to adventure." The herald's summons may be to live, as in the present instance, or, at a later moment of the biography, to die. It may sound the call to some high historical undertaking. Or it may mark the dawn of religious illumination. As apprehended by the mystic, it marks what has been termed "the awakening of the self."[3] In the case of the princess of the fairy tale, it signified no more than the coming of adolescence. But whether small or great, and no matter what the stage or grade of life, the call rings up the curtain, always, on a mystery of transfiguration—a rite, or moment, of spiritual passage, which, when complete, amounts to a dying and a birth. The familiar life horizon has been outgrown; the old concepts, ideals, and emotional patterns no longer fit; the time for the passing of a threshold is at hand.

Typical of the circumstances of the call are the dark forest, the great tree, the babbling spring, and the loathly, underestimated appearance of the carrier of the power of destiny. We recognize in the scene the symbols of the World Navel. The frog, the little dragon, is the nursery counterpart of the underworld serpent whose head supports the earth and who represents the life-progenitive, demiurgic powers of the abyss. He comes up with the golden sun ball, his dark deep waters having just taken it down: at this moment resembling the great Chinese Dragon of

FIGURE 11. *Apis in the Form of a Bull Transports the Deceased as Osiris to the Underworld* (carved wood, Egypt, c. 700–650 B.C.)

the East, delivering the rising sun in his jaws, or the frog on whose head rides the handsome young immortal, Han Hsiang, carrying in a basket the peaches of immortality. Freud has suggested that all moments of anxiety reproduce the painful feelings of the first separation from the mother—the tightening of the breath, congestion of the blood, etc., of the crisis of birth.[4] Conversely, all moments of separation and new birth produce anxiety. Whether it be the king's child about to be taken from the felicity of her established dual-unity with King Daddy, or God's daughter Eve, now ripe to depart from the idyl of the Garden, or again, the supremely concentrated Future Buddha breaking past the last horizons of the created world, the same archetypal images are activated, symbolizing danger, reassurance, trial, passage, and the strange holiness of the mysteries of birth.

The disgusting and rejected frog or dragon of the fairy tale brings up the sun ball in its mouth; for the frog, the serpent, the rejected one, is the representative of that unconscious deep ("so deep that the bottom cannot be seen") wherein are hoarded all of the rejected, unadmitted, unrecognized, unknown, or undeveloped factors, laws, and elements of existence. Those are the pearls of the fabled submarine palaces of the nixies, tritons, and water guardians; the jewels that give light to the demon cities of the underworld; the fire seeds in the ocean of immortality which supports the earth and surrounds it like a snake; the stars in the bosom of immortal night. Those are the nuggets in the gold hoard of the dragon; the guarded apples of the Hesperides; the filaments of the Golden Fleece. The herald or announcer of the adventure, therefore, is often dark, loathly, or terrifying, judged evil by the world; yet if one could follow, the way would be opened through the walls of day into the dark where the jewels glow. Or the herald is a beast (as in the fairy tale), representative of the repressed instinctual fecundity within ourselves, or again a veiled mysterious figure—the unknown.

The story is told, for example, of King Arthur, and how he made him ready with many knights to ride ahunting.

> As soon as he was in the forest, the King saw a great hart afore him. This hart will I chase, said King Arthur, and so he spurred the horse, and rode after long, and so by fine force he was like to have smitten the hart; whereas the King had chased the hart so long, that his horse lost his breath, and fell down dead; then a yeoman fetched the King another horse. So the King saw the hart embushed, and his horse dead; he set him down by a fountain, and

there he fell in great thoughts. And as he sat so, him thought he heard a noise of hounds, to the sum of thirty. And with that the King saw coming toward him the strangest beast that ever he saw or heard of; so the beast went to the well and drank, and the noise was in the beast's belly like unto the questyng of thirty couple hounds; but all the while the beast drank there was no noise in the beast's belly: and therewith the beast departed with a great noise, whereof the King had great marvel.[5]

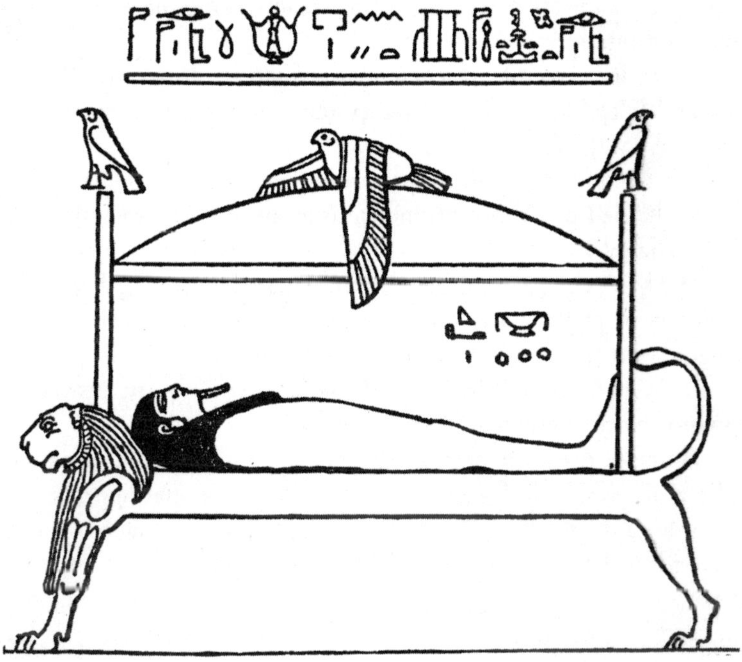

FIGURE 12. *Isis in the Form of a Hawk Joins Osiris in the Underworld* (carved stone, Ptolemaic, Egypt, c. first century A.D.)

Or we have the case—from a very different portion of the world—of an Arapaho girl of the North American plains. She spied a porcupine near a cottonwood tree. She tried to hit the animal, but it ran behind the tree and began to climb. The girl started after, to catch it, but it continued just out of reach. "Well!" she said, "I am climbing to catch the porcupine, for I want those quills, and if necessary I will go to the top." The porcupine reached the top of the tree, but as she approached and was about to lay hands on it, the cottonwood tree suddenly lengthened, and the porcupine resumed his climb. Looking down, she saw her friends craning up at her and beckoning her to descend; but having passed under the influence of the porcupine, and fearful for the great distance between herself and the ground, she continued to mount the tree, until she became the merest speck to those looking from below, and with the porcupine she finally reached the sky.[6]

Two dreams will suffice to illustrate the spontaneous appearance of the figure of the herald in the psyche that is ripe for transformation. The first is the dream of a young man seeking the way to a new world-orientation:

"I am in a green land where many sheep are at pasture. It is the 'land of sheep.' In the land of sheep stands an unknown woman and points the way."[7]

The second is the dream of a young girl whose girl companion has lately died of consumption; she is afraid that she may have the disease herself.

"I was in a blossoming garden; the sun was just going down with a blood-red glow. Then there appeared before me a black, noble knight, who spoke to me with a very serious, deep and frightening voice: 'Wilt thou go with me?' Without attending my answer, he took me by the hand, and carried me away."[8]

Whether dream or myth, in these adventures there is an atmosphere of irresistible fascination about the figure that appears suddenly as guide, marking a new period, a new stage, in the biography. That which has to be faced, and is somehow profoundly familiar to the unconscious—though unknown, surprising, and even frightening to the conscious personality—makes itself known; and what formerly was meaningful may become strangely emptied of value: like the world of the king's child, with the sudden disappearance into the well of the golden ball. Thereafter, even though the hero returns for a while to his familiar occupations, they may be found unfruitful. A series of signs of increasing force then will become visible, until—as in the following legend of "The Four Signs," which is the most celebrated example of the call to adventure in the literature of the world—the summons can no longer be denied.

The young prince Gautama Śākyamūni, the Future Buddha, had been protected by his father from all knowledge of age, sickness, death, or monkhood, lest he should be moved to thoughts of life renunciation; for it had been prophesied at his birth that he was to become either a world emperor or a Buddha. The king—prejudiced in favor of the royal vocation—provided his son with three palaces and forty thousand dancing girls to keep his mind attached to the world. But these only served to advance the inevitable; for while still relatively young, the youth exhausted for himself the fields of fleshly joy and became ripe for the other experience. The moment he was ready, the proper heralds automatically appeared:

> Now on a certain day the Future Buddha wished to go to the park, and told his charioteer to make ready the chariot. Accordingly the man brought out a sumptuous and elegant chariot, and, adorning it richly, he harnessed to it four state horses of the Sindhava breed, as white as the petals of the white lotus, and announced to the Future Buddha that everything was ready. And the Future Buddha mounted the chariot, which was like to a palace of the gods, and proceeded toward the park.
>
> "The time for the enlightenment of the prince Siddhartha draweth nigh," thought the gods; "we must show him a sign": and they changed one of their number into a decrepit old man, broken-toothed, gray-haired, crooked and bent of body, leaning on a staff, and trembling, and showed him to the Future Buddha, but so that only he and the charioteer saw him.
>
> Then said the Future Buddha to the charioteer, "Friend, pray, who is this man? Even his hair is not like that of other men." And when he heard the answer, he said, "Shame on birth, since to every one that is born old age must come." And agitated in heart, he thereupon returned and ascended his palace.
>
> "Why has my son returned so quickly?" asked the king.
>
> "Sire, he has seen an old man," was the reply; "and because he has seen an old man, he is about to retire from the world."
>
> "Do you want to kill me, that you say such things? Quickly get ready some plays to be performed before my son. If we can but get him to enjoying pleasure, he will cease to think of retiring from the world." Then the king extended the guard to half a league in each direction.
>
> Again on a certain day, as the Future Buddha was going to the park, he saw a diseased man whom the gods had fashioned; and having again made inquiry, he returned, agitated in heart, and ascended his palace.
>
> And the king made the same inquiry and gave the same order as before; and again extending the guard, placed them for three quarters of a league around.
>
> And again on a certain day, as the Future Buddha was going to the park, he saw a dead man whom the gods had fashioned;

> and having again made inquiry, he returned, agitated in heart, and ascended his palace.
>
> And the king made the same inquiry and gave the same orders as before; and again extending the guard placed them for a league around.
>
> And again on a certain day, as the Future Buddha was going to the park, he saw a monk, carefully and decently clad, whom the gods had fashioned; and he asked his charioteer, "Pray, who is this man?" "Sire, this is one who has retired from the world"; and the charioteer thereupon proceeded to sound the praises of retirement from the world. The thought of retiring from the world was a pleasing one to the Future Buddha.[9]

This first stage of the mythological journey—which we have designated the "call to adventure"—signifies that destiny has summoned the hero and transferred his spiritual center of gravity from within the pale of his society to a zone unknown. This fateful region of both treasure and danger may be variously represented: as a distant land, a forest, a kingdom underground, beneath the waves, or above the sky, a secret island, lofty mountaintop, or profound dream state; but it is always a place of strangely fluid and polymorphous beings, unimaginable torments, superhuman deeds, and impossible delight. The hero can go forth of his own volition to accomplish the adventure, as did Theseus when he arrived in his father's city, Athens, and heard the horrible history of the Minotaur; or he may be carried or sent abroad by some benign or malignant agent, as was Odysseus, driven about the Mediterranean by the winds of the angered god Poseidon. The adventure may begin as a mere blunder, as did that of the princess of the fairy tale; or still again, one may be only casually strolling, when some passing phenomenon catches the wandering eye and lures one away from the frequented paths of man. Examples might be multiplied, *ad infinitum,* from every corner of the world.

In the above section, and throughout the following pages, I have made no attempt to exhaust the evidence. To have done so (after the manner, for example, of Frazer, in *The Golden Bough*) would have enlarged my chapters prodigiously without making the main line of the monomyth any clearer. Instead, I am giving in each section a few striking examples from a number of widely scattered, representative traditions. During the course of the work I shift my sources gradually, so that the reader may savor the peculiar qualities of the various styles. By the time he comes to the last page, he will have reviewed an immense number of mythologies. Should he wish to prove whether all might have been cited for every section of the monomyth, he need only turn to some of the source volumes enumerated in the bibliography and ramble through a few of the multitude of tales.

---

2. *Refusal of the Call*

OFTEN IN ACTUAL LIFE, and not infrequently in the myths and popular tales, we encounter the dull case of the call unanswered; for it is always possible to turn the ear to other interests. Refusal of the summons converts the adventure into its negative. Walled in boredom, hard work, or "culture," the subject loses the power of significant affirmative action and becomes a victim to be saved. His flowering world becomes a wasteland of dry stones and his life feels meaningless—even though, like King Minos, he may through titanic effort succeed in building an empire of renown. Whatever house he builds, it will be a house of death: a labyrinth of cyclopean walls to hide from him his Minotaur. All he can do is create new problems for himself and await the gradual approach of his disintegration.

"Because I have called, and ye refused... I also will laugh at your calamity; I will mock when your fear cometh; when your fear cometh as desolation, and your destruction cometh as a whirlwind; when distress and anguish cometh upon you.... For the turning away of the simple shall slay them, and the prosperity of fools shall destroy them."[10]

Time Jesum transeuntem et non revertentem: "Dread the passage of Jesus, for he does not return."[11]

The myths and folktales of the whole world make clear that the refusal is essentially a refusal to give up what one takes to be one's own interest. The future is regarded not in terms of an unremitting series of deaths and births, but as though one's present system of ideals, virtues, goals, and advantages were to be fixed and made secure. King Minos retained the divine bull, when the sacrifice would have signified submission to the will of the god of his society; for he preferred what he conceived to be his economic advantage. Thus he failed to advance into the life-role that he had assumed—and we have seen with what calamitous effect. The divinity itself became his terror; for, obviously, if one is oneself one's god, then God himself, the will of God, the power that would destroy one's egocentric system, becomes a monster.

I fled Him, down the nights and down the days;
I fled Him, down the arches of the years;
I fled Him, down the labyrinthine ways
Of my own mind; and in the mist of tears
I hid from Him, and under running laughter.[12]

One is harassed, both day and night, by the divine being that is the image of the living self within the locked labyrinth of one's own disoriented psyche. The ways to the gates have all been lost: there is no exit. One can only cling, like Satan, furiously, to oneself and be in hell; or else break, and be annihilate at last, in God.

"Ah, fondest, blindest, weakest,
I am He Whom thou seekest!
Thou dravest love from thee, who dravest Me."[13]

The same harrowing, mysterious voice was to be heard in the call of the Greek Apollo to the fleeing maiden Daphne, daughter of the river Peneus, as he pursued her over the plain. "O nymph, O Peneus' daughter, stay!" the deity called to her—like the frog to the princess of the fairy tale.

"I who pursue thee am no enemy. Thou knowest not whom thou fleest, and for that reason dost thou flee. Run with less speed, I pray, and hold thy flight. I, too, will follow with less speed. Nay, stop and ask who thy lover is."

He would have said more [the story goes], but the maiden pursued her frightened way and left him with words unfinished, even in her desertion seeming fair. The winds bared her limbs, the opposing breezes set her garments aflutter as she ran, and a light air flung her locks streaming behind her. Her beauty was enhanced by flight. But the chase drew to an end, for the youthful god would not longer waste his time in coaxing words, and, urged on by love, he pursued at utmost speed. Just as when a Gallic hound has seen a hare in an open plain, and seeks his prey on flying feet, but the hare, safety; he, just about to fasten on her, now, even now thinks he has her, and grazes her very heels with his outstretched muzzle; but she knows not whether or not she be already caught, and barely escapes from those sharp fangs and leaves behind the jaws just closing on her: so ran the god and maid, he sped by hope and she by fear. But he ran the more swiftly, borne on the wings of love, gave her no time to rest, hung over her fleeing shoulders and breathed on the hair that streamed over her neck. Now was her strength all gone, and, pale with fear and utterly overcome by the toil of her swift flight, seeing the waters of her father's river near, she cried: "O father, help! If your waters hold divinity, change and destroy this beauty by which I pleased o'er well." Scarce had she thus prayed when a down-dragging numbness seized her limbs, and her soft sides were begirt with thin bark. Her hair was changed to leaves, her arms to branches. Her feet, but now so swift, grew fast in sluggish roots, and her head was now but a tree's top. Her gleaming beauty alone remained.[14]

FIGURE 13. *Apollo and Daphne* (carved ivory, Coptic, Egypt, fifth century A.D.)

This is indeed a dull and unrewarding finish. Apollo, the sun, the lord of time and ripeness, no longer pressed his frightening suit, but instead, simply named the laurel his favorite tree and ironically recommended its leaves to the fashioners of victory wreaths. The girl had retreated to the image of her parent and there found protection—like the unsuccessful husband whose dream of mother love preserved him from the state of cleaving to a wife.[15]

The literature of psychoanalysis abounds in examples of such desperate fixations. What they represent is an impotence to put off the infantile ego, with its sphere of emotional relationships and ideals. One is bound in by the walls of childhood; the father and mother stand as threshold guardians, and the timorous soul, fearful of some punishment,* fails to make the passage through the door and come to birth in the world without.

Dr. Jung has reported a dream that resembles very closely the image of the myth of Daphne. The dreamer is the same young man who found himself (see above, p. 46) in the land of the sheep—the land, that is to say, of unindependence. A voice within him says, "I must first get away from the father"; then a few nights later: "a snake draws a circle about the dreamer, and he stands like a tree, grown fast to the earth."[16] This is an image of the magic circle drawn about the personality by the dragon power of the fixating parent.† Brynhild, in the same way, was protected in her virginity, arrested in her daughter state for years, by the circle of the fire of all-father Wotan. She slept in timelessness until the coming of Siegfried.

Little Briar-rose (Sleeping Beauty) was put to sleep by a jealous hag (an unconscious evil-mother image). And not only the child, her entire world went off to sleep; but at last, "after long, long years," there came a prince to wake her.

> The king and queen (the conscious good-parent images), who had just come home and were entering the hall, began to fall asleep, and with them the whole estate. All the horses slept in the stalls, the dogs in the yard, the pigeons on the roof, the flies on the walls, yes, the fire that flickered on the hearth grew still and slumbered, and the roast ceased to simmer. And the cook, who was about to pull the hair of the scullery boy because he had forgotten something, let him go and fell off to sleep. And the wind

---

* See Freud: castration complex.

† The serpent (in mythology a symbol of the terrestrial waters) corresponds precisely to Daphne's father, the river Peneus.

> went down, and not a leaf stirred in the trees. Then around the castle a hedge of thorns began to grow, which became taller every year, and finally shut off the whole estate. It grew up taller than the castle, so that nothing more was seen, not even the weather-cock on the roof.[17]

A Persian city once was "enstoned to stone"—king and queen, soldiers, inhabitants, and all—because its people refused the call of Allah.[18] Lot's wife became a pillar of salt for looking back, when she had been summoned forth from her city by Jehovah.[19] And there is the tale of the Wandering Jew, cursed to remain on earth until the Day of Judgment, because when Christ had passed him carrying the cross, this man among the people standing along the way called, "Go faster! A little speed!" The unrecognized, insulted Savior turned and said to him, "I go, but you shall be waiting here for me when I return."[20]

Some of the victims remain spellbound forever (at least, so far as we are told), but others are destined to be saved. Brynhild was preserved for her proper hero and little Briar-rose was rescued by a prince. Also, the young man transformed into a tree dreamed subsequently of the unknown woman who pointed the way, as a mysterious guide to paths unknown.[21] Not all who hesitate are lost. The psyche has many secrets in reserve. And these are not disclosed unless required. So it is that sometimes the predicament following an obstinate refusal of the call proves to be the occasion of a providential revelation of some unsuspected principle of release.

Willed introversion, in fact, is one of the classic implements of creative genius and can be employed as a deliberate device. It drives the psychic energies into depth and activates the lost continent of unconscious infantile and archetypal images. The result, of course, may be a disintegration of consciousness more or less complete (neurosis, psychosis: the plight of spellbound Daphne); but on the other hand, if the personality is able to absorb and integrate the new forces, there will be experienced an almost super-human degree of self-consciousness and masterful control. This is a basic principle of the Indian disciplines of yoga. It has been the way, also, of many creative spirits in the West.[22] It cannot be described, quite, as an answer to any specific call. Rather, it is a deliberate, terrific refusal to respond to anything but the deepest, highest, richest answer to the as-yet-unknown demand of some waiting void within: a kind of total strike, or rejection of the offered terms of life, as a result of which some power of transformation carries the problem to a plane of new magnitudes, where it is suddenly and finally resolved.

This is the aspect of the hero-problem illustrated in the wondrous Arabian Nights adventure of the Prince Kamar al-Zaman and the Princess Budur. The young and handsome prince, the only son of King Shahriman of Persia, persistently refused the repeated suggestions, requests, demands, and finally injunctions, of his father, that he should do the normal thing and take to himself a wife. The first time the subject was broached to him, the lad responded: "O my father, know that I have no lust to marry nor doth my soul incline to women; for that concerning their craft and perfidy I have read many books and heard much talk, even as saith the poet:

Now, an of women ask ye, I reply:—
In their affairs I'm versed a doctor rare!
When man's head grizzles and his money dwindles,
In their affection he hath naught for share.

And another said:

Rebel against women and so shalt thou serve Allah the more;
The youth who gives women the rein must forfeit all hope to soar.
They'll baulk him when seeking the strange device, Excelsior,
Tho' waste he a thousand of years in the study of science and lore."

And when he had ended his verses he continued, "O my father, wedlock is a thing whereto I will never consent; no, not though I drink the cup of death."

When the Sultan Shahriman heard these words from his son, light became darkness in his sight and he was full of grief; yet, for the great love he bore him, he was unwilling to repeat his wishes and was not angry, but showed him all manner of kindness.

After a year, the father pressed again his question, but the youth persisted in refusal, with further stanzas from the poets. The king consulted with his wazir, and the minister advised:

> O king, wait another year and, if after that thou be minded to speak to him on the matter of marriage, speak not to him privily, but address him on a day of state, when all the emirs and wazirs are present with the whole of the army standing before thee. And when all are in crowd then send for thy son, Kamar al-Zaman, and summon him; and, when he cometh, broach to him the matter of marriage before the wazirs and grandees and officers of state and captains; for he will surely be bashful and daunted by their presence and will not dare to oppose thy will.

When the moment came, however, and King Shahriman gave his command before the state, the prince bowed his head awhile, then raising it towards his father, and, being moved by youthful folly and boyish ignorance, replied: "But for myself I will never marry; no, not though I drink the cup of death! As for thee, thou art great in age and small of wit: hast thou not, twice ere this day and before this occasion, questioned me of the matter of marriage, and I refused my consent? Indeed thou dotest and art not fit to govern a flock of sheep!" So saying Kamar al-Zaman unclapsed his hands from behind his back and tucked up his sleeves above his elbows before his father, being in a fit of fury; moreover, he added many words to his sire, knowing not what he said, in the trouble of his spirits.

The king was confounded and ashamed, since this befell in the presence of his grandees and soldier-officers assembled on a high festival and state occasion; but presently the majesty of kingship took him, and he cried out at his son and made him tremble. Then he called to the guards standing before him and commanded, "Seize him!" So they came forward and laid hands on him and, binding him, brought him before his sire, who bade them pinion his elbows behind his back and in this guise make him stand before the presence. And the prince bowed down his head for fear and apprehension, and his brow and face were beaded and spangled with sweat; and shame and confusion troubled him sorely. Thereupon his father abused him and reviled him and cried, "Woe to thee, thou son of adultery and nursling of abomination! How durst thou answer me in this wise before my captains and soldiers? But hitherto none hath chastised thee. Knowest thou not that this deed thou hast done were a disgrace to him had it been done by the meanest of my subjects?" And the king ordered his mamelukes to loose his elbow-bonds and imprison him in one of the bastions of the citadel.

So they took the prince and thrust him into an old tower in which there was a dilapidated salon, and in its midst a ruined well, after having first swept it and cleansed its floor-rags and set therein a couch on which they laid a mattress, a leathern rug, and a cushion. And then they brought a great lantern and a wax candle; for that place was dark, even by day. And lastly the mamelukes led Kamar al-Zaman thither, and stationed a eunuch at the door. And when all this was done, the prince threw himself on the couch, sad-spirited, and heavyhearted, blaming himself and repenting of his injurious conduct to his father.

Meanwhile in the distant empire of China, the daughter of King Ghazur, Lord of the Islands and the Seas and the Seven Palaces, was in like case. When her beauty had become known and her name and fame been bruited abroad in the neighboring countries, all the kings had sent to her father to demand her of him in marriage, and he had consulted her on the matter, but she had disliked the very word *wedlock.* "O my father," she had answered, "I have no mind to marry; no, not at all; for I am a sovereign lady and a queen suzerain ruling over men, and I have no desire for a man who shall rule over me." And the more suits she refused, the more her suitors' eagerness increased and all the royalties of the inner Islands of China sent presents and rarities to her father with letters asking her in marriage. So he pressed her again and again with advice on the matter of espousals; but she ever opposed to him refusals, till at last she turned upon him angrily and cried: "O my father, if thou name matrimony to me once more, I will go into my chamber and take a sword and, fixing its hilt on the ground, will set its point to my waist; then will I press upon it, till it come forth from my back, and so slay myself."

Now when the king heard these words, the light became darkness in his sight and his heart burned for her as with a flame of fire, because he feared lest she should kill herself; and he was filled with perplexity concerning her affair and the kings her suitors. So he said to her: "If thou be determined not to marry and there be no help for it: abstain from going and coming in and out." Then he placed her in a house and shut her up in a chamber, appointing ten old women as duennas to guard her, and forbade her to go forth to the Seven Palaces. Moreover, he made it appear that he was incensed against her, and sent letters to all the kings, giving them to know that she had been stricken with madness by the Jinn.[23]

With the hero and the heroine both following the negative way, and between them the continent of Asia, it will require a miracle to consummate the union of this eternally predestined pair. Whence can such a power come to break the life-negating spell and dissolve the wrath of the two childhood fathers?

The reply to this question would remain the same throughout the mythologies of the world. For, as is written so frequently in the sacred pages of the Koran: "Well able is Allah to save." The sole problem is what the machinery of the miracle is to be. And that is a secret to be opened only in the following stages of this Arabian Nights' entertainment.

3. *Supernatural Aid*

For those who have not refused the call, the first encounter of the hero-journey is with a protective figure (often a little old crone or old man) who provides the adventurer with amulets against the dragon forces he is about to pass.

An East African tribe, for example, the Wachaga of Tanganyika, tell of a very poor man named Kyazimba, who set out in desperation for the land where the sun rises. And he had traveled long and grown tired, and was simply standing, looking hopelessly in the direction of his search, when he heard someone approaching from behind. He turned and perceived a decrepit little woman. She came up and wished to know his business. When he had told her, she wrapped her garment around him, and, soaring from the earth, transported him to the zenith, where the sun pauses in the middle of the day. Then with a mighty din a great company of men came from eastward to that place, and in the midst of them was a brilliant chieftain, who, when he had arrived, slaughtered an ox and sat down to feast with his retainers. The old woman asked his help for Kyazimba. The chieftain blessed the man and sent him home. And it is recorded that he lived in prosperity ever after.[24]

Among the American Indians of the Southwest the favorite personage in this benignant role is Spider Woman—a grandmotherly little dame who lives underground. The Twin War Gods of the Navaho on the way to the house of their father, the Sun, had hardly departed from their home, following a holy trail, when they came upon this wonderful little figure:

> The boys traveled rapidly in the holy trail, and soon after sunrise, near Dsilnaotil, saw smoke arising from the ground. They went to the place where the smoke rose, and they found it came from the smoke hole of a subterranean chamber. A ladder, black from smoke, projected through the hole. Looking down into the chamber they saw an old woman, the Spider Woman, who glanced up at them and said: "Welcome, children. Enter. Who are you, and whence do

you come together walking?" They made no answer, but descended the ladder. When they reached the floor she again spoke to them, asking: "Whither do you two go walking together?" "Nowhere in particular," they answered; "we came here because we had nowhere else to go." She asked this question four times, and each time she received a similar answer. Then she said: "Perhaps you would seek your father?" "Yes," they answered, "if we only knew the way to his dwelling." "Ah!" said the woman, "it is a long and dangerous way to the house of your father, the Sun. There are many monsters dwelling between here and there, and perhaps, when you get there, your father may not be glad to see you, and may punish you for coming. You must pass four places of danger—the rocks that crush the traveler, the reeds that cut him to pieces, the cane cactuses that tear him to pieces, and the boiling sands that overwhelm him. But I shall give you something to subdue your enemies and preserve your lives." She gave them a charm called "feather of the alien gods," which consisted of a hoop with two life-feathers (feathers plucked from a living eagle) attached, and another life-feather to preserve their existence. She taught them also this magic formula, which, if repeated to their enemies, would subdue their anger: "Put your feet down with pollen. Put your hands down with pollen. Put your head down with pollen. Then your feet are pollen; your hands are pollen; your body is pollen; your mind is pollen; your voice is pollen. The trail is beautiful. Be still."[25]*

FIGURE 14. *The Rocks That Crush, the Reeds That Cut* (sand painting, Navaho, North America, A.D. 1943)

* Pollen is a symbol of spiritual energy among the American Indians of the Southwest. It is used profusely in all ceremonials, both to drive evil away and to mark out the symbolical path of life.

The helpful crone and fairy godmother is a familiar feature of European fairy lore; in Christian saints' legends the role is commonly played by the Virgin. The Virgin by her intercession can win the mercy of the Father. Spider Woman with her web can control the movements of the Sun. The hero who has come under the protection of the Cosmic Mother cannot be harmed. The thread of Ariadne brought Theseus safely through the adventure of the labyrinth. This is the guiding power that runs through the work of Dante in the female figures of Beatrice and the Virgin, and appears in Goethe's *Faust* successively as Gretchen, Helen of Troy, and the Virgin. "Thou art the living fount of hope," prays Dante, at the end of his safe passage through the perils of the Three Worlds; "Lady, thou art so great and so availest, that whoso would have grace, and has not recourse to thee, would have his desire fly without wings. Thy benignity not only succors him who asks, but oftentimes freely foreruns the asking. In thee mercy, in thee pity, in thee magnificence, in thee whatever of goodness is in any creature, are united."[26]

What such a figure represents is the benign, protecting power of destiny. The fantasy is a reassurance—a promise that the peace of Paradise, which was known first within the mother womb, is not to be lost; that it supports the present and stands in the future as well as in the past (is omega as well as alpha); that though omnipotence may seem to be endangered by the threshold passages and life awakenings, protective power is always and ever present within the sanctuary of the heart and even immanent within, or just behind, the unfamiliar features of the world. One has only to know and trust, and the ageless guardians will appear. Having responded to his own call, and continuing to follow courageously as the consequences unfold, the hero finds all the forces of the unconscious at his side. Mother Nature herself supports the mighty task. And in so far as the hero's act coincides with that for which his society itself is ready, he seems to ride on the great rhythm of the historical process. "I feel myself," said Napoleon at the opening of his Russian campaign, "driven towards an end that I do not know. As soon as I shall have reached it, as soon as I shall become unnecessary, an atom will suffice to shatter me. Till then, not all the forces of mankind can do anything against me."[27]

Not infrequently, the supernatural helper is masculine in form. In fairy lore it may be some little fellow of the wood, some wizard, hermit, shepherd, or smith, who appears, to supply the amulets and advice that the hero will require. The higher mythologies develop

FIGURE 15. *Virgil Leading Dante* (ink on vellum, Italy, fourteenth century A.D.)

the role in the great figure of the guide, the teacher, the ferryman, the conductor of souls to the afterworld. In classical myth this is Hermes-Mercury; in Egyptian, usually Thoth (the ibis god, the baboon god); in Christian, the Holy Ghost.[28] Goethe presents the masculine guide in *Faust* as Mephistopheles—and not infrequently the dangerous aspect of the "mercurial" figure is stressed; for he is the lurer of the innocent soul into realms of trial. In Dante's vision the part is played by Virgil, who yields to Beatrice at the threshold of Paradise. Protective and dangerous, motherly and fatherly at the same time, this supernatural principle of guardianship and direction unites in itself all the ambiguities of the unconscious—thus signifying the support of our conscious personality by that other, larger system, but also the inscrutability of the guide that we are following, to the peril of all our rational ends.

The following dream supplies a vivid example of the fusion of opposites in the unconscious: "I dreamed that I had gone into a street of brothels and to one of the girls. As I entered, she changed into a man, who was lying, half clothed, on a sofa. He said: 'It doesn't disturb you (that I am now a man)?' The man looked old, and he had white sideburns. He reminded me of a certain chief forester who was a good friend of my father."[29] "All dreams," Dr. Stekel observes, "have a bisexual tendency. Where the bisexuality cannot be perceived, it is hidden in the latent dream content."[30]

The hero to whom such a helper appears is typically one who has responded to the call. The call, in fact, was the first announcement of the approach of this initiatory priest. But even to those who apparently have hardened their hearts the supernatural guardian may appear; for, as we have seen: "Well able is Allah to save."

And so it happened, as it were by chance, that in the ancient and deserted tower where Kamar al-Zaman, the Persian prince, lay sleeping, there was an old Roman well,* and this was inhabited by a Jinniyah of the seed of Iblis the Accursed, by name Maymunah, daughter of Al-Dimiryat, a renowned king of the Jinn.

Compare Maymunah the Jinn to the frog of the fairy tale. In pre-Mohammedan Arabia the Jinn (singular: *m.* Jinni; *f.* Jinniyah) were haunting-demons of the deserts and wilderness. Hairy and misformed, or else shaped as animals, ostriches, or serpents, they were very dangerous to unprotected persons. The Prophet Mohammed admitted the existence of these heathen spirits,[31] and incorporated them in the Mohammedan system, which recognizes three created intelligences under Allah: Angels formed of light, Jinn of subtle fire, and Man of the dust of the earth. The Mohammedan Jinn have the power of putting on any form they please, but not grosser than the essence of fire and smoke, and they can thus make themselves visible to mortals. There are three orders of Jinn: flyers, walkers, and divers. Many are supposed to have accepted the True Faith, and these are regarded as good; the rest are bad. The latter dwell and work in close association with the Fallen Angels, whose chief is Iblis ("the Despairer").

And as Kamar al-Zaman continued sleeping till the first third of the night, Maymunah came up out of the Roman well and made for the firmament, thinking to listen by stealth to the converse of the angels; but when she reached the mouth of the well, and saw a light shining in the tower room, contrary to custom, she marveled, drew nigh, entered within the door, and beheld the couch spread, whereon was a human form with a wax candle burning at his head and the lantern at his feet. She folded her wings and stood by the bed, and, drawing back the coverlid, discovered Kamar al-Zaman's face. And she was

* The well is symbolical of the unconscious. Compare that of the fairy story of the Frog King, pp. 41–42.

motionless for a full hour in admiration and wonderment. "Blessed be Allah," she exclaimed when she recovered, "the best of Creators!" for she was of the true-believing Jinn.

Then she promised herself that she would do no hurt to Kamar al-Zaman, and became concerned lest, resting in this desert place, he should be slain by one of her relatives, the Marids.* Bending over him, she kissed him between the eyes, and presently drew back the sheet over his face; and after a while she spread her wings and, soaring into the air, flew upwards till she drew near to the lowest of the heavens.

Now as chance or destiny would have it, the soaring Ifritah Maymunah suddenly heard in her neighborhood the noisy flapping of wings. Directing herself by the sound, she found it coming from an Ifrit called Dahnash. So she swooped down on him like a sparrow hawk, and when he was aware of her and knew her to be Maymunah, the daughter of the king of the Jinn, he was sore afraid, and his side muscles quivered, and he implored her to forbear. But she challenged him to declare whence he should be coming at this hour of the night. He replied that he was returning from the Islands of the Inland Sea in the parts of China, the realms of King Ghayur, Lord of the Islands and the Seas and the Seven Palaces.

"There," said he, "I saw a daughter of his, than whom Allah hath made none fairer in her time." And he launched into great praise of the Princess Budur. "She hath a nose," said he,

> like the edge of a burnished blade and cheeks like purple wine or anemones blood-red: her lips as coral and cornelian shine and the water of her mouth is sweeter than old wine; its taste would quench hell's fiery pain. Her tongue is moved by wit of high degree and ready repartee: her breast is seduction to all that see (glory be to Him Who fashioned it and finished it!); and joined thereto are two upper arms smooth and rounded; even as saith of her the poet Al-Walahan:
>
> *She has wrists which, did her bangles not contain,*
> *would run from out her sleeves in silvern rain.*

The celebration of her beauty continued, and when Maymunah had heard it all she remained silent in astonishment. Dahnash resumed, and described the mighty king, her father, his treasures, and the Seven Palaces, as well as the history of the daughter's refusal to wed. "And I,"

---

* An Ifrit (Ifritah) is a powerful Jinni (Jinniyah). The Marids are a particularly powerful and dangerous class of Jinn.

said he, "O my lady, go to her every night and take my fill of feeding my sight on her face and I kiss her between the eyes: yet, of my love to her, I do her no hurt." He desired Maymunah to fly back with him to China and look on the beauty, loveliness, stature, and perfection of proportion of the princess. "And after, if thou wilt," said he, "chastise me or enslave me; for it is thine to bid and to forbid."

Maymunah was indignant that anyone should presume to celebrate any creature in the world, after the glimpse she had just had of Kamar al-Zaman. "Faugh! Faugh!" she cried. She laughed at Dahnash and spat in his face. "Verily, this night I have seen a young man," said she, "whom if thou saw though but in a dream, thou wouldst be palsied with admiration and spittle would flow from thy mouth." And she described his case. Dahnash expressed his disbelief that anyone could be more handsome than the Princess Budur, and Maymunah commanded him to come down with her and look.

"I hear and I obey," said Dahnash.

And so they descended and alighted in the salon. Maymunah stationed Dahnash beside the bed and, putting out her hand, drew back the silken coverlet from Kamar al-Zaman's face, when it glittered and glistened and shimmered and shone like the rising sun. She gazed at him for a moment, then turning sharply round upon Dahnash said: "Look, O accursed, and be not the basest of madmen; I am a maid, yet my heart he hath waylaid."

"By Allah, O my Lady, thou art excusable," declared Dahnash; "but there is yet another thing to be considered, and that is, that the estate female differeth from the male. By Allah's might, this thy beloved is the likest of all created things to my mistress in beauty and loveliness and grace and perfection; and it is as though they were both cast alike in the mold of seemlihead."

The light became darkness in Maymunah's sight when she heard those words, and she dealt Dahnash with her wing so fierce a buffet on the head as well-nigh made an end of him. "I conjure thee," she commanded, "by the light of my love's glorious countenance, go at once, O accursed, and bring hither thy mistress whom thou lovest so fondly and foolishly, and return in haste that we may lay the twain together and look at them both as they lie asleep side by side; so shall it appear to us which be the goodlier and more beautiful of the two."

And so, incidentally to something going on in a zone of which he was entirely unconscious, the destiny of the life-reluctant Kamar al-Zaman began to fulfill itself, without the cooperation of his conscious will.[32]

4. *The Crossing of the First Threshold*

WITH THE PERSONIFICATIONS of his destiny to guide and aid him, the hero goes forward in his adventure until he comes to the "threshold guardian" at the entrance to the zone of magnified power. Such custodians bound the world in the four directions—also up and down—standing for the limits of the hero's present sphere, or life horizon. Beyond them is darkness, the unknown, and danger; just as beyond the parental watch is danger to the infant and beyond the protection of his society danger to the member of the tribe. The usual person is more than content, he is even proud, to remain within the indicated bounds, and popular belief gives him every reason to fear so much as the first step into the unexplored. Thus the sailors of the bold vessels of Columbus, breaking the horizon of the medieval mind—sailing, as they thought, into the boundless ocean of immortal being that surrounds the cosmos, like an endless mythological serpent biting its tail[33]—had to be cozened and urged on like children, because of their fear of the fabled leviathans, mermaids, dragon kings, and other monsters of the deep.

The folk mythologies populate with deceitful and dangerous presences every desert place outside the normal traffic of the village. For example, the Hottentots describe an ogre that has been occasionally encountered among the scrubs and dunes. Its eyes are set on its instep, so that to discover what is going on it has to get down on hands and knees, and hold up one foot. The eye then looks behind; otherwise it is gazing continually at the sky. This monster is a hunter of men, whom it tears to shreds with cruel teeth as long as fingers. The creature is said to hunt in packs.[34] Another Hottentot apparition, the Hai-uri, progresses by leaping over clumps of scrub instead of going around them.[35] A dangerous one-legged, one-armed, one-sided figure—the half-man—invisible if viewed from the off side, is encountered in many parts of the earth. In Central Africa it is declared that such a half-man says to the person who has encountered him: "Since you have met with me, let us fight together." If thrown, he

FIGURE 16. *Odysseus and the Sirens* (detail; polychrome-figured white lecythus, Greece, fifth century B.C.)

will plead: "Do not kill me. I will show you lots of medicines"; and then the lucky person becomes a proficient doctor. But if the half-man (called *Chiruwi,* "a mysterious thing") wins, his victim dies.[36]

The regions of the unknown (desert, jungle, deep sea, alien land, etc.) are free fields for the projection of unconscious content. Incestuous *libido* and patricidal *destrudo* are thence reflected back against the individual and his society in forms suggesting threats of violence and fancied dangerous delight—not only as ogres but also as sirens of mysteriously seductive, nostalgic beauty. The Russian peasants know, for example, of the "Wild Women" of the woods who have their abode in mountain caverns where they maintain households, like human beings. They are handsome females, with fine square heads, abundant tresses, and hairy bodies. They fling their breasts over their shoulders when they run and when they nurse their children. They go in groups. With unguents prepared from forest roots they can anoint and render themselves invisible. They like to dance or tickle people to death who wander alone into the forest, and anyone who accidentally chances upon their invisible dancing parties dies. On the other hand, for people who set out food for them, they reap the grain, spin, care for the children, and tidy up the house; and if a girl will comb out hemp for them to spin, they will give her leaves that turn to gold. They enjoy human lovers, have frequently married country youths, and are known to make excellent wives. But like all supernatural brides, the minute the husband offends in the least their whimsical notions of marital propriety, they disappear without a trace.[37]

One more example, to illustrate the libidinous association of the dangerous impish ogre with the principle of seduction, is Dyedushka Vodyanoy, the Russian "Water Grandfather." He is an adroit shapeshifter and is said to drown people who swim at midnight or at noon. Drowned or disinherited girls he marries. He has a special talent for coaxing unhappy women into his toils. He likes to dance on moonlit nights. Whenever a wife of his is about to have a baby, he comes into the villages to seek a midwife. But he can be detected by the water that oozes from the border of his garments. He is bald, tun bellied, puffy cheeked, with green clothing and a tall cap of reeds; but he can also appear as an attractive young man, or as some personage well known in the community. This Water Master is not strong ashore, but in his own element he is supreme. He inhabits the deeps of rivers, streams, and ponds, preferring to be close beside a mill. During the day he remains concealed, like an old trout or salmon, but at night he surfaces, splashing and flopping like a fish, to drive his subaqueous cattle, sheep, and horses ashore to graze, or else to perch up on the mill wheel and quietly comb his long green hair and beard. In the springtime, when he rouses from his long hibernation, he smashes the ice along the rivers, piling up great blocks. Mill wheels he is amused to destroy. But in a favorable temper he drives his fishherds into the fisherman's net or gives warning of coming floods. The midwife who accompanies him he pays richly with silver and gold. His beautiful daughters, tall, pale, and with an air of sadness, transparently costumed in green, torture and torment the drowned. They like to rock on trees, beautifully singing.[38]

The Arcadian god Pan is the best known Classical example of this dangerous presence dwelling just beyond the protected zone of the village boundary. Sylvanus and Faunus were his Latin counterparts.* He was the inventor of the shepherd's pipe, which he played for the dances of the nymphs, and the satyrs were his male companions.† The emotion that he instilled in human beings who by accident adventured into his domain was "panic" fear: a sudden, groundless fright. Any trifling cause then—the break of a twig, the flutter of a leaf—would flood the mind with imagined danger, and in the frantic effort to escape from his own aroused unconscious the victim expired in a flight of dread.

* In Alexandrian times Pan was identified with the ithyphallic Egyptian divinity Min, who was, among other things, the guardian of desert roads.

† Compare Dionysos, the great Thracian counterpart of Pan.

Yet Pan was benign to those who paid him worship, yielding the boons of the divine hygiene of nature: bounty to the farmers, herders, and fisherfolk who dedicated their first fruits to him, and health to all who properly approached his shrines of healing. Also wisdom, the wisdom of Omphalos, the World Navel, was his to bestow; for the crossing of the threshold is the first step into the sacred zone of the universal source. At Lykaion was an oracle, presided over by the nymph Erato, whom Pan inspired, as Apollo the prophetess at Delphi. And Plutarch numbers the ecstasies of the orgiastic rites of Pan along with the ecstasy of Cybele, the Bacchic frenzy of Dionysos, the poetic frenzy inspired by the Muses, the warrior frenzy of the god Ares (= Mars), and, fiercest of all, the frenzy of love, as illustrations of that divine "enthusiasm" that overturns the reason and releases the forces of the destructive-creative dark.

"I dreamed," stated a middle-aged, married gentleman, "that I wanted to get into a wonderful garden. But before it there was a watchman who would not permit me to enter. I saw that my friend, Fräulein Elsa, was within; she wanted to reach me her hand, over the gate. But the watchman prevented that, took me by the arm, and conducted me home. 'Do be sensible—after all!' he said. 'You know that you musn't do that.' "[39]*

This is a dream that brings out the sense of the first, or protective, aspect of the threshold guardian. One had better not challenge the watcher of the established bounds. And yet—it is only by advancing beyond those bounds, provoking the other, destructive aspect of the same power, that the individual passes, either alive or in death, into a new zone of experience. In the language of the pigmies of the Andaman Islands, the word *oko-jumu* ("dreamer," "one who speaks from dreams") designates those highly respected and feared individuals who are distinguished from their fellows by the possession of supernatural talents, which can be acquired only by meeting with the spirits—directly in the jungle, through extraordinary dream, or by death and return.[40] The adventure is always and everywhere a passage beyond the veil of the known into the unknown; the powers that

* The watchman symbolizes, according to Wilhelm Stekel, "consciousness, or, if one prefers, the aggregate of all the morality and restrictions present in consciousness. Freud," continues Dr. Stekel, "would describe the watchman as the 'superego.' But he is really only an 'interego.' Consciousness prevents the breaking through of dangerous wishes and immoral actions. This is the sense in which watchmen, police officials and officers in dreams are in general to be interpreted" (Wilhelm Stekel, *Fortschritte und Technik der Traumdeutung* [Wien-Leipzig-Bern: Verlag für Medizin, Weidmann und Cie., 1935], pp. 37–38).

watch at the boundary are dangerous; to deal with them is risky; yet for anyone with competence and courage the danger fades.

In the Banks Islands of the New Hebrides, if a young man coming back from his fishing on a rock, towards sunset, chances to see

> a girl with her head bedecked with flowers beckoning to him from the slope of the cliff up which his path is leading him; he recognizes the countenance of some girl of his own or a neighboring village; he stands and hesitates and thinks she must be a *mae*;* he looks more closely, and observes that her elbows and knees bend the wrong way; this reveals her true character, and he flies. If a young man can strike the temptress with a dracaena leaf she turns into her own shape and glides away a snake.

But these very snakes, the *mae,* so greatly feared, are believed to become the familiars of those who have intercourse with them.[41] Such demons—at once dangers and bestowers of magic power—every hero must encounter who steps an inch outside the walls of his tradition.

Two vivid Oriental stories will serve to illuminate the ambiguities of this perplexing pass and show how, though the terrors will recede before a genuine psychological readiness, the overbold adventurer beyond his depth may be shamelessly undone.

The first is of a caravan leader from Benares, who made bold to conduct his richly loaded expedition of five hundred carts into a waterless demon wilderness. Forewarned of dangers, he had taken the precaution to set huge chatties filled with water in the carts, so that, rationally considered, his prospect of making the passage of not more than sixty desert leagues was of the best. But when he had reached the middle of the crossing, the ogre who inhabited that wilderness thought, "I will make these men throw away the water they took." So he created a cart to delight the heart, drawn by pure white young oxen, the wheels smeared with mud, and came down the road from the opposite direction. Both before him and behind marched the demons who formed his retinue, heads wet, garments wet, decked with garlands of water lilies both blue and white, carrying in their hands clusters of lotus flowers both red and white, chewing the fibrous stalks of water lilies, streaming with drops of water and mud. And when the caravan and the demon company drew aside to let each other pass, the ogre greeted the leader in a friendly manner. "Where are you going?" he politely asked. To which the caravan leader replied: "We, sir, are coming from Benares.

* An amphibious sea snake marked with bands of dark and light color, always more or less dreaded whenever it is seen.

But you are approaching decked with water lilies both blue and white, with lotus flowers both red and white in your hands, chewing the fibrous stalks of water lilies, smeared with mud, with drops of water streaming from you. Is it raining along the road by which you came? Are the lakes completely covered with water lilies both blue and white, and lotus flowers both red and white?"

The ogre: "Do you see that dark green streak of woods? Beyond that point the entire forest is one mass of water; it rains all the time; the hollows are full of water; everywhere are lakes completely covered with lotus flowers both red and white." And then, as the carts passed one after another, he inquired: "What goods do you have in this cart—and in that? The last moves very heavily; what goods do you have in that?" "We have water in that," the leader answered. "You have acted wisely, of course, in bringing water thus far; but beyond this point you have no occasion to burden yourself. Break the chatties to pieces, throw away the water, travel at ease." The ogre went his way, and when out of sight, returned again to his own city of ogres.

Now that caravan leader, out of his own foolishness, took the advice of the ogre, broke the chatties, and caused the carts to move forward. Ahead there was not the slightest particle of water. For lack of water to drink the men grew weary. They traveled until sundown, and then unharnessed the carts, drew them up in a contracted circle, and tied the oxen to the wheels. There was neither water for the oxen nor gruel and boiled rice for the men. The weakened men lay down here and there and went to sleep. At midnight the ogres approached from the city of ogres, slew the oxen and men, every one, devoured their flesh, leaving only the bare bones, and, having so done, departed. The bones of their hands and all their other bones lay scattered about in the four directions and the four intermediate directions; five hundred carts stood as full as ever.[42]

The second story is of a different style. It is told of a young prince who had just completed his military studies under a world-renowned teacher. Having received, as a symbol of his distinction, the title Prince Five-weapons, he accepted the five weapons that his teacher gave him, bowed, and, armed with the new weapons, struck out onto the road leading to the city of his father, the king. On the way he came to a certain forest. People at the mouth of the forest warned him. "Sir prince, do not enter this forest," they said; "an ogre lives here, named Sticky-hair; he kills every man he sees."

But the prince was confident and fearless as a maned lion. He entered the forest just the same. When he reached the heart of it, the ogre showed himself. The ogre had increased his stature to the height of a palm tree; he had created for himself a head as big as a summer house with bell-shaped pinnacle, eyes as big as alms bowls, two tusks as big as giant bulbs or buds; he had the beak of a hawk; his belly was covered with blotches; his hands and feet were dark green. "Where are you going?" he demanded. "Halt! You are my prey!"

Prince Five-weapons answered without fear, but with great confidence in the arts and crafts that he had learned. "Ogre," said he, "I knew what I was about when I entered this forest. You would do well to be careful about attacking me; for with an arrow steeped in poison will I pierce your flesh and fell you on the spot!"

Having thus threatened the ogre, the young prince fitted to his bow an arrow steeped in deadly poison and let fly. It stuck right in the ogre's hair. Then he let fly, one after another, fifty arrows. All stuck right to the ogre's hair. The ogre shook off every one of those arrows, letting them fall right at his feet, and approached the young prince.

Prince Five-weapons threatened the ogre a second time, and drawing his sword, delivered a masterly blow. The sword, thirty-three inches long, stuck right to the ogre's hair. Then the prince smote him with a spear. That also stuck right to his hair. Perceiving that the spear had stuck, he smote him with a club. That also stuck right to his hair.

When he saw that the club had stuck, he said: "Master ogre, you have never heard of me before. I am Prince Five-weapons. When I entered this forest infested by you, I took no account of bows and suchlike weapons; when I entered this forest, I took account only of myself. Now I am going to beat you and pound you into powder and dust!" Having thus made known his determination, with a yell he struck the ogre with his right hand. His hand stuck right to the ogre's hair. He struck him with his left hand. That also stuck. He struck him with his right foot. That also stuck. He struck him with his left foot. That also stuck. Thought he: "I will beat you with my head and pound you into powder and dust!" He struck him with his head. That also stuck right to the ogre's hair."*

* It has been pointed out that this adventure of Prince Five-weapons is the earliest known example of the celebrated and well-nigh universal tar-baby story of popular folklore. (See Aurelio M. Espinosa: "Notes on the Origin and History of the Tar-Baby Story," *Journal of American Folklore*, 43 [1930]: 129–209; "A New Classification of the Fundamental Elements of the Tar-Baby Story on the Basis of Two Hundred and Sixty-Seven Versions," *Journal of American Folklore*, 56 [1943]: 31–37; and Ananda K. Coomaraswamy, "A Note on the Stick Fast Motif," *Journal of American Folklore*, 57 [1944]: 128–131.)

FIGURE 17. *Baal with Thunderbolt Spear* (limestone stele, Assyria, fifteenth–thirteenth century B.C.)

Prince Five-weapons, snared five times, stuck fast in five places, dangled from the ogre's body. But for all that, he was unafraid, undaunted. As for the ogre, he thought: "This is some lion of a man, some man of noble birth—no mere man! For although he has been caught by an ogre like me, he appears neither to tremble nor to quake! In all the time I have harried this road, I have never seen a single man to match him! Why, pray, is he not afraid?" Not daring to eat him, he asked: "Youth, why are you not afraid? Why are you not terrified with the fear of death?"

"Ogre, why should I be afraid? For in one life one death is absolutely certain. What's more, I have in my belly a thunderbolt for a weapon. If you eat me, you will not be able to digest that weapon. It will tear your insides into tatters and fragments and will kill you. In that case we'll both perish. That's why I'm not afraid!"

Prince Five-weapons, the reader must know, was referring to the Weapon of Knowledge that was within him. Indeed, this young hero was none other than the Future Buddha, in an earlier incarnation.

The thunderbolt (*vajra*) is one of the major symbols in Buddhist iconography, signifying the spiritual power of Buddhahood (indestructible enlightenment) which shatters the illusory realities of the world. The Absolute, or Adi Buddha, is represented in the images of Tibet as *Vajra-Dhara* (Tibetan: *Dorje-Chang*), "Holder of the Adamantine Bolt."

In the figures of the gods that have come down from ancient Mesopotamia (Sumer and Akkad, Babylonia and Assyria) the thunderbolt, in the same form as the *vajra,* is a conspicuous element (see Figure 62); from these it was inherited by Zeus.

We know also that among primitive peoples warriors may speak of their weapons as thunderbolts. *Sicut in coelo et in terra*: the initiated warrior is an agent of the divine will; his training is not only in manual but also in spiritual skills. Magic (the supernatural power of the thunderbolt), as well as physical force and chemical poison, gives the lethal energy to his blows. A consummate master would require no physical weapon at all; the power of his magic word would suffice.

The parable of Prince Five-weapons illustrates this theme. But it also teaches that the one who relies or prides himself upon his merely empirical, physical character is already undone. "We have here the picture of a hero," writes Dr. Coomaraswamy, "who can be involved in the coils of an aesthetic experience ["the five points" being the five senses], but is able, by an intrinsic moral superiority, to liberate himself, and even to release others."[43]

"What this youth says is true," thought the ogre, terrified with the fear of death. "From the body of this lion of a man, my stomach would not be able to digest a fragment of flesh even so small as a kidney bean. I'll let him go!" And he let Prince Five-weapons go. The Future Buddha preached the Doctrine to him, subdued him, made him self-denying, and then transformed him into a spirit entitled to receive offerings in the forest. Having admonished the ogre to be heedful, the youth departed from the forest, and at the mouth of the forest told his story to human beings; then went his way.[44]

As a symbol of the world to which the five senses glue us, and which cannot be pressed aside by the actions of the physical organs, Sticky-hair was subdued only when the Future Buddha, no longer protected by the five weapons of his momentary name and physical character, resorted to the unnamed, invisible sixth: the divine thunderbolt of the knowledge of the transcendent principle, which is beyond the phenomenal realm of names and forms. Therewith the situation changed. He was no longer caught, but released; for that which he now remembered himself to be is ever free. The force of the monster of phenomenality was dispelled, and he was rendered self-denying. Self-denying, he became divine—a spirit entitled to receive offerings—as is the world itself when known, not as final, but as a mere name and form of that which transcends, yet is immanent within, all names and forms.

The "Wall of Paradise," which conceals God from human sight, is described by Nicholas of Cusa as constituted of the "coincidence of opposites," its gate being guarded by "the highest spirit of reason, who bars the way until he has been overcome."[45] The pairs of opposites (being and not being, life and death, beauty and ugliness, good and evil, and all the other polarities that bind the faculties to hope and fear, and link the organs of action to deeds of defense and acquisition) are the clashing rocks (Symplegades) that crush the traveler, but between which the heroes always pass. This is a motif known throughout the world. The Greeks associated it with two rocky islands of the Euxine Sea, which clashed together, driven by winds; but Jason, in the *Argo*, sailed between, and since that time they have stood apart.[46] The Twin Heroes of the Navaho legend were warned of the same obstacle by Spider Woman; protected, however, by the pollen symbol of the path, and eagle feathers plucked from a living sun bird, they passed between.[47]

As the rising smoke of an offering through the sun door, so goes the hero, released from ego, through the walls of the world—leaving ego stuck to Sticky-hair and passing on.

5. *The Belly of the Whale*

THE IDEA THAT THE PASSAGE of the magical threshold is a transit into a sphere of rebirth is symbolized in the worldwide womb image of the belly of the whale. The hero, instead of conquering or conciliating the power of the threshold, is swallowed into the unknown, and would appear to have died.

Mishe-Nahma, King of Fishes,
In his wrath he darted upward,
Flashing leaped into the sunshine,
Opened his great jaws and swallowed
Both canoe and Hiawatha.[48]

The Eskimo of Bering Strait tell of the trickster-hero Raven, how, one day, as he sat drying his clothes on a beach, he observed a whale-cow swimming gravely close to shore. He called: "Next time you come up for air, dear, open your mouth and shut your eyes." Then he slipped quickly into his raven clothes, pulled on his raven mask, gathered his fire sticks under his arm, and flew out over the water. The whale came up. She did as she had been told. Raven darted through the open jaws and straight into her gullet. The shocked whale-cow snapped and sounded; Raven stood inside and looked around.[49]

The Zulus have a story of two children and their mother swallowed by an elephant. When the woman reached the animal's stomach, "she saw large forests and great rivers, and many high lands; on one side there were many rocks; and there were many people who had built their village there; and many dogs and many cattle; all there inside the elephant."[50]

The Irish hero Finn MacCool was swallowed by a monster of indefinite form, of the type known to the Celtic world as a *peist.* The little German girl Red Ridinghood was swallowed by a wolf. The Polynesian favorite Maui was swallowed by his great-great-grandmother, Hine-nui-te-po. And the whole Greek pantheon, with the sole exception of Zeus, was swallowed by its father, Kronos.

The Greek hero Herakles, pausing at Troy on his way homeward with the belt of the Queen of the Amazons, found that the city was being harassed by a monster sent against it by the sea-god Poseidon. The beast would come ashore and devour people as they moved about on the plain. Beautiful Hesione, the daughter of the king, had just been bound by her father to the sea rocks as a propitiatory sacrifice, and the great visiting hero agreed to rescue her for a price. The monster, in due time, broke to the surface of the water and opened its enormous maw. Herakles took a dive into the throat, cut his way out through the belly, and left the monster dead.

FIGURE 18. *Saturn Swallowing His Children* (detail; oil on plaster, mounted on canvas, Spain, A.D. 1819)

FIGURE 19. *Threshold Guardians, Bearing Thunderbolts* (painted wood, Japan, A.D. 1203)

This popular motif gives emphasis to the lesson that that passage of the threshold is a form of self-annihilation. Its resemblance to the adventure of the Symplegades is obvious. But here, instead of passing outward, beyond the confines of the visible world, the hero goes inward, to be born again. The disappearance corresponds to the passing of a worshiper into the temple—where he is to be quickened by the recollection of who and what he is, namely dust and ashes unless immortal. The temple interior, the belly of the whale, and the heavenly land beyond, above, and below the confines of the world, are one and the same. That is why the approaches of and the entrances to temples are flanked and defended by colossal gargoyles: dragons, lions, devil-slayers with drawn swords, resentful dwarves, winged bulls. These are the threshold guardians to ward away all incapable of encountering the higher silence within. They are preliminary embodiments of the dangerous aspect of the presence, corresponding to the mythological ogres that bound the conventional world, or to the two rows of teeth of the whale. They illustrate the fact that the devotee at the moment of the entry into the temple undergoes a metamorphosis. His secular character remains without; he sheds it as a snake its slough. Once inside he may be said to have died to time and returned to the World Womb, the World Navel, the Earthly Paradise. The mere fact that anyone can physically walk past the temple guardians does not invalidate their significance; for if the intruder is incapable of encompassing the sanctuary, he has effectually remained without. Anyone unable to understand a god sees it as a devil and is thus defended from the approach. Allegorically, then, the passage into a temple and the hero-dive through the jaws of the whale are identical adventures, both denoting, in the picture language, the life-centering, life-renewing act.

"No creature," writes Ananda Coomaraswamy, "can attain a higher grade of nature without ceasing to exist."[51] Indeed, the physical body of the hero may be actually slain, dismembered, and scattered over the land or sea—as in the Egyptian myth of the savior Osiris: he was thrown into a sarcophagus and committed to the Nile by his brother Set,* and when he returned from the dead his brother slew him again, tore the body into fourteen pieces, and scattered these over the land. The Twin Heroes of the Navaho had to pass not only the clashing rocks, but also the reeds that cut the traveler to pieces,

* The sarcophagus or casket is an alternative for the belly of the whale. Compare Moses in the bulrushes.

the boiling sands that overwhelm him. The hero whose attachment to ego is already annihilate passes back and forth across the horizons of the world, in and out of the dragon, as readily as a king through all the rooms of his house. And therein lies his power to save; for his passing and returning demonstrate that through all the contraries of phenomenality the Uncreate-Imperishable remains, and there is nothing to fear.

And so it is that, throughout the world, men whose function it has been to make visible on earth the life-fructifying mystery of the slaying of the dragon have enacted upon their own bodies the great symbolic act, scattering their flesh, like the body of Osiris, for the renovation of the world. In Phrygia, for example, in honor of the crucified and resurrected savior Attis, a pine tree was cut on the twenty-second of March, and brought into the sanctuary of the mother-goddess, Cybele. There it was swathed like a corpse with woolen bands and decked with wreaths of violets. The effigy of a young man was tied to the middle of the stem. Next day took place a ceremonial lament and blowing of trumpets. The twenty-fourth of March was known as the Day of Blood: the high priest drew blood from his arms, which he presented as an offering; the lesser clergy whirled in a dervish-dance, to the sound of drums, horns, flutes, and cymbals, until, rapt in ecstasy, they gashed their bodies with knives to bespatter the altar and tree with their blood; and the novices, in imitation of the god whose death and resurrection they were celebrating, castrated themselves and swooned.[52]

Attis's is the sacrifice that King Minos refused when he withheld the bull from Poseidon. As Frazer has shown, ritual regicide was a general tradition in the ancient world. "In Southern India," he writes, "the king's reign and life terminated with the revolution of the planet Jupiter round the sun. In Greece, on the other hand, the king's fate seems to have hung in the balance at the end of every eight years.... Without being unduly rash we may surmise that the tribute of seven youths and seven maidens whom the Athenians were bound to send to Minos every eight years had some connexion with the renewal of the king's power for another octennial cycle."[53] The bull sacrifice required of King Minos implied that he would sacrifice himself, according to the pattern of the inherited tradition, at the close of his eight-year term. But he seems to have offered, instead, the substitute of the Athenian youths and maidens. That perhaps is how the divine Minos became the monster Minotaur, the self-annihilate king the tyrant Holdfast, and the hieratic state, wherein every man enacts his role, the merchant empire, wherein each is out for himself. Such practices of substitution seem to have become general throughout the antique world toward the close of the great period of the early hieratic states, during the third and second millennia B.C.

And in the same spirit, the king of the south Indian province of Quilacare, at the completion of the twelfth year of his reign, on a day of solemn festival, had a wooden scaffolding constructed, and spread over with hangings of silk. When he had ritually bathed in a tank, with great ceremonies and to the sound of music, he then came to the temple, where he did worship before the divinity. Thereafter, he mounted the scaffolding and, before the people, took some very sharp knives and began to cut off his own nose, and then his ears, and his lips, and all his members, and as much of his flesh as he was able. He threw it away and round about, until so much of his blood was spilled that he began to faint, whereupon he summarily cut his throat.[54]

FIGURE 20. *The Return of Jason* (red-figure kalyx, Etruscan, Italy, c. 470 B.C.)

FIGURE 21. *The Temptation of St. Anthony* (copperplate engraving, Germany, c. A.D. 1470)

CHAPTER II

Initiation

1. *The Road of Trials*

ONCE HAVING TRAVERSED the threshold, the hero moves in a dream landscape of curiously fluid, ambiguous forms, where he must survive a succession of trials. This is a favorite phase of the myth-adventure. It has produced a world literature of miraculous tests and ordeals. The hero is covertly aided by the advice, amulets, and secret agents of the supernatural helper whom he met before his entrance into this region. Or it may be that he here discovers for the first time that there is a benign power everywhere supporting him in his superhuman passage.

One of the best known and most charming examples of the "difficult tasks" motif is that of Psyche's quest for her lost lover, Cupid.[1] Here all the principal roles are reversed: instead of the lover trying to win his bride, it is the bride trying to win her lover; and instead of a cruel father withholding his daughter from the lover, it is the jealous mother, Venus, hiding her son, Cupid, from his bride. When Psyche pleaded with Venus, the goddess grasped her violently by the hair and dashed her head upon the ground, then took a great quantity of wheat, barley, millet, poppy seed, peas, lentils, and beans, mingled these all together in a heap, and commanded the girl to sort them before night. Psyche was aided by an army of ants. Venus told her, next, to gather the golden wool of certain dangerous wild sheep, sharp of horn and poisonous of bite, that inhabited an inaccessible valley in a dangerous wood. But a green reed instructed her how to gather from the reeds round about the golden locks shed by the sheep in their passage. The goddess now required a bottle of water from a freezing spring high on a towering rock beset by sleepless dragons. An eagle approached, and accomplished the marvelous task. Psyche was ordered, finally, to bring from the abyss of the underworld a box full of supernatural beauty. But a high tower told her how to go down to the world below, gave her coins for Charon and sops for Cerberus, and sped her on her way.

Psyche's voyage to the underworld is but one of innumerable such adventures undertaken by the heroes of fairy tale and myth. Among the most perilous are those of the shamans of the peoples of the farthest north (the Lapps, Siberians, Eskimo, and certain American Indian tribes), when they go to seek out and recover the lost or abducted souls of the sick. The shaman of the Siberians is clothed for the adventure in a magical costume representing a bird or reindeer, the shadow principle of the shaman himself, the shape of his soul. His drum is his animal—his eagle, reindeer, or horse; he is said to fly or ride on it. The stick that he carries is another of his aids. And he is attended by a host of invisible familiars.

An early voyager among the Lapps has left a vivid description of the weird performance of one of these strange emissaries into the kingdoms of the dead.[2] Since the yonder world is a place of everlasting night, the ceremonial of the shaman has to take place after dark. The friends and neighbors gather in the flickering, dimly lighted hut of the patient, and follow attentively the gesticulations of the magician. First he summons the helping spirits; these arrive, invisible to all but himself. Two women in ceremonial attire, but without belts and wearing linen hoods, a man without hood or belt, and a girl not as yet adult are in attendance.

The shaman uncovers his head, loosens his belt and shoestrings, covers his face with his hands and begins to twirl in a variety of circles. Suddenly, with very violent gestures, he shouts: "Fit out the reindeer! Ready to boat!" Snatching up an ax, he begins striking himself about the knees with it and swinging it in the direction of the three women. He drags burning logs out of the fire with his naked hands. He dashes three times around each of the women and finally collapses, "like a dead man." During the whole time, no one has been permitted to touch him. While he reposes now in trance, he is to be watched so closely that not even a fly may settle upon him. His spirit has departed, and he is viewing the sacred mountains

FIGURE 22. *Psyche and Charon* (oil on canvas, England, c. A.D. 1873)

with their inhabiting gods. The women in attendance whisper to each other, trying to guess in what part of the yonder world he now may be.

The women may be unable to locate the shaman's position in the yonder world, in which case his spirit may fail to return to the body. Or the wandering spirit of an enemy shaman may engage him in battle or else lead him astray. It is said that there have been many shamans who failed to return.[3]

If they mention the correct mountain, the shaman stirs either a hand or a foot. At length he begins to return. In a low, weak voice he utters the words he has heard in the world below. Then the women begin to sing. The shaman slowly awakes, declaring both the cause of the illness and the manner of sacrifice to be made. Then he announces the length of time it will take for the patient to grow well.

"On his laborious journey," reports another observer,

> the shaman has to encounter and master a number of differing obstacles (*pudak*) which are not always easily overcome. After he has wandered through dark forests and over massive ranges of mountains, where he occasionally comes across the bones of other

> shamans and their animal mounts who have died along the way, he reaches an opening in the ground. The most difficult stages of the adventure now begin, when the depths of the underworld with their remarkable manifestations open before him. . . . After he has appeased the watchers of the kingdom of the dead and made his way past the numerous perils, he comes at last to the Lord of the Underworld, Erlik himself. And the latter rushes against him, horribly bellowing; but if the shaman is sufficiently skillful he can soothe the monster back again with promises of luxurious offerings. This moment of the dialogue with Erlik is the crisis of the ceremonial. The shaman passes into an ecstasy.[4]

"In every primitive tribe," writes Dr. Géza Róheim, "we find the medicine man in the center of society and it is easy to show that the medicine man is either a neurotic or a psychotic or at least that his art is based on the same mechanisms as a neurosis or a psychosis. Human groups are actuated by their group ideals, and these are always based on the infantile situation."[5] "The infancy situation is modified or inverted by the process of maturation, again modified by the necessary adjustment to reality, yet it is there and supplies those unseen libidinal ties without which no human groups could exist."[6] The medicine men, therefore, are simply making both visible and public the systems of symbolic fantasy that are present in the psyche of every adult member of their society. "They are the leaders in this infantile game and the lightning conductors of common anxiety. They fight the demons so that others can hunt the prey and in general fight reality."[7]

And so it happens that if anyone—in whatever society—undertakes for himself the perilous journey into the darkness by descending, either intentionally or unintentionally, into the crooked lanes of his own spiritual labyrinth, he soon finds himself in a landscape of symbolical figures (any one of which may swallow him) which is no less marvelous than the wild Siberian world of the *pudak* and sacred mountains. In the vocabulary of the mystics this is the second stage of the Way, that of the "purification of the self," when the senses are "cleansed and humbled," and the energies and interests "concentrated upon transcendental things";[8] or in a vocabulary of more modern turn: this is the process of dissolving, transcending, or transmuting the infantile images of our personal past. In our dreams the ageless perils, gargoyles, trials, secret helpers, and instructive figures are nightly still encountered; and in their forms we may see reflected not only the whole picture of our present case, but also the clue to what we must do to be saved.

"I stood before a dark cave, wanting to go in," was the dream of a patient at the beginning of his analysis; "and I shuddered at the thought that I might not be able to find my way back."[9] "I saw one beast after another," Emanuel Swedenborg recorded in his dream book, for the night of October 19–20, 1744, "and they spread their wings, and were dragons. I was flying over them, but one of them was supporting me."[10*] And the dramatist Friedrich Hebbel recorded, a century later (April 13, 1844): "In my dream I was being drawn with great force through the sea; there were terrifying abysses, with here and there a rock to which it was possible to hold."[11] Themistocles dreamed that a snake wound itself around his body, then crept up to his neck and when it touched his face became an eagle that took him in its talons and, carrying him upward, bore him a long distance, and set him down on a golden herald's staff that suddenly appeared, so safely that he was all at once relieved of his great anxiety and fear.[12]

The specific psychological difficulties of the dreamer frequently are revealed with touching simplicity and force:

"I had to climb a mountain. There were all kinds of obstacles in the way. I had now to jump over a ditch, now to get over a hedge, and finally to stand still because I had lost my breath." This was the dream of a stutterer.[13]

"I stood beside a lake that appeared to be completely still. A storm came up abruptly and high waves arose, so that my whole face was splashed"; the dream of a girl afraid of blushing (ereuthophobia), whose face, when she blushed, would become wet with perspiration.[14]

"I was following a girl who was going ahead of me, along the dark street. I could see her from behind only and admired her beautiful figure. A mighty desire seized me, and I was running after her. Suddenly a beam, as though released from a spring, came across the street and blocked the way. I awoke with my heart pounding." The patient was a homosexual, the transverse beam, a phallic symbol.[15]

"I got into a car, but did not know how to drive. A man who sat behind me gave me instructions. Finally, things were going quite well and we came to a plaza, where there were a number of women standing.

* Swedenborg's own comment on this dream was as follows: "Dragons of this kind, which do not reveal themselves as dragons until one sees their wings, symbolize false love. I am just now writing on this subject" (Ježower, *Das Buch der Träume*, p. 490).

The mother of my fiancée received me with great joy." The man was impotent, but had found an instructor in the psychoanalyst.[16]

"A stone had broken my windshield. I was now open to the storm and rain. Tears came to my eyes. Could I ever reach my destination in this car?" The dreamer was a young woman who had lost her virginity and could not get over it.[17]

"I saw half of a horse lying on the ground. It had only one wing and was trying to arise, but was unable to do so." The patient was a poet, who had to earn his daily bread by working as a journalist.[18]

"I was bitten by an infant." The dreamer was suffering from a psychosexual infantilism.[19]

"I am locked with my brother in a dark room. He has a large knife in his hand. I am afraid of him. 'You will drive me crazy and bring me to the madhouse,' I tell him. He laughs with malicious pleasure, replying: 'You will always be caught with me. A chain is wrapped around the two of us.' I glanced at my legs and noticed for the first time the thick iron chain that bound together my brother and myself." The brother, comments Dr. Stekel, was the patient's illness.[20]

"I am going over a narrow bridge," dreams a sixteen-year-old girl. "Suddenly it breaks under me and I plunge into the water. An officer dives in after me, and brings me, with his strong arms, to the bank. Suddenly it seems to me then that I am a dead body. The officer too looks very pale, like a corpse."[21]*

"The dreamer is absolutely abandoned and alone in a deep hole of a cellar. The walls of his room keep getting narrower and narrower, so that he cannot stir." In this image are combined the ideas of mother womb, imprisonment, cell, and grave.[22]

"I am dreaming that I have to go through endless corridors. Then I remain for a long time in a little room that looks like the bathing pool in the public baths. They compel me to leave the pool, and I have to pass again through a moist, slippery shaft, until I come through a little latticed door into the open. I feel like one newly born, and I think: 'This means a spiritual rebirth for me, through my analysis.' "[23]

There can be no question: the psychological dangers through

---

* "Naturally," writes Dr. Stekel, "'to be dead' here means 'to be alive.' She begins to live and the officer 'lives' with her. They die together. This throws a glaring light on the popular fantasy of the double-suicide."

It should be noted also that this dream includes the well-nigh universal mythological image of the sword bridge (the razor's edge, p. 16), which appears in the romance of Lancelot's rescue of Queen Guinevere from the castle of King Death.

which earlier generations were guided by the symbols and spiritual exercises of their mythological and religious inheritance, we today (in so far as we are unbelievers, or, if believers, in so far as our inherited beliefs fail to represent the real problems of contemporary life) must face alone, or, at best, with only tentative, impromptu, and not often very effective guidance. This is our problem as modern, "enlightened" individuals, for whom all gods and devils have been rationalized out of existence.* Nevertheless, in the multitude of myths and legends that have been preserved to us, or collected from the ends of the earth, we may yet see delineated something of our still human course. To hear and profit, however, one may have to submit somehow to purgation and surrender. And that is part of our problem: just how to do that. "Or do ye think that ye shall enter the Garden of Bliss without such trials as came to those who passed away before you?"[24]

The oldest recorded account of the passage through the gates of metamorphosis is the Sumerian myth of the goddess Inanna's descent to the nether world.

From the "great above" she set her mind toward
the "great below,"
The goddess, from the "great above" she set her
mind toward the "great below,"
Inanna, from the "great above" she set her mind
toward the "great below."

My lady abandoned heaven, abandoned earth,
To the nether world she descended,
Inanna abandoned heaven, abandoned earth,
To the nether world she descended,
Abandoned lordship, abandoned ladyship,
To the nether world she descended.

She adorned herself with her queenly robes and jewels. Seven divine decrees she fastened at her belt. She was ready to enter the "land of no return," the nether world of death and darkness, governed by her enemy and sister goddess, Ereshkigal. In fear, lest her sister should put her to death, Inanna instructed Ninshubur, her messenger, to go to heaven and set up a hue and cry for her in the assembly hall of the gods if after three days she should have failed to return.

---

* "The problem is not new," writes Dr. C. G. Jung, "for all ages before us have believed in gods in some form or other. Only an unparalleled impoverishment of symbolism could enable us to rediscover the gods as psychic factors, that is, as archetypes of the unconscious. . . . Heaven has become for us the cosmic space of the physicists, and the divine empyrean a fair memory of things that once were. But 'the heart glows,' and a secret unrest gnaws at the roots of our being." (Jung, "Archetypes of the Collective Unconscious," par. 50.)

Inanna descended. She approached the temple made of lapis lazuli, and at the gate was met by the chief gatekeeper, who demanded to know who she was and why she had come. "I am the queen of heaven, the place where the sun rises," she replied. "If thou art the queen of heaven," he said, "the place where the sun rises, why, pray, hast thou come to the land of no return? On the road whose traveler returns not, how has thy heart led thee?" Inanna declared that she had come to attend the funeral rites of her sister's husband, the lord Gugalanna; whereupon Neti, the gatekeeper, bid her stay until he should report to Ereshkigal. Neti was instructed to open to the queen of heaven the seven gates, but to abide by the custom and remove at each portal a part of her clothing.

To the pure Inanna he says:
"Come, Inanna, enter."

Upon her entering the first gate,
The shugurra, the "crown of the plain" of her head, was removed.
"What, pray, is this?"
"Extraordinarily, O Inanna, have the decrees of
the nether world been perfected,
O Inanna, do not question the rites of the nether world."

Upon her entering the second gate,
The rod of lapis lazuli was removed.
"What, pray, is this?"
"Extraordinarily, O Inanna, have the decrees of
the nether world been perfected,
O Inanna, do not question the rites of the nether world."

Upon her entering the third gate,
The small lapis lazuli stones of her neck were removed.
"What, pray, is this?"
"Extraordinarily, O Inanna, have the decrees of
the nether world been perfected,
O Inanna, do not question the rites of the nether world."

Upon her entering the fourth gate,
The sparkling stones of her breast were removed.
"What, pray, is this?"
"Extraordinarily, O Inanna, have the decrees of
the nether world been perfected,
O Inanna, do not question the rites of the nether world."

Upon her entering the fifth gate,
The gold ring of her hand was removed.
"What, pray, is this?"

"Extraordinarily, O Inanna, have the decrees of
the nether world been perfected,
O Inanna, do not question the rites of the nether world."

Upon her entering the sixth gate,
The breastplate of her breast was removed.
"What, pray, is this?"
"Extraordinarily, O Inanna, have the decrees of
the nether world been perfected,
O Inanna, do not question the rites of the nether world."

Upon her entering the seventh gate,
All the garments of ladyship of her body were removed.
"What, pray, is this?"
"Extraordinarily, O Inanna, have the decrees of
the nether world been perfected,
O Inanna, do not question the rites of the nether world."

Naked, she was brought before the throne. She bowed low. The seven judges of the nether world, the Anunnaki, sat before the throne of Ereshkigal, and they fastened their eyes upon Inanna—the eyes of death.

At their word, the word which tortures the spirit,
The sick woman was turned into a corpse,
The corpse was hung from a stake.[25]

Inanna and Ereshkigal, the two sisters, light and dark respectively, together represent, according to the antique manner of symbolization, the one goddess in two aspects; and their confrontation epitomizes the whole sense of the difficult road of trials. The hero, whether god or goddess, man or woman, the figure in a myth or the dreamer of a dream, discovers and assimilates his opposite (his own unsuspected self) either by swallowing it or by being swallowed. One by one the resistances are broken. He must put aside his pride, his virtue, beauty, and life, and bow or submit to the absolutely intolerable. Then he finds that he and his opposite are not of differing species, but one flesh.*

The ordeal is a deepening of the problem of the first threshold and the question is still in balance: Can the ego put itself to death? For many-headed is this surrounding Hydra; one head cut off, two more appear—unless the right caustic is applied to the mutilated

* Or, as James Joyce has phrased it: "equals of opposites, evolved by a one-same power of nature or of spirit, as the sole condition and means of its himundher manifestation and polarised for reunion by the symphysis of their antipathies" (Joyce, *Finnegans Wake*, p. 92).

stump. The original departure into the land of trials represented only the beginning of the long and really perilous path of initiatory conquests and moments of illumination. Dragons have now to be slain and surprising barriers passed—again, again, and again. Meanwhile there will be a multitude of preliminary victories, unretainable ecstasies, and momentary glimpses of the wonderful land.

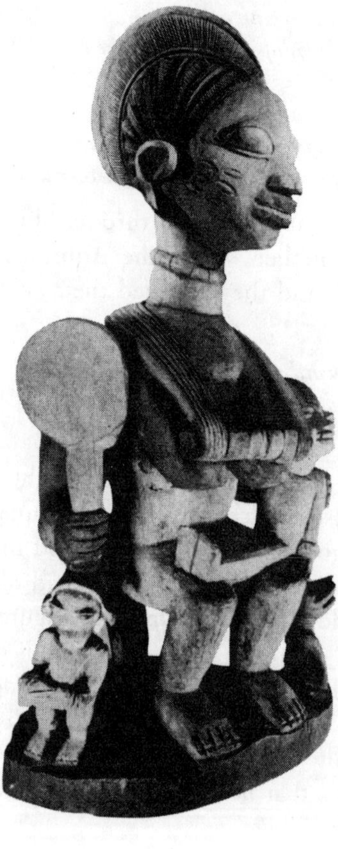

FIGURE 23. *Mother of the Gods* (carved wood, Egba-Yoruba, Nigeria, date uncertain)

2. *The Meeting with the Goddess*

THE ULTIMATE ADVENTURE, when all the barriers and ogres have been overcome, is commonly represented as a mystical marriage (ἱερὸς γάμος) of the triumphant hero-soul with the Queen Goddess of the World. This is the crisis at the nadir, at the zenith, or at the uttermost edge of the earth, at the central point of the cosmos, in the tabernacle of the temple, or within the darkness of the deepest chamber of the heart.

In the west of Ireland they still tell the tale of the Prince of the Lonesome Isle and the Lady of Tubber Tintye. Hoping to heal the Queen of Erin, the heroic youth had undertaken to go for three bottles of the water of Tubber Tintye, the flaming fairy well. Following the advice of a supernatural aunt whom he encountered on the way, and riding a wonderful, dirty, lean little shaggy horse that she gave to him, he crossed a river of fire and escaped the touch of a grove of poison trees. The horse with the speed of the wind shot past the end of the castle of Tubber Tintye; the prince sprang from its back through an open window, and came down inside, safe and sound.

> The whole place, enormous in extent, was filled with sleeping giants and monsters of sea and land—great whales, long slippery eels, bears, and beasts of every form and kind. The prince passed through them and over them till he came to a great stairway. At the head of the stairway he went into a chamber, where he found the most beautiful woman he had ever seen, stretched on a couch asleep. "I'll have nothing to say to you," thought he, and went on to the next; and so he looked into twelve chambers. In each was a woman more beautiful than the one before. But when he reached the thirteenth chamber and opened the door, the flash of gold took the sight from his eyes. He stood awhile till the sight came back, and then entered. In the great bright chamber was a golden couch, resting on wheels of gold. The wheels turned continually; the couch went round and round, never stopping night or day.

> On the couch lay the Queen of Tubber Tintye; and if her twelve maidens were beautiful, they would not be beautiful if seen near her. At the foot of the couch was Tubber Tintye itself—the well of fire. There was a golden cover upon the well, and it went around continually with the couch of the Queen.
>
> "Upon my word," said the prince, "I'll rest here a while." And he went up on the couch and never left it for six days and nights.[26]

The Lady of the House of Sleep is a familiar figure in fairy tale and myth. We have already spoken of her, under the forms of Brynhild and little Briar-rose.[27] She is the paragon of all paragons of beauty, the reply to all desire, the bliss-bestowing goal of every hero's earthly and unearthly quest. She is mother, sister, mistress, bride. Whatever in the world has lured, whatever has seemed to promise joy, has been premonitory of her existence—in the deep of sleep, if not in the cities and forests of the world. For she is the incarnation of the promise of perfection; the soul's assurance that, at the conclusion of its exile in a world of organized inadequacies, the bliss that once was known will be known again; the comforting, the nourishing, the "good" mother—young and beautiful—who was known to us, and even tasted, in the remotest past. Time sealed her away, yet she is dwelling still, like one who sleeps in timelessness, at the bottom of the timeless sea.

The remembered image is not only benign, however; for the "bad" mother too—(1) the absent, unattainable mother, against whom aggressive fantasies are directed, and from whom a counter-aggression is feared; (2) the hampering, forbidding, punishing mother; (3) the mother who would hold to herself the growing child trying to push away; and finally (4) the desired but forbidden mother (Oedipus complex) whose presence is a lure to dangerous desire (castration complex)—persists in the hidden land of the adult's infant recollection and is sometimes even the greater force. She is at the root of such unattainable great goddess figures as that of the chaste and terrible Diana—whose absolute ruin of the young sportsman Actaeon illustrates what a blast of fear is contained in such symbols of the mind's and body's blocked desire.

Actaeon chanced to see the dangerous goddess at noon; that fateful moment when the sun breaks in its youthful, strong ascent, balances, and begins the mighty plunge to death. He had left his companions to rest, together with his blooded dogs, after a morning of running game, and without conscious purpose had gone wandering,

FIGURE 24. *Diana and Actaeon* (marble metope, Hellenic, Sicily, c. 460 B.C.)

straying from his familiar hunting groves and fields, exploring through the neighboring woods. He discovered a vale, thick grown with cypresses and pine. He penetrated curiously into its fastness. There was a grotto within it, watered by a gentle, purling spring and with a stream that widened to a grassy pool. This shaded nook was the resort of Diana, and at that moment she was bathing among her nymphs, absolutely naked. She had put aside her hunting spear, her quiver, her unstrung bow, as well as her sandals and her robe. And one of the nude nymphs had bound up her tresses into a knot; some of the others were pouring water from capacious urns.

When the young, roving male broke into the pleasant haunt, a shriek of female terror went up, and all the bodies crowded about their mistress, trying to hide her from the profane eye. But she stood above them, head and shoulders. The youth had seen, and was continuing to see. She glanced for her bow, but it was out of reach, so she quickly took up what was at hand, namely water, and flung it into Actaeon's face. "Now you are free to tell, if you can," she cried at him angrily, "that you have seen the goddess nude."

Antlers sprouted on his head. His neck grew great and long, his eartips sharp. His arms lengthened to legs, and his hands and feet became hooves. Terrified, he bounded—marveling that he should move so rapidly. But when he paused for breath and drink and beheld his features in a clear pool, he reared back aghast.

A terrible fate then befell Actaeon. His own hounds, catching the scent of the great stag, came baying through the wood. In a moment of joy at hearing them he paused, but then spontaneously took fright and fled. The pack followed, gradually gaining. When they had come to his heels, the first of them flying at his flank, he tried to cry their names, but the sound in his throat was not human. They fixed him with their fangs. He went down, and his own hunting companions, shouting encouragement at the dogs, arrived in time to deliver the *coup de grâce.* Diana, miraculously aware of the flight and death, could now rest appeased.[28]

The mythological figure of the Universal Mother imputes to the cosmos the feminine attributes of the first, nourishing and protecting presence. The fantasy is primarily spontaneous; for there exists a close and obvious correspondence between the attitude of the young child toward its mother and that of the adult toward the surrounding material world.[29] But there has been also, in numerous religious traditions, a consciously controlled pedagogical utilization of this archetypal image for the purpose of the purging, balancing, and initiation of the mind into the nature of the visible world.

In the Tantric books of medieval and modern India the abode of the goddess is called Mani-dvipa, "The Island of Jewels." Her couch-and-throne is there, in a grove of wish-fulfilling trees. The beaches of the isle are of golden sands. They are laved by the still waters of the ocean of the nectar of immortality. The goddess is red with the fire of life; the earth, the solar system, the galaxies of far-extending space, all swell within her womb. For she is the world creatrix, ever mother, ever virgin. She encompasses the encompassing, nourishes the nourishing, and is the life of everything that lives.

The sacred writings (Śastras) of Hinduism are divided into four classes: (1) Śruti, which are regarded as direct divine revelation; these include the four Vedas (ancient books of psalms) and certain of the Upaniṣads (ancient books of philosophy); (2) Smṛti, which include the traditional teachings of the orthodox sages, canonical instructions for domestic ceremonials, and certain works of secular and religious law, as well as the great Hindu epic, the Mahābhārata, which of course includes the Bhagavad Gītā; (3) Purāṇa, which are the Hindu mythological and epic works par excellence; these treat of cosmogonic, theological, astronomical, and physical knowledge; and (4) Tantra, texts describing techniques and rituals for the worship of deities, and for the attainment of supranormal power. Among the Tantras are a group of particularly important scriptures (called Āgamas) which are supposed to have been revealed directly by the Universal God Śiva and his Goddess Pārvatī. (They are termed, therefore, "The Fifth Veda.") These support a mystical tradition known specifically as "The Tantra," which has exercised a pervasive influence on the later forms of Hindu and Buddhist iconography. Tantric symbolism was carried by medieval Buddhism out of India into Tibet, China, and Japan.

She is also the death of everything that dies. The whole round of existence is accomplished within her sway, from birth, through adolescence, maturity, and senescence, to the grave. She is the womb and the tomb: the sow that eats her farrow. Thus she unites the "good" and the "bad," exhibiting the two modes of the remembered mother, not as personal only, but as universal. The devotee is expected to contemplate the two with equal equanimity. Through this exercise his spirit is purged of its infantile, inappropriate sentimentalities and resentments, and his mind opened to the inscrutable presence which exists, not primarily as "good" and "bad" with respect to his childlike human convenience, his weal and woe, but as the law and image of the nature of being.

The great Hindu mystic of the nineteenth century Ramakrishna (1836–1886) was a priest in a temple newly erected to the Cosmic Mother at Dakshineswar, a suburb of Calcutta. The temple image displayed the divinity in her two aspects simultaneously, the terrible and the benign. Her four arms exhibited the symbols of her universal power: the upper left hand brandishing a bloody saber, the lower gripping by the hair a severed human head; the upper right was lifted in the "fear not" gesture, the lower extended in bestowal of boons. As necklace she wore a garland of human heads; her kilt was a girdle of human arms; her long tongue was out to lick blood. She was Cosmic Power, the totality of the universe, the harmonization of all the pairs of opposites, combining wonderfully the terror of absolute destruction with an impersonal yet motherly reassurance.

As change, the river of time, the fluidity of life, the goddess at once creates, preserves, and destroys. Her name is Kālī, the Black One; her title: The Ferry across the Ocean of Existence.[30]

FIGURE 25. *Devouring Kālī* (carved wood, Nepal, eighteenth–nineteenth century A.D.)

One quiet afternoon Ramakrishna beheld a beautiful woman ascend from the Ganges and approach the grove in which he was meditating. He perceived that she was about to give birth to a child. In a moment the babe was born, and she gently nursed it. Presently, however, she assumed a horrible aspect, took the infant in her now ugly jaws and crushed it, chewed it. Swallowing it, she returned again to the Ganges, where she disappeared.[31]

Only geniuses capable of the highest realization can support the full revelation of the sublimity of this goddess. For lesser men she reduces her effulgence and permits herself to appear in forms concordant with their undeveloped powers. Fully to behold her would be a terrible accident for any person not spiritually prepared: as witness the unlucky case of the lusty young buck Actaeon. No saint was he, but a sportsman unprepared for the revelation of the form that must be beheld without the normal human (i.e., infantile) over- and undertones of desire, surprise, and fear.

Woman, in the picture language of mythology, represents the totality of what can be known. The hero is the one who comes to know. As he progresses in the slow initiation which is life, the form of the goddess undergoes for him a series of transfigurations: she can never be greater than himself, though she can always promise more than he is yet capable of comprehending. She lures, she guides, she bids him burst his fetters. And if he can match her import, the two, the knower and the known, will be released from every limitation. Woman is the guide to the sublime acme of sensuous adventure. By deficient eyes she is reduced to inferior states; by the evil eye of ignorance she is spellbound to banality and ugliness. But she is redeemed by the eyes of understanding. The hero who can take her as she is, without undue commotion but with the kindness and assurance she requires, is potentially the king, the incarnate god, of her created world.

A story, for example, is told of the five sons of the Irish king Eochaid: of how, having gone one day ahunting, they found themselves astray, shut in on every hand. Thirsty, they set off, one by one, to look for water. Fergus was the first:

> and he lights on a well, over which he finds an old woman standing sentry. The fashion of the hag is this: blacker than coal every joint and segment of her was, from crown to ground; comparable to a wild horse's tail the grey wiry mass of hair that pierced her scalp's upper surface; with her sickle of a greenish looking tusk that was in her head, and curled till it touched her ear, she could

> lop the verdant branch of an oak in full bearing; blackened and smoke-bleared eyes she had; nose awry, wide-nostrilled; a wrinkled and freckled belly, variously unwholesome; warped crooked shins, garnished with massive ankles and a pair of capacious shovels; knotty knees she had and livid nails. The beldame's whole description in fact was disgusting. "That's the way it is, is it?" said the lad, and "that's the very way," she answered. "Is it guarding the well thou art?" he asked, and she said: "it is." "Dost thou licence me to take away some water?" "I do," she consented, "yet only so that I have of thee one kiss on my cheek." "Not so," said he. "Then water shall not be conceded by me." "My word I give," he went on, "that sooner than give thee a kiss I would perish of thirst!" Then the young man departed to the place where his brethren were, and told them that he had not gotten water.

Olioll, Brian, and Fiachra, likewise, went on the quest and equally attained to the identical well. Each solicited the old thing for water, but denied her the kiss.

Finally it was Niall who went, and he came to the very well.

> "Let me have water, woman!" he cried. "I will give it," said she, "and bestow on me a kiss." He answered: "forby giving thee a kiss, I will even hug thee!" Then he bends to embrace her, and gives her a kiss. Which operation ended, and when he looked at her, in the whole world was not a young woman of gait more graceful, in universal semblance fairer than she: to be likened to the last-fallen snow lying in trenches every portion of her was, from crown to sole; plump and queenly forearms, fingers long and taper, straight legs of a lovely hue she had; two sandals of the white bronze betwixt her smooth and soft white feet and the earth; about her was an ample mantle of the choicest fleece pure crimson, and in the garment a brooch of white silver; she had lustrous teeth of pearl, great regal eyes, mouth red as the rowanberry. "Here, woman, is a galaxy of charms," said the young man. "That is true indeed." "And who art thou?" he pursued. "'Royal Rule' am I," she answered, and uttered this:
>
> "King of Tara! I am Royal Rule...."
>
> "Go now," she said, "to thy brethren, and take with thee water; moreover, thine and thy children's for ever the kingdom and supreme power shall be.... And as at the first thou hast seen me ugly, brutish, loathly—in the end, beautiful—even so is royal rule: for without battles, without fierce conflict, it may not be won; but in the result, he that is king of no matter what shows comely and handsome forth."[32]

Such is royal rule? Such is life itself. The goddess guardian of the inexhaustible well—whether as Fergus, or as Actaeon, or as the Prince of the Lonesome Isle discovered her—requires that the hero should be endowed with what the troubadours and minnesingers termed the "gentle heart." Not by the animal desire of an Actaeon, not by the fastidious revulsion of such as Fergus, can she be comprehended and rightly served, but only by gentleness: *aware* ("gentle sympathy") it was named in the romantic courtly poetry of tenth- to twelfth-century Japan.

Within the gentle heart Love shelters himself,
As birds within the green shade of the grove.
Before the gentle heart, in nature's scheme,
Love was not, nor the gentle heart ere Love.
For with the sun, at once,
So sprang the light immediately; nor was
Its birth before the sun's.
And Love hath his effect in gentleness
Of very self; even as
Within the middle fire the heat's excess.[33]

The meeting with the goddess (who is incarnate in every woman) is the final test of the talent of the hero to win the boon of love (charity: *amor fati*), which is life itself enjoyed as the encasement of eternity.

And when the adventurer, in this context, is not a youth but a maid, she is the one who, by her qualities, her beauty, or her yearning, is fit to become the consort of an immortal. Then the heavenly husband descends to her and conducts her to his bed—whether she will or no. And if she has shunned him, the scales fall from her eyes; if she has sought him, her desire finds its peace.

The Arapaho girl who followed the porcupine up the stretching tree was enticed to the camp-circle of the people of the sky. There she became the wife of a heavenly youth. It was he who, under the form of the luring porcupine, had seduced her to his supernatural home.

The king's daughter of the nursery tale, the day following the adventure at the well, heard a thumping at her castle door: the frog had arrived to press her to her bargain. And in spite of her great disgust, he followed her to her chair at table, shared the meal from her little golden plate and cup, even insisted on going to sleep with her in her little silken bed. In a tantrum she plucked him from the floor and flung him at the wall. When he fell, he was no frog but a king's son with kind and beautiful eyes. And then we hear that they were married and were driven in a beautiful coach back to the young man's waiting kingdom, where the two became a king and queen.

Or once again: when Psyche had accomplished all of the difficult tasks, Jupiter himself gave to her a draft of the elixir of immortality; so that she is now and forever united with Cupid, her beloved, in the paradise of perfected form.

The Greek Orthodox and Roman Catholic churches celebrate the same mystery in the Feast of the Assumption:

"The Virgin Mary is taken up into the bridal chamber of heaven, where the King of Kings sits on his starry throne."

"O Virgin most prudent, whither goest thou, bright as the morn? all beautiful and sweet art thou, O daughter of Zion, fair as the moon, elect as the sun."[34]

FIGURE 26. *Vierge Ouvrante (Opening Virgin)* (polychrome wood, France, fifteenth century A.D.)

3. *Woman as the Temptress*

THE MYSTICAL MARRIAGE with the queen goddess of the world represents the hero's total mastery of life; for the woman is life, the hero its knower and master. And the testings of the hero, which were preliminary to his ultimate experience and deed, were symbolical of those crises of realization by means of which his consciousness came to be amplified and made capable of enduring the full possession of the mother-destroyer, his inevitable bride. With that he knows that he and the father are one: he is in the father's place.

Thus phrased, in extremest terms, the problem may sound remote from the affairs of normal human creatures. Nevertheless, every failure to cope with a life situation must be laid, in the end, to a restriction of consciousness. Wars and temper tantrums are the makeshifts of ignorance; regrets are illuminations come too late. The whole sense of the ubiquitous myth of the hero's passage is that it shall serve as a general pattern for men and women, wherever they may stand along the scale. Therefore it is formulated in the broadest terms. The individual has only to discover his own position with reference to this general human formula, and let it then assist him past his restricting walls. Who and where are his ogres? Those are the reflections of the unsolved enigmas of his own humanity. What are his ideals? Those are the symptoms of his grasp of life.

In the office of the modern psychoanalyst, the stages of the hero-adventure come to light again in the dreams and hallucinations of the patient. Depth beyond depth of self-ignorance is fathomed, with the analyst in the role of the helper, the initiatory priest. And always, after the first thrills of getting under way, the adventure develops into a journey of darkness, horror, disgust, and phantasmagoric fears.

The crux of the curious difficulty lies in the fact that our conscious views of what life ought to be seldom correspond to what life really is. Generally we refuse to admit within ourselves, or within our friends, the fullness of that pushing, self-protective, malodorous, carnivorous, lecherous fever which is the very nature of the organic cell.

Rather, we tend to perfume, whitewash, and reinterpret; meanwhile imagining that all the flies in the ointment, all the hairs in the soup, are the faults of some unpleasant someone else.

But when it suddenly dawns on us, or is forced to our attention, that everything we think or do is necessarily tainted with the odor of the flesh, then, not uncommonly, there is experienced a moment of revulsion: life, the acts of life, the organs of life, woman in particular as the great symbol of life, become intolerable to the pure, the pure, pure soul.

O, that this too too solid flesh would melt,
Thaw and resolve itself into a dew!
Or that the Everlasting had not fix'd
His canon 'gainst self-slaughter! O God! God!

So exclaims the great spokesman of this moment, Hamlet:

How weary, stale, flat, and unprofitable
Seem to me all the uses of this world!
Fie on't! ah fie! 'tis an unweeded garden,
That grows to seed; things rank and gross in nature
Possess it merely. That it should come to this![35]

The innocent delight of Oedipus in his first possession of the queen turns to an agony of spirit when he learns who the woman is. Like Hamlet, he is beset by the moral image of the father. Like Hamlet, he turns from the fair features of the world to search the darkness for a higher kingdom than this of the incest and adultery ridden, luxurious, and incorrigible mother. The seeker of the life beyond life must press beyond her, surpass the temptations of her call, and soar to the immaculate ether beyond.

For a God called him—called him many times,
From many sides at once: "Ho, Oedipus,
Thou Oedipus, why are we tarrying?
It is full long that thou art stayed for; come!"[36]

Where this Oedipus-Hamlet revulsion remains to beset the soul, there the world, the body, and woman above all become the symbols no longer of victory but of defeat. A monastic-puritanical, world-negating ethical system then radically and immediately transfigures all the images of myth. No longer can the hero rest in innocence with the goddess of the flesh; for she is become the queen of sin.

"So long as a man has any regard for this corpse-like body," writes the Hindu monk Śaṅkarāchārya,

> he is impure, and suffers from his enemies as well as from birth, disease and death; but when he thinks of himself as pure, as the essence of the Good, and the Immovable, he becomes free.... Throw far away this limitation of a body which is inert and filthy by nature. Think of it no longer. For a thing that has been vomited (as you should vomit forth your body) can excite only disgust when it is recalled again to mind.[37]

This is a point of view familiar to the West from the lives and writings of the saints.

> When Saint Peter observed that his daughter, Petronilla, was too beautiful, he obtained from God the favor that she should fall sick of a fever. Now one day when his disciples were by him, Titus said to him: "You who cure all maladies, why do you not fix it so that Petronilla can get up from her bed?" And Peter replied to him: "Because I am satisfied with her condition as it is." This was by no means as much as to say he had not the power to cure her; for, immediately, he said to her: "Get up, Petronilla, and make haste to wait on us." The young girl, cured, got up and came to serve them. But when she had finished, her father said to her: "Petronilla, return to your bed!" She returned, and was straightway taken again with the fever. And later, when she had begun to be perfect in her love of God, her father restored her to perfect health.
>
> At that time a noble gentleman named Flaccus, struck by her beauty, came to bid for her hand in marriage. She replied: "If you wish to marry me, send a group of young girls to conduct me to your home!" But when these had arrived, Petronilla directly set herself to fast and pray. Receiving communion, she lay back in her bed, and after three days rendered her soul up to God.[38]
>
> As a child Saint Bernard of Clairvaux suffered from headaches. A young woman came to visit him one day, to soothe his sufferings with her songs. But the indignant child drove her from the room. And God rewarded him for his zeal; for he got up from his bed immediately, and was cured.
>
> Now the ancient enemy of man, perceiving little Bernard to be of such wholesome disposition, exerted himself to set traps for his chastity. When the child, however, at the instigation of the devil, one day had stood staring at a lady for some time, suddenly he blushed for himself, and entered the icy water of a pond in penance, where he remained until frozen to his bones. Another time, when he was asleep, a young girl came naked to his bed. Bernard, becoming aware of her, yielded in silence the part of the bed in which he lay, and rolling over to the other side returned

> to sleep. Having stroked and caressed him for some time, the unhappy creature presently was so taken with shame, in spite of her shamelessness, that she got up and fled, full of horror at herself and of admiration for the young man.
>
> Still again, when Bernard together with some friends one time had accepted the hospitality of the home of a certain wealthy lady, she, observing his beauty, was seized with a passion to sleep with him. She arose that night from her bed, and came and placed herself at the side of her guest. But he, the minute he felt someone close to him, began to shout: "Thief! Thief!" Immediately thereupon, the woman scurried away, the entire house was on its feet, lanterns were lit, and everybody hunted around for the burglar. But since none was found, all returned to their beds and to sleep, with the sole exception of this lady, who, unable to close her eyes, again arose and slipped into the bed of her guest. Bernard began to shout: "Thief!" And again the alarms and investigations! After that, even a third time this lady brought herself to be spurned in like fashion; so that finally she gave up her wicked project, out of either fear or discouragement. On the road next day the companions of Bernard asked him why he had had so many dreams about thieves. And he replied to them: "I had really to repel the attacks of a thief; for my hostess tried to rob me of a treasure, which, had I lost it, I should never have been able to regain."
>
> All of which convinced Bernard that it was a pretty risky thing to live together with the serpent. So he planned to be quit of the world and enter the monastic order of the Cistercians.[39]

Not even monastery walls, however, not even the remoteness of the desert, can defend against the female presences; for as long as the hermit's flesh clings to his bones and pulses warm, the images of life are alert to storm his mind. Saint Anthony, practicing his austerities in the Egyptian Thebaid, was troubled by voluptuous hallucinations perpetrated by female devils attracted to his magnetic solitude. Apparitions of this order, with loins of irresistible attraction and breasts bursting to be touched, are known to all the hermit-resorts of history. "*Ah! bel ermite! bel ermite!... Si tu posais ton doigt sur mon épaule, ce serait comme une traînée de feu dans tes veines. La possession de la moindre place de mon corps t'emplira d'une joie plus véhémente que la conquête d'un empire. Avance tes lévres....*"[40]*

---

* [This succubus is the spirit of the Queen of Sheba: Ah! Beautiful hermitess, beautiful hermitess!... If you set your finger against my flesh, it would be as a strand of fire through thy veins. The possession of the least part of my body should fill thee with a joy more vehement than an empire's conquest. Bring on thy lips....—Ed.]

Writes the New Englander Cotton Mather:

> *The Wilderness* through which we are passing to the Promised Land is all filled with Fiery flying serpents. But, blessed be God, none of them have hitherto so fastened upon us as to confound us utterly! All our way to Heaven lies by *Dens of Lions* and the *Mounts of Leopards*; there are incredible Droves of Devils in our way.... We are poor travellers in a world which is as well the Devil's Field, as the Devil's *Gaol*; a world in which every Nook whereof, the Devil is encamped with Bands of Robbers to pester all that have their faces looking Zionward.[41]

4. *Atonement with the Father*

"THE BOW OF GOD'S WRATH is bent, and the Arrow made ready on the String; and Justice bends the Arrow at your Heart, and strains the Bow; and it is nothing but the mere Pleasure of God, and that of an angry God, without any Promise or Obligation at all, that keeps the Arrow one Moment from being made drunk with your Blood...."

With these words Jonathan Edwards threatened the hearts of his New England congregation by disclosing to them, unmitigated, the ogre aspect of the father. He riveted them to the pews with images of the mythological ordeal; for though the Puritan prohibited the graven image, yet he allowed himself the verbal. "The Wrath," Jonathan Edwards thundered,

> the Wrath of God is like great Waters that are dammed for the present; they increase more and more, and rise higher and higher till an Outlet is given; and the longer the Stream is stopt, the more rapid and mighty is its Course when once it is let loose. 'Tis true, that Judgment against your evil Works has not been executed hitherto; the Floods of God's Vengeance have been withheld; but your Guilt in the mean Time is constantly increasing, and you are every Day treasuring up more Wrath; the Waters are continually rising, and waxing more and more mighty; and there is nothing but the mere Pleasure of God that holds the Waters back that are unwilling to be stopt, and press hard to go forward; if God should only

> withdraw his Hand from the Flood-gate, it would immediately fly open, and the fiery Floods of the Fierceness of the Wrath of God would rush forth with inconceivable Fury, and would come upon you with omnipotent Power; and if your Strength were Ten thousand Times greater than it is, yea Ten thousand Times greater than the Strength of the stoutest, sturdiest Devil in Hell, it would be nothing to withstand or endure it....

Having threatened with the element water, Pastor Jonathan next turns to the image of fire.

> The God that holds you over the Pit of Hell, much as one holds a Spider or some lothsome Insect over the Fire, abhors you, and is dreadfully provoked: his Wrath towards you burns like Fire; he looks upon you as Worthy of nothing else but to be cast into the Fire; he is of purer Eyes than to bear to have you in his Sight; you are Ten thousand Times so abominable in his Eyes as the most hateful venomous Serpent is in ours. You have offended him infinitely more than ever a stubborn Rebel did his Prince; and yet 'tis nothing but his Hand that holds you from falling into the Fire every Moment....
>
> O Sinner!... You hang by a slender Thread, with the Flames of Divine Wrath flashing about it, and ready every Moment to singe it, and burn it asunder; and you have no Interest in any Mediator, and nothing to lay hold of to save yourself, nothing to keep off the Flames of Wrath, nothing of your own, nothing that you ever have done, nothing that you can do, to induce God to spare you one Moment....

But now, at last, the great resolving image of the second birth—only for a moment, however:

> Thus are all you that never passed under a great Change of Heart, by the mighty Power of the Spirit of GOD upon your souls, all that were never born again, and made new Creatures, and raised from being dead in Sin, to a State of new, and before altogether unexperienced Light and Life (however you may have reformed your Life in many Things, and may have had religious Affections, and may keep up a Form of Religion in your Families and Closets, and in the House of God, and may be strict in it) you are thus in the Hands of an angry God; 'tis nothing but his mere Pleasure that keeps you from being this Moment swallowed up in everlasting Destruction.[42]

"God's mere pleasure," which defends the sinner from the arrow, the flood, and the flames, is termed in the traditional vocabulary of

Christianity God's "mercy"; and "the mighty power of the spirit of God," by which the heart is changed, that is God's "grace." In most mythologies, the images of mercy and grace are rendered as vividly as those of justice and wrath, so that a balance is maintained, and the heart is buoyed rather than scourged along its way. "Fear not!" says the hand gesture of the god Śiva, as he dances before his devotee the dance of the universal destruction. "Fear not, for all rests well in God. The forms that come and go—and of which your body is but one—are the flashes of my dancing limbs. Know Me in all, and of what shall you be afraid?" The magic of the sacraments (made effective through the passion of Jesus Christ, or by virtue of the meditations of the Buddha), the protective power of primitive amulets and charms, and the supernatural helpers of the myths and fairy tales of the world, are mankind's assurances that the arrow, the flames, and the flood are not as brutal as they seem.

FIGURE 27. *Creation* (detail; fresco, Italy, A.D. 1508–1512)

For the ogre aspect of the father is a reflex of the victim's own ego—derived from the sensational nursery scene that has been left behind, but projected before; and the fixating idolatry of that pedagogical nonthing is itself the fault that keeps one steeped in a sense of sin, sealing the potentially adult spirit from a better balanced, more realistic view of the father, and therewith of the world. Atonement (at-one-ment) consists in no more than the abandonment of that

FIGURE 28. *Śiva, Lord of the Cosmic Dance* (cast bronze, India, c. tenth–twelfth century A.D.)

The symbolism of this eloquent image has been well expounded by Ananda K. Coomaraswamy,[43] and by Heinrich Zimmer.[44] Briefly: the extended right hand holds the drum, the beat of which is the beat of time, time being the first principle of creation; the extended left holds the flame, which is the flame of the destruction of the created world; the second right hand is held in the gesture of "fear not," while the second left, pointing to the lifted left foot, is held in a position symbolizing "elephant" (the elephant is the "breaker of the way through the jungle of the world," i.e., the divine guide); the right foot is planted on the back of a dwarf, the demon "Non-knowing," which signifies the passage of souls from God into matter, but the left is lifted, showing the release of the soul: the left is the foot to which the "elephant-hand" is pointing and supplies the reason for the assurance, "Fear not." The God's head is balanced, serene and still, in the midst of the dynamism of creation and destruction which is symbolized by the rocking arms and the rhythm of the slowly stamping right heel. This means that at the center all is still. Śiva's right earring is a man's, his left, woman's; for the God includes and is beyond the pairs of opposites. Śiva's facial expression is neither sorrowful nor joyous, but is the visage of the Unmoved Mover, beyond, yet present within, the world's bliss and pain. The wildly streaming locks represent the long-untended hair of the Indian yogi, now flying in the dance of life; for the presence known in the joys and sorrows of life, and that found through withdrawn meditation, are but two aspects of the same, universal, non-dual, Being-Consciousness-Bliss (*sat-cit-ānanda*). Śiva's bracelets, arm bands, ankle rings, and brahminical thread,[45] are living serpents. This means that he is made beautiful by the Serpent Power—the mysterious Creative Energy of God, which is the material and the formal cause of his own self-manifestation in, and as, the universe with all its beings. In Śiva's hair may be seen a skull, symbolic of death, the forehead ornament of the Lord of Destruction, as well as a crescent moon, symbolic of birth and increase, which are his other boons to the world. Also, there is in his hair the flower of a datura—from which plant an intoxicant is prepared (compare the wine of Dionysos and the wine of the Mass). A little image of the goddess Ganges is hidden in his locks; for it is he who receives on his head the impact of the descent of the divine Ganges from heaven, letting the life- and salvation-bestowing waters then flow gently to the earth for the physical and spiritual refreshment of mankind. The dance posture of the God may be visualized as the symbolic syllable *AUM* (ओं or ॐ) which is the verbal equivalent of the four states of consciousness and their fields of experience. (A: waking consciousness; U: dream consciousness; M: dreamless sleep; the silence around the sacred syllable is the Unmanifest Transcendent.[46]) The God is thus within the worshiper as well as without.

Such a figure illustrates the function and value of a graven image, and shows why long sermons are unnecessary among idol-worshipers. The devotee is permitted to soak in the meaning of the divine symbol in deep silence and in his own good time. Furthermore, just as the god wears arm bands and ankle rings, so does the devotee; and these mean what the god's mean. They are made of gold instead of serpents, gold (the metal that does not corrode) symbolizing immortality; i.e., immortality is the mysterious creative energy of God, which is the beauty of the body.

Many other details of life and local custom are similarly duplicated, interpreted, and thus validated, in the details of the anthropomorphic idols. In this way, the whole of life is made into a support for meditation. One lives in the midst of a silent sermon all the time.

self-generated double monster—the dragon thought to be God (superego)* and the dragon thought to be Sin (repressed id). But this requires an abandonment of the attachment to ego itself; and that is what is difficult. One must have a faith that the father is merciful, and then a reliance on that mercy. Therewith, the center of belief is transferred outside of the bedeviling god's tight scaly ring, and the dreadful ogres dissolve.

It is in this ordeal that the hero may derive hope and assurance from the helpful female figure, by whose magic (pollen charms or power of intercession) he is protected through all the frightening experiences of the father's ego-shattering initiation. For if it is impossible to trust the terrifying father-face, then one's faith must be centered elsewhere (Spider Woman, Blessed Mother); and with that reliance for support, one endures the crisis—only to find, in the end, that the father and mother reflect each other, and are in essence the same.

When the Twin Warriors of the Navaho, having departed from Spider Woman with her advice and protective charms, had made their perilous way between the rocks that crush, through the reeds that cut to pieces, and the cactus plants that tear to pieces, and then across the boiling sands, they came at last to the house of the Sun, their father. The door was guarded by two bears. These arose and growled; but the words that Spider Woman had taught the boys made the animals crouch down again. After the bears, there threatened a pair of serpents, then winds, then lightnings: the guardians of the ultimate threshold.† All were readily appeased, however, with the words of the prayer.

Built of turquoise, the house of the Sun was great and square, and it stood on the shore of a mighty water. The boys entered it, and they beheld a woman sitting in the west, two handsome young men in the south, two handsome young women in the north. The young women stood up without a word, wrapped the newcomers in four sky-coverings, and placed them on a shelf. The boys lay quietly. Presently a rattle hanging over the door shook four times and one of the young women said, "Our father is coming."

The bearer of the sun strode into his home, removed the sun from his back, and hung it on a peg on the west wall of the room, where it shook and clanged for some time, going "tla, tla, tla, tla." He turned to the older woman and demanded angrily: "Who were

---

* Or "interego" (see above, p. 67, footnote).

† Compare the numerous thresholds crossed by Inanna; see above, pp. 88–89.

those two that entered here today?" But the woman did not reply. The young people looked at one another. The bearer of the sun put his question angrily four times before the woman said to him at last: "It would be well for you not to say too much. Two young men came hither today, seeking their father. You have told me that you pay no visits when you go abroad, and that you have met no woman but me. Whose sons, then, are these?" She pointed to the bundle on the shelf, and the children smiled significantly at one another.

The bearer of the sun took the bundle from the shelf, unrolled the four robes (the robes of dawn, blue sky, yellow evening light, and darkness), and the boys fell out on the floor. He immediately seized them. Fiercely, he flung them at some great sharp spikes of white shell that stood in the east. The boys tightly clutched their life-feathers and bounded back. The man hurled them, equally, at spikes of turquoise in the south, haliotis in the west, and black rock in the north. The boys always clutched their life-feathers tightly and came bounding back. "I wish it were indeed true," said the Sun, "that they were my children."

Four symbolical colors, representing the points of the compass, play a prominent role in Navaho iconography and cult. They are white, blue, yellow, and black, signifying, respectively, east, south, west, and north. These correspond to the red, white, green, and black on the hat of the African trickster divinity Edshu (see pp. 36–37); for the House of the Father, like the Father himself, symbolizes the Center.

The Twin Heroes are tested against the symbols of the four directions, to discover whether they partake of the faults and limitations of any one of the quarters.

The terrible father assayed then to steam the boys to death in an overheated sweatlodge. They were aided by the winds, who provided a protected retreat within the lodge in which to hide. "Yes, these are my children," said the Sun when they emerged—but that was only a ruse; for he was still planning to trick them. The final ordeal was a smoking-pipe filled with poison. A spiny caterpillar warned the boys and gave them something to put into their mouths. They smoked the pipe without harm, passing it back and forth to one another till it was finished. They even said it tasted sweet. The Sun was proud. He was completely satisfied. "Now, my children," he asked, "what is it you want from me? Why do you seek me?" The Twin Heroes had won the full confidence of the Sun, their father.[47]

The need for great care on the part of the father, admitting to his house only those who have been thoroughly tested, is illustrated by the unhappy exploit of the lad Phaëthon, described in a famous tale of the Greeks. Born of a virgin in Ethiopia and taunted by his playmates to search the question of his father, he set off across Persia and India to find the palace of the Sun—for his mother had told him that his father was Phoebus, the god who drove the solar chariot.

"The palace of the Sun stood high on lofty columns, bright with glittering gold and bronze that shone like fire. Gleaming ivory crowned the gables above; the double folding doors were radiant with burnished silver. And the workmanship was more beautiful than the materials."

Climbing the steep path, Phaëthon arrived beneath the roof. And he discovered Phoebus sitting on an emerald throne, surrounded by the Hours and the Seasons, and by Day, Month, Year, and Century. The bold youngster had to halt at the threshold, his mortal eyes unable to bear the light; but the father gently spoke to him across the hall.

"Why have you come?" the father asked. "What do you seek, O Phaëthon—a son no father need deny?"

The lad respectfully replied: "O my father (if thou grantest me the right to use that name)! Phoebus! Light of the entire world! Grant me a proof, my father, by which all may know me for thy true son."

The great god set his glittering crown aside and bade the boy approach. He gathered him into his arms. Then he promised, sealing the promise with a binding oath, that any proof the lad desired would be granted.

What Phaëthon desired was his father's chariot, and the right to drive the winged horses for a day.

"Such a request," said the father, "proves my promise to have been rashly made." He put the boy a little away from him and sought to dissuade him from the demand. "In your ignorance," said he, "you are asking for more than can be granted even to the gods. Each of the gods may do as he will, and yet none, save myself, has the power to take his place in my chariot of fire; no, not even Zeus."

Phoebus reasoned. Phaëthon was adamant. Unable to retract the oath, the father delayed as long as time would allow, but was finally forced to conduct his stubborn son to the prodigious chariot: its axle of gold and the pole of gold, its wheels with golden tires and a ring of silver spokes. The yoke was set with chrysolites and jewels. The Hours were already leading the four horses from their lofty stalls, breathing fire and filled with ambrosial food. They put upon them the clanking bridles; the great animals pawed at the bars. Phoebus anointed Phaëthon's face with an ointment to protect it against the flames and then placed on his head the radiant crown.

"If, at least, you can obey your father's warnings," the divinity advised,

> spare the lash and hold tightly to the reins. The horses go fast enough of themselves. And do not follow the straight road directly through the five zones of heaven, but turn off at the fork to the left—the tracks of my wheels you will clearly see. Furthermore, so that the sky and earth may have equal heat, be careful to go neither too high nor too low; for if you go too high you will burn up the skies, and if you go too low ignite the earth. In the middle is the safest path.
>
> But hurry! While I am speaking, dewy Night has reached her goal on the western shore. We are summoned. Behold, the dawn is glowing. Boy, may Fortune aid and conduct you better than you can guide yourself. Here, grasp the reins.

Tethys, the goddess of the sea, had dropped the bars, and the horses, with a jolt, abruptly started; cleaving with their feet the clouds; beating the air with their wings; outrunning all the winds that were rising from the same eastern quarter. Immediately—the chariot was so light without its accustomed weight—the car began to rock about like a ship tossing without ballast on the waves. The driver, panic-stricken, forgot the reins, and knew nothing of the road. Wildly mounting, the team grazed the heights of the sky and startled the remotest constellations. The Great and Little Bear were scorched. The Serpent lying curled about the polar stars grew warm, and with the heat grew dangerously fierce. Boötes took flight, encumbered with his plough. The Scorpion struck with his tail.

The chariot, having roared for some time through unknown regions of the air, knocking against the stars, next plunged down crazily to the clouds just above the ground; and the Moon beheld, in amazement, her brother's horses running below her own. The clouds evaporated. The earth burst into flame. Mountains blazed; cities perished with their walls; nations were reduced to ashes. That was the time the peoples of Ethiopia became black; for the blood was drawn to the surface of their bodies by the heat. Libya became a desert. The Nile fled in terror to the ends of the earth and hid its head, and it is hidden yet.

Mother Earth, shielding her scorched brow with her hand, choking with hot smoke, lifted her great voice and called upon

FIGURE 29. *The Fall of Phaëthon* (ink on parchment, Italy, A.D. 1533)

Jove, the father of all things, to save his world. "Look around!" she cried at him. "The heavens are asmoke from pole to pole. Great Jove, if the sea perish, and the land, and all the realms of the sky, then we are back again in the chaos of the beginning! Take thought! Take thought for the safety of our universe! Save from the flames whatever yet remains!"

Jove, the Almighty Father, hastily summoned the gods to witness that unless some measure were quickly taken all was lost. Thereupon he hurried to the zenith, took a thunderbolt in his right hand, and flung it from beside his ear. The car shattered; the horses, terrified, broke loose; Phaëthon, fire raging in his hair, descended like a falling star. And the river Po received his burning frame.

The Naiads of that land consigned his body to a tomb, whereupon this epitaph:

Here Phaëthon lies: in Phoebus' car he fared,
And though he greatly failed, more greatly dared.[48]

This tale of indulgent parenthood illustrates the antique idea that when the roles of life are assumed by the improperly initiated, chaos supervenes. When the child outgrows the popular idyl of the mother breast and turns to face the world of specialized adult action, it passes, spiritually, into the sphere of the father—who becomes, for his son, the sign of the future task, and for his daughter, of the future husband. Whether he knows it or not, and no matter what his position in society, the father is the initiating priest through whom the young being passes on into the larger world. And just as, formerly, the mother represented the "good" and "evil," so now does he, but with this complication—that there is a new element of rivalry in the picture: the son against the father for the mastery of the universe, and the daughter against the mother to *be* the mastered world.

The traditional idea of initiation combines an introduction of the candidate into the techniques, duties, and prerogatives of his vocation with a radical readjustment of his emotional relationship to the parental images. The mystagogue (father or father-substitute) is to entrust the symbols of office only to a son who has been effectually purged of all inappropriate infantile cathexes—for whom the just, impersonal exercise of the powers will not be rendered impossible by unconscious (or perhaps even conscious and rationalized) motives of self-aggrandizement, personal preference, or resentment. Ideally, the invested one has been divested of his mere humanity and is representative of an impersonal cosmic force. He is the twice-born: he has become himself the father. And he is competent, consequently, now to enact himself the role of the initiator, the guide, the sun door, through whom one may pass from the infantile illusions of "good" and "evil" to an experience of the majesty of cosmic law, purged of hope and fear, and at peace in the understanding of the revelation of being.

"Once I dreamed," declared a little boy, "that I was captured by cannon balls [*sic*]. They all began to jump and yell. I was surprised to see myself in my own parlor. There was a fire, and a kettle was over it full of boiling water. They threw me into it and once in a while the cook used to come over and stick a fork into me to see if I was cooked. Then he took me out and gave me to the chief, who was just going to bite me when I woke up."[49]

"I dreamed that I was at table with my wife," states a civilized gentleman.

> During the course of the meal I reached over and took our second child, a baby, and in a matter-of-fact fashion proceeded to put him into a green soup bowl, full of hot water or some hot liquid; for he came out cooked thoroughly, like chicken fricassee.
>
> I laid the viand on a bread board at the table and cut it up with my knife. When we had eaten all of it except a small part like a chicken gizzard I looked up, worried, to my wife and asked her, "Are you sure you wanted me to do this? Did you intend to have him for supper?"
>
> She answered, with a domestic frown, "After he was so well cooked, there was nothing else to do." I was just about to finish the last piece, when I woke up.[50]

This archetypal nightmare of the ogre father is made actual in the ordeals of primitive initiation. The boys of the Australian Murngin tribe, as we have seen, are first frightened and sent running to their mothers. The Great Father Snake is calling for their foreskins.* This places the women in the role of protectresses. A prodigious horn is blown, named Yurlunggur, which is supposed to be the call of the Great Father Snake, who has emerged from his hole. When the men come for the boys, the women grab up spears and pretend not only to fight but also to wail and cry, because the little fellows are going to be taken away and "eaten." The men's triangular dancing ground is the body of the Great Father Snake. There the boys are shown, during

* See above, p. 7.

many nights, numerous dances symbolical of the various totem ancestors, and are taught the myths that explain the existing order of the world. Also, they are sent on a long journey to neighboring and distant clans, imitative of the mythological wanderings of the phallic ancestors.[51] In this way, "within" the Great Father Snake as it were, they are introduced to an interesting new object world that compensates them for their loss of the mother; and the male phallus, instead of the female breast, is made the central point (*axis mundi*) of the imagination.

The culminating instruction of the long series of rites is the release of the boy's own hero-penis from the protection of its foreskin, through the frightening and painful attack upon it of the circumciser:

"The father [i.e., circumciser] is the one who *separates* the child from the mother," writes Dr. Róheim. "What is cut off the boy is really the mother. . . . The glans in the foreskin is the child in the mother."[52]

It is interesting to note the continuance to this day of the rite of circumcision in the Hebrew and Mohammedan cults, where the Feminine element has been scrupulously purged from the official, strictly monotheistic mythology. "God forgiveth not the sin of joining other gods with Him," we read in the Koran. "The Pagans, leaving Allah, call but upon female deities."[53]

Among the Arunta, for example, the sound of the bull-roarers is heard from all sides when the moment has arrived for this decisive break from the past. It is night, and in the weird light of the fire suddenly appear the circumciser and his assistant.

The noise of the bull-roarers is the voice of the great demon of the ceremony, and the pair of operators are its apparition. With their beards thrust into their mouths, signifying anger, their legs widely extended, and their arms stretched forward, the two men stand perfectly still, the actual operator in front, holding in his right hand the small flint knife with which the operation is to be conducted, and his assistant pressing close up behind him, so that the two bodies are in contact with each other. Then a man approaches through the firelight, balancing a shield on his head and at the same time snapping the thumb and first finger of each hand. The bull-roarers are making a tremendous din, which can be heard by the women and children in their distant camp. The man with the shield on his head goes down on one knee just a little in front of the operator, and immediately one of the boys is lifted from the ground by a number of his uncles, who carry him feet foremost and place him on the shield, while in deep, loud tones a chant is thundered forth by all the men. The operation is swiftly performed, the fearsome figures retire immediately from the lighted area, and the boy, in a more or less dazed condition, is attended to, and congratulated by the men to whose estate he has now just arrived. "You have done well," they say; "you did not cry out."[54]

The native Australian mythologies teach that the first initiation rites were carried out in such a way that all the young men were killed.[55] The ritual is thus shown to be, among other things, a dramatized expression of the Oedipal aggression of the elder generation; and the circumcision, a mitigated castration.[56] But the rites provide also for the cannibal, patricidal impulse of the younger, rising group of males, and at the same time reveal the benign self-giving aspect of the archetypal father; for during the long period of symbolical instruction, there is a time when the initiates are forced to live only on the fresh-drawn blood of the older men. "The natives," we are told,

> are particularly interested in the Christian communion rite, and having heard about it from missionaries they compare it to the blood-drinking rituals of their own.[57]
>
> In the evening the men come and take their places according to tribal precedence, the boy lying with his head on his father's thighs. He must make no movement or he will die. The father blindfolds him with his hands because if the boy should witness the following proceedings it is believed that his *father and mother will both die.* The wooden vessel or a bark vessel is placed near one of the boy's mother's brothers, who, having tied his arm lightly, pierces the upper part with a nosebone and holds the arm over the vessel until a certain amount of blood has been taken. The man next to him pierces his arm, and so on, until the vessel is filled. It may hold two quarts or so. The boy takes a long draught of the blood. Should his stomach rebel, the father holds his throat to prevent his ejecting the blood, because if it happens *his father, mother, sisters, and brothers would all die.* The remainder of the blood is thrown over him.
>
> From this time on, sometimes for a whole moon, the boy is allowed no other food than human blood, Yamminga, the mythical ancestor, having made this law.... Sometimes the blood is dried in the vessel and then the guardian cuts it in sections with his nosebone, and it is eaten by the boy, the two end sections first. The sections must be regularly divided or the boy will die.[58]

Frequently the men who give their blood faint and remain in a state of coma for an hour or more because of exhaustion.[59] "In former times," writes another observer, "this blood (drunk ceremonially by the novices) was obtained from a man who was killed for the purpose, and portions of his body were eaten."[60] "Here," comments Dr. Róheim, "we come as near to a ritual representation of the killing and eating of the primal father as we can ever get."

In one recorded case, two of the boys looked up when they were not supposed to. "Then the old men went forward, each with a stone knife in hand. Stooping over the two boys they opened veins in each. Out flowed the blood, and the other men all raised a death cry. The boys were lifeless. The old *wirreenuns* (medicine men), dipping their stone knives in the blood, touched with them the lips of all present.... The bodies of the Boorah victims were cooked. Each man who had been to five Boorahs ate a piece of this flesh; no others were allowed to see this done"[61]

There can be no doubt that no matter how unilluminated the stark-naked Australian savages may seem to us, their symbolical ceremonials represent a survival into modern times of an incredibly old system of spiritual instruction, the far-flung evidences of which are to be found not only in all the lands and islands bordering the Indian Ocean, but also among the remains of the archaic centers of what we tend to regard as our own very special brand of civilization. Just how much the old men know, it is difficult to judge from the published accounts of our Occidental observers. But it can be seen from a comparison of the figures of Australian ritual with those familiar to us from higher cultures, that the great themes, the ageless archetypes, and their operation upon the soul remain the same.

For an astounding revelation of the survival in contemporary Melanesia of a symbolic system essentially identical with that of the Egypto-Babylonian, Trojan-Cretan "labyrinth complex" of the second millennium B.C., see John Layard's *Stone Men of Malekula*.[62] W. F. J. Knight has discussed the evident relationship of the Malekulan "journey of the soul to the underworld" with the classical descent of Aeneas, and the Babylonian of Gilgamesh,[63] while W. J. Perry thought he could recognize evidences of this culture-continuity running all the way from Egypt and Sumer out through the Oceanic area to North America.[64] Many scholars have pointed out the close correspondences between the details of the classical Greek and primitive Australian rites of initiation.[65]

It is still uncertain by what means and in what eras the mythological and cultural patterns of the various archaic civilizations may have been disseminated to the farthest corners of the earth; yet it can be stated categorically that few (if any) of the so-called "primitive cultures" studied by our anthropologists represent autochthonous growths. They are, rather, local adaptations, provincial degenerations, and immensely old fossilizations of folkways that were developed in very different lands, often under much less simple circumstances, and by other races.[66]

Come, O Dithyrambos,
Enter this my male womb.[67]

This cry of Zeus, the Thunder-hurler, to the child, his son, Dionysos, sounds the leitmotif of the Greek mysteries of the initiatory second birth. "And bull-voices roar thereto from somewhere out of the unseen, fearful semblances, and from a drum an image as it were of thunder underground is borne on the air heavy with dread."[68] The word "Dithyrambos" itself, as an epithet of the killed and resurrected Dionysos, was understood by the Greeks to signify "him of the double door," him who had survived the awesome miracle of the second birth. And we know that the choral songs (dithyrambs) and dark, blood-reeking rites in celebration of the god—associated with the renewal of vegetation, the renewal of the moon, the renewal of the sun, the renewal of the soul, and solemnized at the season of the resurrection of the year god—represent the ritual beginnings of the Attic tragedy. Throughout the ancient world such myths and rites abounded: the deaths and resurrections of Tammuz, Adonis, Mithra, Virbius, Attis, and Osiris, and of their various animal representatives (goats and sheep, bulls, pigs, horses, fish, and birds) are known to every student of comparative religion; the popular carnival games of the Whitsuntide Louts, Green Georges, John Barleycorns, and Kostrubonkos, Carrying-out-Winter, Bringing-in-Summer, and Killing of the Christmas Wren have continued the tradition, in a mood of frolic, into our contemporary calendar;[69] and through the Christian church (in the mythology of the Fall and Redemption, Crucifixion, and Resurrection, the "second birth" of baptism, the initiatory blow on the cheek at confirmation, the symbolical eating of the Flesh and drinking of the Blood) solemnly, and sometimes effectively, we are united to those immortal images of initiatory might, through the sacramental operation of which man, since the beginning of his day on earth, has dispelled the terrors of his phenomenality and won through to the all-transfiguring vision of immortal being. "For if the blood of bulls and of goats, and the ashes of an heifer sprinkling the unclean, sanctifieth to the purifying of the flesh: how much more shall the blood of Christ, who through the eternal Spirit offered himself without spot to God, purge your conscience from dead works to serve the living God?"[70]

There is a folktale told by the Basumbwa of East Africa, of a man whose dead father appeared to him, driving the cattle of Death, and conducted him along a path that went into the ground, as into a vast burrow. They came to an extensive area where there were some people. The father hid the son and went off to sleep. The Great Chief, Death, appeared the next morning. One side of him was beautiful; but the other side was rotten, maggots were dropping to the ground. His attendants were gathering the maggots. The attendants washed the sores, and when they had finished, Death said: "The one born today: if he goes trading, he will be robbed. The woman who conceives today: she will die with the child conceived. The man who cultivates today: his crops have perished. The one who is to go into the jungle has been eaten by the lion."

Death thus pronounced the universal curse, and returned to rest. But the following morning, when he appeared, his attendants washed and perfumed the beautiful side, massaging it with oil. When they

FIGURE 30. *The Sorceror* (rock engraving with black paint fill-in, Paleolithic, France, c. 10,000 B.C.)

FIGURE 31. *The Universal Father, Viracocha, Weeping* (bronze, pre-Incan, Argentina, c. A.D. 650–750)

had finished, Death pronounced the blessing: "The one born today: may he become wealthy. May the woman who conceives today give birth to a child who will live to be old. The one born today: let him go into the market; may he strike good bargains; may he trade with the blind. The man who is to enter the jungle: may he kill game; may he discover even elephants. Because today I pronounce the benediction."

The father then said to the son: "If you had arrived today, many things would have come into your possession. But now it is clear that poverty has been ordained for you. Tomorrow you had better go."

And the son returned to his home.[71]

The Sun in the Underworld, Lord of the Dead, is the other side of the same radiant king who rules and gives the day; for "Who is it that sustains you from the sky and from the earth? And who is it that brings out the living from the dead and the dead from the living? And who is it that rules and regulates all affairs?"[72] We recall the Wachaga tale of the very poor man, Kyazimba, who was transported by a crone to the zenith, where the Sun rests at noon;[73] there the Great Chief bestowed on him prosperity. And we recall the trickster-god Edshu, described in a tale from the other coast of Africa:[74] spreading strife was his greatest joy. These are differing views of the same dreadful Providence. In him are contained and from him proceed the contradictions, good and evil, death and life, pain and pleasure, boons and deprivation. As the person of the sun door, he is the fountainhead of all the pairs of opposites. "With Him are the keys of the Unseen.... In the end, unto Him will be your return; then will He show you the truth of all that ye did."[75]

The mystery of the apparently self-contradictory father is rendered tellingly in the figure of a great divinity of prehistoric Peru, named Viracocha. His tiara is the sun; he grasps a thunderbolt in either hand; and from his eyes descend, in the form of tears, the rains that refresh the life of the valleys of the world. Viracocha is the Universal God, the creator of all things; and yet, in the legends of his appearances upon the earth, he is shown wandering as a beggar, in rags and reviled. One is reminded of the Gospel of Mary and Joseph at the inn-doors of Bethlehem,[76] and of the classical story of the begging of Jove and Mercury at the home of Baucis and Philemon.[77] One is reminded also of the unrecognized Edshu. This is a theme frequently encountered in mythology; its sense is caught in the words of the Koran: "whithersoever ye turn, there is the Presence of Allah."[78] "Though He is hidden in all things," say the Hindus, "that Soul shines not forth; yet He is seen by subtle seers with superior, subtle intellect."[79] "Split the stick," runs a Gnostic aphorism, "and there is Jesus."[80]

Viracocha, therefore, in this manner of manifesting his ubiquity, participates in the character of the highest of the universal gods. Furthermore his synthesis of sun-god and storm-god is familiar. We know it through the Hebrew mythology of Yahweh, in whom the traits of two gods are united (Yahweh, a storm-god, and El, a solar); it is apparent in the Navaho personification of the father of the Twin Warriors; it is obvious in the character of Zeus, as well as in the thunderbolt and halo of certain forms of the Buddha image. The meaning is that the grace that pours into the universe through the sun door is the same as the energy of the bolt that annihilates and is itself indestructible: the delusion-shattering light of the Imperishable is the same as the light that creates. Or again, in terms of a secondary polarity of nature: the fire blazing in the sun glows also in the fertilizing storm; the energy behind the elemental pair of opposites, fire and water, is one and the same.

But the most extraordinary and profoundly moving of the traits of Viracocha, this nobly conceived Peruvian rendition of the universal god, is the detail that is peculiarly his own, namely that of the tears. The living waters are the tears of God. Herewith the world-discrediting insight of the monk, "All life is sorrowful," is combined with the world-begetting affirmative of the father: "Life must be!" In full awareness of the life anguish of the creatures of his hand, in full consciousness of the roaring wilderness of pains, the brain-splitting fires of the deluded, self-ravaging, lustful, angry universe of his creation, this divinity acquiesces in the deed of supplying life to life. To withhold the seminal waters would be to annihilate; yet to give them forth is to create this world that we know. For the essence of time is flux, dissolution of the momentarily existent; and the essence of life is time. In his mercy, in his love for the forms of time, this demiurgic man of men yields countenance to the sea of pangs; but in his full awareness of what he is doing, the seminal waters of the life that he gives are the tears of his eyes.

The paradox of creation, the coming of the forms of time out of eternity, is the germinal secret of the father. It can never be quite explained. Therefore, in every system of theology there is an umbilical point, an Achilles tendon which the finger of mother life has touched, and where the possibility of perfect knowledge has been impaired. The problem of the hero is to pierce himself (and therewith his world) precisely through that point; to shatter and annihilate that key knot of his limited existence.

The problem of the hero going to meet the father is to open his soul beyond terror to such a degree that he will be ripe to understand how the sickening and insane tragedies of this vast and ruthless cosmos are completely validated in the majesty of Being. The hero transcends life with its peculiar blind spot and for a moment rises to a glimpse of the source. He beholds the face of the father, understands—and the two are atoned.

In the biblical story of Job, the Lord makes no attempt to justify in human or any other terms the ill pay meted out to his virtuous servant, "a simple and upright man, and fearing God, and avoiding evil." Nor was it for any sins of their own that Job's servants were slain by the Chaldean troops, his sons and daughters crushed by a collapsing roof. When his friends arrive to console him, they declare, with a pious faith in God's justice, that Job must have done some evil to have deserved to be so frightfully afflicted. But the honest, courageous, horizon-searching sufferer insists that his deeds have been good; whereupon the comforter, Elihu, charges him with blasphemy, as naming himself more just than God.

When the Lord himself answers Job out of the whirlwind, He makes no attempt to vindicate His work in ethical terms, but only magnifies His Presence, bidding Job do likewise on earth in human emulation of the way of heaven:

> Gird up thy loins now like a man; I will demand of thee, and declare thou unto me. Wilt thou also disannul my judgment? Wilt thou condemn me, that thou mayst be righteous? Hast thou an arm like God? or canst thou thunder with a voice like him? Deck thyself now with majesty and excellency; and array thyself with glory and beauty. Cast abroad the rage of thy wrath: and behold every one that is proud and abase him. Look on every one that is proud, and bring him low; and tread down the wicked in their place. Hide them in the dust together; and bind their faces in secret. Then I will also confess unto thee that thine own hand can save thee.[81]

There is no word of explanation, no mention of the dubious wager with Satan described in chapter one of the Book of Job; only a thunder-and-lightning demonstration of the fact of facts, namely that man cannot measure the will of God, which derives from a center beyond the range of human categories. Categories, indeed, are totally shattered by the Almighty of the Book of Job, and remain shattered to the last. Nevertheless, to Job himself the revelation appears to have made soul-satisfying sense. He was a hero who, by his courage in the fiery furnace, his unreadiness to break down and grovel before a popular conception of the character of the All Highest, had proven himself capable of facing a greater revelation than the one that satisfied his friends. We cannot interpret his words of the last chapter as those of a man merely intimidated. They are the words of one who has *seen* something surpassing anything that has been *said* by way of justification. "I have heard of thee by the hearing of the ear: but now mine eye seeth thee. Wherefore I abhor myself, and repent in dust and ashes."[82] The pious comforters are humbled; Job is rewarded with a fresh house, fresh servants, and fresh daughters and sons. "After this lived Job an hundred and forty years, and saw his sons, and his sons' sons, even four generations. So Job died, being old and full of days."[83]

For the son who has grown really to know the father, the agonies of the ordeal are readily borne; the world is no longer a vale of tears but a bliss-yielding, perpetual manifestation of the Presence. Contrast with the wrath of the angry God known to Jonathan Edwards and his flock, the following tender lyric from the miserable Eastern European ghettos of that same century:

Oh, Lord of the Universe
I will sing Thee a song.
Where canst Thou be found,
And where canst Thou not be found?
Where I pass—there art Thou.
Where I remain—there, too, Thou art.
Thou, Thou, and only Thou.

Doth it go well—'tis thanks to Thee.
Doth it go ill—ah, 'tis also thanks to Thee.

Thou art, Thou hast been, and Thou wilt be.
Thou didst reign, Thou reignest, and Thou wilt reign.

Thine is Heaven, Thine is Earth.
Thou fillest the high regions,
And Thou fillest the low regions.
Wheresoever I turn, Thou, oh Thou, art there.[84]

5. Apotheosis

ONE OF THE MOST POWERFUL and beloved of the Bodhisattvas of the Mahāyāna Buddhism of Tibet, China, and Japan is the Lotus Bearer, Avalokiteśvara, "The Lord Looking Down in Pity," so called because he regards with compassion all sentient creatures suffering the evils of existence. To him goes the millionfold-repeated prayer of the prayer wheels and temple gongs of Tibet: *Om mani padme hum,* "The jewel is in the lotus." To him go perhaps more prayers per minute than to any single divinity known to man; for when, during his final life on earth as a human being, he shattered for himself the bounds of the last threshold (which moment opened to him the timelessness of the void beyond the frustrating mirage-enigmas of the named and bounded cosmos), he paused: he made a vow that before entering the void he would bring all creatures without exception to enlightenment; and since then he has permeated the whole texture of existence with the divine grace of his assisting presence, so that the least prayer addressed to him, throughout the vast spiritual empire of the Buddha, is graciously heard. Under differing forms he traverses the ten thousand worlds, and appears in the hour of need and prayer. He reveals himself in human form with two arms, in superhuman forms with four arms, or with six, or twelve, or a thousand, and he holds in one of his left hands the lotus of the world.

Like the Buddha himself, this godlike being is a pattern of the divine state to which the human hero attains who has gone beyond the last terrors of ignorance. "When the envelopment of consciousness has been annihilated, then he becomes free of all fear, beyond the reach of change."[85] This is the release potential within us all, and which anyone can attain—through herohood; for, as we read: "All things are Buddha-things";[86] or again (and this is the other way of making the same statement): "All beings are without self."

FIGURE 32. *Bodhisattva* (temple banner, Tibet, nineteenth century A.D.)

Hīnayāna or Theravada Buddhism (the Buddhism surviving in Ceylon, Burma, and Thailand) reveres the Buddha as a human hero, a supreme saint and sage. Mahāyāna Buddhism, on the other hand (the Buddhism of the north), regards the Enlightened One as a world savior, an incarnation of the universal principle of enlightenment.

A Bodhisattva is a personage on the point of Buddhahood: according to the Hīnayāna view, an adept who will become a Buddha in a subsequent reincarnation; according to the Mahāyāna view (as the following paragraphs will show), a type of world savior, representing particularly the universal principle of compassion. The word *bodhisattva* (Sanskrit) means: "whose being or essence is enlightenment."

Mahāyāna Buddhism has developed a pantheon of many Bodhisattvas and many past and future Buddhas. These all inflect the manifested powers of the transcendent, one and only Ādi-Buddha ("Primal Buddha"),[87] who is the highest conceivable source and ultimate boundary of all being, suspended in the void of nonbeing like a wonderful bubble.

The world is filled and illumined by, but does not hold, the Bodhisattva ("he whose being is enlightenment"); rather, it is he who holds the world, the lotus. Pain and pleasure do not enclose him, he encloses them—and with profound repose. And since he is what all of us may be, his presence, his image, the mere naming of him, helps.

> He wears a garland of eight thousand rays, in which is seen fully reflected a state of perfect beauty. The color of his body is purple gold. His palms have the mixed color of five hundred lotuses, while each finger tip has eighty-four thousand signet-marks, and each mark eighty-four thousand colors; each color has eighty-four thousand rays which are soft and mild and shine over all things that exist. With these jewel hands he draws and embraces all beings. The halo surrounding his head is studded with five hundred Buddhas, miraculously transformed, each attended by five hundred Bodhisattvas, who are attended, in turn, by numberless gods. And when he puts his feet down to the ground, the flowers of diamonds and jewels that are scattered cover everything in all directions. The color of his face is gold. While in his towering crown of gems stands a Buddha, two hundred and fifty miles high.[88]

In China and Japan this sublimely gentle Bodhisattva is represented not only in male form, but also as female. Kwan Yin of China, Kannon of Japan—the Madonna of the Far East—is precisely this benevolent regarder of the world. She will be found in every Buddhist temple of the farthest Orient. She is blessed alike to the simple and to the wise; for behind her vow there lies a profound intuition, world-redeeming, world-sustaining. The pause on the threshold of *nirvāṇa,* the resolution to forego until the end of time (which never ends) immersion in the untroubled pool of eternity, represents a realization that the distinction between eternity and time is only apparent—made, perforce, by the rational mind, but dissolved in the perfect knowledge of the mind that has transcended the pairs of opposites. What is understood is that time and eternity are two aspects of the same experience-whole, two planes of the same nondual ineffable; i.e., the jewel of eternity is in the lotus of birth and death: *om mani padme hum.*

The first wonder to be noted here is the androgynous character of the Bodhisattva: masculine Avalokiteśvara, feminine Kwan Yin.

FIGURE 33. *Kwan Yin, the Avalokiteśvara Bodhisattva* (painted wood, China, eleventh–thirteenth century A.D.)

Male-female gods are not uncommon in the world of myth. They emerge always with a certain mystery; for they conduct the mind beyond objective experience into a symbolic realm where duality is left behind. Awonawilona, chief god of the pueblo of Zuni, the maker and container of all, is sometimes spoken of as he, but is actually he-she. The Great Original of the Chinese chronicles, the holy woman T'ai Yuan, combined in her person the masculine Yang and the feminine Yin.

Yang, the light, active, masculine principle, and *Yin*, the dark, passive, and feminine, in their interaction underlie and constitute the whole world of forms ("the ten thousand things"). They proceed from and together make manifest *Tao*: the source and law of being. *Tao* means "road," or "way." *Tao* is the way or course of nature, destiny, cosmic order; the Absolute made manifest. *Tao* is therefore also "truth," "right conduct." *Yang* and *Yin* together as *Tao* are depicted thus: ☯. *Tao* underlies the cosmos. *Tao* inhabits every created thing.

The kabbalistic teachings of the medieval Jews, as well as the Gnostic Christian writings of the second century, represent the Word Made Flesh as androgynous—which was indeed the state of Adam as he was created, before the female aspect, Eve, was removed into another form. And among the Greeks, not only Hermaphrodite (the child of Hermes and Aphrodite),[89] but Eros too, the divinity of love (the first of the gods, according to Plato),[90] were in sex both female and male.

"So God created man in his own image, in the image of God created he him; male and female created he them."[91] The question may arise in the mind as to the nature of the image of God; but the answer is already given in the text, and is clear enough. "When the Holy One, Blessed be He, created the first man, He created him androgynous."[92] The removal of the feminine into another form symbolizes the beginning of the fall from perfection into duality; and it was naturally followed by the discovery of the duality of good and evil, exile from the garden where God walks on earth, and thereupon the building of the Wall of Paradise, constituted of the "coincidence of opposites,"[93] by which Man (now man and woman) is cut off from not only the vision but even the recollection of the image of God.

This is the biblical version of a myth known to many lands. It represents one of the basic ways of symbolizing the mystery of creation: the devolvement of eternity into time, the breaking of the one into the two and then the many, as well as the generation of new life through the reconjunction of the two. This image stands at the beginning of the cosmogonic cycle,[94] and with equal propriety at the conclusion of the hero-task, at the moment when the wall of Paradise is dissolved, the divine form found and recollected, and wisdom regained.[95]

Tiresias, the blinded seer, was both male and female: his eyes were closed to the broken forms of the light-world of the pairs of opposites, yet he saw in his own interior darkness the destiny of Oedipus.[96] Śiva appears united in a single body with Śakti, his spouse—he the right side, she the left—in the manifestation known as Ardhanārīśvara, "The Half-Woman Lord."[97] The ancestral images of certain African and Melanesian tribes show on one being the breasts of the mother and the beard and penis of the father.[98] And in Australia, about a year following the ordeal of the circumcision, the candidate for full

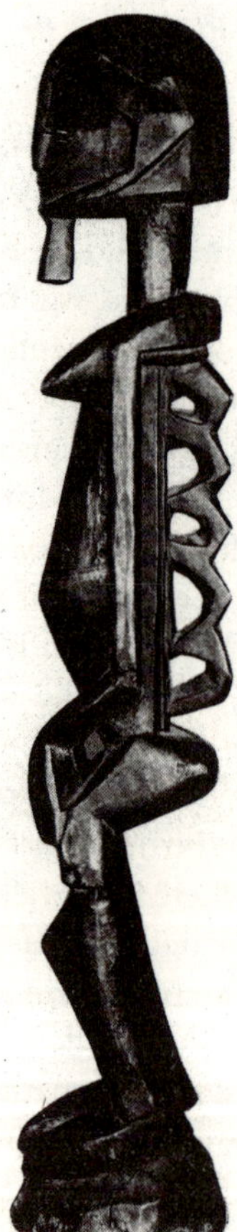

FIGURE 34. *Androgynous Ancestor* (carved wood, Mali, twentieth century A.D.)

manhood undergoes a second ritual operation—that of subincision (a slitting open of the underside of the penis, to form a permanent cleft into the urethra). The opening is termed the "penis womb." It is a symbolical male vagina. The hero has become, by virtue of the ceremonial, more than man.[99]

The blood for ceremonial painting and for gluing white bird's-down to the body is derived by the Australian fathers from their subincision holes. They break open again the old wounds, and let it flow.[100] It symbolizes at once the menstrual blood of the vagina and the semen of the male, as well as urine, water, and male milk. The flowing shows that the old men have the source of life and nourishment within themselves;[101] i.e., that they and the inexhaustible world fountain are the same.[102]

The call of the Great Father Snake was alarming to the child; the mother was protection. But the father came. He was the guide and initiator into the mysteries of the unknown. As the original intruder into the paradise of the infant with its mother, the father is the archetypal enemy; hence, throughout life all enemies are symbolical (to the unconscious) of the father. "Whatever is killed becomes the father."[103] Hence the veneration in headhunting communities (in New Guinea, for example) of the heads brought home from vendetta raids.[104] Hence, too, the irresistible compulsion to make war: the impulse to destroy the father is continually transforming itself into public violence. The old men of the immediate community or race protect themselves from their growing sons by the psychological magic of their totem ceremonials. They enact the ogre father, and then reveal themselves to be the feeding mother too. A new and larger paradise is thus established. But this paradise does not include the traditional enemy tribes, or races, against whom aggression is still systematically projected. All of the "good" father-mother content is saved for home, while the "bad" is flung abroad and about: "for who is this uncircumcised Philistine, that he should defy the armies of the living God?"[105] "And slacken not in following up the enemy: if ye are suffering hardships, they are suffering similar hardships; but ye have hope from Allah, while they have none."[106]

Totem, tribal, racial, and aggressively missionizing cults represent only partial solutions of the psychological problem of subduing hate by love; they only partially initiate. Ego is not annihilated in them; rather, it is enlarged; instead of thinking only of himself, the individual becomes dedicated to the whole of *his* society. The rest of the world meanwhile (that is to say, by far the greater portion of mankind) is left outside the sphere of his sympathy and protection because outside the sphere of the protection of his god. And there takes place, then, that dramatic divorce of the two principles of love and hate which the pages of history so bountifully illustrate. Instead of clearing his own heart the zealot tries to clear the world. The laws of the City of God are applied only to his in-group (tribe, church, nation, class, or what not) while the fire of a perpetual holy war is hurled (with good conscience, and indeed a sense of pious service) against whatever uncircumcised, barbarian, heathen, "native," or alien people happens to occupy the position of neighbor.[107]

The world is full of the resultant mutually contending bands: totem-, flag-, and party-worshipers. Even the so-called Christian nations—which are supposed to be following a "World" Redeemer—are better known to history for their colonial barbarity and internecine strife than for any practical display of that unconditioned love, synonymous with the effective conquest of ego, ego's world, and ego's tribal god, which was taught by their professed supreme Lord:

> I say unto you, Love your enemies, do good to them which hate you. Bless them that curse you, and pray for them which despitefully use you. And unto him that smiteth thee on the one cheek offer also the other; and him that taketh away thy cloke forbid not to take thy coat also. Give to every man that asketh of thee; and of him that taketh away thy goods ask them not again. And as ye would that men should do to you, do ye also to them likewise. For if ye love them which love you, what thank have ye? for sinners also love those that love them. And if ye do good to them which do good to you, what thank have ye? for sinners also do even the same. And if ye lend to them of whom ye hope to receive, what thank have ye? for sinners also lend to sinners, to receive as much again. But love ye your enemies, and do good, and lend, hoping for nothing again; and your reward shall be great, and ye shall be the children of the Highest: for he is kind unto the unthankful and to the evil. Be ye therefore merciful, as your Father also is merciful.[108]

Compare the following Christian letter:

In the Year of Our Lord 1682

To ye aged and beloved, Mr. John Higginson:

There be now at sea a ship called *Welcome,* which has on board 100 or more of the heretics and malignants called Quakers, with W. Penn, who is the chief scamp, at the head of them. The General Court has accordingly given sacred orders to Master Malachi Huscott, of the brig *Porpoise,* to waylay the

> said *Welcome* slyly as near the Cape of Cod as may be, and make captive the said Penn and his ungodly crew, so that the Lord may be glorified and not mocked on the soil of this new country with the heathen worship of these people. Much spoil can be made of selling the whole lot to Barbadoes, where slaves fetch good prices in rum and sugar and we shall not only do the Lord great good by punishing the wicked, but we shall make great good for His Minister and people.
>
> Yours in the bowels of Christ,
>
> COTTON MATHER[109]

Once we have broken free of the prejudices of our own provincially limited ecclesiastical, tribal, or national rendition of the world archetypes, it becomes possible to understand that the supreme initiation is not that of the local motherly fathers, who then project aggression onto the neighbors for their own defense. The good news, which the World Redeemer brings and which so many have been glad to hear, zealous to preach, but reluctant, apparently, to demonstrate, is that God is love, that He can be, and is to be, loved, and that all without exception are his children.[110] Such comparatively trivial matters as the remaining details of the credo, the techniques of worship, and devices of episcopal organization (which have so absorbed the interest of Occidental theologians that they are today seriously discussed as the principal questions of religion), are merely pedantic snares, unless kept ancillary to the major teaching. Indeed, where not so kept, they have a regressive effect: they reduce the father image back again to the dimensions of the totem. And this, of course, is what has happened throughout the Christian world. One would think that we had been called upon to decide or to know whom, of all of us, the Father prefers. Whereas, the teaching is much less flattering: "Judge not, that ye be not judged."[111] The World Savior's cross, in spite of the behavior of its professed priests, is a vastly more democratic symbol than the local flag.[112]

Dr. Karl Menninger has pointed out[113] that though Jewish rabbis, Protestant ministers, and Catholic priests can sometimes be brought to reconcile, on a broad basis, their theoretical differences, yet whenever they begin to describe the rules and regulations by which eternal life is to be achieved, they hopelessly differ. "Up to this point the program is impeccable," writes Dr. Menninger. "But if no one knows for certain what the rules and regulations are, it all becomes an absurdity." The reply to this, of course, is that given by Ramakrishna:

> God has made different religions to suit different aspirants, times, and countries. All doctrines are only so many paths; but a path is by no means God Himself. Indeed, one can reach God if one follows any of the paths with whole hearted devotion.... One may eat a cake with icing either straight or sidewise. It will taste sweet either way.[114]

The understanding of the final—and critical—implications of the world-redemptive words and symbols of the tradition of Christendom has been so disarranged, during the tumultuous centuries that have elapsed since St. Augustine's declaration of the holy war of the *Civitas Dei* against the *Civitas Diaboli,* that the modern thinker wishing to know the meaning of a world religion (i.e., of a doctrine of universal love) must turn his mind to the other great (and much older) universal communion: that of the Buddha, where the primary word still is *peace*—peace to all beings.

I do not mention Islam, because there, too, the doctrine is preached in terms of the holy war and thus obscured. It is certainly true that there, as well as here, many have known that the proper field of battle is not geographical but psychological (compare Rumi: "What is 'beheading'? Slaying the carnal soul in the holy war."[115]); nevertheless, the popular and orthodox expression of both the Mohammedan and the Christian doctrines has been so ferocious that it requires a very sophisticated reading to discern in either mission the operation of love.

The following Tibetan verses, for example, from two hymns of the poet-saint Milarepa, were composed about the time that Pope Urban II was preaching the First Crusade:

Amid the City of Illusoriness of the Six World-Planes
The chief factor is the sin and obscuration born of evil works;
Therein the being followeth dictates of likes and dislikes,
And findeth ne'er the time to know Equality:
Avoid, O my son, likes and dislikes.[116]

If ye realize the Emptiness of All Things, Compassion
will arise within your hearts;
If ye lose all differentiation between yourselves and others, fit
to serve others ye will be;
And when in serving others ye shall win success, then shall ye
meet with me;
And finding me, ye shall attain to Buddhahood.[117]

"The Emptiness of All Things" (Sanskrit: *śūnyatā,* "voidness") refers, on the one hand, to the illusory nature of the phenomenal world and on the other, to the impropriety of attributing such qualities as we may know from our experience of the phenomenal world to the imperishable.

In the Heavenly Radiance of the Voidness,
There existeth not shadow of thing or concept,
Yet it pervadeth all objects of knowledge;
Obeisance to the Immutable Voidness.[118]

Peace is at the heart of all because Avalokiteśvara–Kwan Yin, the mighty Bodhisattva, Boundless Love, includes, regards, and dwells within (without exception) every sentient being. The perfection of the delicate wings of an insect, broken in the passage of time, he regards—and he himself is both their perfection and their disintegration. The perennial agony of man, self-torturing, deluded, tangled in the net of his own tenuous delirium, frustrated, yet having within himself, undiscovered, absolutely unutilized, the secret of release: this too he regards—and is. Serene above man, the angels; below man, the demons and unhappy dead: these all are drawn to the Bodhisattva by the rays of his jewel hands, and they are he, as he is they. The bounded, shackled centers of consciousness, myriad-fold, on every plane of existence (not only in this present universe, limited by the Milky Way, but beyond, into the reaches of space), galaxy beyond galaxy, world beyond world of universes, coming into being out of the timeless pool of the void, bursting into life, and like a bubble therewith vanishing: time and time again: lives by the multitude: all suffering: each bounded in the tenuous, tight circle of itself—lashing, killing, hating, and desiring peace beyond victory: these all are the children, the mad figures of the transitory yet inexhaustible, long world dream of the All-Regarding, whose essence is the essence of Emptiness: "The Lord Looking Down in Pity."

But the name means also: "The Lord Who Is Seen Within."* We are all reflexes of the image of the Bodhisattva. The sufferer within us is that divine being. We and that protecting father are one. This is the redeeming insight. That protecting father is every man we meet. And so it must be known that, though this ignorant, limited, self-defending, suffering body may regard itself as threatened by some other—the enemy—that one too is the God. The ogre breaks us, but the hero, the fit candidate, undergoes the initiation "like a man"; and behold, it was the father: we in Him and He in us.[119] The dear, protecting mother of our body could not defend us from the Great Father Serpent; the mortal, tangible body that she gave us was delivered into his frightening power. But death was not the end. New life, new birth, new knowledge of existence (so that we live not in this

* *Avalokita* (Sanskrit) = "looking down," but also, "seen"; *iśvara* = "Lord"; hence, both "The Lord Looking Down [in Pity]," and "The Lord Seen [Within]" (*a* and *i* combine into *e* in Sanskrit: hence *Avalokiteśvara*). See W. Y. Evans-Wentz, *Tibetan Yoga and Secret Doctrines* (London: Oxford University Press, 1935), p. 233, note 2.

physique only, but in all bodies, all physiques of the world, as the Bodhisattva) was given us. That father was himself the womb, the mother, of a second birth.[120]

This is the meaning of the image of the bisexual god. He is the mystery of the theme of initiation. We are taken from the mother, chewed into fragments, and assimilated to the world-annihilating body of the ogre for whom all the precious forms and beings are only the courses of a feast; but then, miraculously reborn, we are more than we were. If the God is a tribal, racial, national, or sectarian archetype, we are the warriors of his cause; but if he is a lord of the universe itself, we then go forth as knowers to whom *all* men are brothers. And in either case, the childhood parent images and ideas of "good" and "evil" have been surpassed. We no longer desire and fear; we are what was desired and feared. All the gods, Bodhisattvas, and Buddhas have been subsumed in us, as in the halo of the mighty holder of the lotus of the world.

> Come [therefore], and let us return unto the Lord: for he hath torn, and he will heal us; he hath smitten, and he will bind us up. After two days will he revive us: in the third day he will raise us up, and we shall live in his sight. Then shall we know, if we follow on to know the Lord: his going forth is prepared as the morning; and he shall come unto us as the rain, as the latter and former rain unto the earth.[121]

This is the sense of the first wonder of the Bodhisattva: the androgynous character of the presence. Therewith the two apparently opposite mythological adventures come together: the Meeting with the Goddess, and the Atonement with the Father. For in the first the initiate learns that male and female are (as phrased in the Bṛhadāranyaka Upaniṣad) "two halves of a split pea";[122] whereas in the second, the Father is found to be antecedent to the division of sex: the pronoun "He" was a manner of speech, the myth of Sonship a guiding line to be erased. And in both cases it is found (or rather, recollected) that the hero himself is that which he had come to find.

The second wonder to be noted in the Bodhisattva myth is its annihilation of the distinction between life and release-from-life—which is symbolized (as we have observed) in the Bodhisattva's renunciation of *nirvāṇa*. Briefly, *nirvāṇa* means "the Extinguishing of the Threefold Fire of Desire, Hostility, and Delusion." As the reader will recall: in the legend of the Temptation under the Bo Tree (see above, pp. 24–25) the antagonist of the Future Buddha was

Kāma-Māra, literally "Desire-Hostility," or "Love and Death," the magician of Delusion. He was a personification of the Threefold Fire and of the difficulties of the last test, a final threshold guardian to be passed by the universal hero on his supreme adventure to *nirvāṇa.*

"The verb *nirvā* (Sanskrit) is, literally, 'to blow out,' not transitively, but as a fire ceases to draw.... Deprived of fuel, the fire of life is 'pacified,' i.e., quenched, when the mind has been curbed, one attains to the 'peace of Nirvana,' 'despiration in God.'... It is by ceasing to feed our fires that the peace is reached, of which it is well said in another tradition that 'it passeth understanding'"[123] The word "de-spiration" is contrived from a literal Latinization of the Sanskrit *nirvāṇa, nir* = "out, forth, outward, out of, out from, away, away from"; *vāṇa* = "blown"; *nirvāṇa* = "blown out, gone out, extinguished."

Having subdued within himself to the critical point of the ultimate ember the Threefold Fire, which is the moving power of the universe, the Savior beheld reflected, as in a mirror all around him, the last projected fantasies of his primitive physical will to live like other human beings—the will to live according to the normal motives of desire and hostility, in a delusory ambient of phenomenal causes, ends, and means. He was assailed by the last fury of the disregarded flesh. And this was the moment on which all depended; for from one coal could arise again the whole conflagration.

This greatly celebrated legend affords an excellent example of the close relationship maintained in the Orient between myth, psychology, and metaphysics. The vivid personifications prepare the intellect for the doctrine of the interdependence of the inner and the outer worlds. No doubt the reader has been struck by a certain resemblance of this ancient mythological doctrine of the dynamics of the psyche to the teachings of the modern Freudian school. According to the latter, the life-wish (*eros* or *libido,* corresponding to the Buddhist *Kāma,* "desire") and the death-wish (*thanatos* or *destrudo,* which is identical with the Buddhist *Māra,* "hostility or death") are the two drives that not only move the individual from within but also animate for him the surrounding world.[124] Moreover, the unconsciously grounded delusions from which desires and hostilities arise are in both systems dispelled by psychological analysis (Sanskrit: *viveka*) and illumination (Sanskrit: *vidyā*). Yet the aims of the two teachings—the traditional and the modern—are not exactly the same.

Psychoanalysis is a technique to cure excessively suffering individuals of the unconsciously misdirected desires and hostilities that weave around them their private webs of unreal terrors and ambivalent attractions; the patient released from these finds himself able to participate with comparative satisfaction in the more realistic fears, hostilities, erotic and religious practices, business enterprises, wars, pastimes, and household tasks offered to him by his particular culture. But for the one who has deliberately undertaken the difficult and dangerous journey beyond the village compound, these interests, too, are to be regarded as based on error. Therefore the aim of the religious teaching is not to cure the individual back again to the general delusion, but to detach him from delusion altogether; and this not by readjusting the desire (*eros*) and hostility (*thanatos*)—for that would only originate a new context of delusion—but by *extinguishing* the impulses to the very root, according to the method of the celebrated Buddhist Eightfold Path:

> Right Belief, Right Intentions,
> Right Speech, Right Actions,
> Right Livelihood, Right Endeavoring,
> Right Mindfulness, Right Concentration.

With the final "extirpation of delusion, desire, and hostility" (*nirvāṇa*) the mind knows that it is not what it thought: thought goes. The mind rests in its true state. And here it may dwell until the body drops away.

> *Stars, darkness, a lamp, a phantom, dew, a bubble,*
> *A dream, a flash of lightning, and a cloud:*
> *Thus we should look upon all that was made.*[125]

The Bodhisattva, however, does not abandon life. Turning his regard from the inner sphere of thought-transcending truth (which can be described only as "emptiness," since it surpasses speech) outward again to the phenomenal world, he perceives without the same ocean of being that he found within. "Form is emptiness, emptiness indeed is form. Emptiness is not different from form, form is not different from emptiness. What is form, that is emptiness; what is emptiness, that is form. And the same applies to perception, name, conception, and knowledge."[126] Having surpassed the delusions of his formerly self-assertive, self-defensive, self-concerned ego, he knows without and within the same repose. What he beholds without is the visual aspect of the magnitudinous, thought-transcending emptiness on which his own experiences of ego, form, perceptions, speech, conceptions, and

FIGURE 35. *Bodhidharma* (paint on silk, Japan, sixteenth century A.D.)

knowledge ride. And he is filled with compassion for the self-terrorized beings who live in fright of their own nightmare. He rises, returns to them, and dwells with them as an egoless center, through whom the principle of emptiness is made manifest in its own simplicity. And this is his great "compassionate act"; for by it the truth is revealed that in the understanding of one in whom the Threefold Fire of Desire, Hostility, and Delusion is dead, this world *is nirvāṇa.* "Gift waves" go out from such a one for the liberation of us all. "This our worldly life is an activity of *nirvāna* itself, not the slightest distinction exists between them."[127]

And so it may be said that the modern therapeutic goal of the cure back to life is attained through the ancient religious discipline, after all; only the circle traveled by the Bodhisattva is a large one; and the departure from the world is regarded not as a fault, but as the first step into that noble path at the remotest turn of which illumination is to be won concerning the deep emptiness of the universal round. Such an ideal is well known, also, to Hinduism: the one freed in life (*jīvan mukta*), desireless, compassionate, and wise, "with the heart concentrated by yoga, viewing all things with equal regard, beholds himself in all beings and all beings in himself. In whatever way he leads his life, that one lives in God."[128]

The story is told of a Confucian scholar who besought the twenty-eighth Buddhist patriarch, Bodhidharma, "to pacify his soul." Bodhidharma retorted, "Produce it and I will pacify it." The Confucian replied, "That is my trouble, I cannot find it." Bodhidharma said, "Your wish is granted." The Confucian understood and departed in peace.[129]

Those who know, not only that the Everlasting lives in them but that what they, and all things, really are *is* the Everlasting, dwell in the groves of the wish-fulfilling trees, drink the brew of immortality, and listen everywhere to the unheard music of eternal concord. These are the immortals. The Taoist landscape paintings of China and Japan depict supremely the heavenliness of this terrestrial state. The four benevolent animals, the phoenix, the unicorn, the tortoise, and the dragon, dwell amongst the willow gardens, the bamboos, and the plums, and amid the mists of sacred mountains, close to the honored spheres. Sages, with craggy bodies but spirits eternally young, meditate among these peaks, or ride curious, symbolic animals across immortal tides, or converse delightfully over teacups to the flute of Lan Ts'ai-ho.

The mistress of the earthly paradise of the Chinese immortals is the fairy goddess Hsi Wang Mu, "The Golden Mother of the Tortoise." She dwells in a palace on the K'un-lun Mountain, which is surrounded by fragrant flowers, battlements of jewels and a garden wall of gold.* She is formed of the pure quintessence of the western air. Her quests at her periodical "Feast of the Peaches" (celebrated when the peaches ripen, once in every six thousand years) are served by the Golden Mother's gracious daughters, in bowers and pavilions by the Lake of Gems. Waters play there from a remarkable fountain. Phoenix marrow, dragon liver, and other meats are tasted; the peaches

* This is the Wall of Paradise; see above, pp. 73 and 131. We are now *inside*. Hsi Wang Mu is the feminine aspect of the Lord who walks in the Garden, who created man in his own image, male and female (Book of Genesis, 1:27).

and the wine bestow immortality. Music from invisible instruments is heard, songs that are not from mortal lips; and the dances of the visible damsels are the manifestations of the joy of eternity in time.[130]

The tea ceremonies of Japan are conceived in the spirit of the Taoist earthly paradise. The tearoom, called "the abode of fancy," is an ephemeral structure built to enclose a moment of poetic intuition. Called too "the abode of vacancy," it is devoid of ornamentation. Temporarily it contains a single picture or flower-arrangement. The teahouse is called "the abode of the unsymmetrical": the unsymmetrical suggests movement; the purposely unfinished leaves a vacuum into which the imagination of the beholder can pour.

FIGURE 36. *Tea Ceremony: Abode of Vacancy* (photograph by Joseph Campbell, Japan, A.D. 1958)

The guest approaches by the garden path, and must stoop through the low entrance. He makes obeisance to the picture or flower-arrangement, to the singing kettle, and takes his place on the floor. The simplest object, framed by the controlled simplicity of the teahouse, stands out in mysterious beauty, its silence holding the secret of temporal existence. Each guest is permitted to complete the experience in relation to himself. The members of the company thus contemplate the universe in miniature, and become aware of their hidden fellowship with the immortals.

The great tea masters were concerned to make of the divine wonder an experienced moment; then out of the teahouse the influence was carried into the home; and out of the home distilled into the nation.[131] During the long and peaceful Tokugawa period (1603–1868), before the arrival of Commodore Perry in 1854, the texture of Japanese life became so imbued with significant formalization that existence to the slightest detail was a conscious expression of eternity, the landscape itself a shrine. Similarly, throughout the Orient, throughout the ancient world, and in the pre-Columbian Americas, society and nature represented to the mind the inexpressible. "The plants, rocks, fire, water, all are alive. They watch us and see our needs. They see when we have nothing to protect us," declared an old Apache storyteller, "and it is then that they reveal themselves and speak to us."[132] This is what the Buddhist calls "the sermon of the inanimate."

A certain Hindu ascetic who lay down to rest beside the holy Ganges placed his feet up on a Śiva-symbol (a "*liṅgam-yonī,*" a combined phallus and vulva, symbolizing the union of the God with his Spouse). A passing priest observed the man reposing thus and rebuked him. "How can you dare to profane this symbol of God by resting your feet on it?" demanded the priest. The ascetic replied, "Good sir, I am sorry; but will you kindly take my feet and place them where there is no such sacred *liṅgam*?" The priest seized the ankles of the ascetic and lifted them to the right, but when he set them down a phallus sprang from the ground and they rested as before. He moved them again; another phallus received them. "Ah, I see!" said the priest, humbled; and he made obeisance to the reposing saint and went his way.

The third wonder of the Bodhisattva myth is that the first wonder (namely, the bisexual form) is symbolical of the second (the identity of eternity and time). For in the language of the divine pictures, the world of time is the great mother womb. The life therein, begotten by the father, is compounded of her darkness and his light.[133] We are conceived in her and dwell removed from the father, but when we pass from the womb of time at death (which is our birth to eternity) we are given into his hands. The wise realize, even within this womb, that they have come from and are returning to the father; while the very wise know that she and he are in substance one.

FIGURE 37. *Liṅgam-Yonī* (carved stone, Vietnam, c. ninth century A.D.)

This is the meaning of those Tibetan images of the union of the Buddhas and Bodhisattvas with their own feminine aspects that have seemed so indecent to many Christian critics. According to one of the traditional ways of looking at these supports of meditation, the female form (Tibetan: *yum*) is to be regarded as time and the male (*yab*) as eternity. The union of the two is productive of the world, in which all things are at once temporal and eternal, created in the image of this self-knowing male-female God. The initiate, through meditation, is led to the recollection of this Form of forms (*yab-yum*) within himself. Or on the other hand, the male figure may be regarded as symbolizing the initiating principle, the method; in which case the female denotes the goal to which initiation leads. But this goal is *nirvāṇa* (eternity). And so it is that both the male and the female are to be envisioned, alternately, as time and eternity. That is to say, the two are the same, each is both, and the dual form (*yab-yum*) is only an effect of illusion, which itself, however, is not different from enlightenment.

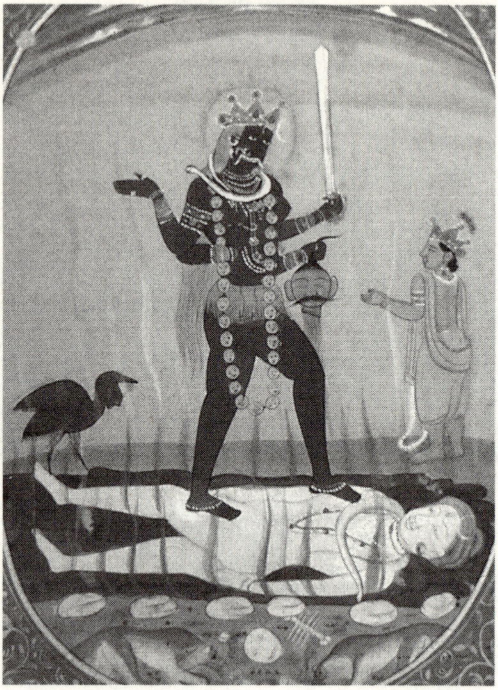

FIGURE 38. *Kālī Astride Śiva* (gouache on paper, India, date uncertain)

Comparatively, the Hindu goddess Kālī[134] is shown standing on the prostrate form of the god Śiva, her spouse. What Jung, drawing on the language of alchemy, called the *mysterium coniunctionis,* the mystery of the great union, is a standard motif in myths throughout the world, but particularly in the Orient. The Hindu goddess Kālī is frequently shown standing on the prostrate form of the god Śiva, her spouse. She brandishes the sword of death, i.e., spiritual discipline. The blood-dripping human head tells the devotee that he that loseth his life for her sake shall find it. The gestures of "fear not" and "bestowing boons" teach that she protects her children, that the pairs of opposites of the universal agony are not what they seem, and that for one centered in eternity the phantasmagoria of temporal "goods" and "evils" is but a reflex of the mind—as the goddess herself, though apparently trampling down the god, is actually his blissful dream.

Beneath the goddess of the Island of Jewels[135] two aspects of the god are represented: the one, face upward, in union with her, is the creative, world-enjoying aspect; but the other, turned away, is the *deus absconditus,* the divine essence in and by itself, beyond event and change, inactive, dormant, void, beyond even the wonder of the hermaphroditic mystery.[136]

This is a supreme statement of the great paradox by which the wall of the pairs of opposites is shattered and the candidate admitted to the vision of the God, who when he created man in his own image created him male and female. In the male's right hand is held a thunderbolt that is the counterpart of himself, while in his left he holds a bell, symbolizing the goddess. The thunderbolt is both the method and eternity, whereas the bell is "illumined mind"; its note is the beautiful sound of eternity that is heard by the pure mind throughout creation, and therefore within itself.[137]

Precisely the same bell is rung in the Christian Mass at the moment when God, through the power of the words of the consecration, descends into the bread and wine. And the Christian reading of the meaning also is the same: *Et Verbum caro factum est,** i.e., "The Jewel is in the Lotus": *Om mani padme hum.*

Compare the Kauṣītaki Upaniṣad, 1:4, describing the hero who has reached the Brahmā-world: "Just as one driving a chariot looks down upon the two chariot wheels, thus he looks down upon day and night, thus upon good deeds and evil deeds, and upon all the pairs of opposites. This one, devoid of good deeds, devoid of evil deeds, a knower of God, unto very God he goes."

In this section the following have been equated:

The Void	The World
Eternity	Time
Nirvāṇa	*Saṃsāra*
Truth	Illusoriness
Enlightenment	Compassion
The God	The Goddess
The Enemy	The Friend
Death	Birth
The Thunderbolt	The Bell
The Jewel	The Lotus
Subject	Object
Yab	Yum
Yang	Yin

Tao
Supreme Buddha
Bodhisattva
Jīvan Mukta
The Word Made Flesh

* "And the Word was made flesh"; verse of the Angelus, celebrating the conception of Jesus in Mary's womb.

6. The Ultimate Boon

When the Prince of the Lonesome Island had remained six nights and days on the golden couch with the sleeping Queen of Tubber Tintye, the couch resting on wheels of gold and the wheels turning continually—the couch going round and round, never stopping night or day—on the seventh morning he said, "It is time for me now to leave this place." So he came down and filled the three bottles with water from the flaming well. In the golden chamber was a table of gold, and on the table a leg of mutton with a loaf of bread; and if all the men of Erin were to eat for a twelvemonth from the table, the mutton and the bread would be in the same form after the eating as before.

The Prince sat down, ate his fill of the loaf and the leg of mutton, and left them as he had found them. Then he rose up, took his three bottles, put them in his wallet, and was leaving the chamber, when he said to himself: "It would be a shame to go away without leaving something by which the Queen may know who was here while she slept." So he wrote a letter, saying that the son of the King of Erin and the Queen of the Lonesome Island had spent six days and nights in the golden chamber of Tubber Tintye, had taken away three bottles of water from the flaming well, and had eaten from the table of gold. Putting his letter under the pillow of the Queen, he went out, stood in the open window, sprang on the back of the lean and shaggy little horse, and passed the trees and the river unharmed.[138]

The ease with which the adventure is here accomplished signifies that the hero is a superior man, a born king. Such ease distinguishes numerous fairy tales and all legends of the deeds of incarnate gods. Where the usual hero would face a test, the elect encounters no delaying obstacle and makes no mistake. The well is the World Navel, its flaming water the indestructible essence of existence, the bed going round and round being the World Axis. The sleeping castle is that ultimate abyss to which the descending consciousness submerges in dream, where the individual life is on the point of dissolving into undifferentiated energy: and it would be death to dissolve; yet death, also, to lack the fire. The motif (derived from an infantile fantasy) of the inexhaustible dish, symbolizing the perpetual life-giving, form-building powers of the universal source, is a fairy-tale counterpart of the mythological image of the cornucopian banquet of the gods. The bringing together of the two great symbols of the meeting with the goddess and the fire theft reveals with simplicity and clarity the status of the anthropomorphic powers in the realm of myth. They are not ends in themselves, but guardians, embodiments, or bestowers, of the liquor, the milk, the food, the fire, the grace, of indestructible life.

Such imagery can be readily interpreted as primarily, even though perhaps not ultimately, psychological; for it is possible to observe, in the earliest phases of the development of the infant, symptoms of a dawning "mythology" of a state beyond the vicissitudes of time. These appear as reactions to, and spontaneous defenses against, the body-destruction fantasies that assail the child when it is deprived of the mother breast.[139] "The infant reacts with a temper tantrum and the fantasy that goes with the temper tantrum is to tear everything out of the mother's body.... The child then fears retaliation for these impulses, i.e., that everything will be scooped out of its own inside."[140] Anxieties for the integrity of its body, fantasies of restitution, a silent, deep requirement for indestructibility and protection against the "bad" forces from within and without, begin to direct the shaping psyche; and these remain as determining factors in the later neurotic, and even normal, life activities, spiritual efforts, religious beliefs, and ritual practices of the adult.

The profession, for example, of the medicine man, this nucleus of all primitive societies, "originates... on the basis of the infantile body-destruction fantasies, by means of a series of defence mechanisms."[141] In Australia a basic conception is that the spirits have removed the intestines of the medicine man and substituted pebbles, quartz crystals, a quantity of rope, and sometimes also a little snake endowed with power.[142]

> The first formula is abreaction in fantasy (my inside has already been destroyed) followed by reaction-formation (my inside is not something corruptible and full of faeces, but incorruptible, full of quartz crystals). The second is projection: "It is not I who am trying to penetrate into the body but foreign sorcerers who shoot disease-substances into people." The third formula is restitution:

> "I am not trying to destroy people's insides, I am healing them." At the same time, however, the original fantasy element of the valuable body-contents torn out of the mother returns in the healing technique: to suck, to pull, to rub something out of the patient.[143]

Another image of indestructibility is represented in the folk idea of the spiritual "double"—an external soul not afflicted by the losses and injuries of the present body, but existing safely in some place removed.[144] "My death," said a certain ogre, "is far from here and hard to find, on the wide ocean. In that sea is an island, and on the island there grows a green oak, and beneath the oak is an iron chest, and in the chest is a small basket, and in the basket is a hare, and in the hare is a duck, and in the duck is an egg; and he who finds the egg and breaks it, kills me at the same time."[145] Compare the dream of a successful modern businesswoman:

> I was stranded on a desert island. There was a Catholic priest there also. He had been doing something about putting boards from one island to another so people could pass. We passed to another island and there asked a woman where I'd gone. She replied that I was diving with some divers. Then I went somewhere to the interior of the island where was a body of beautiful water full of gems and jewels and the other "I" was down there in a diving suit. I stood there looking down and watching myself.[146]

There is a charming Hindu tale of a king's daughter who would marry only the man that found and awakened her double, in the Land of the Lotus of the Sun, at the bottom of the sea.[147] The initiated Australian, after his marriage, is conducted by his grandfather to a sacred cave and there shown a small slab of wood inscribed with allegorical designs: "This," he is told, "is your body; this and you are the same. Do not take it to another place or you will feel pain."[148] The Manicheans and the Gnostic Christians of the first centuries A.D. taught that when the soul of the blessed arrives in heaven it is met by saints and angels bearing its "vesture of light," which has been preserved for it.

The supreme boon desired for the Indestructible Body is uninterrupted residence in the Paradise of the Milk That Never Fails:

> Rejoice ye with Jerusalem, and be glad with her, all ye that love her: rejoice for joy with her, all ye that mourn for her: that ye may suck, and be satisfied with the breasts of her consolations; that ye may milk out, and be delighted with the abundance of her glory.

> For thus saith the Lord, Behold, I will extend peace to her like a river... then shall ye suck, ye shall be borne upon her sides, and be dandled upon her knees.[149]

FIGURE 39. *Isis Giving Bread and Water to the Soul* (Egypt, date uncertain)

Soul and body food, heart's ease, is the gift of "All Heal," the nipple inexhaustible. Mt. Olympus rises to the heavens; gods and heroes banquet there on ambrosia (*α*, not, *βροτός*, mortal). In Wotan's mountain hall, four hundred and thirty-two thousand heroes consume the undiminished flesh of Sachrimnir, the Cosmic Boar, washing it down with a milk that runs from the udders of the she goat Heidrun: she feeds on the leaves of Yggdrasil, the World Ash. Within the fairy hills of Erin, the deathless Tuatha De Danaan consume the self-renewing pigs of Manannan, drinking copiously of Guibne's ale. In Persia, the gods in the mountain garden on Mt. Hara Berezaiti drink immortal *haoma,* distilled from the Gaokerena Tree, the tree of life. The Japanese gods drink *sake,* the Polynesian *ave,* the Aztec gods drink the blood of men and maids. And the redeemed of Yahweh, in their roof garden, are served the inexhaustible, delicious flesh of the monsters Behemoth, Leviathan, and Ziz, while drinking the liquors of the four sweet rivers of paradise.[150]

It is obvious that the infantile fantasies which we all cherish still in the unconscious play continually into myth, fairy tale, and the teachings of the church, as symbols of indestructible being. This is helpful, for the mind feels at home with the images, and seems to be remembering something already known. But the circumstance is obstructive too, for the feelings come to rest in the symbols and resist passionately every effort to go beyond. The prodigious gulf between those childishly blissful multitudes who fill the world with piety and the truly free breaks open at the line where the symbols give way and are transcended. "O ye," writes Dante, departing from the Terrestrial Paradise, "O ye who in a little bark, desirous to listen, have followed behind my craft which singing passes on, turn to see again your shores; put not out upon the deep; for haply, losing me, ye would remain astray. The water which I take was never crossed. Minerva breathes, and Apollo guides me, and nine Muses point out to me the Bears."[151] Here is the line beyond which thinking does not go, beyond which all feeling is truly dead: like the last stop on a mountain railroad from which climbers step away, and to which they return, there to converse with those who love mountain air but cannot risk the heights. The ineffable teaching of the beatitude beyond imagination comes to us clothed, necessarily, in figures reminiscent of the imagined beatitude of infancy; hence the deceptive childishness of the tales. Hence, too, the inadequacy of any merely psychological reading.

In the published psychoanalytical literature, the dream sources of the symbols are analyzed, as well as their latent meanings for the unconscious, and the effects of their operation upon the psyche; but the further fact that great teachers have employed them consciously as metaphors remains unregarded: the tacit assumption being that the great teachers of the past were neurotics (except, of course, a number of the Greeks and Romans) who mistook their uncriticized fantasies for revelation. In the same spirit, the revelations of psychoanalysis are regarded by many laymen to be productions of the "salacious mind" of Dr. Freud.

The sophistication of the humor of the infantile imagery, when inflected in a skillful mythological rendition of metaphysical doctrine, emerges magnificently in one of the best known of the great myths of the Oriental world: the Hindu account of the primordial battle between the titans and the gods for the liquor of immortality. An ancient earth being, Kaśyapa, "The Turtle Man," had married thirteen of the daughters of a still more ancient demiurgic patriarch, Dakṣa, "The Lord of Virtue." Two of these daughters, Diti and Aditī by name, had given birth respectively to the titans and the gods. In an unending series of family battles, however, many of these sons of Kaśyapa were being slain. But now the high priest of the titans, by great austerities and meditations, gained the favor of Śiva, Lord of the Universe. Śiva bestowed on him a charm to revive the dead. This gave to the titans an advantage which the gods, in the next battle, were quick to perceive. They retired in confusion to consult together, and addressed themselves to the high divinities Brahmā and Viṣṇu.

FIGURE 40. *Brahmā, Viṣṇu, and Śiva with Their Consorts* (painted miniature, India, early nineteenth century A.D.)

Brahmā, Viṣṇu, and Śiva, respectively Creator, Preserver, and Destroyer, constitute a trinity in Hinduism, as three aspects of the operation of the one creative substance. After the seventh century B.C., Brahmā, declining in importance, became merely the creative agent of Viṣṇu. Thus Hinduism today is divided into two main camps, one devoted primarily to the creator-preserver Viṣṇu, the other to Śiva, the world-destroyer, who unites the soul to the eternal. But these two are ultimately one. In the present myth, it is through their joint operation that the elixir of life is obtained.

They were advised to conclude with their brother-enemies a temporary truce, during which the titans should be induced to help them churn the Milky Ocean of immortal life for its butter—Amṛta (*a* not, *mṛta,* mortal), "the nectar of deathlessness." Flattered by the invitation, which they regarded as an admission of their superiority, the titans were delighted to participate; and so the epochal cooperative adventure at the beginning of the four ages of the world cycle began. Mount Mandara was selected as the churning stick. Vāsuki, the King of Serpents, consented to become the churning rope with which to twirl it. Viṣṇu himself, in the form of a tortoise, dove into the Milky Ocean to support with his back the base of the mountain. The gods laid hold of one end of the serpent, after it had been wrapped around the mountain, the titans the other. And the company then churned for a thousand years.

The first thing to arise from the surface of the sea was a black, poisonous smoke, called Kālakuta, "Black Summit," namely the highest concentration of the power of death. "Drink me," said Kālakuta; and the operation could not proceed until someone should be found capable of drinking it up. Śiva, sitting aloof and afar, was approached. Magnificently, he relaxed from his position of deeply indrawn meditation and proceeded to the scene of the churning of the Milky Ocean. Taking the tincture of death in a cup, he swallowed it at a gulp, and by his yoga-power held it in his throat. The throat turned blue. Hence Śiva is addressed as "Blue Neck," Nīlakantha.

The churning now being resumed, presently there began coming up out of the inexhaustible depths precious forms of concentrated power. Apsarases (nymphs) appeared, Lakṣmī, the goddess of fortune, the milk-white horse named Ucchaiḥśravas, "Neighing Aloud," the pearl of gems, Kaustubha, and other objects to the number of thirteen. Last to appear was the skilled physician of the gods, Dhanvantari, holding in his hand the moon, the cup of the nectar of life.

Now began immediately a great battle for possession of the invaluable drink. One of the titans, Rāhu, managed to steal a sip, but was beheaded before the liquor passed his throat; his body decayed but the head remained immortal. And this head now goes pursuing the moon forever through the skies, trying again to seize it. When it succeeds, the cup passes easily through its mouth and out again at its throat: that is why we have eclipses of the moon.

But Viṣṇu, concerned lest the gods should lose the advantage, transformed himself into a beautiful dancing damsel. And while the titans, who were lusty fellows, stood spellbound by the girl's charm, she took up the moon-cup of Amṛta, teased them with it for a moment, and then suddenly passed it over to the gods. Viṣṇu immediately again transformed himself into a mighty hero, joined the gods against the titans, and helped drive away the enemy to the crags and dark canyons of the world beneath. The gods now dine on the Amṛta forever, in their beautiful palaces on the summit of the central mountain of the world, Mount Sumeru.[152]

Humor is the touchstone of the truly mythological as distinct from the more literal-minded and sentimental theological mood. The gods as icons are not ends in themselves. Their entertaining myths transport the mind and spirit, not *up to,* but *past* them, into the yonder void; from which perspective the more heavily freighted theological dogmas then appear to have been only pedagogical lures: their function, to cart the unadroit intellect away from its concrete clutter of facts and events to a comparatively rarefied zone, where, as a final boon, all existence—whether heavenly, earthly, or infernal—may at last be seen transmuted into the semblance of a lightly passing, recurrent, mere childhood dream of bliss and fright. "From one point of view all those divinities exist," a Tibetan lama recently replied to the question of an understanding Occidental visitor, "from another they are not real."[153] This is the orthodox teaching of the ancient Tantras: "All of these visualized deities are but symbols representing the various things that occur on the Path";[154] as well as a doctrine of the contemporary psychoanalytical schools.[155] And the same meta-theological insight seems to be what is suggested in Dante's final verses, where the illuminated voyager at last is able to lift his courageous eyes beyond the beatific vision of Father, Son, and Holy Ghost, to the one Eternal Light.[156]

The gods and goddesses then are to be understood as embodiments and custodians of the elixir of Imperishable Being but not themselves the Ultimate in its primary state. What the hero seeks through his intercourse with them is therefore not finally themselves, but their grace, i.e., the power of their sustaining substance. This miraculous energy-substance and this alone is the Imperishable; the names and forms of the deities who everywhere embody, dispense, and represent it come and go. This is the miraculous energy of the thunderbolts of Zeus, Yahweh, and the Supreme Buddha, the fertility of the rain of Viracocha, the virtue announced by the bell rung in the Mass at the consecration,[157] and the light of the ultimate illumination of the saint and sage. Its guardians dare release it only to the duly proven.

But the gods may be oversevere, overcautious, in which case the hero must trick them of their treasure. Such was the problem of Prometheus. When in this mood even the highest gods appear as malignant, life-hoarding ogres, and the hero who deceives, slays, or appeases them is honored as the savior of the world.

Maui of Polynesia went against Mahu-ika, the guardian of fire, to wring from him his treasure and transport it back to mankind. Maui went straight up to the giant Mahu-ika and said to him: "Clear away the brush from this level field of ours so that we may contend together in friendly rivalry." Maui, it must be told, was a great hero and a master of devices.

Mahu-ika inquired, "What feat of mutual prowess and emulation shall it be?"

"The feat of tossing," Maui replied.

To this Mahu-ika agreed; then Maui asked, "Who shall begin?"

Mahu-ika answered, "I shall."

Maui signified his consent, so Mahu-ika took hold of Maui and tossed him up in the air; he rose high above and fell right down into Mahu-ika's hands; again Mahu-ika tossed Maui up, chanting: "Tossing, tossing—up you go!"

Up went Maui, and then Mahu-ika chanted this incantation:

Up you go to the first level,
Up you go to the second level,
Up you go to the third level,
Up you go to the fourth level,
Up you go to the fifth level,
Up you go to the sixth level,
Up you go to the seventh level,
Up you go to the eighth level,
Up you go to the ninth level,
Up you go to the tenth level!

Maui turned over and over in the air and started to come down again, and he fell right beside Mahu-ika; then Maui said, "You're having all the fun!"

"Why indeed!" Mahu-ika exclaimed. "Do you imagine you can send a whale flying up into the air?"

"I can try!" Maui answered.

So Maui took hold of Mahu-ika and tossed him up, chanting: "Tossing, tossing—up you go!"

Up flew Mahu-ika, and now Maui chanted this spell:

Up you go to the first level,
Up you go to the second level,
Up you go to the third level,
Up you go to the fourth level,
Up you go to the fifth level,
Up you go to the sixth level,
Up you go to the seventh level,
Up you go to the eighth level,
Up you go to the ninth level,
Up you go—way up in the air!

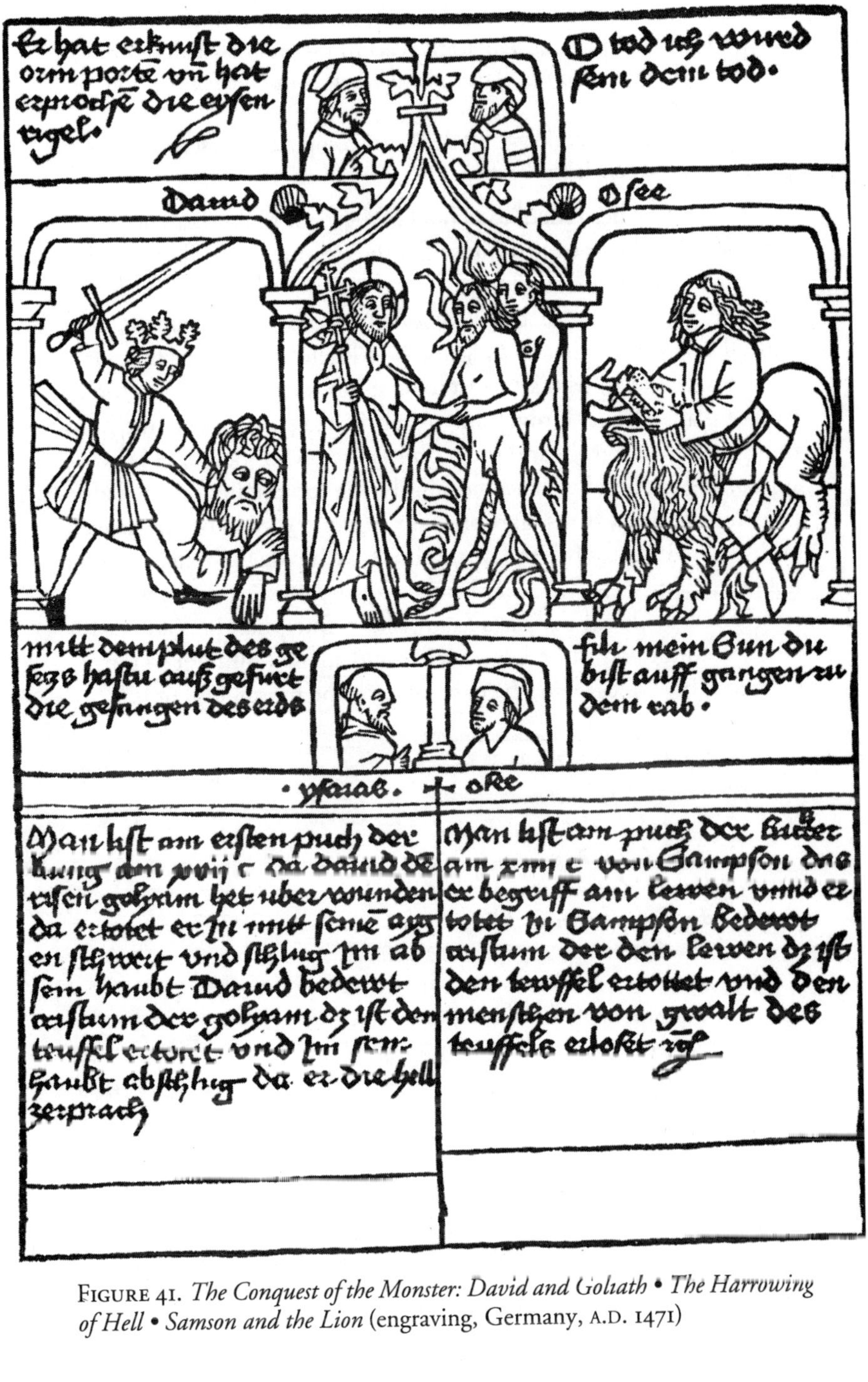

FIGURE 41. *The Conquest of the Monster: David and Goliath • The Harrowing of Hell • Samson and the Lion* (engraving, Germany, A.D. 1471)

> Mahu-ika turned over and over in the air and commenced to fall back; and when he had nearly reached the ground Maui called out these magic words: "That man up there—may he fall right on his head!"
>
> Mahu-ika fell down; his neck was completely telescoped together, and so Mahu-ika died.

At once the hero Maui took hold of the giant Mahu-ika's head and cut it off, then he possessed himself of the treasure of the flame, which he bestowed upon the world.[158]

The greatest tale of the elixir quest in the Mesopotamian, prebiblical tradition is that of Gilgamesh, a legendary king of the Sumerian city of Erech, who set forth to attain the watercress of immortality, the plant "Never Grow Old." After he had passed safely the lions that guard the foothills and the scorpion men who watch the heaven-supporting mountains, he came, amidst the mountains, to a paradise garden of flowers, fruits, and precious stones. Pressing on, he arrived at the sea that surrounds the world. In a cave beside the waters dwelt a manifestation of the Goddess Ishtar, Siduri-Sabitu, and this woman, closely veiled, closed the gates against him. But when he told her his tale, she admitted him to her presence and advised him not to pursue his quest, but to learn and be content with the mortal joys of life:

Gilgamesh, why dost thou run about this way?
The life that thou art seeking, thou wilt never find.
When the gods created man,
    they put death upon mankind,
    and held life in their own hands.
Fill thy belly, Gilgamesh;
    day and night enjoy thyself;
    prepare each day some pleasant occasion.
Day and night be frolicsome and gay;
    let thy clothes be handsome,
    thy head shampooed, thy body bathed.
Regard the little one who takes thy hand.
Let thy wife be happy against thy bosom.

This passage, missing from the standard Assyrian edition of the legend, appears in a much earlier Babylonian fragmentary text.[159] It has been frequently remarked that the advice of the sibyl is hedonistic, but it should be noted also that the passage represents an initiatory test, not the moral philosophy of the ancient Babylonians. As in India, centuries later, when a student approaches a teacher to ask the secret of immortal life, he is first put off with a description of the joys of the mortal.[160] Only if he persists is he admitted to the next initiation.

But when Gilgamesh persisted, Siduri-Sabitu gave him permission to pass and apprised him of the dangers of the way.

The woman instructed him to seek the ferryman Ursanapi, whom he found chopping wood in the forest and guarded by a group of attendants. Gilgamesh shattered these attendants (they were called "those who rejoice to live," "those of stone") and the ferryman consented to convey him across the waters of death. It was a voyage of one and one-half months. The passenger was warned not to touch the waters.

Now the far land that they were approaching was the residence of Utnapishtim, the hero of the primordial deluge,* here abiding with his wife in immortal peace. From afar Utnapishtim spied the approaching little craft alone on the endless waters, and he wondered in his heart:

Why are "those of stone" of the boat shattered,
And someone who is not of my service sailing in the boat?
That one who is coming: is he not a man?

Gilgamesh, on landing, had to listen to the patriarch's long recitation of the story of the deluge. Then Utnapishtim bid his visitor sleep, and he slept for six days. Utnapishtim had his wife bake seven loaves and place them by the head of Gilgamesh as he lay asleep beside the boat. And Utnapishtim touched Gilgamesh, and he awoke, and the host ordered the ferryman Ursanapi to give the guest a bath in a certain pool and then fresh garments. Following that, Utnapishtim announced to Gilgamesh the secret of the plant.

Gilgamesh, something secret I will disclose to thee,
and give thee thine instruction:
That plant is like a brier in the field;
its thorn, like that of the rose, will pierce thy hand.
But if thy hand attain to that plant,
thou wilt return to thy native land.

The plant was growing at the bottom of the cosmic sea.

Ursanapi ferried the hero out again into the waters. Gilgamesh tied stones to his feet and plunged. Down he rushed, beyond every bound of endurance, while the ferryman remained in the boat. And when the diver had reached the bottom of the bottomless sea, he plucked the plant, though it mutilated his hand, cut off the stones,

* Babylonian prototype of the biblical Noah.

FIGURE 42. *The Branch of Immortal Life* (alabaster wall panel, Assyria, c. 885–860 B.C.)

Though the hero was warned against touching these waters on the journey out, he now can enter them with impunity. This is a measure of the power gained through his visit with the old Lord and Lady of the Everlasting Island. Utnapishtim-Noah, the flood hero, is an archetypal father figure; his island, the World Navel, is a prefigurement of the later Greco-Roman "Islands of the Blessed."

and made again for the surface. When he broke the surface and the ferryman had hauled him back into the boat, he announced in triumph:

> *Ursanapi, this plant is the one...*
> *By which Man may attain to full vigor.*
> *I will bring it back to Erech of the sheep-pens....*
> *Its name is: "In his age, Man becomes young again."*
> *I will eat of it and return to the condition of my youth.*

They proceeded across the sea. When they had landed, Gilgamesh bathed in a cool water-hole and lay down to rest. But while he slept, a serpent smelled the wonderful perfume of the plant, darted forth, and carried it away. Eating it, the snake immediately gained the power of sloughing its skin, and so renewed its youth. But Gilgamesh, when he awoke, sat down and wept, "and the tears ran down the wall of his nose."[161]

To this very day, the possibility of physical immortality charms the heart of man. The Utopian play by Bernard Shaw, *Back to Methuselah*, produced in 1921, converted the theme into a modern socio-biological parable. Four hundred years earlier the more literal-minded Juan Ponce de León discovered Florida in a search for the land of "Bimini," where he had expected to find the fountain of youth. While centuries before and far away, the Chinese philosopher Ko Hung spent the latter years of a long lifetime preparing pills of immortality. "Take three pounds of genuine cinnabar," Ko Hung wrote,

> and one pound of white honey. Mix them. Dry the mixture in the sun. Then roast it over a fire until it can be shaped into pills. Take ten pills the size of a hemp seed every morning. Inside of a year, white hair will turn black, decayed teeth will grow again, and the body will become sleek and glistening. If an old man takes this medicine for a long period of time, he will develop into a young man. The one who takes it constantly will enjoy eternal life, and will not die.[162]

A friend one day arrived to pay a visit to the solitary experimenter and philosopher, but all he found were Ko Hung's empty clothes. The old man was gone; he had passed into the realm of the immortals.[163]

The research for *physical* immortality proceeds from a misunderstanding of the traditional teaching. On the contrary, the basic problem is: to enlarge the pupil of the eye, so that the *body* with its attendant personality will no longer obstruct the view. Immortality is then experienced as a present fact: "It is here! It is here!"[164]

FIGURE 43. *Bodhisattva* (carved stone, Cambodia, twelfth century A.D.)

> All things are in process, rising and returning. Plants come to blossom, but only to return to the root. Returning to the root is like seeking tranquility. Seeking tranquility is like moving toward destiny. To move toward destiny is like eternity. To know eternity is enlightenment, and not to recognize eternity brings disorder and evil.
>
> Knowing eternity makes one comprehensive; comprehension makes one broadminded; breadth of vision brings nobility; nobility is like heaven.
>
> The heavenly is like Tao. Tao is the Eternal. The decay of the body is not to be feared.[165]

The Japanese have a proverb: "The gods only laugh when men pray to them for wealth." The boon bestowed on the worshiper is always scaled to his stature and to the nature of his dominant desire: the boon is simply a symbol of life energy stepped down to the requirements of a certain specific case. The irony, of course, lies in the fact that, whereas the hero who has won the favor of the god may beg for the boon of perfect illumination, what he generally seeks are longer years to live, weapons with which to slay his neighbor, or the health of his child.

The Greeks tell of King Midas, who had the luck to win from Bacchus the offer of whatsoever boon he might desire. He asked that everything he touched should be turned to gold. When he went his way, he plucked, experimentally, the twig of an oak tree and it was immediately gold; he took up a stone, it had turned to gold; an apple was a golden nugget in his hand. Ecstatic, he ordered prepared a magnificent feast to celebrate the miracle. But when he sat down and set his fingers to the roast, it was transmuted; at his lips the wine became liquid gold. And when his little daughter, whom he loved beyond anything on earth, came to console him in his misery, she became, the moment he embraced her, a pretty golden statue.

The agony of breaking through personal limitations is the agony of spiritual growth. Art, literature, myth and cult, philosophy, and ascetic disciplines are instruments to help the individual past his limiting horizons into spheres of ever-expanding realization. As he crosses threshold after threshold, conquering dragon after dragon, the stature of the divinity that he summons to his highest wish increases, until it subsumes the cosmos. Finally, the mind breaks the bounding sphere of the cosmos to a realization transcending all experiences of form—all symbolizations, all divinities: a realization of the ineluctable void.

So it is that when Dante had taken the last step in his spiritual adventure, and came before the ultimate symbolic vision of the Triune God in the Celestial Rose, he had still one more illumination to experience, even beyond the forms of the Father, Son, and Holy Ghost. "Bernard," he writes, "made a sign to me, and smiled, that I should look upward; but I was already, of myself, such as he wished; for my sight, becoming pure, was entering more and more, through the radiance of the lofty Light which in Itself is true. Thenceforward my vision was greater than our speech, which yields to such a sight, and the memory yields to such excess."[166]

"There goes neither the eye, nor speech, nor the mind: we know It not; nor do we see how to teach one about It. Different It is from all that are known, and It is beyond the unknown as well."[167]

This is the highest and ultimate crucifixion, not only of the hero, but of his god as well. Here the Son and the Father alike are annihilated—as personality-masks over the unnamed. For just as the figments of a dream derive from the life energy of one dreamer, representing only fluid splitting and complications of that single force, so do all the forms of all the worlds, whether terrestrial or divine, reflect the universal force of a single inscrutable mystery: the power that constructs the atom and controls the orbits of the stars.

That font of life is the core of the individual, and within himself he will find it—if he can tear the coverings away. The pagan Germanic divinity Othin (Wotan) gave an eye to split the veil of light into the knowledge of this infinite dark, and then underwent for it the passion of a crucifixion:

I ween that I hung on the windy tree,
Hung there for nights full nine;
With the spear I was wounded, and offered I was
To Othin, myself to myself,
On the tree that none may ever know
What root beneath it runs.[168]

The Buddha's victory beneath the Bo Tree is the classic Oriental example of this deed. With the sword of his mind he pierced the bubble of the universe—and it shattered into nought. The whole world of natural experience, as well as the continents, heavens, and hells of traditional religious belief, exploded—together with their gods and demons. But the miracle of miracles was that though all exploded, all was nevertheless thereby renewed, revivified, and made glorious with the effulgence of true being. Indeed, the gods of the redeemed heavens raised their voices in harmonious acclaim of the man-hero who had penetrated beyond them to the void that was their life and source:

> Flags and banners erected on the eastern rim of the world let their streamers fly to the western rim of the world; likewise those erected on the western rim of the world, to the eastern rim of the world; those erected on the northern rim of the world, to the southern rim of the world; and those erected on the southern rim of the world, to the northern rim of the world; while those erected on the level of the earth let theirs fly until they beat against the Brahma-world; and those of the Brahma-world let theirs hang down to the level of the earth. Throughout the ten thousand worlds the flowering trees bloomed; the fruit trees were weighted down by the burden of their fruit; trunk-lotuses bloomed on the trunks of trees; branch-lotuses on the branches of trees; vine-lotuses on the vines; hanging-lotuses in the sky; and stalk-lotuses burst through the rocks and came up by sevens. The system of ten thousand worlds was like a bouquet of flowers sent whirling through the air, or like a thick carpet of flowers; in the intermundane spaces the eight-thousand-league-long hells, which not even the light of seven suns had formerly been able to illumine, were now flooded with radiance; the eighty-four-thousand-league-deep ocean became sweet to the taste; the rivers checked their flowing; the blind from birth received their sight; the deaf from birth their hearing; the crippled from birth the use of their limbs; and the bonds and fetters of captives broke and fell off.[169]

FIGURE 44. *The Return of the Prodigal* (oil on canvas, Holland, A.D. 1662)

CHAPTER III

Return

1. Refusal of the Return

When the hero-quest has been accomplished, through penetration to the source, or through the grace of some male or female, human or animal personification, the adventurer still must return with his life-transmuting trophy. The full round, the norm of the monomyth, requires that the hero shall now begin the labor of bringing the runes of wisdom, the Golden Fleece, or his sleeping princess back into the kingdom of humanity, where the boon may redound to the renewing of the community, the nation, the planet, or the ten thousand worlds.

But the responsibility has been frequently refused. Even the Buddha, after his triumph, doubted whether the message of realization could be communicated, and saints are reported to have passed away while in the supernal ecstasy. Numerous indeed are the heroes fabled to have taken up residence forever in the blessed isle of the unaging Goddess of Immortal Being.

A moving tale is told of an ancient Hindu warrior-king named Muchukunda. He was born from his father's left side, the father having swallowed by mistake a fertility potion that the Brahmins had prepared for his wife;* and in keeping with the promising symbolism of this miracle, the motherless marvel, fruit of the male womb, grew to be such a king among kings that when the gods, at one period, were suffering defeat in their perpetual contest with the demons, they

* This detail is a rationalization of rebirth from the hermaphroditic, initiating father.

called upon him for help. He assisted them to a mighty victory, and they, in their divine pleasure, granted him the realization of his highest wish. But what should such a king, himself almost omnipotent, desire? What greatest boon of boons could be conceived of by such a master among men? King Muchukunda, so runs the story, was very tired after his battle: all he asked was that he might be granted sleep without end, and that any person chancing to arouse him should be burned to a crisp by the first glance of his eye.

The boon was bestowed. In a cavern chamber, deep within the womb of the mountain, King Muchukunda retired to sleep, and there slumbered through the revolving eons. Individuals, peoples, civilizations, world ages, came into being out of the void and dropped back into it again, while the old king, in his state of subconscious bliss, endured. Timeless as the Freudian unconscious beneath the dramatic time world of our fluctuating ego-experience, the old mountain man, the drinker of deep sleep, lived on and on.

His awakening came—but with a surprising turn that throws into new perspective the whole problem of the hero-circuit, as well as the mystery of the mighty king's request for sleep as the highest conceivable boon,

Viṣṇu, the Lord of the World, had become incarnate in the person of a beautiful youth named Kṛṣṇa (Krishna), who having saved the land of India from a tyrannical race of demons, had assumed the throne. And he had been ruling in Utopian peace, when a horde of barbarians suddenly invaded from the northwest. Kṛṣṇa the king went against them, but in keeping with his divine nature, won the victory playfully, by simple ruse. Unarmed and garlanded with lotuses, he came out of his stronghold and tempted the enemy king to pursue and catch him, then dodged into a cave. When the barbarian followed, he discovered someone lying there in the chamber, asleep.

"Oh!" thought he. "So he has lured me here and now he feigns to be a harmless sleeper."

He kicked the figure lying on the ground before him, and it stirred. It was King Muchukunda. The figure rose and the eyes that had been closed for unnumbered cycles of creation, world history, and dissolution, opened slowly to the light. The first glance that went forth struck the enemy king, who burst into a torch of flame and was reduced immediately to a smoking heap of ash. Muchukunda turned and the second glance struck the garlanded, beautiful youth, whom the awakened old king straightway recognized by his radiance as an incarnation of God. And Muchukunda bowed before his savior with the following prayer.

> My Lord God! When I lived and wrought as a man, I lived and wrought—straying restlessly; through many lives, birth after birth, I sought and suffered, nowhere knowing cease or rest. Distress I took for joy. Mirages appearing over the desert I mistook for refreshing waters. Delights I grasped, and what I obtained was misery. Kingly power and earthly possession, riches and might, friends and sons, wife and followers, everything that lures the senses: I wanted them all, because I believed that these would bring me beatitude. But the moment anything was mine it changed its nature, and became as a burning fire.
>
> Then I found my way into the company of the gods, and they welcomed me as a companion. But where, still, surcease? Where rest? The creatures of this world, gods included, are all tricked, my Lord God, by your playful ruses; that is why they continue in their futile round of birth, life agony, old age, and death. Between lives, they confront the lord of the dead and are forced to endure hells of every degree of pitiless pain. And it all comes from you!
>
> My Lord God, deluded by your playful ruses, I too was a prey of the world, wandering in a labyrinth of error, netted in the meshes of ego-consciousness. Now, therefore, I take refuge in your Presence—the boundless, the adorable—desiring only freedom from it all.

When Muchukunda stepped from his cave, he saw that men, since his departure, had become reduced in stature. He was as a giant among them. And so he departed from them again, retreated to the highest mountains, and there dedicated himself to the ascetic practices that should finally release him from his last attachment to the forms of being.[1]

Muchukunda, in other words, instead of returning, decided to retreat one degree still further from the world. And who shall say that his decision was altogether without reason?

2. *The Magic Flight*

IF THE HERO in his triumph wins the blessing of the goddess or the god and is then explicitly commissioned to return to the world with some elixir for the restoration of society, the final stage of his adventure is supported by all the powers of his supernatural patron. On the other hand, if the trophy has been attained against the opposition of its guardian, or if the hero's wish to return to the world has been resented by the gods or demons, then the last stage of the mythological round becames a lively, often comical, pursuit. This flight may be complicated by marvels of magical obstruction and evasion.

FIGURE 45*a*. *Gorgon-Sister Pursuing Perseus, Who Is Fleeing with the Head of Medusa* (red-figure amphora, Greece, fifth century B.C.)

The Welsh tell, for instance, of a hero, Gwion Bach, who found himself in the Land Under Waves. Specifically, he was at the bottom of Lake Bala, in Merionethshire, in the north of Wales. And there lived at the bottom of this lake an ancient giant, Tegid the Bald, together with his wife, Caridwen. The latter, in one of her aspects, was a patroness of grain and fertile crops, and in another, a goddess of poetry and letters. She was the owner of an immense kettle and desired to prepare therein a brew of science and inspiration. With the aid of necromantic books she contrived a black concoction which she then set over a fire to brew for a year, at the end of which period three blessed drops should be obtained of the grace of inspiration.

And she put our hero, Gwion Bach, to stir the cauldron, and a blind man named Morda to keep the fire kindled beneath it, and she charged them that they should not suffer it to cease boiling for the space of a year and a day. And she herself, according to the books of the astronomers, and in planetary hours, gathered every day of all charm-bearing herbs. And one day, towards the end of the year,

FIGURE 45*b*. *Perseus Fleeing with the Head of Medusa in His Wallet* (red-figure amphora, Greece, fifth century B.C.)

as Caridwen was culling plants and making incantations, it chanced that three drops of the charmed liquor flew out of the cauldron and fell upon the finger of Gwion Bach. And by reason of their great heat he put his finger in his mouth, and the instant he put those marvel-working drops into his mouth he foresaw everything that was to come, and perceived that his chief care must be to guard against the wiles of Caridwen, for vast was her skill. And in very great fear he fled towards his own land. And the cauldron burst in two, because all the liquor within it except the three charm-bearing drops was poisonous, so that the horses of Gwyddno Garanhir were poisoned by the water of the stream into which the liquor of the cauldron ran, and the confluence of that stream was called the Poison of the Horses of Gwyddno from that time forth.

> Thereupon came in Caridwen and saw all the toil of the whole year lost. And she seized a billet of wood and struck the blind Morda on the head until one of his eyes fell out upon his cheek. And he said, "Wrongfully hast thou disfigured me, for I am innocent. Thy loss was not because of me." "Thou speakest truth," said Caridwen, "it was Gwion Bach who robbed me."
>
> And she went forth after him, running. And he saw her, and changed himself into a hare and fled. But she changed herself into a greyhound and turned him. And he ran towards a river, and became a fish. And she in the form of an otter-bitch chased him under the water, until he was fain to turn himself into a bird of the air. She, as a hawk, followed him and gave him no rest in the sky. And just as she was about to stoop upon him, and he was in fear of death, he espied a heap of winnowed wheat on the floor of a barn, and he dropped among the wheat, and turned himself into one of the grains. Then she transformed herself into a high-crested black hen, and went to the wheat and scratched it with her feet, and found him out and swallowed him. And, as the story says, she bore him nine months, and when she was delivered of him, she could not find it in her heart to kill him, by reason of his beauty. So she wrapped him in a leathern bag, and cast him into the sea to the mercy of God, on the twenty-ninth day of April.[2]

The tale of Gwion Bach comes to us through "Taliesin" in *The Mabinogion,* a collection of Welsh romances translated by Lady Charlotte Guest in four volumes between 1838 and 1849. Taliesin, "Chief of the Bards of the West," may have been an actual historical personage of the sixth century A.D., contemporary with the chieftain who became the "King Arthur" of later romance. The bard's legend and poems survive in a thirteenth-century manuscript, "The Book of Taliesin," which is one of the "Four Ancient Books of Wales."

FIGURE 46. *Caridwen in the Shape of a Greyhound Pursuing Gwion Bach in the Shape of a Hare* (lithograph, Britain, A.D. 1877)

A *mabinog* (Welsh) is a bard's apprentice. The term *mabinogi*, "juvenile instruction," denotes the traditional material (myths, legends, poems, etc.) taught to a *mabinog*, and which it was his duty to acquire by heart. *Mabinogion*, the plural of *mabinogi*, was the name given by Guest to her translation of eleven romances from the "Ancient Books."

The bardic lore of Wales, like that of Scotland and Ireland, descends from a very old and abundant pagan-Celtic fund of myth. This was transformed and revivified by the Christian missionaries and chroniclers (fifth century and following), who recorded the old stories and sought painstakingly to co-ordinate them with the Bible. During the tenth century, a brilliant period of romance production, centering primarily in Ireland, converted the inheritance into an important contemporary force. Celtic bards went out to the courts of Christian Europe; Celtic themes were rehearsed by the pagan Scandinavian scalds. A great part of our European fairy lore, as well as the foundation of the Arthurian tradition, traces back to this first great creative period of Occidental romance.[3]

The flight is a favorite episode of the folktale, where it is developed under many lively forms.

The Buriat of Irkutsk (Siberia), for example, declare that Morgon-Kara, their first shaman, was so competent that he could bring back souls from the dead. And so the Lord of the Dead complained to the High God of Heaven, and God decided to pose the shaman a test. He got possession of the soul of a certain man and slipped it into a bottle, covering the opening with the ball of his thumb. The man grew ill, and his relatives sent for Morgon-Kara. The shaman looked everywhere for the missing soul. He searched the forest, the waters, the mountain gorges, the land of the dead, and at last mounted, "sitting on his drum," to the world above, where again he was forced to search for a long time. Presently he observed that the High God of Heaven was keeping a bottle covered with the ball of his thumb, and, studying the circumstance, perceived that inside the bottle was the very soul he had come to find. The wily shaman changed himself into a wasp. He flew at God and gave him such a hot sting on the forehead that the thumb jerked from the opening and the captive got away. Then the next thing God knew, there was this shaman, Morgon-Kara, sitting on his drum again, and going down to earth with the recovered soul. The flight in this case, however, was not entirely successful. Becoming terribly angry, God immediately diminished the power of the shaman forever by splitting his drum in two. And so that is why shaman drums, which originally (according to this story of the Buriat) were fitted with two heads of skin, from that day to this have had only one.[4]

A popular variety of the magic flight is that in which objects are left behind to speak for the fugitive and thus delay pursuit. The New Zealand Maori tell of a fisherman who one day came home to find that his wife had swallowed their two sons. She was lying groaning on the floor. He asked her what the trouble was, and she declared that she was ill. He demanded to know where the two boys were, and she told him they had gone away. But he knew that she was lying. With his magic, he caused her to disgorge them: they came out alive and whole. Then that man was afraid of his wife, and he determined to escape from her as soon as he could, together with the boys.

When the ogress went to fetch water, the man, by his magic, caused the water to decrease and retreat ahead of her, so that she had to go a considerable way. Then by gestures he instructed the huts, the clumps of trees growing near the village, the filth dump, and the temple on top of the hill to answer for him when his wife should return and call. He made away with the boys to his canoe, and they hoisted sail. The woman came back, and, not finding anyone about, began to call. First the filth pit replied. She moved in that direction and called again. The houses answered; then the trees. One after another, the various objects in the neighborhood responded to her, and she ran, increasingly bewildered, in every direction. She became weak and began to pant and sob and then, at last, realized what had been done to her. She hastened to the temple on the hilltop and peered out to sea, where the canoe was a mere speck on the horizon.[5]

Another well-known variety of the magic flight is one in which a number of delaying obstacles are tossed behind by the wildly fleeing hero.

> A little brother and sister were playing by a spring, and as they did so suddenly tumbled in. There was a waterhag down there, and this waterhag said, "Now I have you! Now you shall work your heads off for me!" And she carried them away with her. She gave to the little girl a tangle of filthy flax to spin and made her fetch water in a bottomless tub; the boy had to chop a tree with a blunt ax; and all they ever had to eat were stone-hard lumps of dough. So at last the children became so impatient that they waited until one Sunday, when the hag had gone to church, and escaped. When church let out, the hag discovered that her birds had flown, and so made after them with mighty bounds.
>
> But the children espied her from afar, and the little girl threw back a hairbrush, which immediately turned into a big brush-mountain with thousands and thousands of bristles over which the hag found it very difficult to climb; nevertheless, she finally appeared. As soon as the children saw her, the boy threw back a comb, which immediately turned into a big comb-mountain with a thousand times a thousand spikes; but the hag knew how to catch hold of these, and at last she made her way through. Then the little girl threw back a mirror, and this turned into a mirror-mountain, which was so smooth that the hag was unable to get over. Thought she: "I shall hurry back home and get my ax and chop the mirror-mountain in two." But by the time she got back and demolished the glass, the children were long since far away, and the waterhag had to trudge back again to her spring.[6]

The powers of the abyss are not to be challenged lightly. In the Orient, a great point is made of the danger of undertaking the psychologically disturbing practices of yoga without competent supervision. The meditations of the postulant have to be adjusted to his progress, so that the imagination may be defended at every step by *devatas* (envisioned, adequate deities) until the moment comes for the prepared spirit to step alone beyond. As Dr. Jung has very wisely observed:

> The incomparably useful function of the dogmatic symbol [is that] it protects a person from a direct experience of God as long as he does not mischievously expose himself. But if... he leaves home and family, lives too long alone, and gazes too deeply into the dark mirror, then the awful event of the meeting may befall him. Yet even then the traditional symbol, come to full flower through the centuries, may operate like a healing draught and divert the fatal incursion of the living godhead into the hallowed spaces of the church.[7]

The magic objects tossed behind by the panic-ridden hero—protective interpretations, principles, symbols, rationalizations, anything—delay and absorb the power of the started Hound of Heaven, permitting the adventurer to come back into his fold safe and with perhaps a boon. But the toll required is not always slight.

One of the most shocking of the obstacle flights is that of the Greek hero Jason. He had set forth to win the Golden Fleece. Putting to sea in the magnificent *Argo* with a great company of warriors, he had sailed in the direction of the Black Sea, and, though delayed by many fabulous dangers, arrived, at last, miles beyond the Bosporus, at the city and palace of King Aeëtes. Behind the palace was the grove and tree of the dragon-guarded prize.

Now the daughter of the king, Medea, conceived an overpowering passion for the illustrious foreign visitor and, when her father imposed an impossible task as the price of the Golden Fleece, compounded charms that enabled him to succeed. The task was to plough a certain field, employing bulls of flaming breath and brazen feet, then to sow the field with dragon's teeth and slay the armed men who should immediately spring into being. But with his body and armor anointed with Medea's charm, Jason mastered the bulls; and when the army sprang from the dragon seed, he tossed a stone into their midst, which turned them face to face, and they slew each other to the man.

The infatuated young woman conducted Jason to the oak from which hung the Fleece. The guarding dragon was distinguished by a crest, a three-forked tongue, and nastily hooked fangs; but with the juice of a certain herb the couple put the formidable monster to sleep. Then Jason snatched the prize. Medea ran with him, and the *Argo* put to sea. But the king was soon in swift pursuit. And when Medea perceived that his sails were cutting down their lead, she persuaded Jason to kill Apsyrtos, her younger brother whom she had carried off, and toss the pieces of the dismembered body into the sea. This forced King Aeëtes, her father, to put about, rescue the fragments, and go ashore to give them decent burial. Meanwhile the *Argo* ran with the wind and passed from his ken.[8]

In the Japanese "Records of Ancient Matters" appears another harrowing tale, but of very different import: that of the descent to the underworld of the primeval all-father Izanagi, to recover from the land of the Yellow Stream his deceased sister-spouse Izanami. She met him at the door to the lower world, and he said to her: "Thine Augustness, my lovely younger sister! The lands that I and thou made are not yet finished making; so come back!" She replied: "Lamentable indeed that thou camest not sooner! I have eaten of the food of the Land of the Yellow Stream. Nevertheless, as I am overpowered by the honor of the entry here of Thine Augustness, my lovely elder brother, I wish to return. Moreover, I will discuss the matter particularly with the deities of the Yellow Stream. Be careful, do not look at me!"

She retired into the palace; but as she tarried there very long, he could not wait. He broke off one of the end-teeth of the comb that was stuck in the august left bunch of his hair, and, lighting it as a little torch, he went in and looked. What he saw were maggots swarming, and Izanami rotting.

Aghast at the sight, Izanagi fled back. Izanami said: "Thou hast put me to shame."

Izanami sent the Ugly Female of the nether world in pursuit. Izanagi in full flight took the black headdress from his head and cast it down. Instantly it turned into grapes, and, while his pursuer paused to eat them, he continued on his rapid way. But she resumed the pursuit and gained on him. He took and broke the multitudinous and close-toothed comb in the right bunch of his hair and cast it down. Instantly it turned into bamboo sprouts, and, while she pulled them up and ate them, he fled.

Then his younger sister sent in pursuit of him the eight thunder deities with a thousand and five hundred warriors of the Yellow Stream. Drawing the ten-grasp saber that was augustly girded on him, he fled, brandishing this behind him. But the warriors still pursued. Reaching the frontier pass between the world of the living and the land of the Yellow Stream, he took three peaches that were growing there, waited, and when the army came against him, hurled them. The peaches from the world of the living smote the warriors of the land of the Yellow Stream, who turned and fled.

Her Augustness Izanami, last of all, came out herself. So he drew up a rock which it would take a thousand men to lift, and with it blocked up the pass. And with the rock between them, they stood opposite to one another and exchanged leave-takings. Izanami said: "My lovely elder brother, Thine Augustness! If thou dost behave like this, henceforth I shall cause to die every day one thousand of thy people in thy realm." Izanagi answered: "My lovely younger sister, Thine Augustness! If thou dost so, then I will cause every day one thousand and five hundred women to give birth."[9]

Having moved a step beyond the creative sphere of all-father Izanagi into the field of dissolution, Izanami had sought to protect her brother-husband. When he had seen more than he could bear, he lost his innocence of death but, with his august will to live, drew up as a mighty rock that protecting veil which we all have held, ever since, between our eyes and the grave.

The Greek myth of Orpheus and Eurydice, and hundreds of analogous tales throughout the world, suggest, as does this ancient legend of the farthest East, that in spite of the failure recorded, a possibility exists of a return of the lover with his lost love from beyond the terrible threshold. It is always some little fault, some slight yet critical symptom of human frailty, that makes impossible the open interrelationship between the worlds; so that one is tempted to believe, almost, that if the small, marring accident could be avoided, all would be well. In the Polynesian versions of the romance, however, where the fleeing couple usually escape, and in the Greek satyr-play of Alcestis, where we also have a happy return, the effect is not reassuring, but only superhuman. The myths of failure touch us with the tragedy of life, but those of success only with their own incredibility. And yet, if the monomyth is to fulfill its promise, not human failure or superhuman success but human success is what we shall have to be shown. That is the problem of the crisis of the threshold of the return. We shall first consider it in the superhuman symbols and then seek the practical teaching for historic man.

3. *Rescue from Without*

THE HERO may have to be brought back from his supernatural adventure by assistance from without. That is to say, the world may have to come and get him. For the bliss of the deep abode is not lightly abandoned in favor of the self-scattering of the wakened state. "Who having cast off the world," we read, "would desire to return again? He would be only *there*."[10] And yet, in so far as one is alive, life will call. Society is jealous of those who remain away from it, and will come knocking at the door. If the hero—like Muchukunda—is

FIGURE 47. *The Resurrection of Osiris* (carved stone, Ptolemaic, Egypt, c. 282–145 B.C.)

unwilling, the disturber suffers an ugly shock; but on the other hand, if the summoned one is only delayed—sealed in by the beatitude of the state of perfect being (which resembles death)—an apparent rescue is effected, and the adventurer returns.

When Raven of the Eskimo tale had darted with his fire sticks into the belly of the whale-cow, he discovered himself at the entrance of a handsome room, at the farther end of which burned a lamp. He was surprised to see sitting there a beautiful girl. The room was dry and clean, the whale's spine supporting the ceiling and the ribs forming the walls. From a tube that ran along the backbone, oil dripped slowly into the lamp.

When Raven entered the room, the woman looked up and cried: "How did you get here? You are the first man to enter this place." Raven told what he had done, and she bade him take a seat on the opposite side of the room. This woman was the soul (*inua*) of the whale. She spread a meal before the visitor, gave him berries and oil, and told him, meanwhile, how she had gathered the berries the year before. Raven remained four days as guest of the *inua* in the belly of the whale, and during the entire period was trying to ascertain what kind of tube that could be, running along the ceiling. Every time the woman left the room, she forbade him to touch it. But now, when she again went out, he walked over to the lamp, stretched out his claw, and caught on it a big drop, which he licked off with his tongue. It was so sweet that he repeated the act, and then proceeded to catch drop after drop, as fast as they fell. Presently, however, his greed found this too slow, and so he reached up, broke off a piece of the tube, and ate it. Hardly had he done so, when a great gush of oil poured into the room, extinguished the light, and the chamber itself began to roll heavily back and forth. This rolling went on for four days. Raven was almost dead with fatigue and with the terrible noise that stormed around him all the while. But then everything quieted down and the room lay still; for Raven had broken one of the heart-arteries, and the whale-cow had died. The *inua* never returned. The body of the whale was washed ashore.

But now Raven was a prisoner. While he pondered what he should do, he heard two men talking, up on the back of the animal, and they decided to summon all the people from the village to help with the whale. Very soon they had cut a hole in the upper part of the great body.* When it was large enough, and all the people had gone off with pieces of meat to carry them high up on the shore, Raven stepped out unnoticed. But no sooner had he reached the ground than he remembered he had left his fire sticks within. He took off his coat and mask, and pretty soon the people saw a small, black man, wrapped up in a queer animal skin approaching them. They looked at him curiously. The man offered to help, rolled up his sleeves, and set to work.

In a little while, one of the people working in the interior of the whale shouted, "Look what I have found! Fire sticks in the belly of the whale!" Raven said, "My, but this is bad! My daughter once told me that when fire sticks are found inside a whale that people have cut open, many of these people will die! I'm for running!" He rolled down his sleeves again and made away. The people hurried to follow his example. And so that was how Raven, who then doubled back, had, for a time, the whole feast to himself.[11]

One of the most important and delightful of the myths of the Shintō tradition of Japan—already old when chronicled in the eighth

* In many myths of the hero in the whale's belly he is rescued by birds that peck open the side of his prison.

century A.D. in the "Records of Ancient Matters"—is that of the drawing forth of the beautiful sun-goddess Amaterasu from a heavenly rock-dwelling during the critical first period of the world.

Shintō, "The Way of the Gods," the tradition native to the Japanese as distinguished from the imported Butsudō, or "Way of the Buddha," is a way of devotion to the guardians of life and custom (local spirits, ancestral powers, heroes, the divine king, one's living parents, and one's living children) as distinguished from the powers that yield release from the round (Bodhisattvas and Buddhas). The way of worship is primarily that of preserving and cultivating purity of heart: "What is ablution? It is not merely cleansing the body with holy water, but following the Right and Moral Way."[12] "What pleases the Deity is virtue and sincerity, not any number of material offerings."[13]

Amaterasu, ancestress of the Royal House, is the chief divinity of the numerous folk pantheon, yet herself only the highest manifestation of the unseen, transcendent yet immanent, Universal God: "The Eight Hundred Myriads of Gods are but differing manifestations of one unique Deity, Kunitokotachi-no-Kami, The Eternally Standing Divine Being of the Earth, The Great Unity of All Things in the Universe, The Primordial Being of Heaven and Earth, eternally existing from the beginning to the end of the world."[14] "What deity does Amaterasu worship in abstinence in the Plain of High Heaven? She worships her own Self within as a Deity, endeavoring to cultivate divine virtue in her own person by means of inner purity and thus becoming one with the Deity."[15]

Since the Deity is immanent in all things, all things are to be regarded as divine, from the pots and pans of the kitchen to the Emperor: this is Shintō, "The Way of the Gods." The Emperor being in the highest position receives the greatest reverence, but not reverence different in kind from that bestowed upon all things. "The awe-inspiring Deity manifests Itself, even in the single leaf of a tree or a delicate blade of grass."[16] The function of reverence in Shintō is to honor that Deity in all things; the function of purity to sustain Its manifestation in oneself—following the august model of the divine self-worship of the goddess Amaterasu. "With the unseen God who seeth all secret things in the silence, the heart of the man sincere communes from the earth below" (from a poem by the Emperor Meiji).[17]

This is an example in which the rescued one is somewhat reluctant. The storm-god Susanowo, the brother of Amaterasu, had been misbehaving inexcusably. And though she had tried every means to appease him and had stretched forgiveness far beyond the limit, he continued to destroy her rice fields and to pollute her institutions. As a final insult, he broke a hole in the top of her weaving-hall and let fall through it a "heavenly piebald horse which he had flayed with a backward flaying," at sight of which all the ladies of the goddess, who were busily weaving the august garments of the deities, were so much alarmed that they died of fear.

Amaterasu, terrified at the sight, retired into a heavenly cave, closed the door behind her, and made it fast. This was a terrible thing for her to do; for the permanent disappearance of the sun would have meant as much as the end of the universe—the end, before it had even properly begun. With her disappearance the whole plain of high heaven and all the central land of reed plains became dark. Evil spirits ran riot through the world; numerous portents of woe arose; and the voices of the myriad of deities were like unto the flies in the fifth moon as they swarmed.

Therefore the eight millions of gods assembled in a divine assembly in the bed of the tranquil river of heaven and bid one of their number, the deity named Thought-Includer, to devise a plan. As the result of their consultation, many things of divine efficacy were produced, among them a mirror, a sword, and cloth offerings. A great tree was set up and decorated with jewels; cocks were brought that they might keep up a perpetual crowing; bonfires were lit; grand liturgies were recited. The mirror, eight feet long, was tied to the middle branches of the tree. And a merry, noisy dance was performed by a young goddess called Uzume. The eight millions of divinities were so amused that their laughter filled the air, and the plain of high heaven shook.

FIGURE 48. *Amaterasu Emerges from the Cave* (woodblock print, Japan, A.D. 1860)

The sun-goddess in the cave heard the lively uproar and was amazed. She was curious to know what was going on. Slightly opening the door of the heavenly rock-dwelling, she spoke thus from within: "I thought that owing to my retirement the plain of heaven would be dark, and likewise the central land of reed plains would all be dark: how then is it that Uzume makes merry, and that likewise the eight millions of gods all laugh?" Then Uzume spoke, saying: "We rejoice and are glad because there is a deity more illustrious than Thine Augustness." While she was thus speaking, two of the divinities pushed forward the mirror and respectfully showed it to the sun-goddess, Amaterasu; whereupon she, more and more astonished, gradually came forth from the door and gazed upon it. A powerful god took her august hand and drew her out; whereupon another stretched a rope of straw (called the *shimenawa*) behind her, across the entrance, saying: "Thou must not go back further in than this!" Thereupon both the plain of high heaven and the central land of reed plains again were light.[18] The sun may now retreat, for a time, every night—as does life itself, in refreshing sleep; but by the august *shimenawa* she is prevented from disappearing permanently.

The motif of the sun as a goddess, instead of as a god, is a rare and precious survival from an archaic, apparently once widely diffused, mythological context. The great maternal divinity of South Arabia is the feminine sun, Ilat. The word in German for the sun (*die Sonne*) is feminine. Throughout Siberia, as well as in North America, scattered stories survive of a female sun. And in the fairy tale of Red Ridinghood, who was eaten by the wolf but rescued from its belly by the hunter, we may have a remote echo of the same adventure as that of Amaterasu. Traces remain in many lands; but only in Japan do we find the once great mythology still effective in civilization; for the Emperor is a direct descendant of the grandson of Amaterasu, and as ancestress of the royal house she is honored as one of the supreme divinities of the national tradition of Shintō. In her adventures may be sensed a different world-feeling from that of the now better-known mythologies of the solar *god*: a certain tenderness toward the lovely gift of light, a gentle gratitude for things made visible—such as must once have distinguished the religious mood of many peoples.

The mirror, the sword, and the tree, we recognize. The mirror, reflecting the goddess and drawing her forth from the august repose of her divine nonmanifestation, is symbolic of the world, the field of the reflected image. Therein divinity is pleased to regard its own glory, and this pleasure is itself inducement to the act of manifestation or "creation." The sword is the counterpart of the thunderbolt. The tree is the World Axis in its wish-fulfilling, fruitful aspect—the same as that displayed in Christian homes at the season of the winter solstice, which is the moment of the rebirth or return of the sun, a joyous custom inherited from the Germanic paganism that has given to the modern German language its feminine *Sonne*. The dance of Uzume and the uproar of the gods belong to carnival: the world left topsy-turvy by the withdrawal of the supreme divinity, but joyous for the coming renewal.

And the *shimenawa,* the august rope of straw that was stretched behind the goddess when she reappeared, symbolizes the graciousness of the miracle of the light's return. This *shimenawa* is one of the most conspicuous, important, and silently eloquent, of the traditional symbols of the folk religion of Japan. Hung above the entrances of the temples, festooned along the streets at the New Year festival, it denotes the renovation of the world at the threshold of the return. If the Christian cross is the most telling symbol of the mythological passage into the abyss of death, the *shimenawa* is the simplest sign of the resurrection. The two represent the mystery of the boundary between the worlds—the existent nonexistent line.

Amaterasu is an Oriental sister of the great Inanna, the supreme goddess of the ancient Sumerian cuneiform temple-tablets, whose descent we have already followed into the lower world. Inanna, Ishtar, Astarte, Aphrodite, Venus: those were the names she bore in the successive culture periods of the Occidental development—associated, not with the sun, but with the planet that carries her name, and at the same time with the moon, the heavens, and the fruitful earth. In Egypt she became the goddess of the Dog Star, Sirius, whose annual reappearance in the sky announced the earth-fructifying flood season of the river Nile.

Inanna, it will be remembered, descended from the heavens into the hell region of her sister-opposite, the Queen of Death, Ereshkigal. And she left behind Ninshubur, her messenger, with instructions to rescue her should she not return. She arrived naked before the seven judges; they fastened their eyes upon her, she was turned into a corpse, and the corpse—as we have seen—was hung upon a stake.

*After three days and three nights had passed,**
Inanna's messenger Ninshubur,
Her messenger of favorable words,
Her carrier of supporting words,
Filled the heaven with complaints for her,
Cried for her in the assembly shrine,
Rushed about for her in the house of the gods. . . .
Like a pauper in a single garment he dressed for her,
To the Ekur, the house of Enlil, all alone he directed his step.

This is the beginning of the rescue of the goddess, and illustrates the case of one who so knew the power of the zone into which she

* Compare the Christian Credo: "He descended into Hell, the third day He rose again from the dead. . . ."

FIGURE 49. *Goddess Rising* (carved marble, Italy/Greece, c. 460 B.C.)

was entering that she took the precaution to have herself aroused. Ninshubur went first to the god Enlil; but the god said that, Inanna having gone from the great above to the great below, in the nether world the decrees of the nether world should prevail. Ninshubur next went to the god Nanna; but the god said that she had gone from the great above to the great below, and that in the nether world the decrees of the nether world should prevail. Ninshubur went to the god Enki; and the god Enki devised a plan. He fashioned two sexless creatures and entrusted to them the "food of life" and the "water of life" with instructions to proceed to the nether world and sprinkle this food and water sixty times on Inanna's suspended corpse.

Enlil was the Sumerian air-god, Nanna the moon-god, Enki the water-god and god of wisdom. At the time of the composition of our document (third millennium B.C.) Enlil was the chief divinity of the Sumerian pantheon. He was quick to anger. He was the sender of the Flood. Nanna was one of his sons. In the myths the benign god Enki appears typically in the role of the helper. He is the patron and adviser both of Gilgamesh and of the flood hero, Atarhasis-Utnapishtim-Noah. The motif of Enki *vs.* Enlil is carried on by Classical mythology, in the counterplay of Poseidon *vs.* Zeus (Neptune *vs.* Jove).

Upon the corpse hung from a stake they directed the fear
of the rays of fire,
Sixty times the food of life, sixty times the water of life,
they sprinkled upon it,
Inanna arose.

Inanna ascends from the nether world,
The Anunnaki fled,
And whoever of the nether world may have descended
peacefully to the nether world;
When Inanna ascends from the nether world,
Verily the dead hasten ahead of her.

Inanna ascends from the nether world,
The small demons like reeds,
The large demons like tablet styluses,
Walked at her side.
Who walked in front of her, held a staff in hand,
Who walked at her side, carried a weapon on the loin.
They who preceded her,
They who preceded Inanna,
Were beings who know not food, who know not water,
Who eat not sprinkled flour,
Who drink not libated wine,
Who take away the wife from the loins of man,
Who take away the child from the breast of the nursing mother.

Surrounded by this ghostly, ghastly crowd, Inanna wandered through the land of Sumer, from city to city.[19]

These three examples from widely separated culture areas—Raven, Amaterasu, and Inanna—sufficiently illustrate the rescue from without. They show in the final stages of the adventure the continued operation of the supernatural assisting force that has been attending the elect through the whole course of his ordeal. His conciousness having succumbed, the unconscious nevertheless supplies its own balances, and he is born back into the world from which he came. Instead of holding to and saving his ego, as in the pattern of the magic flight, he loses it, and yet, through grace is returned.

This brings us to the final crisis of the round, to which the whole miraculous excursion has been but a prelude—that, namely, of the paradoxical, supremely difficult threshold-crossing of the hero's return from the mystic realm into the land of common day. Whether rescued from without, driven from within, or gently carried along by the guiding divinities, he has yet to re-enter with his boon the long-forgotten atmosphere where men who are fractions imagine themselves to be complete. He has yet to confront society with his ego-shattering, life-redeeming elixir, and take the return blow of reasonable queries, hard resentment, and good people at a loss to comprehend.

FIGURE 50. *The Reappearance of the Hero: Samson with the Temple-Doors • Christ Arisen • Jonah* (engraving, German, A.D. 1471)

4. *The Crossing of the Return Threshold*

THE TWO WORLDS, the divine and the human, can be pictured only as distinct from each other—different as life and death, as day and night. The hero adventures out of the land we know into darkness; there accomplishes his adventure, or again is simply lost to us, imprisoned, or in danger; and his return is described as a coming back out of that yonder zone. Nevertheless—and here is a great key to the understanding of myth and symbol—the two kingdoms are actually one. The realm of the gods is a forgotten dimension of the world we know. And the exploration of that dimension, either willingly or unwillingly, is the whole sense of the deed of the hero. The values and distinctions that in normal life seem important disappear with the terrifying assimilation of the self into what formerly was only otherness. As in the stories of the cannibal ogresses, the fearfulness of this loss of personal individuation can be the whole burden of the transcendental experience for unqualified souls. But the hero-soul goes boldly in—and discovers the hags converted into goddesses and the dragons into the watchdogs of the gods.

There must always remain, however, from the standpoint of normal waking consciousness, a certain baffling inconsistency between the wisdom brought forth from the deep, and the prudence usually found to be effective in the light world. Hence the common divorce of opportunism from virtue and the resultant degeneration of human existence. Martyrdom is for saints, but the common people have their institutions, and these cannot be left to grow like lilies of the field; Peter keeps drawing his sword, as in the garden, to defend the creator and sustainer of the world.[20] The boon brought from the transcendent deep becomes quickly rationalized into nonentity, and the need becomes great for another hero to refresh the word.

How teach again, however, what has been taught correctly and incorrectly learned a thousand times, throughout the millennia of mankind's prudent folly? That is the hero's ultimate difficult task. How render back into light-world language the speech-defying pronouncements of the dark? How represent on a two-dimensional surface a three-dimensional form, or in a three-dimensional image a multi-dimensional meaning? How translate into terms of "yes" and "no" revelations that shatter into meaninglessness every attempt to define the pairs of opposites? How communicate to people who insist on the exclusive evidence of their senses the message of the all-generating void?

Many failures attest to the difficulties of this life-affirmative threshold. The first problem of the returning hero is to accept as real, after an experience of the soul-satisfying vision of fulfillment, the passing joys and sorrows, banalities and noisy obscenities of life. Why re-enter such a world? Why attempt to make plausible, or even interesting, to men and women consumed with passion, the experience of transcendental bliss? As dreams that were momentous by night may seem simply silly in the light of day, so the poet and the prophet can discover themselves playing the idiot before a jury of sober eyes. The easy thing is to commit the whole community to the devil and retire again into the heavenly rock-dwelling, close the door, and make it fast. But if some spiritual obstetrician has meanwhile drawn the *shimenawa* across the retreat, then the work of representing eternity in time, and perceiving in time eternity, cannot be avoided.

The story of Rip van Winkle is an example of the delicate case of the returning hero. Rip moved into the adventurous realm unconsciously, as we all do every night when we go to sleep. In deep sleep, declare the Hindus, the self is unified and blissful; therefore deep sleep is called the cognitional state.[21] But though we are refreshed and sustained by these nightly visits to the source-darkness, our lives are not reformed by them; we return, like Rip, with nothing to show for the experience but our whiskers.

> He looked round for his gun, but in place of the clean, well-oiled fowling-piece, he found an old firelock lying by him, the barrel incrusted with rust, the lock falling off, and the stock worm-eaten ....As he rose to walk, he found himself stiff in the joints, and wanting his usual activity....As he approached the village, he met a number of people, but none whom he knew; which somewhat surprised him, for he had thought himself acquainted with every one in the country round. Their dress, too, was of a different fashion from that to which he was accustomed. They all stared at him with equal marks of surprise, and, whenever they cast their eyes

> upon him, invariably stroked their chins. The constant recurrence of this gesture induced Rip involuntarily to do the same, when, to his astonishment, he found his beard had grown a foot long.... He began to doubt whether both he and the world around him were not bewitched....
>
> The appearance of Rip, with his long, grizzled beard, his rusty fowling-piece, his uncouth dress, and the army of women and children that had gathered at his heels, soon attracted the attention of the tavern politicians. They crowded round him, eyeing him from head to foot with great curiosity. The orator bustled up to him, and, drawing him partly aside, inquired on which side he voted. Rip stared in vacant stupidity. Another short but busy little fellow pulled him by the arm, and, rising on tiptoe, inquired in his ear whether he was a Federal or a Democrat. Rip was equally at a loss to comprehend the question, when a knowing, self-important old gentleman in a sharp cocked hat made his way through the crowd, putting them to the right and left with his elbows as he passed, and, planting himself before van Winkle—with one arm akimbo, the other resting on his cane; his keen eyes and sharp hat penetrating, as it were, into his very soul—demanded in an austere tone what brought him to the election with a gun on his shoulder and a mob at his heels, and whether he meant to breed a riot in the village. "Alas! gentlemen," cried Rip, somewhat dismayed, "I am a poor, quiet man, a native of the place, and a loyal subject to the King, God bless him!"
>
> Here a general shout burst from the bystanders: "A Tory, a Tory! A spy! A refugee! Hustle him! Away with him!" It was with great difficulty that the self-important man in the cocked hat restored order.[22]

More dispiriting than the fate of Rip is the account of what happened to the Irish hero Oisin when he returned from a long sojourn with the daughter of the King of the Land of Youth. Oisin had done better than poor Rip; he had kept his eyes open in the adventurous realm. He had descended consciously (awake) into the kingdom of the unconscious (deep sleep) and had incorporated the values of the subliminal experience into his waking personality. A transmutation had been effected. But precisely because of this highly desirable circumstance, the dangers of his return were the greater. Since his entire personality had been brought into accord with the powers and forms of timelessness, all of him stood to be refuted, blasted, by the impact of the forms and powers of time.

Oisin, the son of Finn MacCool, one day was out hunting with his men in the woods of Erin, when he was approached by the daughter of the King of the Land of Youth. Oisin's men had gone ahead with the day's kill, leaving their master with his three dogs to shift for himself. And the mysterious being had appeared to him with the beautiful body of a woman, but the head of a pig. She declared that the head was due to a Druidic spell, promising that it would vanish the very minute he would marry her. "Well, if that is the state you are in," said he, "and if marriage with me will free you from the spell, I'll not leave the pig's head on you long."

Without delay the pig's head was dispatched and they set out together for Tir na n-Og, the Land of Youth. Oisin dwelt there as a king many happy years. But one day he turned and declared to his supernatural bride:

> "I wish I could be in Erin to-day to see my father and his men."
>
> "If you go," said his wife, "and set foot on the land of Erin, you'll never come back here to me, and you'll become a blind old man. How long do you think it is since you came here?"
>
> "About three years," said Oisin.
>
> "It is three hundred years," said she, "since you came to this kingdom with me. If you must go to Erin, I'll give you this white steed to carry you; but if you come down from the steed or touch the soil of Erin with your foot, the steed will come back that minute, and you'll be where he left you, a poor old man."
>
> "I'll come back, never fear," said Oisin. "Have I not good reason to come back? But I must see my father and my son and my friends in Erin once more; I must have even one look at them."
>
> She prepared the steed for Oisin and said, "This steed will carry you wherever you wish to go."
>
> Oisin never stopped till the steed touched the soil of Erin; and he went on till he came to Knock Patrick in Munster, where he saw a man herding cows. In the field where the cows were grazing there was a broad flat stone.
>
> "Will you come here," said Oisin to the herdsman, "and turn over this stone?"
>
> "Indeed, then, I will not," said the herdsman; "for I could not lift it, nor twenty men more like me."
>
> Oisin rode up to the stone, and, reaching down, caught it with his hand and turned it over. Underneath the stone was the great horn of the Fenians (borabu), which circled round like a sea-shell, and it was the rule that when any of the Fenians of Erin blew the borabu, the others would assemble at once from whatever part of the country they might be in at the time.

The Fenians were the men of Finn MacCool, giants all. Oisin, who was the son of Finn MacCool, had been one of their number. But their day now had long passed, and the inhabitants of the land were no longer the great ones of old. Such legends of archaic giants are common to folk traditions everywhere; see, for instance, the myth recounted above (pp. 167–169) of King Muchukunda. Comparable are the protracted lives of the Hebrew patriarchs: Adam lived nine hundred and thirty years, Seth nine hundred and twelve, Enos nine hundred and five, etc., etc.[23]

"Will you bring this horn to me?" asked Oisin of the herdsman.

"I will not," said the herdsman; "for neither I nor many more like me could raise it from the ground."

With that Oisin moved near the horn, and reaching down took it in his hand; but so eager was he to blow it, that he forgot everything, and slipped in reaching till one foot touched the earth. In an instant the steed was gone, and Oisin lay on the ground a blind old man.[24]

The equating of a single year in Paradise to one hundred of earthly existence is a motif well known to myth. The full round of one hundred signifies totality. Similarly, the three hundred and sixty degrees of the circle signify totality; accordingly the Hindu Purāṇas represent one year of the gods as equal to three hundred and sixty of men. From the standpoint of the Olympians, eon after eon of earthly history rolls by, revealing ever the harmonious form of the total round, so that where men see only change and death, the blessed behold immutable form, world without end. But now the problem is to maintain this cosmic standpoint in the face of an immediate earthly pain or joy. The taste of the fruits of temporal knowledge draws the concentration of the spirit away from the center of the eon to the peripheral crisis of the moment. The balance of perfection is lost, the spirit falters, and the hero falls.

The idea of the insulating horse, to keep the hero out of immediate touch with the earth and yet permit him to promenade among the peoples of the world, is a vivid example of a basic precaution taken generally by the carriers of supernormal power. Montezuma, emperor of Mexico, never set foot on the ground; he was always carried on the shoulders of noblemen, and if he lighted anywhere they laid a rich tapestry for him to walk upon. Within his palace, the king of Persia walked on carpets on which no one else might tread; outside of it he was never seen on foot but only in a chariot or on horseback. Formerly neither the kings of Uganda, nor their mothers, nor their queens might walk on foot outside of the spacious enclosures in which they lived.

Whenever they went forth they were carried on the shoulders of men of the Buffalo clan, several of whom accompanied any of these royal personages on a journey and took it in turn to bear the burden. The king sat astride the bearer's neck with a leg over each shoulder and his feet tucked under the bearer's arms. When one of these royal carriers grew tired, he shot the king onto the shoulders of a second man without allowing the royal feet to touch the ground.[25]

Sir James George Frazer explains in the following graphic way the fact that over the whole earth the divine personage may not touch the ground with his foot.

> Apparently holiness, magical virtue, taboo, or whatever we may call that mysterious quality which is supposed to pervade sacred or tabooed persons, is conceived by the primitive philosopher as a physical substance or fluid, with which the sacred man is charged just as a Leyden jar is charged with electricity; and exactly as the electricity in the jar can be discharged by contact with a good conductor, so the holiness or magical virtue in the man can be discharged and drained away by contact with the earth, which on this theory serves as an excellent conductor for the magical fluid. Hence in order to preserve the charge from running to waste, the sacred or tabooed personage must be carefully prevented from touching the ground; in electrical language he must be insulated, if he is not to be emptied of the precious substance or fluid with which he, as a vial, is filled to the brim. And in many cases apparently the insulation of the tabooed person is recommended as a precaution not merely for his own sake but for the sake of others; for since the virtue of holiness is, so to say, a powerful explosive which the smallest touch may detonate, it is necessary in the interest of the general safety to keep it within narrow bounds, lest breaking out it should blast, blight, and destroy whatever it comes into contact with.[26]

There is, no doubt, a psychological justification for the precaution. The Englishman dressing for dinner in the jungles of Nigeria feels that there is reason in his act. The young artist wearing his whiskers into the lobby of the Ritz will be glad to explain his idiosyncrasy. The Roman collar sets apart the man of the pulpit. A twentieth-century nun floats by in a costume from the Middle Ages. The wife is insulated, more or less, by her ring.

The tales of W. Somerset Maugham describe the metamorphoses that overcome the bearers of the white man's burden who neglect the taboo of the dinner jacket. Many folk songs give testimony to the dangers of the broken ring. And the myths—for example, the myths assembled by Ovid in his great compendium, the *Metamorphoses*—recount again and again the shocking transformations that take place when the insulation between a highly concentrated power center and the lower power field of the surrounding world is, without proper precautions, suddenly taken away. According to the fairy lore of the Celts and Germans, a gnome or elf caught abroad by the sunrise is turned immediately into a stick or a stone.

The returning hero, to complete his adventure, must survive the impact of the world. Rip van Winkle never knew what he had experienced; his return was a joke. Oisin knew, but he lost his centering in it and so collapsed. Kamar al-Zaman had the best luck of all. He experienced awake the bliss of deep sleep, and returned to the light of day with such a convincing talisman of his unbelievable adventure that he was able to retain his self-assurance in the face of every sobering disillusionment.

While he was sleeping in his tower, the two Jinn, Dahnash and Maymunah, transported from distant China the daughter of the Lord of the Islands and the Seas and the Seven Palaces. Her name was the Princess Budur. And they placed this young woman asleep beside the Persian prince, in the very bed. The Jinn uncovered the two faces, and perceived that the couple were as like as twins. "By Allah," declared Dahnash, "O my lady, my beloved is the fairer." But Maymunah, the female spirit, who loved Kamar al-Zaman, retorted: "Not so, the fairer one is mine." Whereupon they wrangled, challenging and counterchallenging, until Dahnash at last suggested they should seek an impartial judge.

Maymunah smote the ground with her foot, and there came out of it an Ifrit blind in one eye, humpbacked, scurvy-skinned, with eye-orbits slit up and down his face; and on his head were seven horns; four locks of hair fell to his heels; his hands were like pitchforks and his legs like masts; and he had nails like the claws of a lion, feet like the hoofs of the wild ass. The monster respectfully kissed the ground before Maymunah and inquired what she would have him do. Instructed that he was to judge between the two young persons lying on the bed, each with an arm under the other's neck, he gazed long upon them, marveling at their loveliness, then turned to Maymunah and Dahnash, and declared his verdict.

"By Allah, if you will have the truth," he said, "the two are of equal beauty. Nor can I make any choice between them, on account of their being a man and a woman. But I have another thought, which is that we wake each of them in turn, without the knowledge of the other, and whichever is the more enamored shall be judged inferior in comeliness."

It was agreed. Dahnash changed himself to the form of a flea and bit Kamar al-Zaman on the neck. Starting from sleep, the youth rubbed the bitten part, scratching it hard because of the smart, and meanwhile turned a little to the side. He found lying beside him something whose breath was sweeter than musk and whose skin softer than cream. He marveled. He sat up. He looked better at what was beside him and discerned that it was a young woman like a pearl or shining sun, like a dome seen from afar on a well-built wall.

Kamar al-Zaman attempted to wake her, but Dahnash had deepened her slumber. The youth shook her. "O my beloved, awake and look at me," he said. But she never stirred. Kamar al-Zaman imagined Budur to be the woman whom his father wished him to marry, and he was filled with eagerness. But he feared that his sire might be hiding somewhere in the room, watching, so he restrained himself, and contented himself with taking the seal-ring from her little finger and slipping it on his own. The Ifrits then returned him to his sleep.

In contrast with the performance of Kamar al-Zaman was that of Budur. She had no thought or fear of anyone watching. Furthermore, Maymunah, who had awakened her, with female malice had gone high up her leg and bitten hard in a place that burned. The beautiful, noble, glorious Budur, discovering her male affinity beside her, and perceiving that he had already taken her ring, unable either to rouse him or to imagine what he had done to her, and ravaged with love, assailed by the open presence of his flesh, lost all control, and attained to a climax of helpless passion.

> Lust was sore upon her, for that the desire of women is fiercer than the desire of men, and she was ashamed of her own shamelessness. Then she plucked his seal-ring from his finger, and put it on her own instead of the ring he had taken, and bussed his inner lips and hands, nor did she leave any part of him unkissed; after which she took him to her breast and embraced him, and, laying one of her hands under his neck and the other under his armpit, nestled close to him and fell asleep at his side.

Dahnash therefore lost the argument. Budur was returned to China. Next morning; when the two young people awoke with the whole of Asia now between them, they turned to right and to left, but discovered no one at their side. They cried out to their respective households, belabored and slew people round about, and went entirely mad. Kamar al-Zaman lay down to languish; his father, the king, sat down at his head, weeping and mourning over him, and never leaving him, night or day. But the Princess Budur had to be manacled; with a chain of iron about her neck, she was made fast to one of her palace windows.[27]

The encounter and separation, for all its wildness, is typical of the sufferings of love. For when a heart insists on its destiny, resisting the general blandishment, then the agony is great; so too the danger. Forces, however, will have been set in motion beyond the reckoning of the senses. Sequences of events from the corners of the world will draw gradually together, and miracles of coincidence bring the inevitable to pass. The talismanic ring from the soul's encounter with its other portion in the place of recollectedness betokens that the heart was there aware of what Rip van Winkle missed; it betokens too a conviction of the waking mind that the reality of the deep is not belied by that of common day. This is the sign of the hero's requirement, now, to knit together his two worlds.

The remainder of the long story of Kamar al-Zaman is a history of the slow yet wonderful operation of a destiny that has been summoned into life. Not everyone has a destiny: only the hero who has plunged to touch it, and has come up again—with a ring.

5. *Master of the Two Worlds*

FREEDOM TO PASS back and forth across the world division, from the perspective of the apparitions of time to that of the causal deep and back—not contaminating the principles of the one with those of the other, yet permitting the mind to know the one by virtue of the other—is the talent of the master. The Cosmic Dancer, declares Nietzsche, does not rest heavily in a single spot, but gaily, lightly, turns and leaps from one position to another. It is possible to speak from only one point at a time, but that does not invalidate the insights of the rest.

The myths do not often display in a single image the mystery of the ready transit. Where they do, the moment is a precious symbol, full of import, to be treasured and contemplated. Such a moment was that of the Transfiguration of the Christ.

> Jesus taketh Peter, James, and John his brother, and bringeth them up into an high mountain apart, and was transfigured before them: and his face did shine as the sun, and his raiment was white as the light. And, behold, there appeared unto them Moses and Elias talking with him. Then answered Peter, and said unto Jesus, Lord, it is good for us to be here; if thou wilt, let us make here three tabernacles; one for thee, and one for Moses, and one for Elias.* While he yet spoke, behold, a bright cloud overshadowed them: and behold a voice out of the cloud, which said, This is my beloved Son, in whom I am well pleased; hear ye him. And when the disciples heard it, they fell on their face, and were sore afraid. And Jesus came and touched them, and said, Arise, and be not afraid. And when they had lifted up their eyes, they saw no man, save Jesus only. And as they came down from the mountain, Jesus charged them, saying, Tell the vision to no man, until the Son of man be risen again from the dead.[28]

Here is the whole myth in a moment: Jesus the guide, the way, the vision, and the companion of the return. The disciples are his initiates, not themselves masters of the mystery, yet introduced to the full experience of the paradox of the two worlds in one. Peter was so frightened he babbled.[29] Flesh had dissolved before their eyes to reveal the Word. They fell upon their faces, and when they arose the door again had closed.

It should be observed that this eternal moment soars beyond Kamar al-Zaman's romantic realization of his individual destiny. Not only do we have here a masterly passage, back and forth, across the world threshold, but we observe a profounder, very much profounder, penetration of the depths. Individual destiny is not the motive and theme of this vision; for the revelation was beheld by three witnesses, not one: it cannot be satisfactorily elucidated simply in psychological terms. Of course, it may be dismissed. We may doubt whether such a scene ever actually took place. But that would not help us any; for we are concerned, at present, with problems of symbolism, not of historicity. We do not particularly care whether Rip van Winkle, Kamar al-Zaman, or Jesus Christ ever actually lived. Their *stories* are

* "For he wist not what to say; for they were sore afraid" (Gospel According to Mark, 9:6).

what concern us: and these stories are so widely distributed over the world—attached to various heroes in various lands—that the question of whether this or that local carrier of the universal theme may or may not have been a historical, living man can be of only secondary moment. The stressing of this historical element will lead to confusion; it will simply obfuscate the picture message.

What, then, is the tenor of the image of the transfiguration? That is the question we have to ask. But in order that it may be confronted on universal grounds, rather than sectarian, we had better review one further example, equally celebrated, of the archetypal event.

The following is taken from the Hindu "Song of the Lord," the Bhagavad Gītā.* The Lord, the beautiful youth Kṛṣṇa, is an incarnation of Viṣṇu, the Universal God; Prince Arjuna is his disciple and friend.

Arjuna said: "O Lord, if you think me able to behold it, then, O master of yogis, reveal to me your Immutable Self." The Lord said:

> Behold my forms by the hundreds and the thousands—manifold and divine, various in shape and hue. Behold all the gods and angels; behold many wonders that no one has ever seen before. Behold here today the whole universe, the moving and the unmoving, and whatever else you may desire to see, all concentrated in my body.—But with these eyes of yours you cannot see me. I give you a divine eye; behold, now, my sovereign yoga-power.

Having spoken thus, the great Lord of yoga revealed to Arjuna his supreme form as Viṣṇu, Lord of the Universe: with many faces and eyes, presenting many wondrous sights, bedecked with many celestial ornaments, armed with many divine uplifted weapons; wearing celestial garlands and vestments, anointed with divine perfumes, all-wonderful, resplendent, boundless, and with faces on all sides. If the radiance of a thousand suns were to burst forth at once in the sky, that would be like the splendor of the Mighty One. There in the person of the God of gods, Arjuna beheld the whole universe, with its manifold divisions, all gathered together in one. Then, overcome with wonder, his hair standing on end, Arjuna bowed his head to the Lord, joined his palms in salutation, and addressed Him:

> In Thy body, O Lord, I behold all the gods and all the diverse hosts of beings—the Lord Brahma, seated on the lotus, all the patriarchs

* The principal text of modern Hindu devotional religiosity: an ethical dialogue of eighteen chapters, appearing in Book VI of the Mahābhārata, which is the Indian counterpart of the *Iliad*.

FIGURE 51. *Kṛṣṇa Leads Arjuna onto the Battlefield* (gouache on carton, India, eighteenth century A.D.)

> and the celestial serpents. I behold Thee with myriads of arms and bellies, with myriads of faces and eyes; I behold Thee, infinite in form, on every side, but I see not Thy end nor Thy middle nor Thy beginning, O Lord of the Universe, O Universal Form! On all sides glowing like a mass of radiance I behold Thee, with Thy diadem, mace, and discus, blazing everywhere like burning fire and the burning sun, passing all measure and difficult to behold. Thou art the Supreme Support of the Universe; Thou art the undying Guardian of the Eternal Law; Thou art, in my belief, the Primal Being.

This vision was opened to Arjuna on a battlefield, the moment just before the blast of the first trumpet calling to combat. With the god as his charioteer, the great prince had driven out into the field between the two battle-ready peoples. His own armies had been assembled against those of a usurping cousin, but now in the enemy ranks he beheld a multitude of men whom he knew and loved. His spirit failed him. "Alas," he said to the divine charioteer, "we are resolved to commit a great sin, in that we are ready to slay our kinsmen to satisfy our greed for the pleasure of a kingdom! Far better would it be for me if the sons of Dhritarashtra, weapons in hand, should slay me in battle, unarmed and unresisting. I will not fight." But thereupon the comely god had summoned him to courage, pouring out to him the wisdom of the Lord, and in the end had opened to him this vision. The prince beholds, dumbfounded, not only his friend transformed into the living personification of the Support of the Universe, but the heroes of the two armies rushing on a wind into the deity's innumerable, terrible mouths. He exclaims in horror:

> When I look upon Thy blazing form reaching to the skies and shining with many colors, when I see Thee with Thy mouth opened wide and Thy great eyes glowing bright, my inmost soul trembles in fear, and I find neither courage nor peace, O Vishnu! When I behold Thy mouths, striking terror with their tusks, like Time's all-consuming fire, I am disoriented and find no peace. Be gracious, O Lord of the Gods, O Abode of the Universe! All these sons of Dhritarashtra, together with the hosts of monarchs, and Bhishma, Drona, and Karna, and the warrior chiefs of our side as well, enter precipitately thy tusked and terrible mouths, frightful to behold. Some are seen caught between Thy teeth, their heads crushed to powder. As the torrents of many rivers rush toward the ocean, so do the heroes of the mortal world rush into Thy fiercely flaming mouths. As moths rush swiftly into a blazing fire to perish there, even so do these creatures swiftly rush into Thy mouths to their own destruction. Thou lickest Thy lips, devouring all the worlds on every side with Thy flaming mouths. Thy fiery rays fill the whole universe with their radiance and scorch it, O Vishnu! Tell me who Thou art, that wearest this frightful form. Salutations to Thee, O God Supreme! Have mercy. I desire to know Thee, who art the Primal One; for I do not understand Thy purpose.
>
> The Lord said:
>
> I am mighty, world-destroying Time, now engaged here in slaying these men. Even without you, all these warriors standing arrayed in the opposing armies shall not live. Therefore stand up and win glory; conquer your enemies and enjoy an opulent kingdom. By Me and none other have they already been slain; be an instrument only, O Arjuna. Kill Drona and Bhishma and Jayadratha and Karna, and the other great warriors as well, who have already been killed by Me. Be not distressed by fear. Fight, and you shall conquer your foes in the battle.

Having heard these words of Kṛṣṇa, Arjuna trembled, folded his hands in adoration, and bowed down. Overwhelmed with fear, he saluted Kṛṣṇa and then addressed Him again, with faltering voice.

> ...Thou art the first of gods, the ancient Soul; Thou art the supreme Resting-place of the universe; Thou art the Knower and

> That which is to be known and the Ultimate Goal. And by Thee is the world pervaded, O Thou of infinite form. Thou art Wind and Death and Fire and Moon and the Lord of Water. Thou art the First Man and the Great-grandsire. Salutations, salutations to Thee! ... I rejoice that I have seen what was never seen before; but my mind is also troubled with fear. Show me that other form of Thine. Be gracious, O Lord of Gods, O Abode of the Universe. I would see Thee as before, with Thy crown and Thy mace and the discus in Thy hand. Assume again Thy four-armed shape, O Thou of a thousand arms and of endless shapes.

The Lord said: "By My grace, through My own yoga-power, O Arjuna, I have shown you this supreme form, resplendent, universal, infinite, and primeval, which none but you has ever seen.... Be not afraid, be not bewildered, on seeing this terrific form of Mine. Free from fear and glad at heart, behold again My other form."

Having thus addressed Arjuna, Kṛṣṇa assumed a graceful shape again and comforted the terrified Pāndava.[30]

The disciple has been blessed with a vision transcending the scope of normal human destiny, and amounting to a glimpse of the essential nature of the cosmos. Not his personal fate, but the fate of mankind, of life as a whole, the atom and all the solar systems, has been opened to him; and this in terms befitting his human understanding; that is to say, in terms of an anthropomorphic vision: the Cosmic Man.

An identical initiation might have been effected by means of the equally valid image of the Cosmic Horse, the Cosmic Eagle, the Cosmic Tree, or the Cosmic Praying Mantis.

> Om. The head of the sacrificial horse is the dawn, its eye the sun, its vital force the air, its open mouth the fire called Vaishvanara, and the body of the sacrificial horse is the year. Its back is heaven, its belly the sky, its hoof the earth, its sides the four quarters, its ribs the intermediate quarters, its members the seasons, its joints the months and fortnights, its feet the days and nights, its bones the stars and its flesh the clouds. Its half-digested food is the sand, its blood-vessels the rivers, its liver and spleen the mountains, its hairs the herbs and trees. Its forepart is the ascending sun, its hind part the descending sun, its yawning is lightning, its shaking the body is thundering, its urinating is raining, and its neighing is voice.[31]

> *.......................... the archetype*
> *Body of life a beaked carnivorous desire*
> *Self-upheld storm-broad wings: but the eyes*
> *Were spouts of blood; the eyes were gashed out; dark blood*
> *Ran from the ruinous eye-pits to the hook of the beak*
> *And rained on the waste spaces of empty heaven.*
> *Yet the great Life continued, yet the great Life*

Was beautiful, and she drank her defeat, and devoured
Her famine for food.[32]

The Cosmic Tree is a well known mythological figure (viz., Yggdrasil, the World Ash, of the Eddas). The Mantis plays a major role in the mythology of the Bushmen of South Africa.

Furthermore, the revelation recorded in "The Song of the Lord" was made in terms befitting Arjuna's caste and race: The Cosmic Man whom he beheld was an aristocrat, like himself, and a Hindu. Correspondingly, in Palestine the Cosmic Man appeared as a Jew, in ancient Germany as a German; among the Basuto he is a Negro, in Japan Japanese. The race and stature of the figure symbolizing the immanent and transcendent Universal is of historical, not semantic, moment; so also the sex: the Cosmic Woman, who appears in the iconography of the Jains,* is as eloquent a symbol as the Cosmic Man.

Symbols are only the *vehicles* of communication; they must not be mistaken for the final term, the *tenor,* of their reference. No matter how attractive or impressive they may seem, they remain but convenient means, accommodated to the understanding. Hence the personality or personalities of God—whether represented in trinitarian, dualistic, or unitarian terms, in polytheistic, monotheistic, or henotheistic terms, pictorially or verbally, as documented fact or as apocalyptic vision—no one should attempt to read or interpret as the final thing. The problem of the theologian is to keep his symbol translucent, so that it may not block out the very light it is supposed to convey. "For then alone do we know God truly," writes Saint Thomas Aquinas, "when we believe that He is far above all that man can possibly think of God."[33] And in the Kena Upaniṣad, in the same spirit: "To know is not to know; not to know is to know."[34] Mistaking a vehicle for its tenor may lead to the spilling not only of valueless ink, but of valuable blood.

The next thing to observe is that the transfiguration of Jesus was witnessed by devotees who had extinguished their personal wills, men who had long since liquidated "life," "personal fate," "destiny," by complete self-abnegation in the Master. "Neither by the Vedas, nor by penances, nor by alms-giving, nor yet by sacrifice, am I to be seen in the form in which you have just now beheld Me," Kṛṣṇa declared, after he had resumed his familiar shape; "but only by devotion

---

* Jainism is a heterodox Hindu religion (i.e., rejecting the authority of the Vedas) which in its iconography reveals certain extraordinarily archaic traits. (See p. 224.) [For Campbell's further thoughts on Jainism and the Cosmic Woman, see Campbell's *Myths of Light,* (Novato, California: New World Library) pp. 93–101.—Ed.]

FIGURE 52. *The Cosmic Lion Goddess, Holding the Sun* (single-leaf manuscript, India, eighteenth century A.D.)

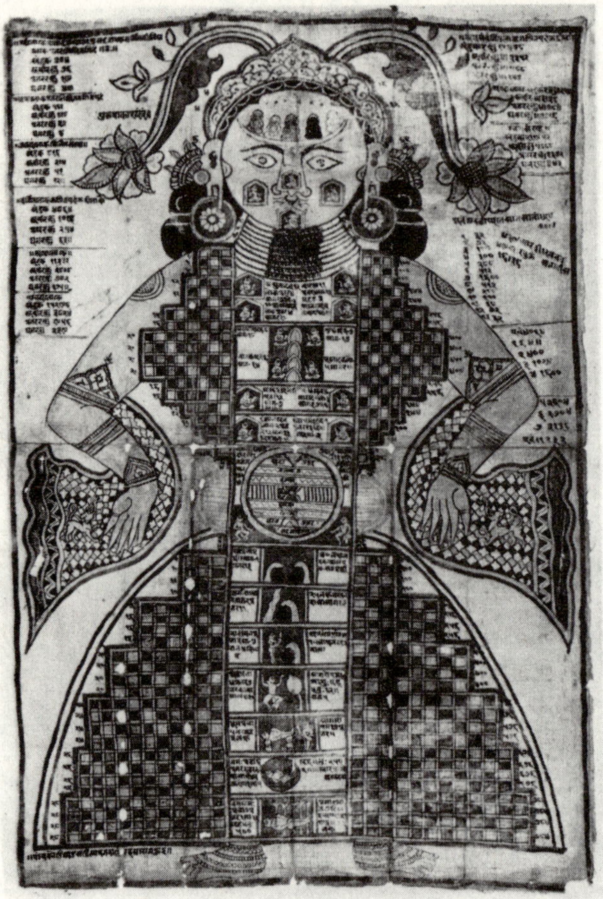

FIGURE 53. *The Cosmic Woman of the Jains* (gouache on cloth, India, eighteenth century A.D.)

to Me may I be known in this form, realized truly, and entered into. He who does My work and regards Me as the Supreme Goal, who is devoted to Me and without hatred for any creature—he comes to me."[35] A corresponding formulation by Jesus makes the point more succinctly: "Whosoever will lose his life for my sake shall find it."[36]

The meaning is very clear; it is the meaning of all religious practice. The individual, through prolonged psychological disciplines, gives up completely all attachment to his personal limitations, idiosyncrasies, hopes and fears, no longer resists the self-annihilation that is prerequisite to rebirth in the realization of truth, and so becomes ripe, at last, for the great at-one-ment. His personal ambitions being totally dissolved, he no longer tries to live but willingly relaxes to whatever may come to pass in him; he becomes, that is to say, an anonymity. The Law lives in him with his unreserved consent.

Many are the figures, particularly in the social and mythological contexts of the Orient, who represent this ultimate state of anonymous presence. The sages of the hermit groves and the wandering mendicants who play a conspicuous role in the life and legends of the East; in myth such figures as the Wandering Jew (despised, unknown, yet with the pearl of great price in his pocket); the tatterdemalion beggar, set upon by dogs; the miraculous mendicant bard whose music stills the heart; or the masquerading god, Zeus, Wotan, Viracocha, Edshu: these are examples.

> Sometimes a fool, sometimes a sage, sometimes possessed of regal splendor; sometimes wandering, sometimes as motionless as a python, sometimes wearing a benignant expression; sometimes honored, sometimes insulted, sometimes unknown—thus lives the man of realization, ever happy with supreme bliss. Just as an actor is always a man, whether he puts on the costume of his role or lays it aside, so is the perfect knower of the Imperishable always the Imperishable, and nothing else.[37]

6. Freedom to Live

WHAT, NOW, IS THE RESULT of the miraculous passage and return?

The battlefield is symbolic of the field of life, where every creature lives on the death of another. A realization of the inevitable guilt of life may so sicken the heart that, like Hamlet or like Arjuna, one may refuse to go on with it. On the other hand, like most of the rest of us, one may invent a false, finally unjustified, image of oneself as an exceptional phenomenon in the world, not guilty as others are, but justified in one's inevitable sinning because one represents the good. Such self-righteousness leads to a misunderstanding, not only of oneself but of the nature of both man and the cosmos. The goal of the myth is to dispel the need for such life ignorance by effecting a reconciliation of the individual consciousness with the universal will. And this is effected through a realization of the true relationship of the passing phenomena of time to the imperishable life that lives and dies in all.

> Even as a person casts off worn-out clothes and puts on others that are new, so the embodied Self casts off worn-out bodies and enters into others that are new. Weapons cut It not; fire burns It not; water wets It not; the wind does not wither It. This Self cannot be cut nor burnt nor wetted nor withered. Eternal, all-pervading, unchanging, immovable, the Self is the same forever.[38]

Man in the world of action loses his centering in the principle of eternity if he is anxious for the outcome of his deeds, but resting them and their fruits on the knees of the Living God he is released by them, as by a sacrifice, from the bondages of the sea of death. "Do without attachment the work you have to do. . . . Surrendering all action to Me, with mind intent on the Self, freeing yourself from longing and selfishness, fight—unperturbed by grief."[39]

Powerful in this insight, calm and free in action, elated that through his hand should flow the grace of Viracocha, the hero is the conscious vehicle of the terrible, wonderful Law, whether his work be that of butcher, jockey, or king.

Gwion Bach, who, having tasted three drops from the poison kettle of inspiration, was eaten by the hag Caridwen, reborn as an infant, and committed to the sea, was found next morning in a fish trap by a hapless and sorely disappointed young man named Elphin, son of the wealthy landholder Gwyddno, whose horses had been killed by the flood of the burst kettle's poison. When the men took up the leathern bag out of the trap and opened it and saw the forehead of the baby boy, they said to Elphin, "Behold a radiant brow (*taliesin*)!" "Taliesin be he called," said Elphin. And he lifted the boy in his arms, and, lamenting his mischance, he placed him sorrowfully behind him. And he made his horse amble gently that before had been trotting, and he carried him as softly as if he had been sitting on the easiest chair in the world. And presently the boy recited aloud a poem in consolation and praise of Elphin, and foretold to him honor and glory.

Fair Elphin, cease to lament!
Let no one be dissatisfied with his own.

To despair will bring no advantage.
No man sees what supports him....
Weak and small as I am,
On the foaming beach of the ocean,
In the day of trouble I shall be
Of more service to thee than three hundred salmon....

When Elphin returned to his father's castle, Gwyddno asked him if he had had a good haul at the weir, and he told him that he had got that which was better than fish. "What was that?" said Gwyddno. "A bard," answered Elphin. Then said Gwyddno, "Alas, what will he profit thee?" And the infant himself replied and said, "He will profit him more than the weir ever profited thee." Asked Gwyddno, "Art thou able to speak, and thou so little?" And the infant answered him, "I am better able to speak than thou to question me." "Let me hear what thou canst say," quoth Gwyddno. Then Taliesin sang a philosophical song.

Now the king one day held court, and Taliesin placed himself in a quiet corner.

> And so when the bards and the heralds came to cry largess, and to proclaim the power of the king and his strength, at the moment that they passed by the corner wherein he was crouching, Taliesin pouted out his lips after them, and played "Blerwm, blerwm," with his finger upon his lips. Neither took they much notice of him as they went by, but proceeded forward till they came before the king, unto whom they made their obeisance with their bodies, as they were wont, without speaking a single word, but pouting out their lips, and making mouths at the king, playing "Blerwm, blerwm," upon their lips with their fingers, as they had seen the boy do elsewhere. This sight caused the king to wonder and to deem within himself that they were drunk with many liquors. Wherefore he commanded one of his lords, who served at the board, to go to them and desire them to collect their wits, and to consider where they stood, and what it was fitting for them to do. And the lord did so gladly. But they ceased not from their folly any more than before. Whereupon he sent to them a second time, and a third, desiring them to go forth from the hall. At the last the king ordered one of his squires to give a blow to the chief of them named Heinin Vardd; and the squire took a broom and struck him on the head, so that he fell back in his seat. Then he arose and went on his knees, and besought leave of the king's grace to show that this their fault was not through want of knowledge, neither through drunkenness, but by the influence of some spirit that was in the hall. And after this Heinin spoke on this wise. "Oh honorable king, be it known to

your grace, that not from the strength of drink, or of too much liquor, are we dumb, without power of speech like drunken men, but through the influence of a spirit that sits in the corner yonder in the form of a child." Forthwith the king commanded the squire to fetch him; and he went to the nook where Taliesin sat, and brought him before the king, who asked him what he was, and whence he came. And he answered the king in verse:

Primary chief bard am I to Elphin,
And my original country is the region of the summer stars;
*Idno and Heinin called me Merddin,**
At length every king will call me Taliesin.

I was with my Lord in the highest sphere,
On the fall of Lucifer into the depth of hell.
I have borne a banner before Alexander;
I know the names of the stars from north to south;
I have been on the galaxy at the throne of the Distributer;
I was in Canaan when Absalom was slain;
I conveyed the Divine Spirit to the level of the vale of Hebron;
I was in the court of Don before the birth of Gwdion.
I was instructor to Eli and Enoc;
I have been winged by the genius of the splendid crosier;
I have been loquacious prior to being gifted with speech;
I was at the place of the crucifixion of the merciful Son of God;
I have been three periods in the prison of Arianrod;
I have been the chief director of the work of the tower of Nimrod;
I am a wonder whose origin is not known.
I have been in Asia with Noah in the ark,
I have seen the destruction of Sodom and Gomorra;
I have been in India when Roma was built,
I am now come here to the Remnant of Troia.
I have been with my Lord in the manger of the ass;
I strengthened Moses through the water of Jordan;
I have been in the firmament with Mary Magdalene;
I have obtained the muse from the cauldron of Caridwen;
I have been bard of the harp to Lleon of Lochlin.
I have been on the White Hill, in the court of Cynvelyn,
For a day and a year in stocks and fetters,
I have suffered hunger for the Son of the Virgin,
I have been fostered in the land of the Deity,
I have been teacher to all intelligences,
I am able to instruct the whole universe.

---

* [Merddin = Merlin, chief wizard of the Arthurian romances.—Ed.]

I shall be until the day of doom on the face of the earth;
And it is not known whether my body is flesh or fish.

Then I was for nine months
In the womb of the hag Caridwen;
I was originally little Gwion,
And at length I am Taliesin.

And when the king and his nobles had heard the song, they wondered much, for they had never heard the like from a boy as young as he.[40]

The larger portion of the bard's song is devoted to the Imperishable, which lives in him, only a brief stanza to the details of his personal biography. Those listening are oriented to the Imperishable in themselves, and then supplied incidentally with an item of information. Though he had feared the terrible hag, he had been swallowed and reborn. Having died to his personal ego, he arose again established in the Self.

The hero is the champion of things becoming, not of things become, because he is. "Before Abraham was, I AM."[41] He does not mistake apparent changelessness in time for the permanence of Being, nor is he fearful of the next moment (or of the "other thing"), as destroying the permanent with its change. "Nothing retains its own form; but Nature, the greater renewer, ever makes up forms from forms. Be sure there's nothing perishes in the whole universe; it does but vary and renew its form."[42] Thus the next moment is permitted to come to pass.—When the Prince of Eternity kissed the Princess of the World, her resistance was allayed.

She opened her eyes, awoke, and looked at him in friendship. Together they came down the stairs, and the king awoke and the queen and the entire courtly estate, and all looked at each other with big eyes. And the horses in the court stood up and shook themselves: the hunting dogs jumped and wagged their tails: the pigeons on the roof drew their little heads out from under their wings, looked around, and flew across the field: the flies on the wall walked again: the fire in the kitchen brightened, flickered, and cooked the dinner: the roast began again to sizzle: and the cook gave the scullery boy a box in the ear that made him yell: and the maid finished plucking the chicken.[43]

The
HERO'S JOURNEY

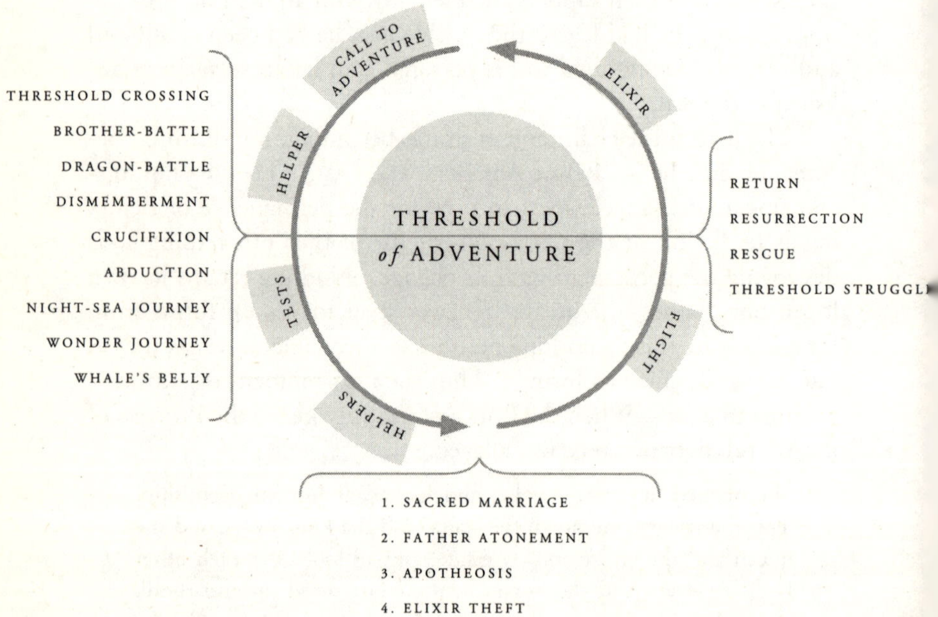

CHAPTER IV

The Keys

THE ADVENTURE CAN BE SUMMARIZED in the opposite diagram.

The mythological hero, setting forth from his common-day hut or castle, is lured, carried away, or else voluntarily proceeds, to the threshold of adventure. There he encounters a shadow presence that guards the passage. The hero may defeat or conciliate this power and go alive into the kingdom of the dark (brother-battle, dragon-battle; offering, charm), or be slain by the opponent and descend in death (dismemberment, crucifixion). Beyond the threshold, then, the hero journeys through a world of unfamiliar yet strangely intimate forces, some of which severely threaten him (tests), some of which give magical aid (helpers). When he arrives at the nadir of the mythological round, he undergoes a supreme ordeal and gains his reward. The triumph may be represented as the hero's sexual union with the goddess-mother of the world (sacred marriage), his recognition by the father-creator (father atonement), his own divinization (apotheosis), or again—if the powers have remained unfriendly to him—his theft of the boon he came to gain (bride-theft, fire-theft); intrinsically it is an expansion of consciousness and therewith of being (illumination, transfiguration, freedom). The final work is that of the return. If the powers have blessed the hero, he now sets forth under their protection (emissary); if not, he flees and is pursued (transformation flight, obstacle flight). At the return threshold the transcendental powers must remain behind; the hero re-emerges from the kingdom of dread (return, resurrection). The boon that he brings restores the world (elixir).

The changes rung on the simple scale of the monomyth defy description. Many tales isolate and greatly enlarge upon one or two of the typical elements of the full cycle (test motif, flight motif, abduction of the bride), others string a number of independent cycles into a single series (as in the *Odyssey*). Differing characters or episodes can become fused, or a single element can reduplicate itself and reappear under many changes.

The outlines of myths and tales are subject to damage and obscuration. Archaic traits are generally eliminated or subdued. Imported materials are revised to fit local landscape, custom, or belief, and always suffer in the process. Furthermore, in the innumerable retellings of a traditional story, accidental or intentional dislocations are inevitable. To account for elements that have become, for one reason or another, meaningless, secondary interpretations are invented, often with considerable skill.[1]

In the Eskimo story of Raven in the belly of the whale, the motif of the fire sticks has suffered a dislocation and subsequent rationalization. The archetype of the hero in the belly of the whale is widely known. The principal deed of the adventurer is usually to make fire with his fire sticks in the interior of the monster, thus bringing about the whale's death and his own release. Fire making in this manner is symbolic of the sex act. The two sticks—socket-stick and spindle—are known respectively as the female and the male; the flame is the newly generated life. The hero making fire in the whale is a variant of the sacred marriage.

But in our Eskimo story this fire-making image underwent a modification. The female principle was personified in the beautiful girl whom Raven encountered in the great room within the animal; meanwhile the conjunction of male and female was symbolized separately in the flow of the oil from the pipe into the burning lamp. Raven's tasting of this oil was his participation in the act. The resultant cataclysm represented the typical crisis of the nadir, the termination of the old eon and initiation of the new. Raven's emergence then symbolized the miracle of rebirth. Thus, the original fire sticks having become superfluous, a clever and amusing epilogue was invented to give them a function in the plot. Having left the fire sticks in the belly of the whale, Raven was able to interpret their rediscovery as an ill-luck omen, frighten the people away, and enjoy the blubber feast alone. This epilogue is an excellent example of secondary elaboration. It plays on the trickster character of the hero but is not an element of the basic story.

In the later stages of many mythologies, the key images hide like needles in great haystacks of secondary anecdote and rationalization; for when a civilization has passed from a mythological to a secular point of view, the older images are no longer felt or quite approved. In Hellenistic Greece and in Imperial Rome, the ancient gods were reduced to mere civic patrons, household pets, and literary favorites. Uncomprehended inherited themes, such as that of the Minotaur—the dark and terrible night aspect of an old Egypto-Cretan representation of the incarnate sun god and divine king—were rationalized and reinterpreted to suit contemporary ends. Mt. Olympus became a Riviera of trite scandals and affairs, and the mother-goddesses hysterical nymphs. The myths were read as superhuman romances. In China, comparably, where the humanistic, moralizing force of Confucianism has fairly emptied the old myth forms of their primal grandeur, the official mythology is today a clutter of anecdotes about the sons and daughters of provincial officials, who, for serving their community one way or another, were elevated by their grateful beneficiaries to the dignity of local gods. And in modern progressive Christianity the Christ—Incarnation of the Logos and Redeemer of the World—is primarily a historical personage, a harmless country wise man of the semi-Oriental past who preached a benign doctrine of "do as you would be done by," yet was executed as a criminal. His death is read as a splendid lesson in integrity and fortitude.

Wherever the poetry of myth is interpreted as biography, history, or science, it is killed. The living images become only remote facts of a distant time or sky. Furthermore, it is never difficult to demonstrate that as science and history mythology is absurd. When a civilization begins to reinterpret its mythology in this way, the life goes out of it, temples become museums, and the link between the two perspectives is dissolved. Such a blight has certainly descended on the Bible and on a great part of the Christian cult.

To bring the images back to life, one has to seek, not interesting applications to modern affairs, but illuminating hints from the inspired past. When these are found, vast areas of half-dead iconography disclose again their permanently human meaning.

On Holy Saturday in the Catholic Church, for example, after the blessing of the new fire,* the blessing of the paschal candle, and the

* Holy Saturday, the day between the Death and Resurrection of Jesus, who is in the belly of Hell. The moment of the renewal of the eon. Compare the motif of the fire sticks discussed above.

reading of the prophecies, the priest puts on a purple cope and, preceded by the processional cross, the candelabra, and the lighted blessed candle, goes to the baptismal font with his ministers and the clergy, while the following tract is sung: "As the hart panteth after the fountains of water, so my soul panteth after Thee, O God! when shall I come and appear before the face of God? My tears have been my bread day and night, while they say to me daily: Where is thy God?"[2]

On arriving at the threshold of the baptistry, the priest pauses to offer up a prayer, then enters and blesses the water of the font, "to the end that a heavenly offspring, conceived by sanctification, may emerge from the immaculate womb of the divine font, reborn new creatures: and that all, however distinguished either by sex in body, or by age in time, may be brought forth to the same infancy by grace, their spiritual mother." He touches the water with his hand, and prays that it may be cleansed of the malice of Satan; makes the sign of the cross over the water; divides the water with his hand and throws some towards the four quarters of the world; breathes thrice upon the water in the form of a cross; then dips the paschal candle in the water and intones: "May the virtue of the Holy Ghost descend into all the water of this font." He withdraws the candle, sinks it back again to a greater depth, and repeats in a higher tone: "May the virtue of the Holy Ghost descend into all the water of this font." Again he withdraws the candle, and for the third time sinks it, to the bottom, repeating in a higher tone still: "May the virtue of the Holy Ghost descend into all the water of this font." Then breathing thrice upon the water he goes on: "And make the whole substance of this water fruitful for regeneration." He then withdraws the candle from the water, and, after a few concluding prayers, the assistant priests sprinkle the people with this blessed water.[3]

The female water spiritually fructified with the male fire of the Holy Ghost is the Christian counterpart of the water of transformation known to all systems of mythological imagery. This rite is a variant of the sacred marriage, which is the source-moment that generates and regenerates the world and man, precisely the mystery symbolized by the Hindu *liṅgam-yonī.* To enter into this font is to plunge into the mythological realm; to break the surface is to cross the threshold into the night-sea. Symbolically, the infant makes the journey when the water is poured on its head; its guide and helpers are the priest and godparents. Its goal is a visit with the parents of its Eternal Self, the Spirit of God and the Womb of Grace.[4] Then it is returned to the parents of the physical body.

Few of us have any inkling of the sense of the rite of baptism, which was our initiation into our Church. Nevertheless, it clearly appears in the words of Jesus: "Verily, verily, I say unto thee, Except a man be born again, he cannot see the kingdom of God." Nicodemus said to him "How can a man be born when he is old? can he enter the second time into his mother's womb and be born?" Jesus answered "Verily, verily, I say unto thee, Except a man be born of water and the spirit, he cannot enter into the kingdom of God."[5]

The popular interpretation of baptism is that it "washes away original sin," with emphasis rather on the cleansing than on the rebirth idea. This is a secondary interpretation. Or if the traditional birth image is remembered, nothing is said of an antecedent marriage. Mythological symbols, however, have to be followed through all their implications before they open out the full system of correspondences through which they represent, by analogy, the millennial adventure of the soul.

FIGURE 54. *The Fountain of Life* (paint on wood, Flanders, c. A.D. 1520)

PART II

THE COSMOGONIC CYCLE

FIGURE 55. *The Aztec Sun Stone* (carved stone, Aztec, Mexico, A.D. 1479)

CHAPTER I

Emanations

I. *From Psychology to Metaphysics*

It is not difficult for the modern intellectual to concede that the symbolism of mythology has a psychological significance. Particularly after the work of the psychoanalysts, there can be little doubt, either that myths are of the nature of dream, or that dreams are symptomatic of the dynamics of the psyche. Sigmund Freud, Carl G. Jung, Wilhelm Stekel, Otto Rank, Karl Abraham, Géza Róheim, and many others have within the past few decades developed a vastly documented modern lore of dream and myth interpretation; and though the doctors differ among themselves, they are united into one great modern movement by a considerable body of common principles. With their discovery that the patterns and logic of fairy tale and myth correspond to those of dream, the long discredited chimeras of archaic man have returned dramatically to the foreground of modern consciousness.

According to this view it appears that through the wonder tales which pretend to describe the lives of the legendary heroes, the powers of the divinities of nature, the spirits of the dead, and the totem ancestors of the group—symbolic expression is given to the unconscious desires, fears, and tensions that underlie the conscious patterns of human behavior. Mythology, in other words, is psychology misread as biography, history, and cosmology. The modern psychologist can translate it back to its proper denotations and thus rescue for the contemporary world a rich and eloquent document of the profoundest depths of human character. Exhibited here, as in a fluoroscope, stand revealed the hidden processes of the enigma *Homo sapiens*—Occidental and Oriental, primitive and civilized, contemporary and archaic. The entire spectacle is before us. We have only to read it, study its constant patterns, analyze its variations, and therewith come to an understanding of the deep forces that have shaped man's destiny and must continue to determine both our private and our public lives.

But if we are to grasp the full value of the materials, we must note that myths are not exactly comparable to dream. Their figures originate from the same sources—the unconscious wells of fantasy—and their grammar is the same, but they are not the spontaneous products of sleep. On the contrary, their patterns are consciously controlled. And their understood function is to serve as a powerful picture language for the communication of traditional wisdom. This is true already of the so-called primitive folk mythologies. The trance-susceptible shaman and the initiated antelope-priest are not unsophisticated in the wisdom of the world, nor unskilled in the principles of communication by analogy. The metaphors by which they live, and through which they operate, have been brooded upon, searched, and discussed for centuries—even millennia; they have served whole societies, furthermore, as the mainstays of thought and life. The culture patterns have been shaped to them. The youth have been educated, and the aged rendered wise, through the study, experience, and understanding of their effective initiatory forms. For they actually touch and bring into play the vital energies of the whole human psyche. They link the unconscious to the fields of practical action, not irrationally, in the manner of a neurotic projection, but in such fashion as to permit a mature and sobering, practical comprehension of the fact-world to play back, as a stern control, into the realms of infantile wish and fear. And if this be true of the comparatively simple folk mythologies (the systems of myth and ritual by which the primitive hunting and fishing tribes support themselves), what may we say of such magnificent cosmic metaphors as those reflected in the great Homeric epics, the *Divine Comedy* of Dante, the Book of Genesis, and the timeless temples of the Orient? Until the most recent decades, these were the support of all human life and the inspiration of philosophy, poetry, and the arts. Where the inherited symbols have been touched by a Lao Tze, Buddha, Zoroaster, Christ, or Mohammed—employed by a consummate master of the spirit as a vehicle of the profoundest moral and metaphysical instruction—obviously we are in the presence rather of immense consciousness than of darkness.

And so, to grasp the full value of the mythological figures that have come down to us, we must understand that they are not only symptoms of the unconscious (as indeed are all human thoughts and acts) but also controlled and intended statements of certain spiritual principles, which have remained as constant throughout the course of human history as the form and nervous structure of the human physique itself. Briefly formulated, the universal doctrine teaches that all the visible structures of the world—all things and beings—are the effects of a ubiquitous power out of which they rise, which supports and fills them during the period of their manifestation, and back into which they must ultimately dissolve. This is the power known to science as energy, to the Melanesians as *mana,* to the Sioux Indians as *wakonda,* the Hindus as Śakti, and the Christians as the power of God. Its manifestation in the psyche is termed, by the psychoanalysts, *libido.*[1] And its manifestation in the cosmos is the structure and flux of the universe itself.

The apprehension of the *source* of this undifferentiated yet everywhere particularized substratum of being is rendered frustrate by the very organs through which the apprehension must be accomplished. The forms of sensibility and the categories of human thought,[2] which are themselves manifestations of this power,* so confine the mind that it is normally impossible not only to see, but even to conceive, beyond the colorful, fluid, infinitely various and bewildering phenomenal spectacle. The function of ritual and myth is to make possible, and then to facilitate, the jump—by analogy. Forms and conceptions that the mind and its senses can comprehend are presented and arranged in such a way as to suggest a truth or openness beyond. And then, the conditions for meditation having been provided, the individual is left alone. Myth is but the penultimate; the ultimate is openness—that void, or being, beyond the categories†—into which the mind must plunge alone and be dissolved. Therefore, God and the gods are only convenient means themselves of the nature of the world of names and forms, though eloquent of, and ultimately conducive to,

* Sanskrit: *māyā-śakti.*

† Beyond the categories, and therefore not defined by either of the pair of opposites called "void" and "being." Such terms are only clues to the transcendency.

the ineffable. They are mere symbols to move and awaken the mind, and to call it past themselves.

The recognition of the secondary nature of the personality of whatever deity is worshiped is characteristic of most of the traditions of the world (see, for example, p. 155, note 154). In Christianity, Mohammedanism, and Judaism, however, the personality of the divinity is taught to be final—which makes it comparatively difficult for the members of these communions to understand how one may go beyond the limitations of their own anthropomorphic divinity. The result has been, on the one hand, a general obfuscation of the symbols, and on the other, a god-ridden bigotry such as is unmatched elsewhere in the history of religion. For a discussion of the possible origin of this aberration, see Sigmund Freud's *Moses and Monotheism.*[3]

Heaven, hell, the mythological age, Olympus and all the other habitations of the gods are interpreted by psychoanalysis as symbols of the unconscious. The key to the modern systems of psychological interpretation therefore is this: the metaphysical realm = the unconscious. Correspondingly, the key to open the door the other way is the same equation in reverse: the unconscious = the metaphysical realm. "For," as Jesus states it, "behold, the kingdom of God is within you."[4] Indeed, the lapse of superconsciousness into the state of unconsciousness is precisely the meaning of the biblical image of the Fall. The constriction of consciousness, to which we owe the fact that we see not the source of the universal power but only the phenomenal forms reflected from that power, turns superconsciousness into unconsciousness and, at the same instant and by the same token, creates the world. Redemption consists in the return to superconsciousness and therewith the dissolution of the world. This is the great theme and formula of the cosmogonic cycle, the mythical image of the world's coming to manifestation and subsequent return into the nonmanifest condition. Equally, the birth, life, and death of the individual may be regarded as a descent into unconsciousness and return. The hero is the one who, while still alive, knows and represents the claims of the superconsciousness which throughout creation is more or less unconscious. The adventure of the hero represents the moment in his life when he achieved illumination—the nuclear moment when, while still alive, he found and opened the road to the light beyond the dark walls of our living death.

And so it is that the cosmic symbols are presented in a spirit of thought-bewildering sublime paradox. The kingdom of God is within, yet without, also; God, however, is but a convenient means to wake the sleeping princess, the soul. Life is her sleep, death the awakening. The hero, the waker of his own soul, is himself but the convenient means of his own dissolution. God, the waker of the soul, is therewith his own immediate death.

Perhaps the most eloquent possible symbol of this mystery is that of the god crucified, the god offered, "himself to himself."[5] Read in one direction, the meaning is the passage of the phenomenal hero into superconsciousness: the body with its five senses—like that of Prince Five-weapons stuck to Sticky-hair—is left hanging to the cross of the knowledge of life and death, pinned in five places (the two hands, the two feet, and the head crowned with thorns).[6] But also, God has descended voluntarily and taken upon himself this phenomenal agony. God assumes the life of man and man releases the God within himself at the mid-point of the cross-arms of the same "coincidence of opposites,"[7] the same sun door through which God descends and Man ascends—each as the other's food.[8]

The modern student may, of course, study these symbols as he will, either as a symptom of others' ignorance, or as a sign to him of his own, either in terms of a reduction of metaphysics to psychology, or vice versa. The traditional way was to meditate on the symbols in both senses. In any case, they are telling metaphors of the destiny of man, man's hope, man's faith, and man's dark mystery.

2. *The Universal Round*

As THE CONSCIOUSNESS of the individual rests on a sea of night into which it descends in slumber and out of which it mysteriously wakes, so, in the imagery of myth, the universe is precipitated out of, and reposes upon, a timelessness back into which it again dissolves. And as the mental and physical health of the individual depends on an orderly flow of vital forces into the field of waking day from the unconscious dark, so again in myth, the continuance of the cosmic order is assured only by a controlled flow of power from the source. The gods are symbolic personifications of the laws governing this flow. The gods come into existence with the dawn of the world and dissolve with the twilight. They are not eternal in the sense that the night is eternal. Only from the shorter span of human existence does the round of a cosmogonic eon seem to endure.

The cosmogonic cycle is normally represented as repeating itself, world without end. During each great round, lesser dissolutions are commonly included, as the cycle of sleep and waking revolves throughout a lifetime. According to an Aztec version, each of the four elements—water, earth, air, and fire—terminates a period of the world: the eon of the waters ended in deluge, that of the earth with an earthquake, that of air with a wind, and the present eon will be destroyed by flame.[9]

According to the Stoic doctrine of the cyclic conflagration, all souls are resolved into the world soul or primal fire. When this universal dissolution is concluded, the formation of a new universe begins (Cicero's *renovatio*), and all things repeat themselves, every divinity, every person, playing again his former part. Seneca gave a description of this destruction in his "De Consolatione ad Marciam," and appears to have looked forward to living again in the cycle to come.[10]

A magnificent vision of the cosmogonic round is presented in the mythology of the Jains. The most recent prophet and savior of this very ancient Indian sect was Mahāvīra, a contemporary of the Buddha (sixth century B.C.). His parents were already followers of a much earlier Jaina savior-prophet, Pārśvanātha, who is represented with snakes springing from his shoulders and is reputed to have flourished 872–772 B.C. Centuries before Pārśvanātha, there lived and died the Jaina savior Neminātha, declared to have been a cousin of the beloved Hindu incarnation Kṛṣṇa. And before him, again, were exactly twenty-one others, going all the way back to Ṛṣabhanātha, who existed in an earlier age of the world, when men and women were always born in wedded couples, were two miles tall, and lived for a period of countless years. Ṛṣabhanātha instructed the people in the seventy-two sciences (writing, arithmetic, reading of omens, etc.), the sixty-four accomplishments of women (cooking, sewing, etc.), and the one hundred arts (pottery, weaving, painting, smithing, barbering, etc.); also, he introduced them to politics and established a kingdom.

Before his day, such innovations would have been superfluous; for the people of the preceding period—who were four miles tall, with one hundred and twenty-eight ribs, enjoying a life span of two periods of countless years—were supplied in all their needs by ten "wish-fulfilling trees" (*kalpa-vṛkṣa*), which gave sweet fruits, leaves that were shaped like pots and pans, leaves that sweetly sang, leaves that gave forth light at night, flowers delightful to see and to smell, food perfect both to sight and to taste, leaves that might serve as jewelry, and bark providing beautiful clothes. One of the trees was like a many-storied palace in which to live; another shed a gentle radiance, like that of many little lamps. The earth was sweet as sugar; the ocean as delicious as wine. And then again, before this happy age, there had been a period happier still—precisely twice as happy—when men and women had been eight miles tall, possessing each two hundred and fifty-six ribs. When those superlative people died, they passed directly to the world of the gods, without ever having heard of religion, for their natural virtue was as perfect as their beauty.

The Jains conceive of time as an endless round. Time is pictured as a wheel with twelve spokes, or ages, classified in two sets of six. The first set is called the "descending" series (*avasarpinī*), and begins with the age of the superlative giant-couples. That paradisiac period endures for ten millions of ten millions of one hundred millions of one hundred million periods of countless years, and then yields slowly to the only half as blissful period when men and women are only four miles tall. In the third period—that of Ṛṣabhanātha, first of the twenty-four world saviors—happiness is mixed with a little sorrow, and virtue with a little vice. At the conclusion of this period, men and women are no longer born together in couples to live together as man and wife.

During the fourth period, the gradual deterioration of the world and its inhabitants steadily continues. The life span and stature of man slowly diminish. Twenty-three world saviors are born; each restating the eternal doctrine of the Jains in terms appropriate to the conditions of his time. Three years, eight and one-half months after the death of the last of the saviors and prophets, Mahāvīra, this period comes to an end.

Our own age, the fifth of the descending series, began in 522 B.C. and will last for twenty-one thousand years. No Jaina savior will be born during this time, and the eternal religion of the Jains will gradually disappear. It is a period of unmitigated and gradually intensifying evil. The tallest human beings are only seven cubits tall, and the longest life span no more than one hundred and twenty-five years. People have only sixteen ribs. They are selfish, unjust, violent, lustful, proud, and avaricious.

But in the sixth of the descending ages, the state of man and his world will be still more horrible. The longest life will be only twenty years; one cubit will be the greatest stature and eight ribs the meager allotment. The days will be hot, the nights cold, disease will be rampant and chastity nonexistent. Tempests will sweep over the earth, and toward the conclusion of the period these will increase. In the end all life, human and animal, and all the vegetable seeds, will be forced to seek shelter in the Ganges, in miserable caves, and in the sea.

The descending series will terminate and the "ascending" series (*utsarpinī*) begin, when the tempest and desolation will have reached the point of the unendurable. For seven days then it will rain, and seven different kinds of rain will fall; the soil will be refreshed, and the seeds will begin to grow. Out of their caves the horrible dwarf-creatures of the arid, bitter earth will venture; and very very gradually there will be perceptible a slight improvement in their morals, health, beauty, and stature; until presently they will be living in a world such as the one we know today. And then a savior will be born, named Padmanātha, to announce again the eternal religion of the Jains; the stature of mankind will approach again the superlative, the beauty of man will surpass the splendor of the sun. At last, the earth will sweeten and the waters turn to wine, the wish-fulfilling trees will yield their bounty of delights to a blissful population of perfectly wedded twins; and the happiness of this community again will be doubled, and the wheel, through ten millions of ten millions of one hundred millions of one hundred million periods of countless years, will approach the point of beginning the downward revolution, which again will lead to the extinction of the eternal religion and the gradually increasing noise of unwholesome merrymaking, warfare, and pestilential winds.[11]

This ever-revolving, twelve-spoked wheel of time of the Jains is a counterpart of the cycle of four ages of the Hindus: the first age a long period of perfect bliss, beauty, and perfection, lasting 4,800 divine years;* the second of somewhat lesser virtue, lasting 3,600 divine years; the third of equally intermingled virtue and vice, lasting 2,400 divine years; and the last, our own, of steadily increasing evil, lasting 1,200 divine years, or 432,000 years according to human calculation. But at the termination of the present period, instead of beginning again immediately to improve (as in the cycle described by the Jains), all is first to be annihilated in a cataclysm of fire and flood,

* A divine year is equal to 360 human years. See above, p. 192.

and thereby reduced to the primordial state of the original, timeless ocean, to remain for a period equal to that of the whole length of the four ages. The world's great ages then begin anew.

FIGURE 56. *The Cosmic Woman of the Jains—Detail of Cosmic Wheel* (gouache on cloth, India, eighteenth century A.D.)

A basic conception of Oriental philosophy is understood to be rendered in this picture-form. Whether the myth was originally an illustration of the philosophical formula, or the latter a distillation out of the myth, it is today impossible to say. Certainly the myth goes back to remote ages, but so too does philosophy. Who is to know what thoughts lay in the minds of the old sages who developed and treasured the myth and handed it on? Very often, during the analysis and penetration of the secrets of archaic symbol, one can only feel that our generally accepted notion of the history of philosophy is founded on a completely false assumption, namely that abstract and metaphysical thought begins where it first appears in our extant records.

The philosophical formula illustrated by the cosmogonic cycle is that of the circulation of consciousness through the three planes of being. The first plane is that of waking experience: cognitive of the hard, gross facts of an outer universe, illuminated by the light of the sun, and common to all. The second plane is that of dream experience: cognitive of the fluid, subtle forms of a private interior world, self-luminous and of one substance with the dreamer. The third plane is that of deep sleep: dreamless, profoundly blissful. In the first are encountered the instructive experiences of life; in the second these are digested, assimilated to the inner forces of the dreamer; while in the third all is enjoyed and known unconsciously, in the "space within the heart," the room of the inner controller, the source and end of all.[12]

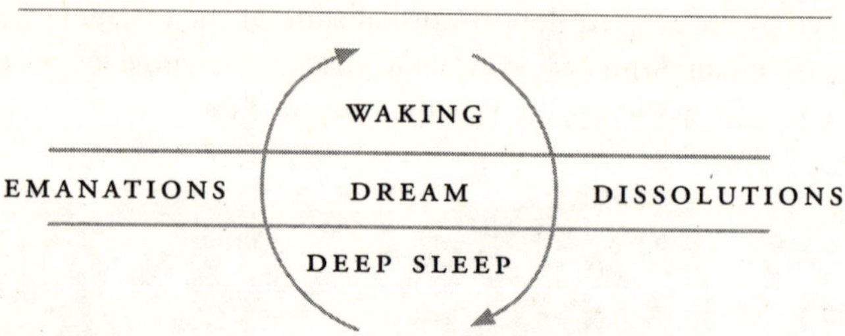

The cosmogonic cycle is to be understood as the passage of universal consciousness from the deep sleep zone of the unmanifest, through dream, to the full day of waking; then back again through dream to the timeless dark. As in the actual experience of every living being, so in the grandiose figure of the living cosmos: in the abyss of sleep the energies are refreshed, in the work of the day they are exhausted; the life of the universe runs down and must be renewed.

The cosmogonic cycle pulses forth into manifestation and back into nonmanifestation amidst a silence of the unknown. The Hindus represent this mystery in the holy syllable *AUM.* Here the sound *A* represents waking consciousness, *U* dream consciousness, *M* deep sleep. The silence surrounding the syllable is the unknown: it is called simply "The Fourth."[13]* The syllable itself is God as creator-preserver-destroyer, but the silence is God Eternal, absolutely uninvolved in all the opening-and-closings of the round.

It is unseen, unrelated, inconceivable,
uninferable, unimaginable, indescribable.
It is the essence of the one self-cognition
common to all states of consciousness.
All phenomena cease in it.
It is peace, it is bliss, it is nonduality.[14]

Myth remains, necessarily, within the cycle, but represents this cycle as surrounded and permeated by the silence. Myth is the revelation of a plenum of silence within and around every atom of existence. Myth is a directing of the mind and heart, by means of profoundly informed figurations, to that ultimate mystery which fills and surrounds all existences. Even in the most comical and apparently frivolous of its moments, mythology is directing the mind to this unmanifest which is just beyond the eye.

"The Aged of the Aged, the Unknown of the Unknown, has a form and yet has no form," we read in a kabbalistic text of the

* Since in Sanskrit *A* and *U* coalesce in *O,* the sacred syllable is pronounced and often written "*OM.*" See the prayers, pp. 127 and 201, above.

medieval Hebrews. "He has a form whereby the universe is preserved, and yet has no form, because he cannot be comprehended."[15] This Aged of the Aged is represented as a face in profile: always in profile, because the hidden side can never be known. This is called "The Great Face," Makroprosopos; from the strands of its white beard the entire world proceeds.

> That beard, the truth of all truths, proceedeth from the place of the ears, and descendeth around the mouth of the Holy One; and descendeth and ascendeth, covering the cheeks which are called the places of copious fragrance; it is white with ornament: and it descendeth in the equilibrium of balanced power, and furnisheth a covering even unto the midst of the breast. That is the beard of adornment, true and perfect, from which flow down thirteen fountains, scattering the most precious balm of splendor. This is disposed in thirteen forms.... And certain dispositions are found in the universe, according to those thirteen dispositions which depend from that venerable beard, and they are opened out into the thirteen gates of mercies.[16]

FIGURE 57. *The Makroprosopos* (engraving, Germany, A.D. 1684)

The white beard of Makroprosopos descends over another head, "The Little Face," Mikroprosopos, represented full face and with a beard of black. And whereas the eye of The Great Face is without lid and never shuts, the eyes of The Little Face open and close in a slow rhythm of universal destiny. This is the opening and closing of the cosmogonic round. The Little Face is named "GOD," the Great Face "I AM."

The text in which we learn of the Makroprosopos and the Mikroprosopos, the Zohar (*zōhar,* "light, splendor"), is a collection of esoteric Hebrew writing given to the world about 1305 by a learned Spanish Jew, Moses de Leon. It was claimed that the material had been drawn from secret originals, going back to the teachings of Simeon ben Yohai, a rabbi of Galilee in the second century A.D. Threatened with death by the Romans, Simeon had hidden for twelve years in a cave; ten centuries later his writings had been found there, and these were the sources of the books of the Zohar.

Simeon's teachings were supposed to have been drawn from the *hokmah nistarah* or hidden wisdom of Moses, i.e., a body of esoteric lore first studied by Moses in Egypt, the land of his birth, then pondered by him during his forty years in the wilderness (where he received special instruction from an angel), and finally incorporated cryptically in the first four books of the Pentateuch, from which it can be extracted by a proper understanding and manipulation of the mystical number-values of the Hebrew alphabet. This lore and the techniques for rediscovering and utilizing it constitute the Kabbala.

It is said that the teachings of the Kabbala (*qabbālāh,* "received or traditional lore") were first entrusted by God himself to a special group of angels in Paradise. After Man had been expelled from the Garden, some of these angels communicated the lessons to Adam, thinking to help him back to felicity thereby. From Adam the teaching passed to Noah, and from Noah to Abraham. Abraham let some of it slip from him while he was in Egypt, and that is why this sublime wisdom can now be found in reduced form in the myths and philosophies of the gentiles. Moses first studied it with the priests of Egypt, but the tradition was refreshed in him by the special instructions of his angels.

Makroprosopos is the Uncreated Uncreating and Mikroprosopos the Uncreated Creating: respectively, the silence and the syllable *AUM,* the unmanifest and the presence immanent in the cosmogonic round.

3. *Out of the Void—Space*

SAINT THOMAS AQUINAS declares: "The name of being wise is reserved to him alone whose consideration is about the end of the universe, which end is also the beginning of the universe."[17] The basic principle of all mythology is this of the beginning in the end. Creation myths are pervaded with a sense of the doom that is continually recalling all created shapes to the imperishable out of which they first emerged. The forms go forth powerfully, but inevitably reach their apogee, break, and return. Mythology, in this sense, is tragic in its view. But in the sense that it places our true being not in the forms that shatter but in the imperishable out of which they again immediately bubble forth, mythology is eminently untragical.[18] Indeed, wherever the mythological mood prevails, tragedy is impossible. A quality rather of dream prevails. True being, meanwhile, is not in the shapes but in the dreamer.

As in dream, the images range from the sublime to the ridiculous. The mind is not permitted to rest with its normal evaluations, but is continually insulted and shocked out of the assurance that now, at last, it has understood. Mythology is defeated when the mind rests solemnly with its favorite or traditional images, defending them as though they themselves were the message that they communicate. These images are to be regarded as no more than shadows from the unfathomable reach beyond, where the eye goeth not, speech goeth not, nor the mind, nor even piety. Like the trivialities of dream, those of myth are big with meaning.

The first phase of the cosmogonic cycle describes the breaking of formlessness into form, as in the following creation chant of the Maoris of New Zealand:

Te Kore (The Void)
Te Kore-tua-tahi (The First Void)
Te Kore-tua-rua (The Second Void)
Te Kore-nui (The Vast Void)
Te Kore-roa (The Far-Extending Void)

Te Kore-para (The Sere Void)
Te Kore-whiwhia (The Unpossessing Void)
Te Kore-rawea (The Delightful Void)
Te Kore-te-tamaua (The Void Fast Bound)
Te Po (The Night)
Te Po-teki (The Hanging Night)
Te Po-terea (The Drifting Night)
Te Po-whawha (The Moaning Night)
Hine-make-moe (The Daughter of Troubled Sleep)
Te Ata (The Dawn)
Te Au-tu-roa (The Abiding Day)
Te Ao-marama (The Bright Day)
Whai-tua (Space)

In space were evolved two existences without shape:

Maku (Moisture [a male])
Mahora-nui-a-rangi (Great Expanse of Heaven [a female])

From these sprang:

Rangi-potiki (The Heavens [a male])
Papa (Earth [a female])

Rangi-potiki and Papa were the parents of the gods.[19]

From the void beyond all voids unfold the world-sustaining emanations, plantlike, mysterious. The tenth of the above series is night; the eighteenth, space or ether, the frame of the visible world; the nineteenth is the male-female polarity; the twentieth is the universe we see. Such a series suggests the depth beyond depth of the mystery of being. The levels correspond to the profundities sounded by the hero in his world-fathoming adventure; they number the spiritual strata known to the mind introverted in meditation. They represent the bottomlessness of the dark night of the soul.*

The Hebrew Kabbala represents the process of creation as a series of emanations (Hebrew: *sephiroth*) out of the I AM of The Great Face. The first is the head itself, in profile, and from this proceed "nine splendid lights." The emanations are represented also as the branches of a cosmic tree, which is upside down, rooted in "the inscrutable height." The world that we see is the reverse image of that tree.

According to the Indian Samkhya philosophers of the eighth

* In the sacred writings of Mahāyāna Buddhism, eighteen "voidnesses" or degrees of the void are enumerated and described. These are experienced by the yogi and by the soul as it passes into death. See Evans-Wentz, *Tibetan Yoga and Secret Doctrine,* pp. 206, 239 f.

century B.C., the void condenses into the element ether or space. From this air is precipitated. From air comes fire, from fire water, and from water the element earth. With each element evolves a sense-function capable of perceiving it: hearing, touch, sight, taste, and smell respectively.[20]

An amusing Chinese myth personifies these emanating elements as five venerable sages, who come stepping out of a ball of chaos, suspended in the void:

> Before heaven and earth had become separated from each other, everything was a great ball of mist, called chaos. At that time, the spirits of the five elements took shape, and then developed into five ancients. The first was called the Yellow Ancient, and he was the master of earth. The second was called the Red Ancient, and he was the master of fire. The third was called the Dark Ancient, and he was the master of water. The fourth was called the Wood Prince, and he was the master of wood. The fifth was called the Metal Mother, and she was the mistress of metals.*
>
> Now each of these five ancients set in motion the primordial spirit from which he had proceeded, so that water and earth sank downward; the heavens soared aloft and the earth became fast in the depths. Then the water gathered into rivers and lakes, and the mountains and plains appeared. The heavens cleared and the earth divided; then there were sun, moon, and all the stars, sand, clouds, rain, and dew. The Yellow Ancient gave play to the purest power of the earth, and to this were added the operations of fire and water. Then there sprang into being the grasses and trees, birds and animals, and the generations of the snakes and insects, and fishes and turtles. The Wood Prince and the Metal Mother brought light and darkness together and thereby created the human race, as man and woman. Thus gradually appeared the world. . . .[21]

* The five elements according to the Chinese system are earth, fire, water, wood, and gold.

4. *Within Space—Life*

THE FIRST EFFECT of the cosmogonic emanations is the framing of the world stage of space; the second is the production of life within the frame: life polarized for self-reproduction under the dual form of the male and female. It is possible to represent the entire process in sexual terms, as a pregnancy and birth. This idea is superbly rendered in another metaphysical genealogy of the Maoris:

From the conception the increase,
From the increase the thought,
From the thought the remembrance,
From the remembrance the consciousness,
From the consciousness the desire.

The word became fruitful;
It dwelt with the feeble glimmering;
It brought forth night:
The great night, the long night,
The lowest night, the loftiest night,
The thick night, to be felt,
The night to be touched,
The night not to be seen,
The night ending in death.

From the nothing the begetting,
From the nothing the increase,
From the nothing the abundance,
The power of increasing,
The living breath.
It dwelt with the empty space, and produced
the atmosphere which is above us.

The atmosphere which floats above the earth,
The great firmament above us,
dwelt with the early dawn,
And the moon sprang forth;
The atmosphere above us,
dwelt with the glowing sky,

FIGURE 58. *Tangaroaā, Producing Gods and Men* (carved wood, Rurutu Island, early eighteenth century A.D.)

And thence proceeded the sun;
Moon and sun were thrown up above,
as the chief eyes of heaven:
Then the Heavens became light:
the early dawn, the early day,
The mid-day: the blaze of day from the sky.
The sky above dwelt with Hawaiki,
and produced land.[22]

About the middle of the nineteenth century, Paiore, a high chieftain of the Polynesian island of Anaa, drew a picture of the beginnings of creation. The first detail of this illustration was a little circle containing two elements, Te Tumu, "The Foundation" (a male), and Te Papa, "The Stratum Rock" (a female).[23]

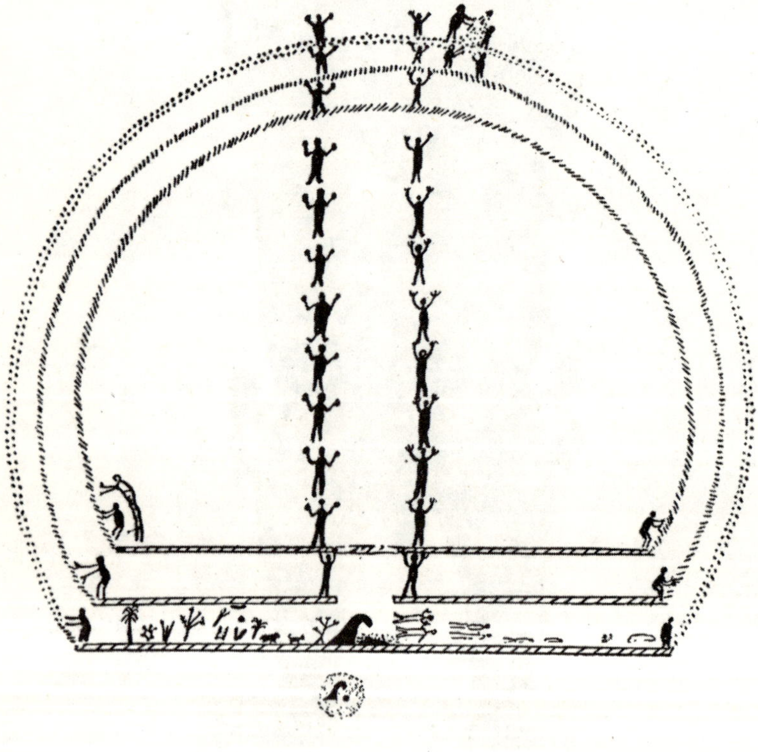

FIGURE 59. *Tuamotuan Creation Chart—Below: The Cosmic Egg. Above: The People Appear, and Shape the Universe* (Tuamotua, nineteenth century A.D.)

> The universe [said Paiore] was like an egg, which contained Te Tumu and Te Papa. It at last burst and produced three layers superposed—one layer below supporting two above. On the lowest layer remained Te Tumu and Te Papa, who created man, animals, and plants.
>
> The first man was Matata, produced without arms; he died shortly after he had come into being. The second man was Aitu, who came with one arm but without legs; and he died like his elder brother. Finally, the third man was Hoatea (Sky-space), and he was perfectly formed. After this came a woman named Hoatu (Fruitfulness of Earth). She became the wife of Hoatea and from them descended the human race.
>
> When the lowest layer of earth became filled with creation, the people made an opening in the middle of the layer above, so that they could get upon it also, and there they established themselves, taking with them plants and animals from below. Then they raised the third layer (so that it should form a ceiling to the second)... and ultimately established themselves up there also, so that human beings had three abodes.
>
> Above the earth were the skies, also superposed, reaching down and supported by their respective horizons, some being attached to those of the earth; and the people continued to work, expanding one sky above another in the same manner, until all were set in order.[24]

The main portion of Paiore's illustration shows the people spreading out the world, standing on each other's shoulders to elevate the skies. On the lowest stratum of this world appear the two original elements, Te Tumu and Te Papa. To the left of them are the plants and animals of their begetting. Over to the right are to be seen the first man, malformed, and the first successful men and women. In the upper sky appears a fire surrounded by four figures, representing an early event in the history of the world: "The creation of the universe was scarcely terminated when Tangaroaā, who delighted in doing evil, set fire to the highest heaven, seeking thus to destroy everything. But fortunately the fire was seen spreading by Tamatua, Oru, and Ruanuku, who quickly ascended from the earth and extinguished the flames."[25]

The image of the cosmic egg is known to many mythologies; it appears in the Greek Orphic, Egyptian, Finnish, Buddhistic, and Japanese. "In the beginning this world was merely nonbeing," we read in a sacred work of the Hindus;

> It was existent. It developed. It turned into an egg. It lay for the period of a year. It was split asunder. One of the two eggshell parts became silver, one gold. That which was of silver is the earth. That which was of gold is the sky. What was the outer membrane is the mountains. What was the inner membrane is cloud and mist. What were the veins are the rivers. What was the fluid within is the ocean. Now, what was born therefrom is yonder sun.[26]

The shell of the cosmic egg is the world frame of space, while the fertile seed-power within typifies the inexhaustible life dynamism of nature.

"Space is boundless by re-entrant form, not by great extension. *That which is* is a shell floating in the infinitude of *that which is not.*" This succinct formulation by a modern physicist, illustrating the world picture as he saw it in 1928,[27] gives precisely the sense of the mythological cosmic egg. Furthermore, the evolution of life, described by our modern science of biology, is the theme of the early stages of the cosmogonic cycle. Finally, the world destruction, which the physicists tell us must come with the exhaustion of our sun and ultimate running down of the whole cosmos,[28] stands presaged in the scar left by the fire of Tangaroaā: the world-destructive effects of the creator-destroyer will increase gradually until, at last, in the second course of the cosmogonic cycle, all will devolve into the sea of bliss.

Not uncommonly the cosmic egg bursts to disclose, swelling from within, an awesome figure in human form. This is the anthropomorphic personification of the power of generation, the Mighty Living One, as it is called in the Kabbala. "Mighty Ta'aroa whose curse was death, he is the creator of the world." Thus we hear from Tahiti, another of the South Sea Isles.* "He was alone. He had no father nor indeed a mother. Ta'aroa simply lived in the void. There was no land, nor sky, nor sea. Land was nebulous: there was no foundation. Ta'aroa then said:

> *O space for land, O space for sky,*
> *Useless world below existing in nebulous state,*
> *Continuing and continuing from time immemorial,*
> *Useless world below, extend!*

"The face of Ta'aroa appeared outside. The shell of Ta'aroa fell away and became land. Ta'aroa looked: Land had come into existence, sea had come into existence, sky had come into existence. Ta'aroa lived god-like contemplating his work."[29]

---

* Ta'aroa (Tahitian dialect) is Tangaroaā.

An Egyptian myth reveals the demiurge creating the world by an act of masturbation.[30] A Hindu myth displays him in yogic meditation, with the forms of his inner vision breaking forth from him (to his own astonishment) and standing then around him as a pantheon of brilliant gods.[31] And in another account from India the all-father is represented as first splitting into male and female, then procreating all the creatures according to kind:

> In the beginning, this universe was only the Self, in human form. He looked around and saw nothing but himself. Then, at the beginning, he cried out, "I am he." Whence came the name, *I.* That is why, even today, when a person is addressed, he first declares, "It is I," and then announces the other name that he goes by.
>
> He was afraid. That is why people are afraid to be alone. He thought, "But what am I afraid of? There is nothing but myself." Whereupon his fear was gone....
>
> He was unhappy. That is why people are not happy when they are alone. He wanted a mate. He became as big as a woman and man embracing. He divided this body, which was himself, in two parts. From that there came husband and wife.... Therefore this human body (before one marries a wife) is like one of the halves of a split pea.... He united with her; and from that were born men.
>
> She considered: "How can he unite with me after producing me from himself? Well then, let me hide myself." She became a cow; but he became a bull and united with her; from that were born cattle. She became a mare, he a stallion; she became a she-ass, he a he-ass and united with her; from that were born the one-hoofed animals. She became a she-goat, he a he-goat; she became a ewe, he a ram and united with her; from that were born goats and sheep. Thus did he project everything that exists in pairs, down to the ants.
>
> Then he knew: "Indeed I am myself the creation, for I have projected the entire world." Whence he was called Creation....[32]

The enduring substratum of the individual and of the progenitor of the universe are one and the same, according to these mythologies; that is why the demiurge in this myth is called the Self. The Oriental mystic discovers this deep-reposing, enduring presence in its original androgynous state when he plunges in meditation into his own interior.

> *Him on whom the sky, the earth, and the atmosphere*
> *Are woven, and the mind, together with all the life-breaths,*
> *Him alone know as the one Soul. Other*
> *Words dismiss. He is the bridge to immortality.*[33]

Thus it appears that though these myths of creation narrate of the remotest past, they speak at the same time of the present origin of the individual. "Each soul and spirit," we read in the Hebrew Zohar,

> prior to its entering into this world, consists of a male and female united into one being. When it descends on this earth the two parts separate and animate two different bodies. At the time of marriage, the Holy One, blessed be He, who knows all souls and spirits, unites them again as they were before, and they again constitute one body and one soul, forming as it were the right and left of one individual.... This union, however, is influenced by the deeds of the man and by the ways in which he walks. If the man is pure and his conduct is pleasing in the sight of God, he is united with that female part of his soul which was his component part prior to his birth.[34]

This kabbalistic text is a commentary to the scene in Genesis where Adam gives forth Eve. A similar conception appears in Plato's *Symposium.* According to this mysticism of sexual love, the ultimate experience of love is a realization that beneath the illusion of two-ness dwells identity: "each is both." This realization can expand into a discovery that beneath the multitudinous individualities of the whole surrounding universe—human, animal, vegetable, even mineral—dwells identity; whereupon the love experience becomes cosmic, and the beloved who first opened the vision is magnified as the mirror of creation. The man or woman knowing this experience is possessed of what Schopenhauer called "the science of beauty everywhere." He "goes up and down these worlds, eating what he desires, assuming what forms he desires," and he sits singing the song of universal unity, which begins: "Oh, wonderful! Oh, wonderful! Oh, wonderful!"[35]

5. The Breaking of the One into the Manifold

THE FORWARD ROLL of the cosmogonic round precipitates the One into the many. Herewith a great crisis, a rift, splits the created world into two apparently contradictory planes of being. In Paiore's chart the people emerge from the lower darknesses and immediately go to work to elevate the sky.[36] They are revealed as moving with an apparent independence. They hold councils, they decide, they plan; they take over the work of arranging the world. Yet we know that behind the scenes the Unmoved Mover is at work, like a puppetmaster.

In mythology, wherever the Unmoved Mover, the Mighty Living One, holds the center of attention, there is a miraculous spontaneity about the shaping of the universe. The elements condense and move into play of their own accord, or at the Creator's slightest word; the portions of the self-shattering cosmic egg go to their stations without aid. But when the perspective shifts, to focus on living beings, when the panorama of space and nature is faced from the standpoint of the personages ordained to inhabit it, then a sudden transformation overshadows the cosmic scene. No longer do the forms of the world appear to move in the patterns of a living, growing, harmonious thing, but stand recalcitrant, or at best inert. The props of the universal stage have to be adjusted, even beaten into shape. The earth brings forth thorns and thistles; man eats bread in the sweat of his brow.

Two modes of myth therefore confront us. According to one, the demiurgic forces continue to operate of themselves; according to the other, they give up the initiative and even set themselves against the further progress of the cosmogonic round. The difficulties represented in this latter form of myth begin even as early as during the long darkness of the original, creature-begetting embrace of the cosmic parents. Let the Maoris introduce us to this terrible theme:

Rangi (the Sky) lay so close on the belly of Papa (Mother Earth) that the children could not break free from the womb.

> They were in an unstable condition, floating about the world of darkness, and this was their appearance: some were crawling... some were upright with arms held up... some lying on their sides... some on their backs, some were stooping, some with their heads bent down, some with legs drawn up... some kneeling... some feeling about in the dark.... They were all within the embrace of Rangi and Papa....
>
> At last the beings who had been begotten by Heaven and Earth, worn out by the continued darkness, consulted among themselves, saying, "Let us now determine what we should do with Rangi and Papa, whether it would be better to slay them or to rend them apart." Then spake Tu-matauenga, the fiercest of the children of Heaven and Earth, "It is well, let us slay them."
>
> Then spake Tane-mahuta, the father of the forests and of all things that inhabit them, or that are constructed from trees. "Nay, not so. It is better to rend them apart, and to let the heaven stand far above us, and the earth lie under our feet. Let the sky become a stranger to us, but the earth remain close to us as our nursing mother."

Several of the brother gods vainly tried to rend apart the heavens and the earth. At last it was Tane-mahuta himself, the father of the forests and of all things that inhabit them, or that are constructed from trees, who succeeded in the titanic project.

> His head is now firmly planted on his mother the earth, his feet he raises up and rests against his father the skies, he strains his back and limbs with mighty effort. Now are rent apart Rangi and Papa, and with cries and groans of woe they shriek aloud.
>
> "Wherefore slay you thus your parents? Why commit you so dreadful a crime as to slay us, as to rend your parents apart?" But Tane-mahuta pauses not, he regards not their shrieks and cries; far, far beneath him he presses down the earth; far, far above him, he thrusts up the sky....[37]

As known to the Greeks, this story is rendered by Hesiod in his account of the separation of Ouranos (Father Heaven) from Gaia (Mother Earth). According to this variant, the Titan Kronos castrated his father with a sickle and pushed him up out of the way.[38] In Egyptian iconography the position of the cosmic couple is inverted: the sky is the mother, the father is the vitality of the earth;[39] but the pattern of the myth remains: the two were pushed asunder by their child, the air god Shu. Again the image comes to us from the ancient cuneiform texts of the Sumerians, dating from the third and fourth

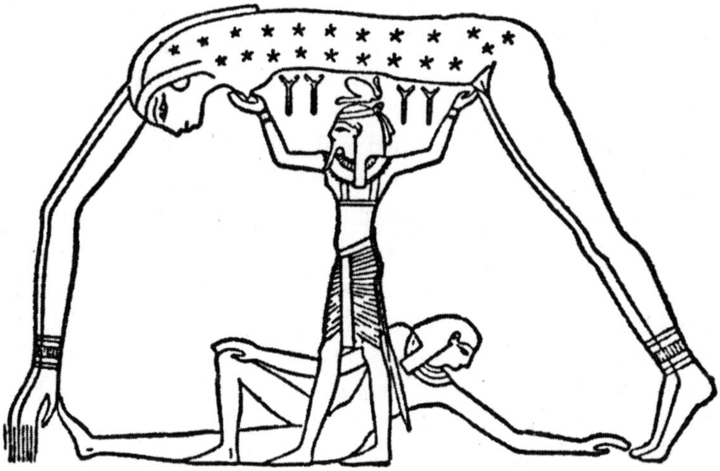

FIGURE 60. *The Separation of Sky and Earth* (Egypt, date uncertain)

millennia B.C. First was the primeval ocean; the primeval ocean generated the cosmic mountain, which consisted of heaven and earth united; An (the Heaven Father) and Ki (the Earth Mother) produced Enlil (the Air God), who presently separated An from Ki and then himself united with his mother to beget mankind.[40]

But if these deeds of the desperate children seem violent, they are as nothing compared with the total carving up of the parent power which we discover recorded in the Icelandic Eddas, and in the Babylonian *Tablets of Creation.* The final insult here is given in the characterization of the demiurgic presence of the abyss as "evil," "dark," "obscene." The bright young warrior-sons, now disdaining the generative source, the personage of the seed-state of deep sleep, summarily slay it, hack it, slice it into lengths, and carpenter it into the structure of the world. This is the pattern for victory of all our later slayings of the dragon, the beginning of the age-long history of the deeds of the hero.

According to the Eddic account, after the "yawning gap"* had given forth in the north a mist-world of cold and in the south a region of fire, and after the heat from the south had played on the rivers of ice that crowded down from the north, a yeasty venom began to be exuded. From this a drizzle arose, which in turn congealed to rime. The rime melted and dripped; life was quickened from the

* *Ginnungagap,* the void, the abyss of chaos into which all devolves at the end of the cycle ("Twilight of the Gods") and out of which then all appears again after a timeless age of reincubation.

drippings in the form of a torpid, gigantic, hermaphroditic, horizontal figure named Ymir. The giant slept, and as it slept it sweated; one of its feet begat with the other a son, while under its left hand germinated a man and wife.

The rime continually melted and dripped, and there condensed from it the cow, Audumla. From her udder flowed four streams of milk, which were drunk for nourishment by Ymir. But the cow, for her own nourishment, licked the iceblocks, which were salty. The evening of the first day she licked, a man's hair came forth from the blocks; the second day a man's head; the third, the entire man was there, and his name was Buri. Now Buri had a son (the mother is not known) named Borr, who married one of the giant daughters of the creatures that had sprung from Ymir. She gave birth to the trinity of Othin, Vili, and Ve, and these then slaughtered sleepful Ymir and carved the body into chunks.

Of Ymir's flesh the earth was fashioned,
And of his sweat the sea;
Crags of his bones, trees of his hair,
And of his skull the sky.
Then of his bones the blithe gods made
Midgard for sons of men;
And of his brain the bitter-mooded
Clouds were all created.[41]

FIGURE 61. *The Murder of Ymir* (lithograph, Denmark, A.D. 1845)

The Poetic Edda is a collection of thirty-four Old Norse poems treating of the pagan Germanic gods and heroes. The poems were composed by a number of singers and poets (scalds) in various parts of the Viking world (one, at least, in Greenland) during the period A.D. 900–1050. The collection was completed, apparently, in Iceland.

The Prose Edda is a handbook for young poets, written in Iceland by the Christian master-poet and chieftain, Snorri Sturluson (1178–1241). It summarizes the pagan Germanic myths and reviews the rules of scaldic rhetoric.

The mythology documented in these texts reveals an earlier, peasant stratum (associated with the thunderer, Thor), a later, aristocratic stratum (that of Wotan-Othin), and a third, distinctly phallic complex (Nyorth, Freya, and Frey). Bardic influences from Ireland mingle with Classical and Oriental themes in this profoundly brooded yet grotesquely humorous world of symbolic forms.

In the Babylonian version the hero is Marduk, the sun-god; the victim is Tiamat—terrifying, dragon-like, attended by swarms of demons—a female personification of the original abyss itself: chaos as the mother of the gods, but now the menace of the world. With bow and trident, club and net, and a convoy of battle-winds, the god mounted his chariot. The four horses, trained to trample underfoot, were flecked with foam.

. . . But Tiamat turned not her neck,
With lips that failed not she uttered rebellious words. . . .
Then the lord raised the thunderbolt, his mighty weapon,
And against Tiamat, who was raging, thus he sent the word:
"Thou art become great, thou hast exalted thyself on high,
And thy heart hath prompted thee to call to battle. . . .
And against the gods my fathers thou hast contrived thy
wicked plan.
Let then thy host be equipped, let thy weapons be girded on!
Stand! I and thou, let us join battle!"

When Tiamat heard these words,
She was like one possessed, she lost her reason.
Tiamat uttered wild, piercing cries,
She trembled and shook to her very foundations.
She recited an incantation, she pronounced her spell,
And the gods of the battle cried out for their weapons.

Then advanced Tiamat and Marduk, the counselor
of the gods;
To the fight they came on, to the battle they drew nigh.
The lord spread out his net and caught her.
And the evil wind that was behind him he let loose
in her face.
The terrible winds filled her belly,

And her courage was taken from her, and her mouth
she opened wide.
He seized the trident and burst her belly,
He severed her inward parts, he pierced her heart.
He overcame her and cut off her life;
He cast down her body and stood upon it.

Having then subdued the remainder of her swarming host, the god of Babylon returned to the mother of the world:

And the lord stood upon Tiamat's hinder parts,
And with his merciless club he smashed her skull.
He cut through the channels of her blood,
And he made the north wind bear it away into secret places. . . .
Then the lord rested, gazing upon her dead body, . . . and
devised a cunning plan,
He split her up like a flat fish into two halves;
One half of her he established as a covering for heaven.
He fixed a bolt, he stationed a watchman,
And bade them not to let her waters come forth.
He passed through the heavens, he surveyed the regions thereof,
And over against the Deep he set the dwelling of Nudimmud.
And the Lord measured the structure of the Deep. . . .[42]

Marduk in this heroic manner pushed back with a ceiling the waters above, and with a floor the waters beneath. Then in the world between he created man.

The myths never tire of illustrating the point that conflict in the created world is not what it seems. Tiamat, though slain and dismembered, was not thereby undone. Had the battle been viewed from another angle, the chaos-monster would have been seen to shatter of her own accord, and her fragments move to their respective stations. Marduk and his whole generation of divinities were but particles of her substance. From the standpoint of those created forms all seemed accomplished as by a mighty arm, amid danger and pain. But from the center of the emanating presence, the flesh was yielded willingly, and the hand that carved it was ultimately no more than an agent of the will of the victim herself.

Herein lies the basic paradox of myth: the paradox of the dual focus. Just as at the opening of the cosmogonic cycle it was possible to say "God is not involved," but at the same time "God is creator-preserver-destroyer," so now at this critical juncture, where the One breaks into the many, destiny "happens," but at the same time "is

FIGURE 62. *Chaos Monster and Sun God* (carved alabaster, Assyria, 885–860 B.C.)

brought about." From the perspective of the source, the world is a majestic harmony of forms pouring into being, exploding, and dissolving. But what the swiftly passing creatures experience is a terrible cacaphony of battle cries and pain. The myths do not deny this agony (the crucifixion); they reveal within, behind, and around it essential peace (the heavenly rose).[43]

The shift of perspective from the repose of the central Cause to the turbulation of the peripheral effects is represented in the Fall of Adam and Eve in the Garden of Eden. They ate of the forbidden fruit, "And the eyes of them both were opened."[44] The bliss of Paradise was closed to them and they beheld the created field from the other side of a transforming veil. Henceforth they should experience the inevitable as the hard to gain.

6. Folk Stories of Creation

The simplicity of the origin stories of the undeveloped folk mythologies stands in contrast to the profoundly suggestive myths of the cosmogonic cycle. No long-sustained attempt to fathom the mysteries behind the veil of space makes itself apparent in these. Through the blank wall of timelessness there breaks and enters a shadowy creator-figure to shape the world of forms. His clay is dreamlike in its duration, fluidity, and ambient power. The earth has not yet hardened; much remains to be done to make it habitable for the future people.

A broad distinction can be made between the mythologies of the truly primitive (fishing, hunting, root-digging, and berry-picking) peoples and those of the civilizations that came into being following the development of the arts of agriculture, dairying, and herding, c. 6000 B.C. Most of what we call primitive, however, is actually colonial, i.e., diffused from some high culture center and adapted to the needs of a simpler society. It is in order to avoid the misleading term "primitive" that I am calling the undeveloped or degenerate traditions "folk mythologies." The term is adequate for the purposes of the present elementary comparative study of the universal forms, though it would certainly not serve for a strict historical analysis.

Old Man was traveling about, declare the Blackfeet of Montana; he was making people and arranging things.

> He came from the south, traveling north, making animals and birds as he passed along. He made the mountains, prairies, timber, and brush first. So he went along, traveling northward, making things as he went, putting rivers here and there, and falls on them, putting red paint here and there in the ground—fixing up the world as we see it today. He made the Milk River (the Teton) and crossed it, and, being tired, went up on a hill and lay down to rest. As he lay on his back, stretched out on the ground, with arms extended, he marked himself out with stones—the shape of his body, head, legs, arms, and everything. There you can see those rocks to-day. After he had rested, he went on northward, and stumbled over a knoll and fell down on his knees. Then he said, "You are a

> bad thing to be stumbling against"; so he raised up two large buttes there, and named them the Knees, and they are called so to this day. He went further north, and with some of the rocks he carried with him he built the Sweet Grass Hills....
>
> One day Old Man determined that he would make a woman and a child; so he formed them both—the woman and the child, her son—of clay. After he had moulded the clay in human shape, he said to the clay, "You must be people," and then he covered it up and left it, and went away. The next morning he went to the place and took the covering off, and saw that the clay shapes had changed a little. The second morning there was still more change, and the third still more. The fourth morning he went to the place, took the covering off, looked at the images, and told them to rise and walk; and they did so. They walked to the river with their Maker, and then he told them that his name was Na'pi, Old Man.
>
> As they were standing by the river, the woman said to him, "How is it? Will we always live, will there be no end to it?" He said: "I have never thought of that. We will have to decide it. I will take this buffalo chip and throw it in the river. If it floats, when people die, in four days they will become alive again; they will die for only four days. But if it sinks, there will be an end to them." He threw the chip in the river, and it floated. The woman turned and picked up a stone, and said: "No, I will throw this stone in the river; if it floats, we will always live, if it sinks people must die, that they may always be sorry for each other." The woman threw the stone into the water, and it sank. "There," said Old Man, "you have chosen. There will be an end to them."[45]

The arranging of the world, the creation of man, and the decision about death are typical themes from the tales of the primitive creator. It is difficult to know how seriously or in what sense these stories were believed. The mythological mode is one not so much of direct as of oblique reference: it is *as if* Old Man had done so-and-so. Many of the tales that appear in the collections under the category of origin stories were certainly regarded more as popular fairy tales than as a book of genesis. Such playful mythologizing is common in all civilizations, higher as well as lower. The simpler members of the populations may regard the resultant images with undue seriousness, but in the main they cannot be said to represent doctrine, or the local "myth." The Maoris, for example, from whom we have some of our finest cosmogonies, have the story of an egg dropped by a bird into the primeval sea; it burst, and out came a man, a woman, a boy, a girl, a pig, a dog, and a canoe. All got into the canoe and drifted to New Zealand.[46] This clearly is a burlesque of the cosmic egg. On the other hand, the Kamchatkans declare, apparently in all seriousness, that God inhabited heaven originally, but then descended to earth. When he traveled about on his snowshoes, the new ground yielded under him like thin and pliant ice. The land has been uneven ever since.[47] Or again, according to the Central Asiatic Kirghiz, when two early people tending a great ox had been without drink for a very long time and were nearly dead of thirst, the animal got water for them by ripping open the ground with its big horns. That is how the lakes in the country of the Kirghiz were made.[48]

A clown figure working in continuous opposition to the well-wishing creator very often appears in myth and folktale, as accounting for the ills and difficulties of existence this side of the veil. The Melanesians of New Britain tell of an obscure being, "the one who was first there," who drew two male figures on the ground, scratched open his own skin, and sprinkled the drawings with his blood. He plucked two large leaves and covered the figures, which became, after a while, two men. The names of the men were To Kabinana and To Karvuvu.

To Kabinana went off alone, climbed a coconut tree that had light yellow nuts, picked two that were still unripe, and threw them to the ground; they broke and became two handsome women. To Karvuvu admired the women and asked how his brother had come by them. "Climb a coconut tree," To Kabinana said, "pick two unripe nuts, and throw them to the ground." But To Karvuvu threw the nuts point downward, and the women who came from them had flat ugly noses.[49]

One day To Kabinana carved a Thum-fish out of wood and let it swim off into the ocean, so that it should be a living fish forever after. Now this Thum-fish drove the Malivaran-fish to the shore, where To Kabinana simply gathered them up from the beach. To Karvuvu admired the Thum-fish and wanted to make one, but when he was taught how, he carved a shark instead. This shark ate the Malivaran-fish instead of driving them ashore. To Karvuvu, crying, went to his brother and said: "I wish I had not made that fish; he does nothing but eat up all the others." "What sort of fish is it?" he was asked. "Well," he answered, "I made a shark." "You really are a disgusting fellow," his brother said. "Now you have fixed it so that our mortal

FIGURE 63. *Khnemu Shapes Pharaoh's Son on a Potter's Wheel While Thoth Marks Life Span* (papyrus, Ptolemaic, Egypt, c. third–first century B.C.)

descendants shall suffer. That fish of yours will eat up all the others, and people too."[50]

Behind this foolishness, it is possible to see that the one cause (the obscure being who cut himself) yields within the frame of the world dual effects—good and evil. The story is not as naïve as it appears.[51] Furthermore, the metaphysical pre-existence of the Platonic archetype of the shark is implied in the curious logic of the final dialogue. This is a conception inherent in every myth. Universal too is the casting of the antagonist, the representative of evil, in the role of the clown. Devils—both the lusty thickheads and the sharp, clever deceivers—are always clowns. Though they may triumph in the world of space and time, both they and their work simply disappear when the perspective shifts to the transcendental. They are the mistakers of shadow for substance: they symbolize the inevitable imperfections of the realm of shadow, and so long as we remain this side the veil cannot be done away.

The Black Tatars of Siberia say that when the demiurge Pajana fashioned the first human beings, he found that he was unable to produce a life-giving spirit for them. So he had to go up to heaven and procure souls from Kudai, the High God, leaving meanwhile a naked dog to guard the figures of his manufacture. The devil, Erlik, arrived while he was away. And Erlik said to the dog: "Thou hast no hair. I will give thee golden hair if thou wilt give into my hands these soulless people." The proposal pleased the dog, and he gave the people he was guarding to the tempter. Erlik defiled them with his spittle, but took flight the moment he saw God approaching to give them life. God saw what had been done, and so he turned the human bodies inside out. That is why we have spittle and impurity in our intestines.[52]

FIGURE 64. *Edshu the Trickster* (carved wood, cowries, and leather; Yoruba; Nigeria; nineteenth–early twentieth century A.D.)

The folk mythologies take up the story of creation only at the moment where the transcendental emanations break into spatial forms. Nevertheless, they do not differ from the great mythologies on any essential point in their evaluations of human circumstance. Their symbolic personages correspond in import—frequently also in trait and deed—to those of the higher iconographies, and the wonder world in which they move is precisely that of the greater revelations: the world and the age between deep sleep and waking consciousness, the zone where the One breaks into the manifold and the many are reconciled in the One.

Breaking free from cosmogonic associations, the negative, clown-devil aspect of the demiurgic power has become a particular favorite in the tales told for amusement. A vivid example is Coyote of the American plains. Reynard the Fox is a European incarnation of this figure.

FIGURE 65. *Tlazolteotl Giving Birth* (carved aplite with garnet inclusions, Aztec, Mexico, late fifteenth–early sixteenth century A.D.)

CHAPTER II

The Virgin Birth

1. Mother Universe

THE WORLD-GENERATING SPIRIT of the father passes into the manifold of earthly experience through a transforming medium—the mother of the world. She is a personification of the primal element named in the second verse of Genesis, where we read that "the spirit of God moved upon *the face of the waters.*" In the Hindu myth, she is the female figure through whom the Self begot all creatures. More abstractly understood, she is the world-bounding frame: "space, time, and causality"—the shell of the cosmic egg. More abstractly still, she is the lure that moved the Self-brooding Absolute to the act of creation.

In mythologies emphasizing the maternal rather than the paternal aspect of the creator, this original female fills the world stage in the beginning, playing the roles that are elsewhere assigned to males. And she is virgin, because her spouse is the Invisible Unknown.

A strange representation of this figure is to be found in the mythology of the Finns. In Runo I of the *Kalevala*[1] it is told how the virgin daughter of the air descended from the sky mansions into the primeval sea, and there for centuries floated on the everlasting waters.

Then a storm arose in fury,
From the East a mighty tempest,
And the sea was wildly foaming,
And the waves dashed ever higher.
Thus the tempest rocked the virgin,

And the billows drove the maiden,
O'er the ocean's azure surface,
On the crest of foaming billows,
Till the wind that blew around her,
And the sea woke life within her.[2]

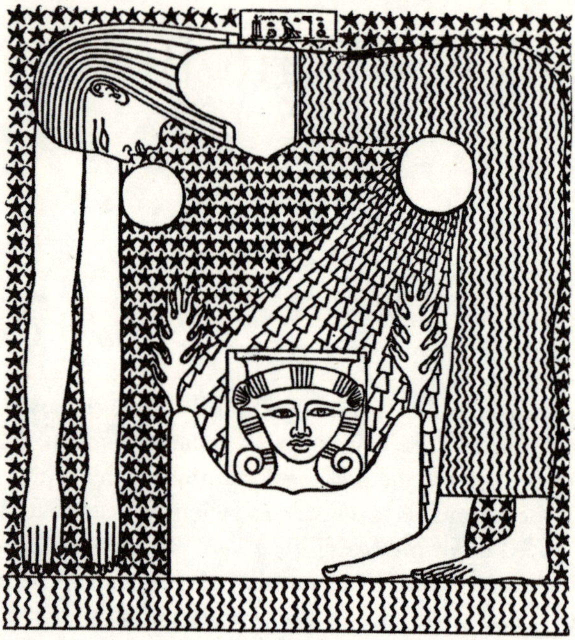

FIGURE 66. *Nut (the Sky) Gives Birth to the Sun; Its Rays Fall on Hathor in the Horizon (Love and Life)* (carved stone, Ptolemaic, Egypt, c. first century B.C.)

The *Kalevala* ("The Land of Heroes") in its present form is the work of Elias Lönnrot (1802–1884), a country physician and student of Finnish philology. Having collected a considerable body of folk poetry around the legendary heroes Väinämöinen, Ilmarinen, Lemminkainen, and Kullervo, he composed these in co-ordinated sequence and cast them in a uniform verse (1835, 1849). The work comes to some 23,000 lines.

A German translation of Lönnrot's *Kalevala* came under the eyes of Henry Wadsworth Longfellow, who thereupon both conceived the plan and chose the meter of his *Song of Hiawatha.*

For seven centuries the Water-Mother floated with the child in her womb, unable to give it birth. She prayed to Ukko, the highest god, and he sent a teal to build its nest on her knee. The teal's eggs fell from the knee and broke; the fragments formed the earth, sky, sun, moon, and clouds. Then the Water-Mother, floating still, herself began the work of the World-Shaper.

When the ninth year had passed over,
*And the summer tenth was passing,**
From the sea her head she lifted,
And her forehead she uplifted,
And she then began Creation,
And she brought the world to order,
On the open ocean's surface,
On the far extending waters.
Wheresoe'er her hand she pointed,
There she formed the jutting headlands;
Wheresoe'er her feet she rested,
There she formed the caves for fishes;
When she dived beneath the water,
There she formed the depths of ocean;
When towards the land she turned her,
There the level shores extended;
Where her feet to land extended,
Spots were formed for salmon netting;
Where her head the land touched lightly,
There the curving bays extended.
Further from the land she floated,
And abode in open water,
And created rocks in ocean,
And the reefs that eyes behold not,
Where the ships are often shattered,
And the sailors' lives are ended.[3]

But the babe remained in her body, growing towards a sentimental middle age:

Still unborn was Väinämöinen:
Still unborn the hard immortal.
Väinämöinen, old and steadfast,
Rested in his mother's body
For the space of thirty summers,
And the sum of thirty winters,
Ever on the placid waters,
And upon the foaming billows.
So he pondered and reflected
How he could continue living

* That is, the tenth summer after the breaking of the eggs of the teal.

In a resting place so gloomy,
In a dwelling far too narrow,
Where he could not see the moonlight,
Neither could behold the sunlight.
Then he spake the words which follow,
And expressed his thoughts in this wise:
"Aid me Moon, and Sun release me,
And the Great Bear lend his counsel,
Through the portal that I know not,
Through the unaccustomed passage.
From the little nest that holds me,
From a dwelling-place so narrow,
To the land conduct the roamer,
To the open air conduct me,
To behold the moon in heaven,
And the splendor of the sunlight;
See the Great Bear's stars above me,
And the shining stars in heaven."
When the moon no freedom gave him,
Neither did the sun release him,
Then he wearied of existence,
And his life became a burden.
Thereupon he moved the portal,
With his finger, fourth in number,
Opened quick the bony gateway,
With the toes upon his left foot,
With his knees beyond the gateway.
Headlong in the water falling,
With his hands the waves repelling,
Thus the man remained in ocean,
And the hero on the billows.[4]

Before Väinämöinen—hero already in his birth—could make his way ashore, the ordeal of a second mother-womb remained to him, that of the elemental cosmic ocean. Unprotected now, he had to undergo the initiation of nature's fundamentally inhuman forces. On the level of water and wind he had to experience again what he already so well knew.

In the sea five years he sojourned,
Waited five years, waited six years,
Seven years also, even eight years,
On the surface of the ocean,
By a nameless promontory,

Near a barren, treeless country.
On the land his knees he planted,
And upon his arms he rested,
Rose that he might view the moonbeams,
And enjoy the pleasant sunlight,
See the Great Bear's stars above him,
And the shining stars in heaven.
Thus was ancient Väinämöinen,
He, the ever famous minstrel,
Born of the divine Creatrix,
Born of Ilmatar, his mother.[5]

2. *Matrix of Destiny*

THE UNIVERSAL GODDESS makes her appearance to men under a multitude of guises; for the effects of creation are multitudinous, complex, and of mutually contradictory kind when experienced from the viewpoint of the created world. The mother of life is at the same time the mother of death; she is masked in the ugly demonesses of famine and disease.

The Sumero-Babylonian astral mythology identified the aspects of the cosmic female with the phases of the planet Venus. As morning star she was the virgin, as evening star the harlot, as lady of the night sky the consort of the moon; and when extinguished under the blaze of the sun she was the hag of hell. Wherever the Mesopotamian influence extended, the traits of the goddess were touched by the light of this fluctuating star.

A myth from southeast Africa, collected from the Wahungwe Makoni tribe of South Rhodesia, displays the aspects of the Venus-mother in co ordination with the first stages of the cosmogonic cycle. Here the original man is the moon; the morning star his first wife, the evening star his second. Just as Väinämöinen emerged from the womb by his own act, so this moon man emerges from the abyssal waters. He and his wives are to be the parents of the creatures of the earth. The story comes to us as follows:

Maori (God) made the first man and called him Mwuetsi (moon). He put him on the bottom of a Dsivoa (lake) and gave him a *ngona* horn filled with *ngona* oil.* Mwuetsi lived in Dsivoa.

Mwuetsi said to Maori: "I want to go on the earth." Maori said: "You will rue it." Mwuetsi said: "None the less, I want to go on the earth." Maori said: "Then go on the earth." Mwuetsi went out of Dsivoa and on to the earth.

The earth was cold and empty. There were no grasses, no bushes, no trees. There were no animals. Mwuetsi wept and said to Maori: "How shall I live here?" Maori said: "I warned you. You have started on the path at the end of which you shall die. I will, however, give you one of your kind." Maori gave Mwuetsi a maiden who was called Massassi, the morning star. Maori said: "Massassi shall be your wife for two years." Maori gave Massassi a fire maker.

In the evening Mwuetsi went into a cave with Massassi. Massassi said: "Help me. We will make a fire. I will gather *chimandra* (kindling) and you can twirl the *rusika* (revolving part of the fire maker)." Massassi gathered kindling. Mwuetsi twirled the *rusika.* When the fire was lighted Mwuetsi lay down on one side of it, Massassi on the other. The fire burned between them.

Mwuetsi thought to himself, "Why has Maori given me this maiden? What shall I do with this maiden, Massassi?" When it was night Mwuetsi took his *ngona* horn. He moistened his index finger with a drop of *ngona* oil. Mwuetsi said, "*Ndini chaambuka mhiri ne mhirir* (I am going to jump over the fire)." [This sentence is many times repeated in a melodramatic, ceremonial tone—Translators.] Mwuetsi jumped over the fire. Mwuetsi approached the maiden, Massassi. Mwuetsi touched Massassi's body with the ointment on his finger. Then Mwuetsi went back to his bed and slept.

When Mwuetsi wakened in the morning he looked over to Massassi. Mwuetsi saw that Massassi's body was swollen. When day broke Massassi began to bear. Massassi bore grasses. Massassi bore bushes. Massassi bore trees. Massassi did not stop bearing till the earth was covered with grasses, bushes, and trees.

The trees grew. They grew till their tops reached the sky. When the tops of the trees reached the sky it began to rain.

Mwuetsi and Massassi lived in plenty. They had fruits and grain. Mwuetsi built a house. Mwuetsi made an iron shovel. Mwuetsi

---

* This horn and oil play a conspicuous role in the folklore of South Rhodesia [the modern-day nation of Zimbabwe—Ed.]. The *ngona* horn is a wonder-working instrument, with the power to create fire and lightning, to impregnate the living, and to resurrect the dead.

made a hoe and planted crops. Massassi plaited fish traps and caught fish. Massassi fetched wood and water. Massassi cooked. Thus Mwuetsi and Massassi lived for two years.

After two years Maori said to Massassi, "The time is up." Maori took Massassi from the earth and put her hack in Dsivoa. Mwuetsi wailed. He wailed and wept and said to Maori: "What shall I do without Massassi? Who will fetch wood and water for me? Who will cook for me?" Eight days long Mwuetsi wept.

Eight days long Mwuetsi wept. Then Maori said: "I have warned you that you are going to your death. But I will give you another woman. I will give you Morongo, the evening star. Morongo will stay with you for two years. Then I shall take her back again." Maori gave Mwuetsi Morongo.

Morongo came to Mwuetsi in the hut. In the evening Mwuetsi wanted to lie down on his side of the fire. Morongo said: "Do not lie down over there. Lie with me." Mwuetsi lay down beside Morongo. Mwuetsi took the *ngona* horn, put some ointment on his index finger. But Morongo said: "Don't be like that. I am not like Massassi. Now smear your loins with *ngona* oil. Smear my loins with *ngona* oil." Mwuetsi did as he was told. Morongo said: "Now couple with me." Mwuetsi coupled with Morongo. Mwuetsi went to sleep.

Towards morning Mwuetsi woke. As he looked over to Morongo he saw that her body was swollen. As day broke Morongo began to give birth. The first day Morongo gave birth to chickens, sheep, goats.

The second night Mwuetsi slept with Morongo again. The next morning she bore eland and cattle.

The third night Mwuetsi slept with Morongo again. The next morning Morongo bore first boys and then girls. The boys who were born in the morning were grown up by nightfall.

On the fourth night Mwuetsi wanted to sleep with Morongo again. But there came a thunderstorm and Maori spoke: "Let be. You are going quickly to your death." Mwuetsi was afraid. The thunderstorm passed over. When it had gone Morongo said to Mwuetsi: "Make a door and then use it to close the entrance to the hut. Then Maori will not be able to see what we are doing. Then you can sleep with me." Mwuetsi made a door. With it he closed the entrance to the hut. Then he slept with Morongo. Mwuetsi slept.

Towards morning Mwuetsi woke. Mwuetsi saw that Morongo's body was swollen. As day broke Morongo began to give birth. Morongo bore lions, leopards, snakes, and scorpions. Maori saw it. Maori said to Mwuetsi: "I warned you."

FIGURE 67. *The Moon King and His People* (rock painting, prehistoric, Zimbabwe, c. 1500 B.C.)

On the fifth night Mwuetsi wanted to sleep with Morongo again. But Morongo said: "Look, your daughters are grown. Couple with your daughters." Mwuetsi looked at his daughters. He saw that they were beautiful and that they were grown up. So he slept with them. They bore children. The children which were born in the morning were full grown by night. And so Mwuetsi became the Mambo (king) of a great people.

But Morongo slept with the snake. Morongo no longer gave birth. She lived with the snake. One day Mwuetsi returned to Morongo and wanted to sleep with her. Morongo said: "Let be." Mwuetsi said: "But I want to." He lay with Morongo. Under Morongo's bed lay the snake. The snake bit Mwuetsi. Mwuetsi sickened.

After the snake had bitten Mwuetsi, Mwuetsi sickened. The next day it did not rain. The plants withered. The rivers and lakes dried. The animals died. The people began to die. Many people died. Mwuetsi's children asked: "What can we do?" Mwuetsi's children said: "We will consult the *hakata* (sacred dice)." The children consulted the *hakata*. The *hakata* said: "Mwuetsi the Mambo is sick and pining. Send Mwuetsi back to the Dsivoa."

Thereupon Mwuetsi's children strangled Mwuetsi and buried him. They buried Morongo with Mwuetsi. Then they chose another man to be Mambo. Morongo, too, had lived for two years in Mwuetsi's Zimbabwe.[6*]

It is clear that each of the three stages of procreation represents an epoch in the development of the world. The pattern for the procession was foreknown, almost as something already observed; this is indicated by the warning of the All Highest. But the Moon Man, the Mighty Living One, would not be denied the realization of his destiny. The conversation at the bottom of the lake is the dialogue of eternity and time, the "Colloquy of the Quick": "To be, or not to be." Unquenchable desire is finally given its rope: movement begins.

The wives and daughters of the Moon Man are the personifications and precipitators of his destiny. With the evolution of his world-creative will the virtues and features of the goddess-mother were metamorphosed. After the birth from the elemental womb, the first two wives were prehuman, suprahuman. But as the cosmogonic round proceeded and the growing moment passed from its primordial to its human historical forms, the mistresses of the cosmic births

* Zimbabwe means roughly "the royal court." The enormous prehistoric ruins near Fort Victoria are called "The Great Zimbabwe"; other stone ruins throughout Southern Rhodesia are called "Little Zimbabwe." [Note by Frobenius and Fox, *African Genesis*.]

withdrew, and the field remained to the women of men. Thereupon the old demiurgic sire in the midst of his community became a metaphysical anachronism. When at last he grew tired of the merely human and yearned back again to the wife of his abundance, the world sickened a moment under the pull of his reaction, but then released itself and ran free. The initiative passed to the community of the children. The symbolic, dream-heavy parental figures subsided into the original abyss. Only man remained on the furnished earth. The cycle had moved on.

3. *Womb of Redemption*

THE WORLD OF HUMAN LIFE is now the problem. Guided by the practical judgment of the kings and the instruction of the priests of the dice of divine revelation (see the *hakata* of Mwuetsi's children, p. 263), the field of consciousness so contracts that the grand lines of the human comedy are lost in a welter of cross-purposes. Men's perspectives become flat, comprehending only the light-reflecting, tangible surfaces of existence. The vista into depth closes over. The significant form of the human agony is lost to view. Society lapses into mistake and disaster. The Little Ego has usurped the judgment seat of the Self.

This is in myth a perpetual theme, in the voices of the prophets a familiar cry. The people yearn for some personality who, in a world of twisted bodies and souls, will represent again the lines of the incarnate image. We are familiar with the myth from our own tradition. It occurs everywhere, under a variety of guises. When the Herod figure (the extreme symbol of the misgoverning, tenacious ego) has brought mankind to the nadir of spiritual abasement, the occult forces of the cycle begin of themselves to move. In an inconspicuous village the maid is born who will maintain herself undefiled of the fashionable errors of her generation: a miniature in the midst of men of the cosmic woman who was the bride of the wind. Her womb, remaining fallow as the primordial abyss, summons to itself by its very readiness the original power that fertilized the void.

"Now on a certain day, while Mary stood near the fountain to fill her pitcher, the angel of the Lord appeared unto her, saying, 'Blessed art thou, Mary, for in thy womb thou hast prepared a habitation for the Lord. Behold, light from heaven shall come and dwell in thee, and through thee shall shine in all the world.'"[7]

The story is recounted everywhere; and with such striking uniformity of the main contours, that the early Christian missionaries were forced to think that the devil himself must be throwing up mockeries of their teaching wherever they set their hand. Fray Pedro Simón reports, in his *Noticias historiales de las conquistes de Tierra Firme en las Indias Occidentales* (Cuenca, 1627), that after work had been begun amongst the peoples of Tunja and Sogamozzo in Colombia, South America,

> the demon of that place began giving contrary doctrines. And among other things, he sought to discredit what the priest had been teaching concerning the Incarnation, declaring that it had not yet come to pass; but that presently the Sun would bring it to pass by taking flesh in the womb of a virgin of the village of Guacheta, causing her to conceive by the rays of the sun while she yet remained a virgin. These tidings were proclaimed throughout the region. And it so happened that the head man of the village named had two virgin daughters, each desirous that the miracle should become accomplished in her. These then began going out from their father's dwellings and garden-enclosure every morning at the first peep of dawn; and mounting one of the numerous hills about the village, in the direction of the sunrise, they disposed themselves in such a way that the first rays of the sun would be free to shine upon them. This going on for a number of days, it was granted the demon by divine permission (whose judgments are incomprehensible) that things should come to pass as he had planned, and in such fashion that one of the daughters became pregnant, as she declared, by the sun. Nine months and she brought into the world a large and valuable *hacuata*, which in their language is an emerald. The woman took this, and, wrapping it in cotton, placed it between her breasts, where she kept it a number of days, at the end of which time it was transformed into a living creature: all by order of the demon. The child was named Goranchacho, and he was reared in the household of the head man, his grandfather, until he was some twenty-four years of age.

Then he proceeded in triumphant procession to the capital of the nation, and was celebrated throughout the provinces as the "Child of the Sun."[8]

Hindu mythology tells of the maiden Pārvatī, daughter of the mountain king, Himalaya, who retreated into the high hills to practice very severe austerities. A tyrant-titan named Taraka had usurped the mastery of the world, and, according to the prophecy, only a son of the High God Śiva could overthrow him. Śiva, however, was the pattern god of yoga—aloof, alone, indrawn in meditation. It was impossible that Śiva should ever be moved to beget a son.

Pārvatī determined to change the world situation by matching Śiva in meditation. Aloof, alone, indrawn into her soul, she too fasted naked beneath the blazing sun, even adding to the heat by building four additional great fires, to each of the four quarters. The handsome body shriveled to a brittle construction of bones, the skin became leathery and hard. Her hair stood matted and wild. The soft liquid eyes burned.

One day a Brahmin youth arrived and asked why anyone so beautiful should be destroying herself with such torture.

"My desire," she replied, "is Śiva, the Highest Object. Śiva is a god of solitude and unshakable concentration. I therefore am practicing these austerities to move him from his state of balance and bring him to me in love."

"Śiva," the youth said, "is a god of destruction. Śiva is the World Annihilator. Śiva's delight is to meditate in burial grounds amidst the reek of corpses; there he beholds the rot of death, and that is congenial to his devastating heart. Śiva's garlands are of living serpents. Śiva is a pauper, furthermore, and no one knows anything of his birth."

The virgin said: "He is beyond the mind of such as you. A pauper, but the fountainhead of wealth; terrifying but the source of grace; snake-garlands or jewel-garlands he can assume or put off at will. How should he have been born, when he is the creator of the uncreated! Śiva is my love."

The youth thereupon put away his disguise—and was Śiva.[9]

4. *Folk Stories of Virgin Motherhood*

THE BUDDHA DESCENDED from heaven to his mother's womb in the shape of a milk-white elephant. The Aztec Coatlicue, "She of the Serpent-woven Skirt," was approached by a god in the form of a ball of feathers. The chapters of Ovid's *Metamorphoses* swarm with nymphs beset by gods in sundry masquerades: Jove as a bull, a swan, a shower of gold. Any leaf accidentally swallowed, any nut, or even the breath of a breeze, may be enough to fertilize the ready womb. The procreating power is everywhere. And according to the whim or destiny of the hour, either a hero-savior or a world-annihilating demon may be conceived—one can never know.

Images of virgin birth abound in the popular tales as well as in myth. One example will suffice: a queer folktale from Tonga, belonging to a little cycle of stories told of the "handsome man," Sinilau. This tale is of particular interest, not because of its extreme absurdity, but because it clearly announces, in unconscious burlesque, every one of the major motifs of the typical life of the hero: virgin birth, quest for the father, ordeal, atonement with the father, the assumption and coronation of the virgin mother, and finally, the heavenly triumph of the true sons while the pretenders are heated hot.

> There was once a certain man and his wife, and the woman was pregnant. When her time came to be delivered of her child she called her husband to come and lift her, that she might give birth. But she bore a clam, and her husband threw her down in anger. She, however, bade him take the clam, and leave it in Sinilau's bathing-pool. Now Sinilau came to bathe, and flung the coconut-husk that he had used to wash himself with on the water. The clam slid along and sucked the coconut-husk, and became pregnant.
>
> One day the woman, the mother of the clam, saw the clam rolling along toward her. She angrily asked the clam why she had come, but the shellfish replied that it was no time for anger, and asked her to curtain off a place in which she could give birth. So a

FIGURE 68. *Coatlicue of the Serpent-woven Skirt, Earth Mother* (carved stone, Aztec, Mexico, late fifteenth century A.D.)

screen was placed, and the clam gave birth to a fine big baby boy. Then she rolled off back to her pool, and the woman cared for the child, who was named Fatai-going-underneath-sandalwood. Time went on, and lo, the clam was again with child, and once more came rolling along to the house that she might give birth there to her child. The performance was repeated and again the clam bore a fine boy, who was named Myrtle-twined-at-random-in-the-fatai. He, too, was left with the woman and her husband to be cared for.

When the two children had grown up to manhood the woman heard that Sinilau was going to hold a festival, and she determined that her two grandsons should be present. So she called the youths, and bade them prepare, adding that the man to whose festival they were going was their father. When they came to where the festival was being held they were gazed at by all the people. There was not a woman but had her eyes fixed on them. As they went along a group of women called to them to turn aside to them, but the two youths refused, and went on, until they came to where the kava was being drunk. There they served the kava.

But Sinilau, angry at their disturbing his festival, ordered two bowls to be brought. Then he bade his men seize one of the youths and cut him up. So the bamboo knife was sharpened to cut him, but when its point was placed on his body it just slipped over his skin, and he cried out:

The knife is placed and slips,
Do thou but sit and gaze at us
Whether we are like thee or not.

Then Sinilau asked what the youth had said, and they repeated the lines to him. So he ordered the two young men to be brought, and asked them who their father was. They replied that he himself was their father. After Sinilau had kissed his newfound sons he told them to go and bring their mother. So they went to the pool and got the clam, and took her to their grandmother, who broke it open, and there stood a lovely woman, named Hina-at-home-in-the-river.

Then they set out on their return to Sinilau. Each of the youths wore a fringed mat, of the sort called *taufohua*; but their mother had on one of the very fine mats called *tuoua*. The two sons went ahead, and Hina followed. When they came to Sinilau they found him sitting with his wives. The youths sat one at each thigh of Sinilau, and Hina sat at his side. Then Sinilau bade the people go and prepare an oven, and heat it hot; and they took the wives and their children, and killed and baked them; but Sinilau was wedded to Hina-at-home-in-the-river.[10]

FIGURE 69. *The Chariot of the Moon* (carved stone, Cambodia, c. A.D. 1113–1150)

CHAPTER III

Transformations of the Hero

1. The Primordial Hero and the Human

WE HAVE COME TWO STAGES: first, from the immediate emanations of the Uncreated Creating to the fluid yet timeless personages of the mythological age; second, from these Created Creating Ones to the sphere of human history. The emanations have condensed, the field of consciousness constricted. Where formerly causal bodies were visible, now only their secondary effects come to focus in the little hard-fact pupil of the human eye. The cosmogonic cycle is now to be carried forward, therefore, not by the gods, who have become invisible, but by the heroes, more or less human in character, through whom the world destiny is realized. This is the line where creation myths begin to give place to legend—as in the Book of Genesis, following the expulsion from the garden. Metaphysics yields to prehistory, which is dim and vague at first, but becomes gradually precise in detail. The heroes become less and less fabulous, until at last, in the final stages of the various local traditions, legend opens into the common daylight of recorded time.

Mwuetsi, the Moon Man, was cut loose, like a fouled anchor; the community of the children floated free into the day-world of waking consciousness. But we are told that there existed among them direct sons of the now submarine father, who, like the children of his first begetting, had grown from infancy to manhood in a single day. These special carriers of cosmic power constituted a spiritual and social aristocracy. Filled with a double charge of the creative energy, they were themselves sources of revelation. Such figures appear on the dawn stage of every legendary past. They are the culture heroes, the city founders.

The Chinese chronicles record that when the earth had solidified and the peoples were settling in the riverlands, Fu Hsi, the "Heavenly Emperor" (2953–2838 B.C.), governed among them. He taught his tribes how to fish with nets, to hunt and to rear domestic animals, divided the people into clans, and instituted matrimony. From a supernatural tablet entrusted to him by a horse-shaped scaly monster out of the waters of the river Meng, he deduced the Eight Diagrams, which remain to this day the fundamental symbols of traditional Chinese thought. He had been born of a miraculous conception, after a gestation of twelve years; his body being that of a serpent, with human arms and the head of an ox.[1]

Shen Nung, his successor, the "Earthly Emperor" (r. 2838–2698 B.C.), was eight feet seven inches tall, with a human body but the head of a bull. He had been miraculously conceived through the influence of a dragon. The embarrassed mother had exposed her infant on a mountainside, but the wild beasts protected and nourished it, and when she learned of this she fetched him home. Shen Nung discovered in one day seventy poisonous plants and their antidotes: through a glass covering to his stomach he could observe the digestion of each herb. Then he composed a pharmacopoeia that is still in use. He was the inventor of the plough and a system of barter; he is worshiped by the Chinese peasant as the "prince of cereals." At the age of one hundred and sixty-eight he was joined to the immortals.[2]

Such serpent kings and minotaurs tell of a past when the emperor was the carrier of a special world-creating, world-sustaining power, very much greater than that represented in the normal human physique. In those times was accomplished the heavy titan-work, the massive establishment of the foundations of our human civilization. But with the progress of the cycle, a period came when the work to be done was no longer proto- or superhuman; it was the labor specifically of man—control of the passions, exploration of the arts, elaboration of the economic and cultural institutions of the state. Now is required no incarnation of the Moon Bull, no Serpent Wisdom of the Eight Diagrams of Destiny, but a perfect human spirit alert to the needs and hopes of the heart. Accordingly, the cosmogonic cycle yields an emperor in human form who shall stand for all generations to come as the model of man the king.

Huang Ti, the "Yellow Emperor" (r. 2697–2597 B.C.), was the third of the august Three. His mother, a concubine of the prince of the province of Chao-tien, conceived him when she one night beheld a golden dazzling light around the constellation of the Great Bear. The child could talk when he was seventy days old and at the age of eleven years suceeded to the throne. His distinguishing endowment was his power to dream: in sleep he could visit the remotest regions and consort with immortals in the supernatural realm. Shortly following his elevation to the throne, Huang Ti fell into a dream that lasted three entire months, during which time he learned the lesson of the control of the heart. After a second dream of comparable length, he returned with the power to teach the people. He instructed them in the control of the forces of nature in their own hearts.

This wonderful man governed China for one hundred years, and during his reign the people enjoyed a veritable golden age. He gathered six great ministers around him, with whose help he composed a calendar, inaugurated mathematical calculations, and taught the making of utensils of wood, pottery, and metal, the building of boats and carriages, the use of money, and the construction of musical instruments of bamboo. He appointed public places for the worship of God. He instituted the bounds and laws of private property. His queen discovered the art of weaving silk. He planted one hundred varieties of grain, vegetables, and trees; favored the development of birds, quadrupeds, reptiles, and insects; taught the uses of water, fire, wood, and earth; and regulated the movements of the tides. Before his death at the age of one hundred and eleven, the phoenix and the unicorn appeared in the gardens of the Empire, in attestation to the perfection of his reign.[3]

2. *Childhood of the Human Hero*

THE EARLIER CULTURE HERO of the snake body and bull head carried within him from birth the spontaneous creative power of the natural world. That was the meaning of his form. The man hero, on the other hand, must "descend" to re-establish connection with the infrahuman. This is the sense, as we have seen, of the adventure of the hero.

But the makers of legend have seldom rested content to regard the world's great heroes as mere human beings who broke past the horizons that limited their fellows and returned with such boons as any man with equal faith and courage might have found. On the contrary, the tendency has always been to endow the hero with extraordinary powers from the moment of birth, or even the moment of conception. The whole hero-life is shown to have been a pageant of marvels with the great central adventure as its culmination.

FIGURE 70. *Pharaoh's Daughter Finding Moses* (detail; oil on canvas, England, A.D. 1886)

This accords with the view that herohood is predestined, rather than simply achieved, and opens the problem of the relationship of biography to character. Jesus, for example, can be regarded as a man who by dint of austerities and meditation attained wisdom; or on the other hand, one may believe that a god descended and took upon himself the enactment of a human career. The first view would lead one to imitate the master literally, in order to break through, in the same way as he, to the transcendent, redemptive experience. But the second states that the hero is rather a symbol to be contemplated than an example to be literally followed. The divine being is a revelation of the omnipotent Self, which dwells within us all. The contemplation of the life thus should be undertaken as a meditation on one's own immanent divinity, not as a prelude to precise imitation, the lesson being, not "Do thus and be good," but "Know this and be God."

This formula is, of course, not precisely that of the common Christian teaching, where, though Jesus is reported to have declared that "the kingdom of God is within," the churches maintain that, since man is created only "in the image" of God, the distinction between the soul and its creator is absolute—thus retaining, as the final reach of their wisdom, the dualistic distinction between man's "eternal soul" and the divinity. The transcending of this pair of opposites is not encouraged (indeed, is rejected as "pantheism" and has sometimes been rewarded with the stake); nevertheless, the prayers and diaries of the Christian mystics abound in ecstatic descriptions of the unitive, soul-shattering experience (see above, p. 31), while Dante's vision at the conclusion of the Divine Comedy (see above, p. 164) certainly goes beyond the orthodox, dualistic, concretistic dogma of the finality of the personalities of the Trinity. Where this dogma is not transcended the myth of Going to the Father is taken literally, as describing man's final goal. (See above, p. 222.)

As for the problem of imitating Jesus as a human model, or meditating upon Him as a god, the history of the Christian attitude may be roughly summarized, as follows: (1) a period of literally following the master, Jesus, by renouncing the world as he did (Primitive Christianity); (2) a period of meditating on Christ Crucified as the divinity within the heart, meanwhile leading one's life in the world as the servant of this god (Early and Medieval Christianity); (3) a rejection of most of the instruments supporting meditation, meanwhile, however, continuing to lead one's life in the world as the servant or vehicle of the god whom one has ceased to visualize (Protestant Christianity); (4) an attempt to interpret Jesus as a model human being, but without accepting his ascetic path (Liberal Christianity). See above, p. 129.

In Part I, "The Adventure of the Hero," we regarded the redemptive deed from the first standpoint, which may be called the psychological. We now must describe it from the second, where it becomes a symbol of the same metaphysical mystery that it was the deed of the hero himself to rediscover and bring to view. In the present chapter, therefore, we shall consider first the miraculous childhood, by which it is shown that a special manifestation of the immanent divine principle has become incarnate in the world, and then, in succession, the various life roles through which the hero may enact his work of destiny. These vary in magnitude, according to the needs of the time.

Stated in the terms already formulated, the hero's first task is to experience consciously the antecedent stages of the cosmogonic cycle; to break back through the epochs of emanation. His second, then, is to return from that abyss to the plane of contemporary life, there to serve as a human transformer of demiurgic potentials. Huang Ti had the power to dream: this was his road of descent and return. Väinämöinen's second or water birth threw him back to an experience of the elemental. In the Tonga tale of the clam wife, the retreat began with the birth of the mother: the brother heroes sprang from an infrahuman womb.

The deeds of the hero in the second part of his personal cycle will be proportionate to the depth of his descent during the first. The sons of the clam wife came up from the animal level; their physical beauty was superlative. Väinämöinen was reborn from the elemental waters and winds; his endowment was to rouse or quell with bardic song the elements of nature and of the human body. Huang Ti sojourned in the kingdom of the spirit; he taught the harmony of the heart. The Buddha broke past even the zone of the creative gods and came back from the void; he announced salvation from the cosmogonic round.

If the deeds of an actual historical figure proclaim him to have been a hero, the builders of his legend will invent for him appropriate adventures in depth. These will be pictured as journeys into miraculous realms, and are to be interpreted as symbolic, on the one hand, of descents into the night-sea of the psyche, and on the other, of the realms or aspects of man's destiny that are made manifest in the respective lives.

King Sargon of Akkad (c. 2550 B.C.) was born of a lowly mother. His father was unknown. Set adrift in a basket of bulrushes on the waters of the Euphrates, he was discovered by Akki the husbandman, whom he was brought up to serve as gardener. The goddess Ishtar favored the youth. Thus he became, at last, king and emperor, renowned as the living god.

Candragupta (fourth century B.C.), the founder of the Hindu Maurya dynasty, was abandoned in an earthen jar at the threshold of a cowshed. A herdsman discovered and fostered the infant. One day when he was playing with his companions a game of High King in the Judgment Seat, little Candragupta commanded that the worst of the offenders should have their hands and feet cut off; then, at his word, the amputated members immediately returned to place. A passing prince, beholding the miraculous game, bought the child for a thousand *harshapanas* and at home discovered by physical signs that he was a Maurya.

Pope Gregory the Great (A.D. 540?–604) was born of noble twins who at the instigation of the devil had committed incest. His penitent mother set him to sea in a little casket. He was found and fostered by fishermen, and at the age of six was sent to a cloister to be educated as a priest. But he desired the life of a knightly warrior. Entering a boat, he was borne miraculously to the country of his parents, where he won the hand of the queen—who presently proved to be his mother. After discovery of this second incest, Gregory remained seventeen years in penance, chained to a rock in the middle of the sea. The keys to the chains were tossed to the waters, but when at the end of the long period they were discovered in the belly of a fish, this was taken to be a providential sign: the penitent was conducted to Rome, where in due course he was elected pope.[4]

Charlemagne (742–814) was persecuted as a child by his elder brothers, and took flight to Saracen Spain. There, under the name of Mainet, he rendered signal services to the king. He converted the king's daughter to the Christian faith, and the two secretly arranged to marry. After further deeds, the royal youth returned to France, where he overthrew his former persecutors and triumphantly assumed the crown. Then he ruled a hundred years, surrounded by a zodiac of twelve peers. According to all reports, his beard and hair were very long and white. (Actually Charles the Great was beardless and bald.) One day, sitting under his judgment tree, he rendered justice to a snake, and in gratitude the reptile bestowed on him a charm that involved him in a love affair with a woman already dead. This amulet fell into a well at Aix: that is why Aix became the emperor's favorite residence. After his long wars against the Saracens, Saxons, Slavs, and Northmen, the ageless emperor died; but he sleeps only, to awake in the hour of his country's need. During the later Middle Ages, he once arose from the dead to participate in a crusade.[5]

Each of these biographies exhibits the variously rationalized theme of the infant exile and return. This is a prominent feature in all legend, folktale, and myth. Usually an effort is made to give it some semblance of physical plausibility. However, when the hero in question is a great patriarch, wizard, prophet, or incarnation, the wonders are permitted to develop beyond all bounds.

The popular Hebrew legend of the birth of father Abraham supplies an example of the frankly supernatural infant exile. The event of the birth had been read by Nimrod in the stars,

> for this impious king was a cunning astrologer, and it was manifest to him that a man would be born in his day who would rise up against him and triumphantly give the lie to his religion. In his terror at the fate foretold him in the stars, he sent for his princes and governors, and asked them to advise him in the matter. They answered, and said: "Our unanimous advice is that thou shouldst build a great house, station a guard at the entrance thereof, and make known in the whole of thy realm that all pregnant women shall repair thither together with their midwives, who are to remain with them when they are delivered. When the days of a woman to be delivered are fulfilled, and the child is born, it shall be the duty of the midwife to kill it, if it be a boy. But if the child be a girl, it shall be kept alive, and the mother shall receive gifts and costly garments, and a herald shall proclaim, 'Thus is done unto the woman who bears a daughter!' "
>
> The king was pleased with this counsel, and he had a proclamation published throughout his whole kingdom, summoning all the architects to build a great house for him, sixty ells high and eighty wide. After it was completed, he issued a second proclamation, summoning all pregnant women thither, and there they were to remain until their confinement. Officers were appointed to take the women to the house, and guards were stationed in it and about it, to prevent the women from escaping thence. He furthermore sent midwives to the house, and commanded them to slay the men children at their mothers' breasts. But if a woman bore a girl, she was to be arrayed in byssus, silk, and embroidered garments, and led forth from the house of detention amid great honors. No less than seventy thousand children were slaughtered thus. Then the angels appeared before God, and spoke, "Seest Thou not what he doth, yon sinner and blasphemer, Nimrod son of Canaan, who slays so many innocent babes that have done no harm?" God answered, and said: "Ye holy angels, I know it and I see it, for I neither slumber nor sleep. I behold and I know the secret things and the things that are revealed,

and ye shall witness what I will do unto this sinner and blasphemer, for I will turn My hand against him to chastise him."

It was about this time that Terah espoused the mother of Abraham and she was with child.... When her time approached, she left the city in great terror and wandered toward the desert, walking along the edge of a valley, until she happened across a cave. She entered this refuge, and on the next day she was seized with the throes, and she gave birth to a son. The whole cave was filled with the light of the child's countenance as with the splendor of the sun, and the mother rejoiced exceedingly. The babe she bore was our father Abraham.

His mother lamented, and said to her son: "Alas that I bore thee at a time when Nimrod is king. For thy sake seventy thousand men-children were slaughtered, and I am seized with terror on account of thee, that he hear of thy existence, and slay thee. Better thou shouldst perish here in this cave than my eye should behold thee dead at my breast." She took the garment in which she was clothed, and wrapped it about the boy. Then she abandoned him in the cave, saying, "May the Lord be with thee, may He not fail thee nor forsake thee."

Thus Abraham was deserted in the cave, without a nurse, and he began to wail. God sent Gabriel down to give him milk to drink, and the angel made it to flow from the little finger of the baby's right hand, and he sucked it until he was ten days old. Then he arose and walked about, and he left the cave and went along the edge of the valley. When the sun sank, and the stars came forth, he said, "These are the gods!" But the dawn came, and the stars could be seen no longer, and then he said, "I will not pay worship to these, for they are no gods." Thereupon the sun came forth, and he spoke, "This is my god, him will I extol." But again the sun set and he said, "He is no god," and beholding the moon, he called him his god to whom he would pay divine homage. Then the moon was obscured, and he cried out: "This, too, is no god! There is One who sets them all in motion."[6]

The Blackfeet of Montana tell of a young monster-slayer, Kut-o-yis, who was discovered by his foster parents when the old man and woman put a clot of buffalo blood to boil in a pot.

Immediately there came from the pot a noise as of a child crying, as if it were being hurt, burnt, or scalded. They looked in the kettle, and saw there a little boy, and they quickly took it out of the water. They were very much surprised.... Now on the fourth day the child spoke, and said, "Lash me in turn to each of these lodge

> poles, and when I get to the last one, I shall fall out of my lashing and be grown up." The old woman did so, and as she lashed him to each lodge pole he could be seen to grow, and finally when they lashed him to the last pole, he was a man.[7]

The folktales commonly support or supplant this theme of the exile with that of the despised one, or the handicapped: the abused youngest son or daughter, the orphan, stepchild, ugly duckling, or the squire of low degree.

A young Pueblo woman, who was helping her mother mix clay for pottery with her foot, felt a splash of mud on her leg but thought no more of it.

> After some days the girl felt something was moving in her belly, but she did not think anything about going to have a baby. She did not tell her mother. But it was growing and growing. One day in the morning she was very sick. In the afternoon she got the baby. Then her mother knew (for the first time) that her daughter was going to have a baby. The mother was very angry about it; but after she looked at the baby, she saw it was not like a baby, she saw it was a round thing with two things sticking out, it was a little jar. "Where did you get this?" said her mother. The girl was just crying. About that time the father came in. "Never mind, I am very glad she had a baby," he said. "But it is not a baby," said her mother. Then the father went to look at it and saw it was a little water jar. After that he was very fond of that little jar. "It is moving," he said. Pretty soon that little water jar was growing. In twenty days it was big. It was able to go around with the children, and it could talk. "Grandfather, take me outdoors, so I can look around," he said. So every morning the grandfather would take him out and he would look at the children, and they were very fond of him and they found out he was a boy, Water Jar Boy. They found out from his talking.[8]

In sum: the child of destiny has to face a long period of obscurity. This is a time of extreme danger, impediment, or disgrace. He is thrown inward to his own depths or outward to the unknown; either way, what he touches is a darkness unexplored. And this is a zone of unsuspected presences, benign as well as malignant: an angel appears, a helpful animal, a fisherman, a hunter, crone, or peasant. Fostered in the animal school, or, like Siegfried, below ground among the gnomes that nourish the roots of the tree of life, or again, alone in some little room (the story has been told a thousand ways), the young world-apprentice learns the lesson of the seed powers, which reside just beyond the sphere of the measured and the named.

The myths agree that an extraordinary capacity is required to face and survive such experience. The infancies abound in anecdotes of precocious strength, cleverness, and wisdom. Herakles strangled a serpent sent against his cradle by the goddess Hera. Maui of Polynesia snared and slowed the sun—to give his mother time to cook her meals. Abraham, as we have seen, arrived at the knowledge of the One God. Jesus confounded the wise men. The baby Buddha had been left one day beneath the shade of a tree; his nurses suddenly noted that the shadow had not moved all afternoon and that the child was sitting fixed in a yogic trance.

The feats of the beloved Hindu savior, Kṛṣṇa, during his infant exile among the cowherds of Gokula and Brindaban, constitute a lively cycle. A certain goblin named Pūtanā came in the shape of a beautiful woman, but with poison in her breasts. She entered the house of Yasoda, the foster mother of the child, and made herself very friendly, presently taking the baby in her lap to give it suck. But Kṛṣṇa drew so hard that he sucked away her life, and she fell dead, reassuming her huge and hideous form. When the foul corpse was cremated, however, it emitted a sweet fragrance; for the divine infant had given the demoness salvation when he had drunk her milk.

Kṛṣṇa was a mischievous little boy. He liked to spirit away the pots of curds when the milkmaids were asleep. He was forever climbing to eat and spill things placed out of his reach on the high shelves. The girls would call him Butter-thief and complain to Yasoda; but he could always invent a story. One afternoon when he was playing in the yard, his foster parent was warned that he was eating clay. She arrived with a switch, but he had wiped his lips, and denied all knowledge of the matter. She opened the dirty mouth to see, but when she peered inside beheld the whole universe, the "Three Worlds." She thought: "How silly I am to imagine that my son could be the Lord of the Three Worlds." Then all was veiled from her again, and the moment passed immediately from her mind. She fondled the little boy and took him home.

The herding folk were accustomed to pay worship to the god Indra, the Hindu counterpart of Zeus, king of heaven and lord of rain. One day when they had made their offering, the lad Kṛṣṇa said to them: "Indra is no supreme deity, though he be king in heaven; he is afraid of the titans. Furthermore, the rain and prosperity for which you are praying depend on the sun, which draws up the waters and makes them fall again. What can Indra do? Whatever comes to pass is determined by the laws of nature and the spirit." Then he turned their attention to the nearby woods, streams, and hills, and especially to Mount Govardhan, as more worthy of their honor than the remote master of the air. And so they offered flowers and fruits and sweetmeats to the mountain.

Kṛṣṇa himself assumed a second form: he took the form of a mountain god and received the offerings of the people, meanwhile remaining in his earlier shape among them, paying worship to the mountain king. The god received the offerings and ate them up.

Indra was enraged, and sent for the king of the clouds, whom he commanded to pour rain over the people until all should be swept away. A flight of storm clouds drew over the district and began to discharge a deluge; it seemed the end of the world was at hand. But the lad Kṛṣṇa filled Mount Govardhan with the heat of his inexhaustible energy, lifted it with his little finger, and bid the people take shelter beneath. The rain struck the mountain, hissed, and evaporated. The torrent fell seven days, but not a drop touched the community of herdsmen.

Then the god realized that the opponent must be an incarnation of the Primal Being. When Kṛṣṇa went out next day to graze the cows, playing music on his flute, the King of Heaven came down on his great white elephant, Airāvata, fell on his face at the feet of the smiling lad, and made submission.[9]

The conclusion of the childhood cycle is the return or recognition of the hero, when, after the long period of obscurity, his true character is revealed. This event may precipitate a considerable crisis; for it amounts to an emergence of powers hitherto excluded from human life. Earlier patterns break to fragments or dissolve; disaster greets the eye. Yet after a moment of apparent havoc, the creative value of the new factor comes to view, and the world takes shape again in unsuspected glory. This theme of crucifixion-resurrection can be illustrated either on the body of the hero himself, or in his effects upon his world. The first alternative we find in the Pueblo story of the water jar.

> The men were going out to hunt rabbits, and Water Jar Boy wanted to go. "Grandfather, could you take me down to the foot of the mesa, I want to hunt rabbits." "Poor grandson, you can't hunt rabbits, you have no legs or arms," said the grandfather. But Water Jar Boy was very anxious to go. "Take me anyway. You are too old and you can't do anything." His mother was crying because her

FIGURE 71. *Kṛṣṇa Holding Mount Govardhan* (color on paper, India, c. A.D. 1790)

The sense of Kṛṣṇa's advice to do worship to the mountain rather than the king of the gods, which to the Western reader may seem strange, is that the Way of Devotion (*bhakti mārga*) must begin with things known and loved by the devotee, not remote, unimaginable conceptions. Since the Godhead is immanent in all, He will make Himself known through any object profoundly regarded. Furthermore, it is the Godhead within the devotee that makes it possible for him to discover Godhead in the world without. This mystery is illustrated in Kṛṣṇa's double presence during the act of worship.

> boy had no legs or arms or eyes. But they used to feed him, in his mouth, in the mouth of the jar. So next morning his grandfather took him down to the south on the flat. Then he rolled along, and pretty soon he saw a rabbit track and he followed the track. Pretty soon the rabbit ran out, and he began to chase it. Just before he got to the marsh there was a rock, and he hit himself against it and broke, and a boy jumped up. He was very glad his skin had been broken and that he was a boy, a big boy. He was wearing lots of beads around his neck and turquoise earrings, and a dance kilt and moccasins, and a buckskin shirt.

Catching a number of rabbits, he returned and presented them to his grandfather, who brought him triumphantly home.[10]

The cosmic energies burning within the vivid Irish warrior Cuchulainn—chief hero of the medieval Ulster Cycle, the so-called Cycle of the Knights of the Red Branch—would suddenly burst like an eruption, both overwhelming himself and smashing everything around.

The legendary cycles of medieval Ireland include: (1) *The Mythological Cycle,* which describes the migrations to the island of prehistoric peoples, their battles, and in particular the deeds of the race of gods known as the Tuatha De Danaan, "Children of the Great Mother, Dana"; (2) *The Annals of the Milesians,* or semi-historical chronicles of the last arriving race, the sons of Milesius, founders of the Celtic dynasties that survived until the arrival of the Anglo-Normans under Henry II in the twelfth century; (3) *The Ulster Cycle of the Knights of the Red Branch,* which treats primarily of the deeds of Cuchulainn (pronounced coohoolinn) at the court of his uncle Conchobar (pronounced conohoor): this cycle greatly influenced the development of the Arthurian tradition, in Wales, Brittany, and England—the court of Conchobar serving as model for that of King Arthur and the deeds of Cuchulainn for those of Arthur's nephew, Sir Gawain (Gawain was the original hero of many of the adventures later assigned to Lancelot, Perceval, and Galahad); (4) *The Cycle of the Fianna:* the Fianna were a company of heroic fighters under the captaincy of Finn MacCool (see p. 192, above); the greatest tale of this cycle being that of the love triangle of Finn, Grianni his bride, and Diarmaid his nephew, many episodes of which come down to us in the celebrated tale of Tristan and Iseult; (5) *Legends of the Irish Saints.*

The "little people" of the popular fairy lore of Christian Ireland are reductions of the earlier pagan divinities, the Tuatha De Danaan.

When he was four years old—so the story goes—he set out to test the "boy corps" of his uncle, King Conchobar, at their own sports. Carrying his hurly of brass, ball of silver, throwing javelin, and toy spear, he proceeded to the court city of Emania, where, without so much as a word of permission, he dived right in among the boys—"thrice fifty in number, who were hurling on the green and practicing martial exercises with Conchobar's son, Follamain, at their head."

The whole field let fly at him. With his fists, forearms, palms, and little shield, he parried the hurlies, balls, and spears that came simultaneously from all directions. Then for the first time in his life he was seized with his battle-frenzy (a bizarre, characteristic transformation later to be known as his "paroxysm" or "distortion") and before anyone could grasp what was coming to pass, he had laid low fifty of the best. Five more of the boy corps went scuttling past the king, where he sat playing chess with Fergus the Eloquent. Conchobar arose and took a hand in the confusion. But Cuchulainn would not lighten his hand until all the youngsters had been placed under his protection and guarantee.[11]

Cuchulainn's first day under arms was the occasion of his full self-manifestation. There was nothing serenely controlled about this performance, nothing of the playful irony that we feel in the deeds of the Hindu Kṛṣṇa. Rather, the abundance of Cuchulainn's power was becoming known for the first time to himself, as well as to everybody else. It broke out of the depths of his being, and then had to be dealt with, impromptu and fast.

The happening was again at the court of King Conchobar, the day Cathbad the Druid declared in prophecy of any stripling who that day should assume arms and armature that "the name of such an one would transcend those of all Ireland's youths besides: his life however would be fleeting short." Cuchulainn forthwith demanded fighting equipment. Seventeen sets of weapons given him he shattered with his strength, until Conchobar invested him with his own outfit. Then he reduced the chariots to fragments. Only that of the king was strong enough to support his trial.

Cuchulainn commanded Conchobar's charioteer to drive him past the distant "Look-out Ford," and they came presently to a remote fortress, the Dun of the Sons of Nechtan, where he cut off the heads of the defenders. He fastened the heads to the sides of the car. On the road back he jumped to the ground and "by sheer running and mere speed" captured two stags of the grandest bulk. With two stones he knocked out of the air two dozen flying swans. And with thongs and other gear he tethered all, both the beasts and the birds, to the chariot.

Levarchan the Prophetess beheld the pageant with alarm as it approached the city and castle of Emania. "The chariot is graced with bleeding heads of his enemies," she declared, "beautiful white birds he has which in the chariot bear him company, and wild unbroken stags bound and tethered to the same." "I know that chariot-fighter," the king said: "even the little boy, my sister's son, who this very day went to the marches. Surely he will have reddened his hand; and should his fury not be timely met, all Emania's young men will perish by him." Very quickly, a method had to be contrived to abate his heat; and one was found. One hundred and fifty women of the castle, and Scandlach their leader at the head of them, "reduced themselves critically to nature's garb, and without subterfuge of any kind trooped out to meet him." The little warrior, embarrassed or perhaps overwhelmed by such a display of womanhood, averted his eyes, at which moment he was seized by the men and soused into a vat of cold water. The staves and hoops of the vessel flew asunder. A second vat boiled. The third became only very hot. Thus Cuchulainn was subdued, and the city saved.[12]

> A beautiful boy indeed was that: seven toes to each foot Cuchulainn had, and to either hand as many fingers; his eyes were bright with seven pupils apiece, each one of which glittered with seven gemlike sparkles. On either cheek he had four moles: a blue, a crimson, a green, and a yellow. Between one ear and the other he had fifty clear-yellow long tresses that were as the yellow wax of bees, or like unto a brooch of the white gold as it glints to the sun unobscured. He wore a green mantle silver-clasped upon his breast and a gold-thread shirt.[13]

But when he was taken by his paroxysm or distortion "he became a fearsome and multiform and wondrous and hitherto unknown being." All over him, from his crown to the ground, his flesh and every limb and joint and point and articulation of him quivered. His feet, shins, and knees shifted themselves and were behind him. The frontal sinews of his head were dragged to the back of his neck, where they showed in lumps bigger than the head of a man-child aged one month.

> One eye became engulfed in his head so far that 'tis a question whether a wild heron could have got at it where it lay against his occiput, to drag it out upon the surface of his cheek; the other eye on the contrary protruded suddenly, and of itself so rested upon the cheek. His mouth was twisted awry till it met his ears... flakes of fire streamed from it. The sounding blows of the heart that pounded within him were as the howl of a ban-dog doing his office, or of a lion in the act of charging bears. Among the aërial clouds over his head were visable the virulent pouring showers and sparks of ruddy fire which the seething of his savage wrath caused to mount up above him. His hair became tangled about his head... over the

> which though a prime apple-tree had been shaken, yet may we surmise that never an apple of them would have reached the ground, but rather that all would have been held impaled each on an individual hair as it bristled on him for fury. His "hero's paroxysm" projected itself out of his forehead, and showed longer as well as thicker than the whetstone of a first-rate man-at-arms. [And finally:] taller, thicker, more rigid, longer than the mast of a great ship was the perpendicular jet of dusky blood which out of his scalp's very central point shot upwards and then was scattered to the four cardinal points; whereby was formed a magic mist of gloom resembling the smoky pall that drapes a regal dwelling, what time a king at night fall of a winter's day draws near to it.[14]

3. *The Hero as Warrior*

THE PLACE OF THE HERO'S BIRTH, or the remote land of exile from which he returns to perform his adult deeds among men, is the mid-point or navel of the world. Just as ripples go out from an underwater spring, so the forms of the universe expand in circles from the source.

"Above the broad, unmoving depths, beneath the nine spheres and the seven floors of heaven, at the central point, the World Navel, the quietest place on earth, where eternal summer rules and the cuckoo everlasting calls, there the White Youth came to consciousness." So begins a hero myth of the Yakuts of Siberia. The White Youth went forth to learn where he was and what his dwelling place was like. Eastward of him lay stretching a broad, fallow field, in the middle of which arose a mighty hill, and on the summit of the hill a gigantic tree. The resin of that tree was transparent and sweet scented, the bark never dried or cracked, the sap shone silver, the luxuriant leaves never wilted, and the catkins resembled a cluster of reversed cups. The summit of the tree rose over the seven heaven-floors and served as a tethering post for the High God, Yryn-ai-tojon; while the roots penetrated into the subterranean abysses, where they formed the pillars of the dwellings of the mythical creatures proper to that zone. The tree held conversation, through its foliage, with the beings of the sky.

When the White Youth turned to face south, he perceived in the midst of a green grassy plain the quiet Lake of Milk that no breath of wind ever stirs; and around the shores of the lake were swamps of curdle. To the north of him a somber forest stood with trees that rustled day and night; and therein was moving every kind of beast. Tall mountains were lifting beyond it, and appeared to be wearing caps of white rabbit fur; they leaned against the sky and protected this middle place from the northern wind. A thicket of scrub stretched out to the west, and beyond it stood a forest of tall firs; behind the forest gleamed a number of blunt-headed solitary peaks.

This was the manner, then, of the world in which the White Youth beheld the light of day. Presently tired, however, of being alone, he went over to the gigantic tree of life. "Honored High Mistress, Mother of my Tree and my Dwelling Place," he prayed; "everything that lives exists in pairs and propagates descendants, but I am alone. I want now to travel and to seek a wife of my own kind; I wish to measure my strength against my kind; I want to become acquainted with men—to live according to the manner of men. Do not deny me thy blessing; I do humbly pray. I bow my head and bend my knee."

FIGURE 72. *Paleolithic Petroglyph* (carved rock, Paleolithic, Algiers, date uncertain)

Then the leaves of the tree began murmuring, and a fine, milk-white rain descended from them upon the White Youth. A warm breath of wind could be felt. The tree began to groan, and out of its roots a female figure emerged to the waist: a woman of middle age, with earnest regard, hair flowing free, and bosom bare. The goddess offered her milk to the youth from a sumptuous breast, and after partaking of it he felt his strength increase a hundredfold. At the same time the goddess promised the youth every happiness and blessed him in such a way that neither water, nor fire, iron, nor anything else should ever do him harm.[15]

From the umbilical spot the hero departs to realize his destiny. His adult deeds pour creative power into the world.

Sang the aged Väinämöinen;
Lakes swelled up, and earth was shaken,
And the coppery mountains trembled,
And the mighty rocks resounded.
And the mountains clove asunder;
On the shore the stones were shattered.[16]

The stanza of the hero-bard resounds with the magic of the word of power; similarly, the sword edge of the hero-warrior flashes with the energy of the creative Source: before it fall the shells of the Outworn.

For the mythological hero is the champion not of things become but of things becoming; the dragon to be slain by him is precisely the monster of the status quo: Holdfast, the keeper of the past. From obscurity the hero emerges, but the enemy is great and conspicuous in the seat of power; he is enemy, dragon, tyrant, because he turns to his own advantage the authority of his position. He is Holdfast not because he keeps the *past* but because he *keeps.*

I am here keeping the distinction between the earlier semi-animal titan-hero (city founder, culture giver) and the later, fully human type. (See pp. 271–275.) The deeds of the latter frequently include the slaying of the former, the Pythons and Minotaurs who were the boon-givers of the past. (A god outgrown becomes immediately a life-destroying demon. The form has to be broken and the energies released.) Not infrequently deeds that belong to the earlier stages of the cycle are assigned to the human hero, or one of the earlier heroes may be humanized and carried on into a later day; but such contaminations and variations do not alter the general formula.

The tyrant is proud, and therein resides his doom. He is proud because he thinks of his strength as his own; thus he is in the clown role, as a mistaker of shadow for substance; it is his destiny to be tricked. The mythological hero, reappearing from the darkness that is the source of the shapes of the day, brings a knowledge of the secret of the tyrant's doom. With a gesture as simple as the pressing of a button, he annihilates the impressive configuration. The hero-deed is a continuous shattering of the crystallizations of the moment. The cycle rolls: mythology focuses on the growing-point. Transformation, fluidity, not stubborn ponderosity, is the characteristic of the living

God. The great figure of the moment exists only to be broken, cut into chunks, and scattered abroad. Briefly: the ogre-tyrant is the champion of the prodigious fact, the hero the champion of creative life.

The world period of the hero in *human* form begins only when villages and cities have expanded over the land. Many monsters remaining from primeval times still lurk in the outlying regions, and through malice or desperation these set themselves against the human community. They have to be cleared away. Furthermore, tyrants of human breed, usurping to themselves the goods of their neighbors, arise, and are the cause of widespread misery. These have to be suppressed. The elementary deeds of the hero are those of the clearing of the field.

Kut-o-yis, or "Blood Clot Boy," when he had been taken from the pot and had grown to manhood in a day, slew the murderous son-in-law of his foster parents, then proceeded against the ogres of the countryside. He exterminated a tribe of cruel bears, with the exception of one female who was about to become a mother. "She pleaded so pitifully for her life, that he spared her. If he had not done this, there would have been no bears in the world." Then he slaughtered a tribe of snakes, but again with the exception of one "who was about to become a mother." Next he deliberately walked along a road which he had been told was dangerous.

> As he was going along, a great windstorm struck him and at last carried him into the mouth of a great fish. This was a sucker-fish and the wind was its sucking. When he got into the stomach of the fish, he saw a great many people. Many of them were dead, but some were still alive. He said to the people, "Ah, there must be a heart somewhere here. We will have a dance." So he painted his face white, his eyes and mouth with black circles, and tied a white rock knife on his head, so that the point stuck up. Some rattles made of hoofs were also brought. Then the people started in to dance. For a while Blood Clot sat making wing-motions with his hands, and singing songs. Then he stood up and danced, jumping up and down until the knife on his head struck the heart. Then he cut the heart down. Next he cut through between the ribs of the fish, and let all the people out.
>
> Again Blood Clot said he must go on his travels. Before starting, the people warned him, saying that after a while he would see a woman who was always challenging people to wrestle with her, but that he must not speak to her. He gave no heed to what they said,

FIGURE 73 *The Pharaoh Narmer Slays a Defeated Foe* (carved schist, Old Kingdom, Egypt, c. 3100 B.C.)

and, after he had gone a little way, he saw a woman who called him to come over. "No," said Blood Clot. "I am in a hurry." However, at the fourth time the woman asked him to come over, he said, "Yes, but you must wait a little while, for I am tired. I wish to rest. When I have rested, I will come over and wrestle with you." Now, while he was resting, he saw many large knives sticking up from the ground almost hidden by straw. Then he knew that the woman killed the people she wrestled with by throwing them down on the knives. When he was rested, he went on. The woman asked him to stand up in the place where he had seen the knives; but he said, "No, I am not quite ready. Let us play a little, before we begin." So he began to play with the woman, but quickly caught hold of her, threw her upon the knives, and cut her in two.

> Blood Clot took up his travels again, and after a while came to a camp where there were some old women. The old women told him that a little farther on he would come to a woman with a swing, but on no account must he ride with her. After a time he came to a place where he saw a swing on the bank of a swift stream. There was a woman swinging on it. He watched her a while, and saw that she killed people by swinging them out and dropping them into the water. When he found this out, he came up to the woman. "You have a swing here; let me see you swing," he said. "No," said the woman, "I want to see you swing." "Well," said Blood Clot, "but you must swing first." "Well," said the woman, "now I shall swing. Watch me. Then I shall see you do it." So the woman swung out over the stream. As she did this, he saw how it worked. Then he said to the woman, "You swing again while I am getting ready"; but as the woman swung out this time, he cut the vine and let her drop into the water. This happened on Cut Bank Creek.[17]

We are familiar with such deeds from our Jack-the-Giant-Killer nursery tales and the classical accounts of the labors of such heroes as Herakles and Theseus. They abound also in the legends of the Christian saints, as in the following charming French tale of Saint Martha.

> There was at that time on the banks of the Rhône, in a forest situated between Avignon and Arles, a dragon, half animal, half fish, larger than an ox, longer than a horse, with teeth as sharp as horns, and great wings at either side of its body; and this monster slew all the travelers and sank all the boats. It had arrived by sea from Galatia. Its parents were the Leviathan—a monster in the form of a serpent that dwelt in the sea—and the Onager—a terrible beast bred in Galatia, which burns with fire everything it touches.
>
> Now Saint Martha, at the earnest request of the people, went against the dragon. Having found it in the forest, in the act of devouring a man, she sprinkled holy water on it and exhibited a crucifix. Immediately, the monster, vanquished, came like a lamb to the side of the saint, who passed her belt around its neck and conducted it to the neighboring village. There the populace slew it with stones and staffs.
>
> And since the dragon had been known to the people under the name of Tarasque, the town took the name of Tarascon, in remembrance. Up to then it had been called Nerluc, which is to say, Black Lake, on account of the somber forests which there bordered the stream.[18]

The warrior-kings of antiquity regarded their work in the spirit of the monster-slayer. This formula, indeed, of the shining hero going against the dragon has been the great device of self-justification for all crusades. Numberless memorial tablets have been composed with the grandiose complacency of the following cuneiform of Sargon of Akkad, destroyer of the ancient cities of the Sumerians, from whom his own people had derived their civilization.

> Sargon, king of Akkad, viceregent of the goddess Ishtar, king of Kish, *pashishu** of the god Anu, King of the Land, great *ishakku*† of the god Enlil: the city of Uruk he smote and its wall he destroyed. With the people of Uruk, he battled and he captured him and in fetters led him through the gate of Enlil. Sargon, king of Akkad, battled with the man of Ur and vanquished him; his city he smote and its wall he destroyed. E-Ninmar he smote and its wall he destroyed, and its entire territory, from Lagash to the sea, he smote. His weapons he washed in the sea....

4. *The Hero as Lover*

THE HEGEMONY WRESTED from the enemy, the freedom won from the malice of the monster, the life energy released from the toils of the tyrant Holdfast—is symbolized as a woman. She is the maiden of the innumerable dragon slayings, the bride abducted from the jealous father, the virgin rescued from the unholy lover. She is the "other portion" of the hero himself—for "each is both": if his stature is that of world monarch she is the world, and if he is a warrior she is fame. She is the image of his destiny which he is to release from the prison of enveloping circumstance. But where he is ignorant of his destiny, or deluded by false considerations, no effort on his part will overcome the obstacles.‡

* One of a class of priests entrusted with the preparation and application of the sacred ointments.

† Chief priest, governing as viceregent of the god.

‡ An amusing and instructive example of a great hero's abject failure will be found in the Finnish *Kalevala*, Runos IV–VIII, where Väinämöinen fails in his wooing, first of Aino, and then of the "maid of Pohjola." The story is much too long for the present context.

The magnificent youth Cuchulainn, at the court of his uncle, Conchobar the king, aroused the anxiety of the barons for the virtue of their wives. They suggested that he should be found a wife of his own. Messengers of the king went out to every province of Ireland, but could find no one he would woo. Then Cuchulainn himself went to a maiden that he knew in Luglochta Loga, "the Gardens of Lugh." And he found her on her playing field, with her foster-sisters around her, teaching them needlework and fine handiwork. Emer lifted up her lovely face and recognized Cuchulainn, and she said: "May you be safe from every harm!"

When the girl's father, Forgall the Wily, was told that the couple had talked together, he contrived to send Cuchulainn off to learn battle skills from Donall the Soldierly in Alba, supposing the youth would never return. And Donall set him a further task, namely, to make the impossible journey to a certain warrior-woman, Scathach, and then compel her to give him instruction in her arts of supernatural valor. Cuchulainn's hero-journey exhibits with extraordinary simplicity and clarity all the essential elements of the classic accomplishment of the impossible task.

The way was across a plain of ill luck: on the hither half of it the feet of men would stick fast; on the farther half the grass would rise and hold them fast on the points of its blades. But a fair youth appeared who presented to Cuchulainn a wheel and an apple. Across the first part of the plain the wheel would roll just ahead, and across the second the apple. Cuchulainn had only to keep to their thin guiding line, without a step to either side, and he would come across to the narrow and dangerous glen beyond.

The residence of Scathach was on an island, and this island was approached by a difficult bridge only: it had two low ends and the midspace high, and whenever anybody leaped on one end of it, the other head would lift itself up and throw him on his back. Cuchulainn was thrown three times. Then his distortion came upon him, and, gathering himself, he jumped on the head of the bridge, and made the hero's salmon-leap, so that he landed on the middle of it; and the other head of the bridge had not fully raised itself up when he reached it, and threw himself from it, and was on the ground of the island.

The warrior-woman Scathach had a daughter—as the monster so often has—and this young maid in her isolation had never beheld anything approaching the beauty of the young man who came down from the mid-air into her mother's fortress. When she had heard from the youth what his project was, she described to him the best manner of approach to persuade her mother to teach him the secrets of supernatural valor. He should go through his hero's salmon-leap to the great yew tree where Scathach was giving instruction to her sons, set his sword between her breasts, and state his demand.

Cuchulainn, following instructions, won from the warrior-sorceress acquaintance with her feats, marriage to her daughter without payment of a bride-price, knowledge of his future, and sexual intercourse with herself. He remained a year, during which he assisted in a great battle against the Amazon Aife, on whom he begot a son. Finally, slaying a hag who disputed with him a narrow path along the edge of a cliff, he started home for Ireland.

One further adventure of battle and love, and Cuchulainn returned to find Forgall the Wily still against him. He simply carried the daughter off this time, and they were married at the court of the king. The adventure itself had given him the capacity to annihilate all opposition. The only annoyance was that uncle Conchobar, the king, exercised on the bride his royal prerogative before she passed officially to the groom.[19]

The motif of the difficult task as prerequisite to the bridal bed has spun the hero-deeds of all time and all the world. In stories of this pattern the parent is in the role of Holdfast; the hero's artful solution of the task amounts to a slaying of the dragon. The tests imposed are difficult beyond measure. They seem to represent an absolute refusal, on the part of the parent ogre, to permit life to go its way; nevertheless, when a fit candidate appears, no task in the world is beyond his skill. Unpredicted helpers, miracles of time and space, further his project; destiny itself (the maiden) lends a hand and betrays a weak spot in the parental system. Barriers, fetters, chasms, fronts of every kind dissolve before the authoritative presence of the hero. The eye of the ordained victor immediately perceives the chink in every fortress of circumstance, and his blow can cleave it wide.

The most eloquent and deep-driving of the traits in this colorful adventure of Cuchulainn is that of the unique, invisible path, which was opened to the hero with the rolling of the wheel and the apple. This is to be read as symbolic and instructive of the miracle of destiny. To a man not led astray from himself by sentiments stemming from the surfaces of what he sees, but courageously responding to the dynamics of his own nature—to a man who is, as Nietzsche phrases it, "a wheel rolling of itself"—difficulties melt and the unpredictable highway opens as he goes.

5. *The Hero as Emperor and as Tyrant*

THE HERO OF ACTION is the agent of the cycle, continuing into the living moment the impulse that first moved the world. Because our eyes are closed to the paradox of the double focus, we regard the deed as accomplished amid danger and great pain by a vigorous arm, whereas from the other perspective it is, like the archetypal dragon-slaying of Tiamat by Marduk, only a bringing to pass of the inevitable.

The supreme hero, however, is not the one who merely continues the dynamics of the cosmogonic round, but he who reopens the eye—so that through all the comings and goings, delights and agonies of the world panorama, the One Presence will be seen again. This requires a deeper wisdom than the other, and results in a pattern not of action but of significant representation. The symbol of the first is the virtuous sword, of the second, the scepter of dominion, or the book of the law. The characteristic adventure of the first is the winning of the bride—the bride is life. The adventure of the second is the going to the father—the father is the invisible unknown.

Adventures of the second type fit directly into the patterns of religious iconography. Even in a simple folktale a depth is suddenly sounded when the son of the virgin one day asks of his mother: "Who is my father?" The question touches the problem of man and the invisible. The familiar myth-motifs of the atonement inevitably follow.

The Pueblo hero, Water Jar Boy, asked the question of his mother.

> "Who is my father?" he said. "I don't know," she said. He asked her again, "Who is my father?" but she just kept on crying and did not answer. "Where is my father's home?" he asked. She could not tell him. "Tomorrow I am going to find my father."—"You cannot find your father," she said. "I never go with any boy, so

> there is no place where you can look for your father." But the boy said, "I have a father, I know where he is living, I am going to see him." The mother did not want him to go, but he wanted to go. So early next morning she fixed a lunch for him, and he went off to the south-east where they called the spring Waiyu powidi, Horse mesa point. He was coming close to that spring, he saw somebody walking a little way from the spring. He went up to him. It was a man. He asked the boy, "Where are you going?"—"I am going to see my father," he said. "Who is your father?" said the man. "Well, my father is living in this spring."—"You will never find your father."—"Well, I want to go into the spring, he is living inside it."—"Who is your father?" said the man again, "Well, I think you are my father," said the boy. "How do you know I am your father?" said the man. "Well, I know you are my father." Then the man just looked at him, to scare him. The boy kept saying, "You are my father." Pretty soon the man said, "Yes, I am your father. I came out of that spring to meet you," and he put his arm around the boy's neck. His father was very glad his boy had come, and he took him down inside the spring.[20]

Where the goal of the hero's effort is the discovery of the unknown father, the basic symbolism remains that of the tests and the self-revealing way. In the above example the test is reduced to the persistent questions and a frightening look. In the earlier tale of the clam wife, the sons were tried with the bamboo knife. We have seen, in our review of the adventure of the hero, to what degrees the severity of the father can go. For the congregation of Jonathan Edwards he became a veritable ogre.

The hero blessed by the father returns to represent the father among men. As teacher (Moses) or as emperor (Huang Ti), his word is law. Since he is now centered in the source, he makes visible the repose and harmony of the central place. He is a reflection of the World Axis from which the concentric circles spread—the World Mountain, the World Tree—he is the perfect microcosmic mirror of the macrocosm. To see him is to perceive the meaning of existence. From his presence boons go out; his word is the wind of life.

But a deterioration may take place in the character of the representative of the father. Such a crisis is described in the Zoroastrian Persian legend of the Emperor of the Golden Age, Jemshid.

> *All looked upon the throne, and heard and saw*
> *Nothing but Jemshid, he alone was King,*

Absorbing every thought; and in their praise
And adoration of that mortal man,
Forgot the worship of the great Creator.
Then proudly he to his nobles spoke,
Intoxicated with their loud applause,
"I am unequalled, for to me the earth
Owes all its science, never did exist
A sovereignty like mine, beneficent
And glorious, driving from the populous land
Disease and want. Domestic joy and rest
Proceed from me, all that is good and great
Waits my behest; the universal voice
Declares the splendor of my government,
Beyond whatever human heart conceived,
And me the only monarch of the world."
—Soon as these words had parted from his lips
Words impious, and insulting to high heaven,
His earthly grandeur faded—then all tongues
Grew clamorous and bold. The day of Jemshid
Passed into gloom, his brightness all obscured.
What said the Moralist? "When thou wert a king
Thy subjects were obedient, but whoever
Proudly neglects the worship of his God
Brings desolation on his house and home."
—And when he marked the insolence of his people,
He knew the wrath of heaven had been provoked,
And terror overcame him.[21]

Persian mythology is rooted in the common Indo-European system that was carried out of the Aral-Caspian steppes into India and Iran, as well as into Europe. The principal divinities of the earliest sacred writings (Avesta) of the Persians correspond very closely to those of the earliest Indian texts (Vedas: see p. 95, above). But the two branches came under greatly differing influences in their new homes, the Vedic tradition submitting gradually to Dravidian Indian forces, the Persian to Sumero-Babylonian.

Early in the first millennium B.C., Persian belief was reorganized by the prophet Zarathustra (Zoroaster) according to a strict dualism of good and evil principles, light and dark, angels and devils. This crisis profoundly affected not only the Persian, but also the subject Hebrew beliefs, and thereby (centuries later) Christianity. It represents a radical departure from the more usual mythological interpretation of good and evil as effects proceeding from a unique source of being that transcends and reconciles all polarity.

Persia was overrun by the zealots of Mohammed, A.D. 642. Those not converted were put to the sword. A poor remnant took refuge in India, where they survive to this day as the Parsis ("Persians") of Bombay. After a period of some three centuries, however, a Mohammedan-Persian literary "Restoration" took place. The great names are: Firdausi (940–1020?), Omar Khayyam (?–1123?), Nizami (1140–1203), Jalal ad-Din Rumi (1207–1273), Saadi (1184–1291), Hafiz (?–1389?), and Jami (1414–1492). Firdausi's *Shah Nameh* ("Epic of Kings") is a rehearsal in simple and stately narrative verse of the story of ancient Persia down to the Mohammedan conquest.

No longer referring the boons of his reign to their transcendent source, the emperor breaks the stereoptic vision which it is his role to sustain. He is no longer the mediator between the two worlds. Man's perspective flattens to include only the human term of the equation, and the experience of a supernal power immediately fails. The upholding idea of the community is lost. Force is all that binds it. The emperor becomes the tyrant ogre (Herod-Nimrod), the usurper from whom the world is now to be saved.

6. *The Hero as World Redeemer*

Two degrees of initiation are to be distinguished in the mansion of the father. From the first the son returns as emissary, but from the second, with the knowledge that "I and the father are one." Heroes of this second, highest illumination are the world redeemers, the so-called incarnations, in the highest sense. Their myths open out to cosmic proportions. Their words carry an authority beyond anything pronounced by the heroes of the scepter and the book.

"All of you watch me. Don't look around," said the hero of the Jicarilla Apache, Killer-of-Enemies;

> Listen to what I say. The world is just as big as my body. The world is as large as my word. And the world is as large as my prayers. The sky is only as large as my words and prayers. The seasons are only as great as my body, my words, and my prayer. It is the same with the waters; my body, my words, my prayer are greater than the waters.
>
> Whoever believes me, whoever listens to what I say, will have long life. One who doesn't listen, who thinks in some evil way, will have a short life.
>
> Don't think I am in the east, south, west, or north. The earth is my body. I am there. I am all over. Don't think I stay only under the earth or up in the sky, or only in the seasons, or on the

> other side of the waters. These are all my body. It is the truth that the underworld, the sky, the seasons, the waters, are all my body. I am all over.
>
> I have already given you that with which you have to make an offering to me. You have two kinds of pipe and you have the mountain tobacco.[22]

The work of the incarnation is to refute by his presence the pretensions of the tyrant ogre. The latter has occluded the source of grace with the shadow of his limited personality; the incarnation, utterly free of such ego-consciousness, is a direct manifestation of the law. On a grandiose scale he enacts the hero-life—performs the hero-deeds, slays the monster—but it is all with the freedom of a work done only to make evident to the eye what might have been accomplished equally well with a mere thought.

Kans, the cruel uncle of Kṛṣṇa, usurper of his own father's throne in the city of Mathurā, heard a voice one day that said to him: "Thy enemy is born, thy death is certain." Kṛṣṇa and his elder brother Balarāma had been spirited to the cowherds from their mother's womb to protect them from this Indian counterpart of Nimrod. And he had sent demons after them—Pūtanā of the poison milk was the first—but all had been undone. Now when his devices had failed, Kans determined to lure the youths to his city. A messenger was sent to invite the cowherds to a sacrifice and great tournament. The invitation was accepted. With the brothers among them, the cowherds came and camped outside the city wall.

Kṛṣṇa and Balarāma, his brother, went in to see the wonders of the town. There were great gardens, palaces, and groves. They encountered a washerman and asked him for some fine clothes; when he laughed and refused, they took the clothes by force and made themselves very gay. Then a hump-backed woman prayed Kṛṣṇa to let her rub sandal-paste on his body. He went up to her, placing his feet on hers, and with two fingers beneath her chin, lifted her up and made her straight and fair. And he said: "When I have slain Kans I shall come back and be with you."

The brothers came to the empty stadium. There the bow of the god Śiva was set up, huge as three palm trees, great and heavy. Kṛṣṇa advanced to the bow, pulled it, and it broke with a mighty noise. Kans in his palace heard the sound and was appalled.

The tyrant sent his troops to kill the brothers in the city. But the lads slew the soldiers and returned to their camp. They told the

FIGURE 74. *Young Maize God* (carved stone, Mayan, Honduras, c. A.D. 680–750)

cowherds they had had an interesting tour, then ate their suppers, and went to bed.

Kans that night had ominous dreams. When he woke, he ordered the stadium prepared for the tournament and the trumpets blown for assembly. Kṛṣṇa and Balarāma arrived as jugglers, followed by the cowherds, their friends. When they entered the gate, there was a furious elephant ready to crush them, mighty as ten thousand common elephants. The driver rode it directly at Kṛṣṇa. Balarāma gave it such a blow with his fist that it halted, started back. The driver rode it again, but the two brothers struck it to the ground, and it was dead.

The youths walked onto the field. Everybody saw what his own nature revealed to him: the wrestlers thought Kṛṣṇa a wrestler, the women thought him the treasure of beauty, the gods knew him as their lord, and Kans thought he was Māra, Death himself. When he had undone every one of the wrestlers sent against him, slaying finally the strongest, he leapt to the royal dais, dragged the tyrant by the hair, and killed him. Men, gods, and saints were delighted, but the king's wives came forth to mourn. Kṛṣṇa, seeing their grief, comforted them with his primal wisdom: "Mother," he said, "do not grieve. No one can live and not die. To imagine oneself as possessing anything is to be mistaken; nobody is father, mother, or son. There is only the continuous round of birth and death."[23]

The legends of the redeemer describe the period of desolation as caused by a moral fault on the part of man (Adam in the garden, Jemshid on the throne). Yet from the standpoint of the cosmogonic cycle, a regular alternation of fair and foul is characteristic of the spectacle of time. Just as in the history of the universe, so also in that of nations: emanation leads to dissolution, youth to age, birth to death, form-creative vitality to the dead weight of inertia. Life surges, precipitating forms, and then ebbs, leaving jetsam behind. The golden age, the reign of the world emperor, alternates, in the pulse of every moment of life, with the waste land, the reign of the tyrant. The god who is the creator becomes the destroyer in the end.

From this point of view the tyrant ogre is no less representative of the father than the earlier world emperor whose position he usurped, or than the brilliant hero (the son) who is to supplant him. He is the representative of the set-fast, as the hero is the carrier of the changing. And since every moment of time bursts free from the fetters of the moment before, so this dragon, Holdfast, is pictured as of the generation immediately preceding that of the savior of the world.

Stated in direct terms: the work of the hero is to slay the tenacious aspect of the father (dragon, tester, ogre king) and release from its ban the vital energies that will feed the universe.

> This can be done either in accordance with the Father's will or against his will; he [the Father] may "choose death for his children's sake," or it may be that the Gods impose the passion upon him, making him their sacrificial victim. These are not contradictory doctrines, but different ways of telling one and the same story; in reality, Slayer and Dragon, sacrificer and victim, are of one mind behind the scenes, where there is no polarity of contraries, but mortal enemies on the stage, where the everlasting war of the Gods and the Titans is displayed. In any case, the Dragon-Father remains a Pleroma, no more diminished by what he exhales than he is increased by what he repossesses. He is the Death, on whom our life depends; and to the question "Is Death one, or many?" the answer is made that "He is one as he is there, but many as he is in his children here."[24]

The hero of yesterday becomes the tyrant of tomorrow, unless he crucifies *himself* today.

From the point of view of the present there is such a recklessness in this deliverance of the future that it appears to be nihilistic. The words of Kṛṣṇa, the world savior, to the wives of the dead Kans carry a frightening overtone; so do the words of Jesus: "I came not to send peace, but a sword. For I am come to set a man at variance against his father, and the daughter against her mother, and the daughter-in-law against her mother-in-law. And a man's foes shall be they of his own household. He that loveth father or mother more than me is not worthy of me: and he that loveth son or daughter more than me is not worthy of me."[25] To protect the unprepared, mythology veils such ultimate revelations under half-obscuring guises, while yet insisting on the gradually instructive form. The savior figure who eliminates the tyrant father and then himself assumes the crown is (like Oedipus) stepping into his sire's stead. To soften the harsh patricide, the legend represents the father as some cruel uncle or usurping Nimrod. Nevertheless, the half hidden fact remains. Once it is glimpsed, the entire spectacle buckles: the son slays the father, but the son and the father are one. The enigmatical figures dissolve back into the primal chaos. This is the wisdom of the end (and rebeginning) of the world.

7. The Hero as Saint

BEFORE WE PROCEED to the last episode of the life, one more hero-type remains to be mentioned: the saint or ascetic, the world-renouncer.

> Endowed with a pure understanding, restraining the self with firmness, turning away from sound and other objects, and abandoning love and hatred; dwelling in solitude, eating but little, controlling the speech, body, and mind, ever engaged in meditation and concentration, and cultivating freedom from passion; forsaking conceit and power, pride and lust, wrath and possessions, tranquil in heart, and free from ego—he becomes worthy of becoming one with the imperishable.[26]

The pattern is that of going to the father, but to the unmanifest rather than the manifest aspect: taking the step that the Bodhisattva renounced: that from which there is no return. Not the paradox of the dual perspective, but the ultimate claim of the unseen is here intended. The ego is burnt out. Like a dead leaf in a breeze, the body continues to move about the earth, but the soul has dissolved already in the ocean of bliss.

Thomas Aquinas, as the result of a mystical experience while celebrating mass in Naples, put his pen and ink on the shelf and left the last chapters of his *Summa Theologica* to be completed by another hand. "My writing days," he stated, "are over; for such things have been revealed to me that all I have written and taught seems of but small account to me, wherefore I hope in my God, that, even as the end has come to my teaching, so it may soon come in my life." Shortly thereafter, in his forty-ninth year, he died.

Beyond life, these heroes are beyond the myth also. Neither do they treat of it anymore, nor can the myth properly treat of them. Their legends are rehearsed, but the pious sentiments and lessons of the biographies are necessarily inadequate; little better than bathos. They have stepped away from the realm of forms, into which the incarnation descends and in which the Bodhisattva remains, the realm

FIGURE 75. *Oedipus Plucking Out His Eyes* (detail; carved stone, Roman, Italy, c. second–third century A.D.)

of the *manifest* profile of The Great Face. Once the *hidden* profile has been discovered, myth is the penultimate, silence the ultimate, word. The moment the spirit passes to the hidden, silence alone remains.

King Oedipus came to know that the woman he had married was his mother, the man he had slain his father; he plucked his eyes out and wandered in penance over the earth. The Freudians declare that each of us is slaying his father, marrying his mother, all the time—only unconsciously: the roundabout symbolic ways of doing this and the rationalizations of the consequent compulsive activity constitute our individual lives and common civilization. Should the feelings chance to become aware of the real import of the world's acts and thoughts, one would know what Oedipus knew: the flesh would suddenly appear to be an ocean of self-violation. This is the sense of the legend of Pope Gregory the Great, born of incest, living in incest. Aghast, he flees to a rock in the sea, and there does penance for his very life.

The tree has now become the cross: the White Youth sucking milk has become the Crucified swallowing gall. Corruption crawls where before was the blossom of spring. Yet beyond this threshold of the cross—for the cross is a way (the sun door), not an end—is beatitude in God.

> He has placed his seal upon me that I may prefer no love to Him.
>
> The winter has passed; the turtle dove sings; the vineyards burst into blossom.
>
> With His own ring my Lord Jesus Christ has wed me, and crowned me with a crown as His bride.
>
> The robe with which the Lord has clothed me is a robe of splendor with gold interwove, and the necklace with which He had adorned me is beyond all price.[27]

8. *Departure of the Hero*

THE LAST ACT in the biography of the hero is that of the death or departure. Here the whole sense of the life is epitomized. Needless to say, the hero would be no hero if death held for him any terror; the first condition is reconciliation with the grave.

> While sitting under the oak of Mamre, Abraham perceived a flashing of light and a smell of sweet odor, and turning around he saw Death coming toward him in great glory and beauty. And Death said unto Abraham: "Think not, Abraham, that this beauty is mine, or that I come thus to every man. Nay, but if any one is righteous like thee, I thus take a crown and come to him, but if he is a sinner, I come in great corruption, and out of their sins I make a crown for my head, and I shake them with great fear, so that they are dismayed." Abraham said to him, "And art thou, indeed, he that is called Death?" He answered, and said, "I am the bitter name," but Abraham answered, "I will not go with thee." And Abraham said to Death, "Show us thy corruption." And Death revealed his

> corruption, showing two heads, the one had the face of a serpent, the other head was like a sword. All the servants of Abraham, looking at the fierce mien of Death, died, but Abraham prayed to the Lord, and he raised them up. As the looks of Death were not able to cause Abraham's soul to depart from him, God removed the soul of Abraham as in a dream, and the archangel Michael took it up into heaven. After great praise and glory had been given to the Lord by the angels who brought Abraham's soul, and after Abraham bowed down to worship, then came the voice of God, saying thus: "Take My friend Abraham into Paradise, where are the tabernacles of My righteous ones and the abodes of My saints Isaac and Jacob in his bosom, where there is no trouble, nor grief, nor sighing, but peace and rejoicing and life unending."[28]

Compare the following dream.

> I was on a bridge where I met a blind fiddler. Everyone was tossing coins into his hat. I came closer and perceived that the musician was not blind. He had a squint, and was looking at me with a crooked glance from the side. Suddenly, there was a little old woman sitting at the side of a road. It was dark and I was afraid. "Where does this road lead?" I thought. A young peasant came along the road and took me by the hand. "Do you want to come home," he said, "and drink coffee?" "Let me go! You are holding too tight!" I cried, and awoke.[29]

The hero, who in his life represented the dual perspective, after his death is still a synthesizing image: like Charlemagne, he sleeps only and will arise in the hour of destiny, or he is among us under another form.

The Aztecs tell of the feathered serpent, Quetzalcoatl, monarch of the ancient city of Tollan in the golden age of its prosperity. He was the teacher of the arts, originator of the calendar, and the giver of maize. He and his people were overcome, at the close of their time, by the stronger magic of an invading race, the Aztecs. Tezcatlipoca, the warrior-hero of the younger people and their era, broke the city of Tollan; and the feathered serpent, king of the golden age, burned his dwellings behind him, buried his treasures in the mountains, transformed his chocolate trees into mesquite, commanded the multi-colored birds, his servants, to fly before him, and departed in great sorrow. And he came to a city called Quauhtitlan, where there was a tree, very tall and large; and he went over to the tree, sat down beneath it, and gazed into a mirror that was brought to him. "I am old," he said; and the place was named "The old Quauhtitlan." Resting again at another place along the way, and looking back in the direction of his Tollan, he wept, and his tears went through a rock. He left in that place the mark of his sitting and the impress of his palms. He was met and challenged, further along, by a group of necromancers, who prohibited him from proceeding until he had left with them the knowledge of working silver, wood, and feathers, and the art of painting. As he crossed the mountains, all of his attendants, who were dwarfs and humpbacks, died of cold. At another place he encountered his antagonist, Tezcatlipoca, who defeated him at a game of ball. At still another he aimed with an arrow at a large *póchotl* tree; the arrow too was an entire *póchotl* tree; so that when he shot it through the first they formed a cross. And so he passed along, leaving many signs and place-names behind him, until, coming at last to the sea, he departed on a raft of serpents. It is not known how he arrived at his destination, Tlapállan, his original home.[30]

Or, according to another tradition, at the shore he immolated himself upon a funeral pyre, and birds with multi-colored feathers arose from his ashes. His soul became the Morning Star.[31]

The life-eager hero can resist death, and postpone his fate for a certain time. It is written that Cuchulainn in his sleep heard a cry, "so terrible and fearful, that he fell out of his bed upon the ground, like a sack, in the east wing of the house." He rushed forth without weapons, followed by Emer, his wife, who carried his arms and garments. And he discovered a chariot harnessed with a chestnut horse that had but one leg, the pole passing through its body and out at the forehead. Within sat a woman, her eyebrows red, and a crimson mantel round her. A very big man walked along beside, also in a coat of crimson, carrying a forked staff of hazelwood and driving a cow.

Cuchulainn claimed the cow as his own, the woman challenged him, and Cuchulainn then demanded to know why she was speaking instead of the big man. She answered that the man was Uargaeth-sceo Luachair-sceo. "Well to be sure," said Cuchulainn, "the length of the name is astonishing!" "The woman to whom you speak," said the big man, "is called Faebor beg-beoil cuimdiuir folt sceubgairit sceo uath." "You are making a fool of me," said Cuchulainn; and he made a leap into the chariot, put his two feet on her two shoulders, and his spear on the parting of her hair. "Do not play your sharp weapons on me!" she said. "Then tell me your true name," said

Cuchulainn. "Go further off from me then," said she; "I am a female satirist, and I carry off this cow as a reward for a poem." "Let us hear your poem," said Cuchulainn. "Only move further off," said the woman; "your shaking over my head will not influence me."

Cuchulainn moved off until he was between the two wheels of the chariot. The woman sang at him a song of challenge and insult. He prepared to spring again, but, in an instant, horse, woman, chariot, man, and cow had disappeared, and on the branch of a tree was a black bird.

"A dangerous enchanted woman you are!" said Cuchulainn to the black bird; for he now realized that she was the battle goddess, Badb, or Morrigan. "If I had only known that it was you, we should not have parted thus." "What you have done," replied the bird, "will bring you ill luck." "You cannot harm me," said Cuchulainn. "Certainly I can," said the woman; "I am guarding your deathbed, and I shall be guarding it henceforth."

Then the enchantress told him that she was taking the cow from the fairy hill of Cruachan to be bred by the bull of the big man, who was Cuailgne; and when her calf was a year old Cuchulainn would die. She herself would come against him when he would be engaged at a certain ford with a man "as strong, as victorious, as dexterous, as terrible, as untiring, as noble, as brave, as great" as himself. "I will become an eel," she said, "and I will throw a noose round thy feet in the ford." Cuchulainn exchanged threats with her, and she disappeared into the ground. But the following year, at the foretold foray at the ford, he overcame her, and actually lived to die another day.[71]

A curious, perhaps playful, echo of the symbolism of salvation in a yonder world dimly sounds in the final passage of the Pueblo folktale of Water Jar Boy.

> A lot of people were living down inside the spring, women and girls. They all ran to the boy and put their arms around him because they were glad their child had come to their house. Thus the boy found his father and his aunts, too. Well, the boy stayed there one night and next day he went back home and told his mother he had found his father. Then his mother got sick and died. Then the boy said to himself, "No use for me to live with these people." So he left them and went to the spring. And there was his mother. That was the way he and his mother went to live with his father. His father was Avaiyo' pi'i (water snake red). He said he could not live with them over at Sikyat'ki. That was the reason he made

FIGURE 76. *Death of the Buddha* (carved stone, India, late fifth century A.D.)

the boy's mother sick so she died and "came over here to live with me," said his father. "Now we will live here together," said Avaiyo' to his son. That's the way that boy and his mother went to the spring to live there.[33]

This story, like that of the clam wife, repeats point for point the mythical narrative. The two stories are charming in their apparent innocence of their power. At the opposite extreme is the account of the death of the Buddha: humorous, like all great myth, but conscious to the last degree.

The Blessed One, accompanied by a large congregation of priests, drew near to the further bank of the Hirannavati river, and to the city of Kusinara and the sal-tree grove Upavattana of the Mallas; and having drawn near, he addressed the venerable Ananda:

"Be so good, Ananda, as to spread me a couch with its head to the north between twin sal-trees. I am weary, Ananda, and wish to lie down."

"Yes, Reverend Sir," said the venerable Ananda to The Blessed One in assent, and spread the couch with its head to the north between twin sal-trees. Then The Blessed One lay down on his right side after the manner of a lion, and placing foot on foot, remained mindful and conscious.

Now at that time the twin sal-trees had completely burst forth into bloom, though it was not the flowering season; and the blossoms scattered themselves over the body of The Tathāgata, and strewed and sprinkled themselves in worship of The Tathāgata.* Also heavenly sandal-wood powder fell from the sky; and this scattered itself over the body of The Tathāgata, and strewed and sprinkled itself in worship of The Tathāgata. And music sounded in the sky in worship of The Tathāgata, and heavenly choruses were heard to sing in worship of The Tathāgata.

During the conversations which then took place, as The Tathāgata lay like a lion on his side, a large priest, the venerable Upavana, stood in front, fanning him. The Blessed One briefly ordered him to step aside; whereupon the body attendant of The Blessed One, Ananda, complained to The Blessed One. "Reverend Sir," he said, "what, pray, was the reason, and what was the cause, that The Blessed One was harsh to the venerable Upavana, saying, 'Step aside, O priest; stand not in front of me'?"

The Blessed One replied:

Ananda, almost all the deities throughout ten worlds have come together to behold The Tathāgata. For an extent, Ananda, of twelve leagues about the city Kusinara and the sal-tree grove Upavattana of the Mallas, there is not a spot of ground large enough to stick the point of a hair into, that is not pervaded by powerful deities. And these deities, Ananda, are angered, saying, "From afar have we come to behold The Tathāgata, for but seldom, and on rare occasions, does a Tathāgata, a saint, and Supreme Buddha arise in the world; and now, to-night, in the last watch, will The Tathāgata pass into Nirvana; but this powerful priest stands in front of The Blessed One, concealing him, and we have no chance to see The Tathāgata, although his last moments are near." Thus Ananda, are these deities angered.

"What are the deities doing, Reverend Sir, whom The Blessed One perceives?"

"Some of the deities, Ananda, are in the air with their minds engrossed by earthly things, and they let fly their hair and cry aloud, and stretch out their arms and cry aloud, and fall headlong to the ground and roll to and fro, saying, 'All too soon will The Blessed One pass into Nirvana; all too soon will The Light of The World vanish from sight!' Some of the deities, Ananda,

---

* Tathāgata: "arrived at or being in (*gata*) such a state or condition (*tathā*)": i.e., an Enlightened One, a Buddha.

are on the earth with their minds engrossed by earthly things, and they let fly their hair and cry aloud, and stretch out their arms and cry aloud, and fall headlong on the ground and roll to and fro, saying, 'All too soon will The Blessed One pass into Nirvana; all too soon will The Happy One pass into Nirvana; all too soon will The Light of The World vanish from sight.' But those deities which are free from passion, mindful and conscious, bear it patiently, saying, 'Transitory are all things. How is it possible that whatever has been born, has come into being, and is organized and perishable, should not perish? That condition is not possible.'"

The last conversations continued for some time, and during the course of them The Blessed One gave consolation to his priests. Then he addressed them:

"And now, O priests, I take my leave of you; all the constituents of being are transitory; work out your salvation with diligence."

And this was the last word of The Tathāgata.

Thereupon The Blessed One entered the first trance; and rising from the first trance, he entered the second trance; and rising from the second trance, he entered the third trance; and rising from the third trance, he entered the fourth trance; and rising from the fourth trance, he entered the realm of the infinity of space; and rising from the realm of the infinity of space, he entered the realm of the infinity of consciousness; and rising from the realm of the infinity of consciousness, he entered the realm of nothingness; and rising from the realm of nothingness, he entered the realm of neither perception nor yet non-perception; and rising from the realm of neither perception nor yet non-perception, he arrived at the cessation of perception and sensation.

Thereupon the venerable Ananda spoke to the venerable Anuruddha as follows:

"Reverend Anuruddha, The Blessed One has passed into Nirvana."

"Nay, brother Ananda, The Blessed One has not yet passed into Nirvana; he has arrived at the cessation of perception and sensation."

Thereupon The Blessed One rising from the cessation of his perception and sensation, entered the realm of neither perception nor yet non-perception; and rising from the realm of neither perception nor yet non-perception, he entered the realm of nothingness; and rising from the realm of nothingness, he entered the realm of infinity of consciousness; and rising from the realm of infinity of consciousness, he entered the realm of the infinity of space; and rising from the realm of the infinity of space, he entered the fourth trance; and rising from the fourth trance, he entered the third trance; and rising from the third trance, he entered the second trance; and rising from the second trance, he entered the first trance; and rising from the first trance, he entered the second trance; and rising from the second trance, he entered the third trance; and rising from the third trance, he entered the fourth trance; and rising from the fourth trance, immediately The Blessed One passed into Nirvana.[34]

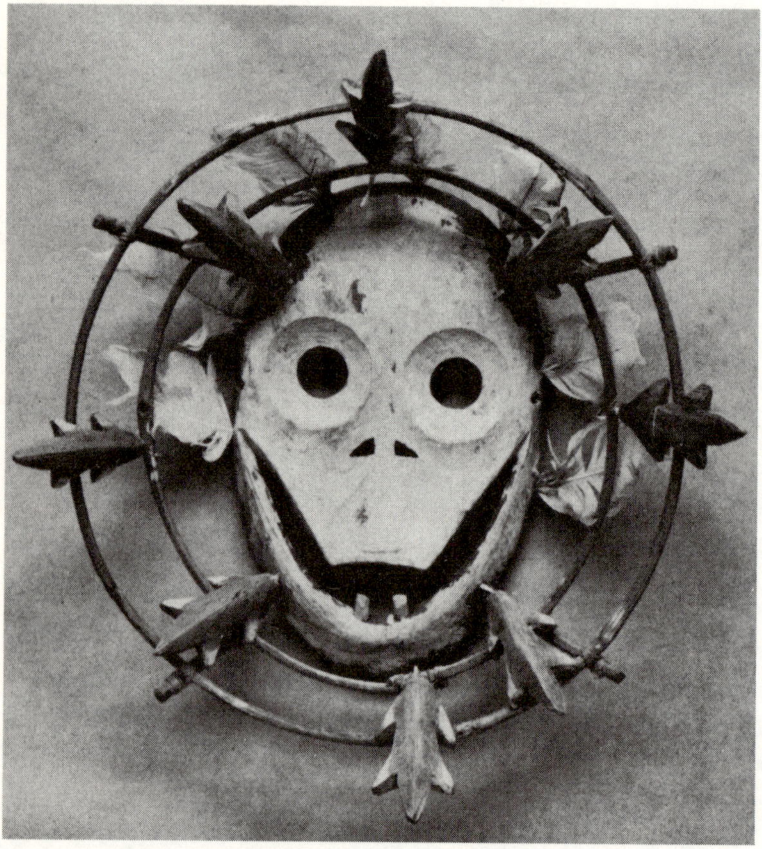

FIGURE 77. *Autumn (Death Mask)* (painted wood, Inuit, North America, date uncertain)

CHAPTER IV

Dissolutions

1. End of the Microcosm

THE MIGHTY HERO of extraordinary powers—able to lift Mount Govardhan on a finger, and to fill himself with the terrible glory of the universe—is each of us: not the physical self visible in the mirror, but the king within. Kṛṣṇa declares: "I am the Self, seated in the hearts of all creatures. I am the beginning, the middle, and the end of all beings."[1] This, precisely, is the sense of the prayers for the dead, at the moment of personal dissolution: that the individual should now return to his pristine knowledge of the world-creative divinity who during life was reflected within his heart.

> When he comes to weakness—whether he come to weakness through old age or through disease—this person frees himself from these limbs just as a mango, or a fig, or a berry releases itself from its bond; and he hastens again, according to the entrance and place of origin, back to life. As noblemen, policemen, chariot-drivers, village-heads wait with food, drink, and lodgings for a king who is coming, and cry: "Here he comes! Here he comes!" so indeed do all things wait for him who has this knowledge and cry: "Here is the Imperishable coming! Here is the Imperishable coming!"[2]

The idea is sounded already in the Coffin Texts of ancient Egypt, where the dead man sings of himself as one with God:

> *I am Atum, I who was alone;*
> *I am Re at his first appearance.*

FIGURE 78. *Osiris, Judge of the Dead* (papyrus, Egypt, c. 1275 B.C.)

I am the Great God, self-generator,
Who fashioned his names, lord of gods,
Whom none approaches among the gods.
I was yesterday, I know tomorrow.
The battle-field of the gods was made when I spoke.
I know the name of that Great God who is therein.
"Praise of Re" is his name.
I am that great Phoenix which is in Heliopolis.[3]

But, as in the death of the Buddha, the power to make a full transit back through the epochs of emanation depends on the character of the man when he was alive. The myths tell of a dangerous journey of the soul, with obstacles to be passed. The Eskimos in Greenland enumerate a boiling kettle, a pelvis bone, a large burning lamp, monster guardians, and two rocks that strike together and open again.[4] Such elements are standard features of world folklore and heroic legend. We have discussed them above, in our chapters of "The Adventure of the Hero." They have received their most elaborate and significant development in the mythology of the soul's last journey.

An Aztec prayer to be said at the deathbed warns the departed of the dangers along the way back to the skeleton god of the dead, Tzontémoc, "He of the Falling Hair."

> Dear child! Thou hast passed through and survived the labors of this life. Now it hath pleased our Lord to carry thee away. For we do not enjoy this world everlastingly, only briefly; our life is like the warming of oneself in the sun. And the Lord hath conferred on us the blessing of knowing and conversing with each other in this existence; but now, at this moment, the god who is called Mictlantecutli, or Aculnahuácatl, or again Tzontémoc, and the goddess known as Mictecacíhuatl, have transported thee away. Thou art brought before His seat; for we all must go there: that place is intended for us all, and it is vast.
>
> We are to have of thee no further recollection. Thou wilt reside in that place most dark, where there is neither light nor window. Thou wilt not return or depart from thence; nor wilt thou think about or concern thyself with the matter of return. Thou wilt be absent from among us for ever more. Poor and orphaned hast thou left thy children, thy grandchildren; nor dost thou know how they will end, how they will pass through the labors of this life. As for ourselves, we shall soon be going there where thou art to be.

The Aztec ancients and officials prepared the body for the funeral, and, when they had properly wrapped it, took a little water and poured it on the head, saying to the deceased: "This thou didst enjoy when thou wert living in the world." And they took a small jug of water and presented it to him, saying: "Here is something for thy journey"; they set it in the fold of his shroud. Then they wrapped the deceased in his blankets, secured him strongly, and placed before him, one at a time, certain papers that had been prepared: "Lo, with this thou wilt be able to go between the mountains that clash." "With this thou wilt pass along the road where the serpent watcheth." "This will satisfy the little green lizard, Xochitónal." "And behold, with this thou wilt make the transit of the eight deserts of freezing cold." "Here is that by which thou wilt go across the eight small hills." "Here is that by which thou wilt survive the wind of the obsidian knives."

The departed was to take a little dog with him, of bright reddish hair. Around its neck they placed a soft thread of cotton; they killed it and cremated it with the corpse. The departed swam on this small animal when he passed the river of the underworld. And, after four years of passage, he arrived with it before the god, to whom he presented his papers and gifts. Whereupon he was admitted, together with his faithful companion, to the "Ninth Abyss."[5]*

The Chinese tell of a crossing of the Fairy Bridge under guidance of the Jade Maiden and the Golden Youth. The Hindus picture a towering firmament of heavens and a many-leveled underworld of hells. The soul gravitates after death to the story appropriate to its relative density, there to digest and assimilate the whole meaning of its past life. When the lesson has been learned, it returns to the world, to prepare itself for the next degree of experience. Thus gradually it makes its way through all the levels of life-value until it has broken past the confines of the cosmic egg. Dante's *Divina Commedia* is an exhaustive review of the stages: "Inferno," the misery of the spirit bound to the prides and actions of the flesh; "Purgatorio," the process of transmuting fleshly into spiritual experience; "Paradiso," the degrees of spiritual realization.

A deep and awesome vision of the journey is that of the Egyptian *Book of the Dead.* The man or woman who has died is identified with and actually called Osiris. The texts open with hymns of praise to Re and Osiris and then proceed to the mysteries of the unswathing of the spirit in the world beneath. In the "Chapter of Giving a Mouth to Osiris N.," we read the phrase: "I rise out of the egg in the hidden land." (Where *N* appears the name of the deceased is given; viz., Osiris Aufankh, Osiris Ani.) This is the announcement of the idea of death as a rebirth. Then, in the "Chapter of Opening the Mouth of Osiris N.," the awakening spirit prays: "May the god Ptah open my mouth, and may the god of my city loose the swathings, even the swathings which are over my mouth." The "Chapter of Making Osiris N. to Possess Memory in the Underworld" and the "Chapter of Giving a Heart to Osiris N. in the Underworld" carry the process of rebirth two stages further. Then begin the chapters of the dangers that the lone voyager has to face and overcome on his way to the throne of the awesome judge.

---

* White dogs and black cannot swim the river, because the white would say: "I have washed myself!" and the black: "I have soiled myself!" Only the bright reddish ones can pass to the shore of the dead.

The Book of the Dead was buried with the mummy as a guide book to the perils of the difficult way, and chapters were recited at the time of burial. At one stage in the preparation of the mummy, the heart of the dead man was cut open and a basalt scarab in a gold setting, symbolic of the sun, was placed therein with the prayer: "My heart, my mother, my heart, my mother; my heart of transformations." This is prescribed in the "Chapter of Not Letting the Heart of Osiris N. Be Taken from Him in the Underworld." Next we read, in the "Chapter of Beating Back the Crocodile":

> Get thee back, O crocodile that dwellest in the west.... Get thee back, O crocodile that dwellest in the south.... Get thee back, O crocodile that dwellest in the north.... The things which are created are in the hollow of my hand, and those which have not yet come into being are in my body. I am clothed and wholly provided with thy magical words, O Re, the which are in heaven above me and in the earth beneath me....

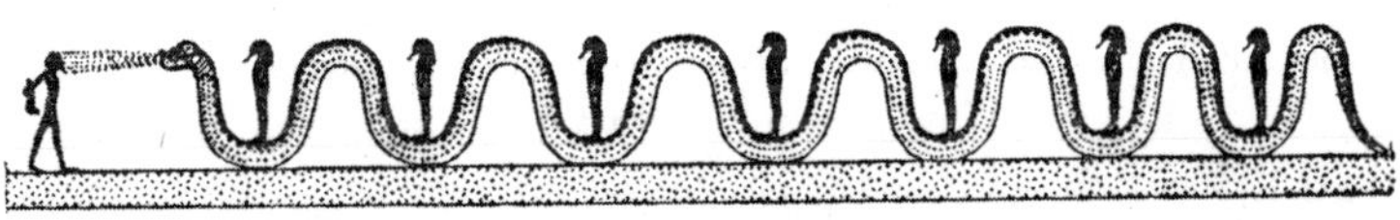

FIGURE 79. *The Serpent Kheti in the Underworld, Consuming with Fire an Enemy of Osiris* (carved alabaster, New Kingdom, Egypt, 1278 B.C.)

The "Chapter of Repulsing Serpents" follows, then the "Chapter of Driving Away Apshait." The soul cries at the latter demon: "Depart from me, O thou who hast lips that gnaw." In the "Chapter of Driving Back the Two Merti Goddesses" the soul declares its purpose, and protects itself by stating its claim to be the son of the father: "...I shine from the Sektet boat, I am Horus the son of Osiris, and I have come to see my father Osiris." The "Chapter of Living by Air in the Underworld" and the "Chapter of Driving Back the Serpent Rerek in the Underworld" carry the hero still further along his way, and then comes the great proclamation of the "Chapter of Driving Away the Slaughterings Which Are Performed in the Underworld":

> My hair is the hair of Nu. My face is the face of the Disk. My eyes are the eyes of Hathor. My ears are the ears of Apuat. My nose is the nose of Khenti-khas. My lips are the lips of Anpu. My teeth are the teeth of Serget. My neck is the neck of the divine goddess Isis. My hands are the hands of Ba-neb-Tattu. My forearms are the forearms

> of Neith, the Lady of Sais. My backbone is the backbone of Suti. My phallus is the phallus of Osiris. My loins are the loins of the Lords of Kher-aba. My chest is the chest of the Mighty One of Terror.... There is no member of my body that is not the member of some God. The god Thoth shieldeth my body altogether, and I am Re day by day. I shall not be dragged back by the arms, and none shall lay violent hold upon my hands....

As in the much later Buddhist image of the Bodhisattva within whose nimbus stand five hundred transformed Buddhas, each attended by five hundred Bodhisattvas, and each of these, in turn, by innumerable gods, so here, the soul comes to the fullness of its stature and power through assimilating the deities that formerly had been thought to be separate from and outside of it. They are projections of its own being; and as it returns to its true state they are all reassumed.

In the "Chapter of Snuffing the Air and of Having the Mastery over the Water of the Underworld," the soul proclaims itself to be the guardian of the cosmic egg: "Hail, thou sycamore-tree of the goddess Nut! Grant thou to me of the water and of the air which dwell in thee. I embrace the throne which is in Hermopolis, and I watch and guard the egg of the Great Cackler. It groweth, I grow; it liveth, I live; it snuffeth the air, I snuff the air, I the Osiris N., in triumph."

FIGURE 80. *The Doubles of Ani and His Wife Drinking Water in the Other World* (papyrus, Ptolemaic, Egypt, c. 240 B.C.)

There follow the "Chapter of Not Letting the Soul of a Man Be Taken from Him in the Underworld" and the "Chapter of Drinking Water in the Underworld and of Not Being Burnt by Fire," and then we come to the great culmination—the "Chapter of Coming Forth by Day in the Underworld," wherein the soul and the universal being are known to be one:

> I am Yesterday, Today, and Tomorrow, and I have the power to be born a second time; I am the divine hidden Soul who createth the gods, and who giveth sepulchral meals unto the denizens of the Underworld of Amentet and of Heaven. I am the rudder of the east, the possessor of two divine faces wherein his beams are seen. I am the lord of the men who are raised up; the lord who cometh forth out of darkness, and whose forms of existence are of the house wherein are the dead. Hail, ye two hawks who are perched upon your resting-places, who harken unto the things which are said by him, who guide the bier to the hidden place, who lead along Re, and who follow him into the uppermost place of the shrine which is in the celestial heights! Hail, lord of the shrine which standeth in the middle of the earth. He is I, and I am he, and Ptah hath covered his sky with crystal....

Thereafter, the soul may range the universe at will, as is shown in the "Chapter of Lifting Up the Feet and of Coming Forth upon the Earth," the "Chapter of Journeying to Heliopolis and of Receiving a Throne Therein," the "Chapter of a Man Transforming Himself into Whatever Form He Pleaseth," the "Chapter of Entering into the Great House," and the "Chapter of Going into the Presence of the Divine Sovereign Princes of Osiris." The chapters of the so-called Negative Confession declare the moral purity of the man who has been redeemed: "I have not done iniquity.... I have not robbed with violence.... I have not done violence to any man.... I have not committed theft.... I have not slain man or woman...." The book concludes with addresses of praise of the gods, and then: the "Chapter of Living Nigh unto Re," the "Chapter of Causing a Man to Come Back to See His House upon Earth," the "Chapter of Making Perfect the Soul," and the "Chapter of Sailing in the Great Sun-Boat of Re."[6]

2. *End of the Macrocosm*

As the created form of the individual must dissolve, so that of the universe also:

> When it is known that after the lapse of a hundred thousand years the cycle is to be renewed, the gods called Loka-byūhas, inhabitants of a heaven of sensual pleasure, wander about through the world, with hair let down and flying in the wind, weeping and wiping away their tears with their hands, and with their clothes red and in great disorder. And thus they make announcement:
>
> "Sirs, after the lapse of a hundred thousand years, the cycle is to be renewed; this world will be destroyed; also the mighty ocean will dry up; and this broad earth, and Sumeru, the monarch of the mountains, will be burnt up and destroyed—up to the Brahma-world will the destruction of the world extend. Therefore, sirs, cultivate friendliness; cultivate compassion, joy, and indifference; wait on your mothers; wait on your fathers; and honor your elders among your kinsfolk."
>
> This is called the Cyclic-Uproar.[7]

The Mayan version of the world-end is represented in an illustration covering the last page of the Dresden Codex.[8] This ancient manuscript records the cycles of the planets and from those deduces calculations of vast cosmic cycles. The serpent numbers which appear toward the close of the text (so-called because of the appearance in them of a serpent symbol) represent world periods of some thirty-four thousand years—twelve and a half million days—and these are recorded again and again.

> In these well-nigh inconceivable periods, all the smaller units may be regarded as coming at last to a more or less exact close. What matter a few score years one way or the other in this virtual eternity? Finally, on the last page of the manuscript, is depicted the Destruction of the World, for which the highest numbers have paved the way. Here we see the rain serpent, stretching across the sky, belching forth torrents of water. Great streams of water

FIGURE 81. *World-end: Rain Serpent and Tiger-claw Goddess* (ink on tree-bark paper, Mayan, Central America, c. A.D. 1200–1250)

> gush from the sun and moon. The old goddess, she of the tiger claws and forbidding aspect, the malevolent patroness of floods and cloudbursts, overturns the bowl of the heavenly waters. The crossbones, dread symbol of death, decorate her skirt, and a writhing snake crowns her head. Below with downward-pointed spear, symbolic of the universal destruction, the black god stalks abroad, a screeching owl raging on his fearsome head. Here, indeed, is portrayed with graphic touch the final all-engulfing cataclysm.[9]

One of the strongest representations appears in the Poetic Edda of the ancient Vikings. Othin (Wotan), the chief of the gods, has asked to know what will be the doom of himself and his pantheon, and the "Wise Woman," a personification of the World Mother herself, Destiny articulate, lets him hear:[10]

> *Brothers shall fight and fell each other,*
> *And sisters' sons shall kinship stain;*
> *Hard is it on earth, with mighty whoredom;*
> *Ax-time, sword-time, shields are sundered,*
> *Wind-time, wolf-time, ere the world falls;*
> *Nor ever shall men each other spare.*

In the land of the giants, Jotunheim, a fair, red rooster shall crow; in Valhalla the rooster Golden Comb; a rust-red bird in Hell. The dog Garm at the cliff-cave, the entrance to the world of the dead, shall open his great jaws and howl. The earth shall tremble, the crags and trees be torn asunder, the sea gush forth upon the land. The fetters of those monsters who were chained back in the beginning shall all burst: Fenris-Wolf shall run free, and advance with lower jaw against the earth, upper against the heavens ("he would gape yet more if there were room for it"); fires shall blaze from his eyes and nostrils. The world-enveloping serpent of the cosmic ocean shall rise in giant wrath and advance beside the wolf upon the land, blowing venom, so that it shall sprinkle all the air and water. Naglfar shall be loosed (the ship made of dead men's nails) and this shall be the transport of the giants. Another ship shall sail with the inhabitants of hell. And the people of fire shall advance from the south.

When the watchman of the gods shall blow the shrieking horn, the warrior sons of Othin will be summoned to the final battle. From all quarters the gods, giants, demons, dwarfs, and elves will be riding for the field. The World Ash, Yggdrasil, will tremble, and nothing then be without fear in heaven and earth.

Othin shall advance against the wolf, Thor against the serpent,

FIGURE 82. *Ragnarök: Fenrir the Wolf Devouring Odin* (carved stone, Viking, Britain, c. A.D. 1000)

Tyr against the dog—the worst monster of all—and Freyr against Surt, the man of flame. Thor shall slay the serpent, stride ten paces from that spot, and because of the venom blown fall dead to the earth. Othin shall be swallowed by the wolf, and thereafter Vidarr, setting one foot upon the lower jaw, shall take the upper jaw of the wolf in his hand and tear asunder the gullet. Loki shall slay Heimdallr and be slain by him. Surt shall cast fire over the earth and burn all the world.

The sun turns black, earth sinks in the sea,
The hot stars down from heaven are whirled;
Fierce grows the steam and the life-feeding flame,
Till fire leaps high about heaven itself.

Now Garm howls loud before Gnipahellir,
The fetters will burst, and the wolf run free;
Much do I know, and more can see
Of the fate of the gods, the mighty in fight.

This vision of Apocalypse comes to us from the Gospel according to Matthew:

> And as Jesus sat upon the Mount of Olives, the disciples came unto him privately, saying, Tell us when shall these things be? and what shall be the sign of thy coming, and of the end of the world?
>
> And Jesus answered and said unto them, Take heed that no man deceive you. For many shall come in my name, saying, I am Christ; and shall deceive many. And ye shall hear of wars and rumors of wars: see that ye be not troubled: for all these things must come to pass, but the end is not yet. For nation shall rise against nation, and kingdom against kingdom: and there shall be famines and pestilences, and earthquakes, in divers places. All these are the beginning of sorrows, Then shall they deliver you up to be afflicted, and shall kill you: and ye shall be hated of all nations for my name's sake. And then shall many be offended, and shall betray one another, and shall hate one another. And many false prophets shall rise, and shall deceive many. And because iniquity shall abound, the love of many shall wax cold. But he that shall endure unto the end, the same shall be saved. And this gospel of the kingdom shall be preached in all the world for a witness unto all nations; and then shall the end come.
>
> When ye therefore shall see the abomination of desolation, spoken of by Daniel the prophet, stand in the holy place, (whoso readeth, let him understand:) Then let them which be in Judaea

flee into the mountains: Let him which is on the housetop not come down to take anything out of his house: Neither let him which is in the field return back to take his clothes. And woe unto them that are with child, and to them that give suck in those days! But pray ye that your flight be not in the winter, neither on the sabbath day: For then shall be great tribulation, such as was not since the beginning of the world to this time, no, nor ever shall be. And except those days should be shortened, there should no flesh be saved: but for the elect's sake those days shall be shortened.

Then if any man shall say unto you: Lo, here is Christ, or there; believe it not. For there shall arise false Christs, and false prophets, and shall show great signs and wonders; insomuch that, if it were possible, they shall deceive the very elect. Behold, I have told you before. Wherefore if they shall say unto you, Behold, he is in the desert; go not forth: behold, he is in the secret chambers; believe it not. For as the lightning cometh out of the east, and shineth even unto the west; so shall also the coming of the Son of man be. For wheresoever the carcase is there will the eagles be gathered together. Immediately after the tribulation of those days shall the sun be darkened, and the moon shall not give her light, and the stars shall fall from heaven, and the powers of the heavens shall be shaken: And then shall appear the sign of the Son of man in heaven: and then shall all the tribes of the earth mourn, and they shall see the Son of man coming in the clouds of heaven with power and great glory. And he shall send his angels with a great sound of a trumpet, and they shall gather together his elect from the four winds, from one end of heaven to the other.... But of that day and hour knoweth no man, no, not the angels of heaven, but my Father only.[11]

FIGURE 83. *Wrestling with Proteus* (carved marble, France, A.D. 1723)

EPILOGUE

Myth and Society

1. *The Shapeshifter*

THERE IS NO FINAL SYSTEM for the interpretation of myths, and there will never be any such thing. Mythology is like the god Proteus, "the ancient one of the sea, whose speech is sooth." The god "will make assay, and take all manner of shapes of things that creep upon the earth, of water likewise, and of fierce fire burning."[1]

The life-voyager wishing to be taught by Proteus must "grasp him steadfastly and press him yet the more," and at length he will appear in his proper shape. But this wily god never discloses even to the skillful questioner the whole content of his wisdom. He will reply only to the question put to him, and what he discloses will be great or trivial, according to the question asked.

> So often as the sun in his course stands high in mid heaven, then forth from the brine comes the ancient one of the sea, whose speech is sooth, before the breath of the West Wind he comes, and the sea's dark ripple covers him. And when he is got forth, he lies down to sleep in the hollow of the caves. And around him the seals, the brood of the fair daughter of the brine, sleep all in a flock, stolen forth from the grey sea water, and bitter is the scent they breathe of the deeps of the salt sea.[2]

The Greek warrior-king Menelaus, who was guided by a helpful daughter of this old sea-father to the wild lair, and instructed by her how to wring from the god his response, desired only to ask the secret of his own personal difficulties and the whereabouts of his personal friends. And the god did not disdain to reply.

Mythology has been interpreted by the modern intellect as a primitive, fumbling effort to explain the world of nature (Frazer); as a production of poetical fantasy from prehistoric times, misunderstood by succeeding ages (Müller); as a repository of allegorical instruction, to shape the individual to his group (Durkheim); as a group dream, symptomatic of archetypal urges within the depths of the human psyche (Jung); as the traditional vehicle of man's profoundest metaphysical insights (Coomaraswamy); and as God's Revelation to His children (the Church). Mythology is all of these. The various judgments are determined by the viewpoints of the judges. For when scrutinized in terms not of what it is but of how it functions, of how it has served mankind in the past, of how it may serve today, mythology shows itself to be as amenable as life itself to the obsessions and requirements of the individual, the race, the age.

2. *The Function of Myth, Cult, and Meditation*

In his life-form the individual is necessarily only a fraction and distortion of the total image of man. He is limited either as male or as female; at any given period of his life he is again limited as child, youth, mature adult, or ancient; furthermore, in his life-role he is necessarily specialized as craftsman, tradesman, servant, or thief, priest, leader, wife, nun, or harlot; he cannot be all. Hence, the totality—the fullness of man—is not in the separate member, but in the body of the society as a whole; the individual can be only an organ. From his group he has derived his techniques of life, the language in which he thinks, the ideas on which he thrives; through the past of that society descended the genes that built his body. If he presumes to cut himself off, either in deed or in thought and feeling, he only breaks connection with the sources of his existence.

The tribal ceremonies of birth, initiation, marriage, burial, installation, and so forth, serve to translate the individual's life-crises and life-deeds into classic, impersonal forms. They disclose him to himself, not as this personality or that, but as the warrior, the bride, the widow, the priest, the chieftain; at the same time rehearsing for the rest of the community the old lesson of the archetypal stages. All participate in the ceremonial according to rank and function. The whole society becomes visible to itself as an imperishable living unit. Generations of individuals pass, like anonymous cells from a living body; but the sustaining, timeless form remains. By an enlargement of vision to embrace this superindividual, each discovers himself enhanced, enriched, supported, and magnified. His role, however unimpressive, is seen to be intrinsic to the beautiful festival-image of man—the image, potential yet necessarily inhibited, within himself.

Social duties continue the lesson of the festival into normal, everyday existence, and the individual is validated still. Conversely, indifference, revolt—or exile—break the vitalizing connectives. From the standpoint of the social unit, the broken-off individual is simply nothing—waste. Whereas the man or woman who can honestly say that he or she has lived the role—whether that of priest, harlot, queen, or slave—*is* something in the full sense of the verb *to be.*

Rites of initiation and installation, then, teach the lesson of the essential oneness of the individual and the group; seasonal festivals open a larger horizon. As the individual is an organ of society, so is the tribe or city—so is humanity entire—only a phase of the mighty organism of the cosmos.

It has been customary to describe the seasonal festivals of so-called native peoples as efforts to control nature. This is a misrepresentation. There is much of the will to control in every act of man, and particularly in those magical ceremonies that are thought to bring rain clouds, cure sickness, or stay the flood; nevertheless the dominant motive in all truly religious (as opposed to black-magical) ceremonial is that of submission to the inevitables of destiny—and in the seasonal festivals this motive is particularly apparent.

No tribal rite has yet been recorded which attempts to keep winter from descending; on the contrary: the rites all prepare the community to endure, together with the rest of nature, the season of the terrible cold. And in the spring, the rites do not seek to compel nature to pour forth immediately corn, beans, and squash for the lean community; on the contrary: the rites dedicate the whole people to the work of nature's season. The wonderful cycle of the year, with its hardships and periods of joy, is celebrated, and delineated, and represented as continued in the life-round of the human group.

Many other symbolizations of this continuity fill the world of the mythologically instructed community. For example, the clans of the American hunting tribes commonly regarded themselves as descended from half-animal, half-human ancestors. These ancestors fathered not only the human members of the clan, but also the animal species after which the clan was named; thus the human members of the beaver clan were blood cousins of the animal beavers, protectors of the species and in turn protected by the animal wisdom of the wood folk. Or another example: The hogan, or mud hut, of the Navahos of New Mexico and Arizona, is constructed on the plan of the Navaho image of the cosmos. The entrance faces east. The eight sides represent the four directions and the points between. Every beam and joist corresponds to an element in the great hogan of the all-embracing earth and sky. And since the soul of man itself is regarded as identical in form with the universe, the mud hut is a representation of the basic harmony of man and world, and a reminder of the hidden life-way of perfection.

But there is another way—in diametric opposition to that of social duty and the popular cult. From the standpoint of the way of duty, anyone in exile from the community is a nothing. From the other point of view, however, this exile is the first step of the quest. Each carries within himself the all; therefore it may be sought and discovered within. The differentiations of sex, age, and occupation are not essential to our character, but mere costumes which we wear for a time on the stage of the world. The image of man within is not to be confounded with the garments. We think of ourselves as Americans, children of the twentieth century, Occidentals, civilized Christians. We are virtuous or sinful. Yet such designations do not tell what it is to be man, they denote only the accidents of geography, birth-date, and income. What is the core of us? What is the basic character of our being?

The asceticism of the medieval saints and of the yogis of India, the Hellenistic mystery initiations, the ancient philosophies of the East and of the West, are techniques for the shifting of the emphasis of individual consciousness away from the garments. The preliminary meditations of the aspirant detach his mind and sentiments from the accidents of life and drive him to the core. "I am not that, not that," he meditates: "not my mother or son who has just died; my body, which is ill or aging; my arm, my eye, my head; not the summation of all these things. I am not my feeling; not my mind; not my power of intuition." By such meditations he is driven to his own profundity and breaks through, at last, to unfathomable realizations. No man can return from such exercises and take very seriously himself as Mr. So-and-so of Such-and-such a township, U.S.A. Society and duties drop away. Mr. So-and-so, having discovered himself big with man, becomes indrawn and aloof.

This is the stage of Narcissus looking into the pool, of the Buddha sitting contemplative under the tree, but it is not the ultimate goal; it is a requisite step, but not the end. The aim is not to *see,* but to realize that one *is,* that essence; then one is free to wander as that essence in the world. Furthermore: the world too is of that essence. The essence of oneself and the essence of the world: these two are one. Hence separateness, withdrawal, is no longer necessary. Wherever the hero may wander, whatever he may do, he is ever in the presence of his own essence—for he has the perfected eye to see. There is no separateness. Thus, just as the way of social participation may lead in the end to a realization of the All in the individual, so that of exile brings the hero to the Self in all.

Centered in this hub-point, the question of selfishness or altruism disappears. The individual has lost himself in the law and been reborn in identity with the whole meaning of the universe. For Him, by Him, the world was made. "O Mohammed," God said, "hadst thou not been, I would not have created the sky."

3. *The Hero Today*

ALL OF WHICH is far indeed from the contemporary view; for the democratic ideal of the self-determining individual, the invention of the power-driven machine, and the development of the scientific method of research have so transformed human life that the long inherited, timeless universe of symbols has collapsed. In the fateful, epoch-announcing words of Nietzsche's Zarathustra: "Dead are all the gods."[3] One knows the tale; it has been told a thousand ways. It is the hero-cycle of the modern age, the wonder-story of mankind's coming to maturity. The spell of the past, the bondage of tradition, was shattered with sure and mighty strokes. The dream-web of myth fell away; the mind opened to full waking consciousness; and modern man emerged from ancient ignorance, like a butterfly from its cocoon, or like the sun at dawn from the womb of mother night.

It is not only that there is no hiding place for the gods from the searching telescope and microscope; there is no such society any more as the gods once supported. The social unit is not a carrier of religious content, but an economic-political organization. Its ideals are not those of the hieratic pantomime, making visible on earth the forms of heaven, but of the secular state, in hard and unremitting competition for material supremacy and resources. Isolated societies, dream-bounded within a mythologically charged horizon, no longer exist except as areas to be exploited. And within the progressive societies themselves, every last vestige of the ancient human heritage of ritual, morality, and art is in full decay.

The problem of mankind today, therefore, is precisely the opposite to that of men in the comparatively stable periods of those great co-ordinating mythologies which now are known as lies. Then all meaning was in the group, in the great anonymous forms, none in the self-expressive individual; today no meaning is in the group—none in the world: all is in the individual. But there the meaning is absolutely unconscious. One does not know toward what one moves. One does not know by what one is propelled. The lines of communication between the conscious and the unconscious zones of the human psyche have all been cut, and we have been split in two.

The hero-deed to be wrought is not today what it was in the century of Galileo. Where then there was darkness, now there is light; but also, where light was, there now is darkness. The modern hero-deed must be that of questing to bring to light again the lost Atlantis of the co-ordinated soul.

Obviously, this work cannot be wrought by turning back, or away, from what has been accomplished by the modern revolution; for the problem is nothing if not that of rendering the modern world spiritually significant—or rather (phrasing the same principle the other way round) nothing if not that of making it possible for men and women to come to full human maturity through the conditions of contemporary life. Indeed, these conditions themselves are what have rendered the ancient formulae ineffective, misleading, and even pernicious. The community today is the planet, not the bounded nation; hence the patterns of projected aggression which formerly served to co-ordinate the in-group now can only break it into factions. The national idea, with the flag as totem, is today an aggrandizer of the nursery ego, not the annihilator of an infantile situation. Its parody-rituals of the parade ground serve the ends of Holdfast, the tyrant dragon, not the God in whom self-interest is annihilate. And the numerous saints of this anticult—namely the patriots whose ubiquitous photographs, draped with flags, serve as official icons—are precisely the local threshold guardians (our demon Sticky-hair) whom it is the first problem of the hero to surpass.

Nor can the great world religions, as at present understood, meet the requirement. For they have become associated with the causes of the factions, as instruments of propaganda and self-congratulation. (Even Buddhism has lately suffered this degradation, in reaction to the lessons of the West.) The universal triumph of the secular state has thrown all religious organizations into such a definitely secondary, and finally ineffectual, position that religious pantomime is hardly more today than a sanctimonious exercise for Sunday morning, whereas business ethics and patriotism stand for the remainder of the week. Such a monkey-holiness is not what the functioning world requires; rather, a transmutation of the whole social order is necessary, so that through every detail and act of secular life the vitalizing image of the universal god-man who is actually immanent and effective in all of us may be somehow made known to consciousness.

And this is not a work that consciousness itself can achieve. Consciousness can no more invent, or even predict, an effective symbol than foretell or control tonight's dream. The whole thing is being worked out on another level, through what is bound to be a long and very frightening process, not only in the depths of every living psyche in the modern world, but also on those titanic battlefields into which the whole planet has lately been converted. We are watching the terrible clash of the Symplegades, through which the soul must pass—identified with neither side.

But there is one thing we may know, namely, that as the new symbols become visible, they will not be identical in the various parts of the globe; the circumstances of local life, race, and tradition must all be compounded in the effective forms. Therefore, it is necessary for men to understand, and be able to see, that through various symbols the same redemption is revealed. "Truth is one," we read in the Vedas; "the sages call it by many names." A single song is being inflected through all the colorations of the human choir. General propaganda for one or another of the local solutions, therefore, is superfluous—or much rather, a menace. The way to become human is to learn to recognize the lineaments of God in all of the wonderful modulations of the face of man.

With this we come to the final hint of what the specific orientation of the modern hero-task must be, and discover the real cause for the disintegration of all of our inherited religious formulae. The center of gravity, that is to say, of the realm of mystery and danger has definitely shifted. For the primitive hunting peoples of those remotest human millennia when the sabertooth tiger, the mammoth, and the lesser presences of the animal kingdom were the primary manifestations of what was alien—the source at once of danger, and of sustenance—the great human problem was to become linked psychologically to the task of sharing the wilderness with these beings. An unconscious identification took place, and this was finally rendered conscious in the half-human, half-animal figures of the mythological totem-ancestors. The animals became the tutors of humanity. Through acts of literal imitation—such as today appear only on the children's playground (or in the madhouse)—an effective annihilation of the human ego was accomplished and society achieved a cohesive organization. Similarly, the tribes supporting themselves on plant-food became cathected to the plant; the life-rituals of planting and reaping were identified with those of human procreation, birth, and progress to maturity. Both the plant and the animal worlds, however, were in the end brought under social control. Whereupon the great field of instructive wonder shifted—to the skies—and mankind enacted the great pantomime of the sacred moon-king, the sacred sun-king, the hieratic, planetary state, and the symbolic festivals of the world-regulating spheres.

Today all of these mysteries have lost their force; their symbols no longer interest our psyche. The notion of a cosmic law, which all existence serves and to which man himself must bend, has long since passed through the preliminary mystical stages represented in the old astrology, and is now simply accepted in mechanical terms as a matter of course. The descent of the Occidental sciences from the heavens to the earth (from seventeenth-century astronomy to nineteenth-century biology), and their concentration today, at last, on man himself (in twentieth-century anthropology and psychology), mark the path of a prodigious transfer of the focal point of human wonder. Not the animal world, not the plant world, not the miracle of the spheres, but man himself is now the crucial mystery. *Man* is that alien presence with whom the forces of egoism must come to terms, through whom the ego is to be crucified and resurrected, and in whose image society is to be reformed. Man, understood however not as "I" but as "Thou": for the ideals and temporal institutions of no tribe, race, continent, social class, or century can be the measure of the inexhaustible and multifariously wonderful divine existence that is the life in all of us.

The modern hero, the modern individual who dares to heed the call and seek the mansion of that presence with whom it is our whole destiny to be atoned, cannot, indeed must not, wait for his community to cast off its slough of pride, fear, rationalized avarice, and sanctified misunderstanding. "Live," Nietzsche says, "as though the day were here." It is not society that is to guide and save the creative hero, but precisely the reverse. And so every one of us shares the supreme ordeal—carries the cross of the redeemer—not in the bright moments of his tribe's great victories, but in the silences of his personal despair.

FIGURE 84. *Earthrise* (photograph, lunar orbit, A.D. 1968)

ACKNOWLEDGMENTS

THIS EDITION WAS PREPARED by the Joseph Campbell Foundation (JCF) as part of the Collected Works of Joseph Campbell (Robert Walter, executive editor; David Kudler, managing editor). All notes marked [Ed.] originated with the JCF editors.

New World Library's editor was Jason Gardner.

The bibliography appears courtesy of the Opus Archive and Research Center, which reserves all rights thereto.

Images of C. G. Jung and Sigmund Freud appear with the permission of HIP/Art Resource, New York.

Image of Franz Boas (page 13) appears with the permission of the Phoebe E. Hearst Museum and the Regents of the University of California.

All other images and quotations appear with the permission of their copyright holders, except where they belong to the public domain. See the endnotes and the illustration list for sources.

Image research assistance was provided by Sabra Moore, by Diana Brown, M.A., and by the associates of the JCF.

ENDNOTES

PREFACE TO THE 1949 EDITION

1 Sigmund Freud, *The Future of an Illusion* (translated by James Strachey et al., Standard Edition, XXI; London: Hogarth Press, 1961), pp. 44–45. (Orig. 1927.)

2 Ṛg Veda: 1.164.46.

PROLOGUE: THE MONOMYTH

1 Clement Wood, *Dreams: Their Meaning and Practical Application* (New York: Greenberg, 1931), p. 124. "The dream material in this book," states the author (p. viii), "is drawn primarily from the thousand and more dreams submitted to me each week for analysis, in connection with my daily feature syndicated throughout the newspapers of the country. This has been supplemented by dreams analysed by me in my private practice." In contrast to most of the dreams presented in the standard works on the subject, those in this popular introduction to Freud come from people not undergoing analysis. They are remarkably ingenuous.

2 Géza Róheim, *The Origin and Function of Culture* (Nervous and Mental Disease Monographs, No. 69, New York, 1943), pp. 17–25.

3 D. T. Burlingham, "Die Einfühlung des Kleinkindes in die Mutter," *Imago*, XXI, p. 429; cited by Géza Róheim, *War, Crime and the Covenant* (*Journal of Clinical Psychopathology, Monograph Series*, No. 1, Monticello, NY, 1945), p. 1.

4 Róheim, *War, Crime and the Covenant*, p. 3.

5 Freud, *The Interpretation of Dreams* (translated by James Strachey, Standard Edition, IV; London: The Hogarth Press, 1953), p. 262. (Orig. 1900.)

6 Freud, *Three Essays on the Theory of Sexuality*, III. "The Transformations of Puberty" (translated by James Strachey, Standard Edition, VII; London: The Hogarth Press, 1953), p. 208. (Orig. 1905.)

7 Sophocles, *Oedipus Tyrannus*, pp. 981–83

8 Wood, *op. cit.*, pp. 92–93.

9 A. van Gennep, *Les rites de passage* (Paris, 1909).

10 Géza Róheim, *The Eternal Ones of the Dream* (New York: International Universities Press, 1945), p. 178.

11 C.G. Jung, *Symbols of Transformation* (translated by R. F. C. Hull, *Collected Works*, vol. 5, New York and London, 2nd ed., 1967), par. 585. (Orig. 1911–12, *Wandlungen und Symbole der Libido,* translated by Beatrice M. Hinkle as *Psychology of the Unconscious,* 1916. Revised by Jung, 1952.)

12 Harold Peake and Herbert John Fleure, *The Way of the Sea* and *Merchant Venturers in Bronze* (New Haven, CT: Yale University Press, 1929 and 1931).

13 Leo Frobenius, *Das unbekannte Afrika* (Munich: Oskar Beck, 1923), pp. 10–11.

14 Ovid, *Metamorphoses,* VIII, 132 ff.; IX, 736 ff.

15 T.S. Eliot, *The Waste Land* (New York: Harcourt, Brace and Company; London: Faber and Faber, 1922), pp. 340–45.

16 Arnold J. Toynbee, *A Study of History* (Oxford University Press, 1934), vol. VI, pp. 169–75.

17 "Forms or images of a collective nature which occur practically all over the earth as constituents of myths and at the same time as autochthonous, individual products of unconscious origin" (C. G. Jung, *Psychology and Religion* [Collected Works, vol. 11; New York and London, 1958], par. 88. Orig. written in English, 1937. See also his *Psychological Types,* index.)

18 Jung, *Psychology and Religion,* par. 89.

19 Friedrich Nietzsche, *Human, All Too Human,* vol. I, p. 13; cited by Jung, *Psychology and Religion,* par. 89, n. 17.

20 Adolph Bastian, *Ethnische Elementargedanken in der Lehre vom Menschen,* Berlin, 1895, vol. I, p. ix.

21 Franz Boas, *The Mind of Primitive Man* (1911), pp. 104, 155, 228.

22 James G. Frazer, *The Golden Bough,* one-volume edition, p. 386. Copyright 1922 by the Macmillan Company and used with their permission.

23 Sigmund Freud, *The Interpretation of Dreams,* translated by James Strachey, Standard Edition, V, pp. 350–51.

24 Jung, *Psychology and Religion,* par. 89.

25 This is Géza Róheim's translation of an Australian Aranda term, *altjiranga mitjina,* which refers to the mythical ancestors who wandered on the earth in the time called *altjiranga nakala,* "ancestor was." The word *altjira* means: (a) a dream, (b) ancestor, beings who appear in the dream, (c) a story (Róheim, *The Eternal Ones of the Dream,* pp. 210–11).

26 Frederick Pierce, *Dreams and Personality* (Copyright 1931 by D. Appleton and Co., publishers), pp. 108–9.

27 Words written over the Gate of Hell:

Per me si va nella città dolente,
Per me si va nell' eterno dolore,
Per me si va tra la Perduta Gente.

—Dante, "Inferno," III, 1–3.

The translation is by Charles Eliot Norton, *The Divine Comedy of Dante Alighieri* (Boston and New York: Houghton Mifflin Company, 1902); this and the other quotations listed in footnotes used by permission of the publishers.

28 Katha Upaniṣad, 3–14. (Unless otherwise noted, my quotations of the *Upanishads* will be taken from Robert Ernest Hume, *The Thirteen Principal Upanishads, Translated from the Sanskrit,* Oxford University Press, 1931.)

The Upaniṣads are a class of Hindu treatises on the nature of man and the universe, forming a late part of the orthodox tradition of speculation. The earliest date from about the eighth century B.C.

29 James Joyce, *A Portrait of the Artist as a Young Man* (New York: The Modern Library; Random House, Inc.), p. 239.

30 Aristotle, *On the Art of Poetry* (translated by Ingram Bywater, with a preface by Gilbert Murray, Oxford University Press, 1920), pp. 14–16.

31 Robinson Jeffers, *Roan Stallion* (New York: Horace Liveright, 1925), p. 20.

32 Euripides, *Bacchae,* p. 1017 (translated by Gilbert Murray).

33 Euripides, *The Cretans,* frg. 475, ap. Porphyry, *De abstinentia,* IV, p. 19, trans. Gilbert Murray. See discussion of this verse by Jane Harrison, *Prolegomena to a Study of Greek Religion* (3rd edition, Cambridge University Press, 1992), pp. 478–500.

34 Ovid, *Metamorphoses,* XV, 165–67, 184–85 (translation by Frank Justus Miller, the Loeb Classical Library).

35 Bhagavad Gītā, 2:18 (translation by Swami Nikhilananda, New York, 1944).

36 The word *monomyth* is from James Joyce, *Finnegans Wake* (New York: Viking Press, Inc., 1939), p. 581.

37 Virgil, *Aeneid,* VI, p. 892.

38 Greatly abridged from *Jataka,* Introduction, i, pp. 58–75 (translated by Henry Clarke Warren, *Buddhism in Translations* [Harvard Oriental Series 3], [Cambridge, MA: Harvard University Press, 1896], pp. 56–87), and the *Lalitavistara* as rendered by Ananda K. Coomaraswamy, *Buddha and the Gospel of Buddhism* (New York: G.P. Putnam's Sons, 1916), pp. 24–38.

39 Exodus, 19:3–5.

40 Louis Ginzberg, *The Legends of the Jews* (Philadelphia: The Jewish Publication Society of America, 1911), vol. III, pp. 90–94.

41 The present volume is not concerned with the historical discussion of this circumstance. That task is reserved for a work now under preparation. [The work mentioned would eventually become Campbell's four-part opus, *The Masks of God*—Ed.] The present volume is a comparative, not genetic, study. Its purpose is to show that essential parallels exist in the myths themselves as well as in the interpretations and applications that the sages have announced for them.

42 Translated by Dom Ansgar Nelson, O.S.B., in *The Soul Afire* (New York: Pantheon Books, 1944), p. 303.

43 Quoted by Epiphanius, *Adversus haereses,* xxvi, 3.

44 See p. 24.

45 This is the serpent that protected the Buddha, the fifth week after his enlightenment. See p. 26.

46 Alice C. Fletcher, *The Hako: A Pawnee Ceremony* (Twenty-second Annual Report, Bureau of American Ethnology, part 2; Washington, DC, 1904), pp. 243–44.

"At the creation of the world," a Pawnee high priest said to Miss Fletcher, in explanation of the divinities honored in the ceremony, "it was arranged that there should be lesser powers. Tirawa-atius, the mighty power, could not come near to man, could not be seen or felt by him, therefore lesser powers were permitted. They were to mediate between man and Tirawa" (*ibid.*, p. 27).

47 See Ananda K. Coomaraswamy, "Symbolism of the Dome," *The Indian Historical Quarterly*, vol. XIV, No. 1 (March 1938).

48 John, 6:55.

49 *Ibid.*, 10:9.

50 *Ibid.*, 6:56.

51 Koran, 5:108.

52 Heraclitus, fragment 102.

53 Heraclitus, fragment 46.

54 William Blake, *The Marriage of Heaven and Hell*, "Proverbs of Hell."

55 Leo Frobenius, *Und Afrika sprach* (Berlin: Vita, Deutsches Verlagshaus, 1912), pp. 243–45. Compare the strikingly similar episode recounted of Othin (Wotan) in the Prose Edda, "Skáldskaparmál" I ("Scandinavian Classics," vol. V, New York, 1929, p. 96). Compare also Jehovah's command in Exodus, 32:27: "Put every man his sword by his side, and go in and out from gate to gate throughout the camp, and slay every man his brother, and every man his companion, and every man his neighbor."

PART I

CHAPTER I: DEPARTURE

1 *Grimm's Fairy Tales*, No. 1, "The Frog King."

2 *The Psychopathology of Everyday Life* (Standard Edition, VI; orig. 1901).

3 Evelyn Underhill, *Mysticism, A Study in the Nature and Development of Man's Spiritual Consciousness* (New York: E.P. Dutton and Co., 1911), Part II, "The Mystic Way," Chapter II, "The Awakening of the Self."

4 Sigmund Freud, *Introductory Lectures on Psycho-Analysis* (translated by James Strachey, Standard Edition, XVI; London: Hogarth Press, 1963), pp. 396–97 (orig. 1916–17).

5 Malory, *Le Morte d'Arthur*, I, p. xix. This pursuit of the hart and view of the "questyng beast" marks the beginning of the mysteries associated with the Quest of the Holy Grail.

6 George A. Dorsey and Alfred L. Kroeber, *Traditions of the Arapaho* (Chicago: Field Columbia Museum, Publication 81, Anthropological Series, vol. V; 1903), p. 300. Reprinted in Stith Thompson's *Tales of the North American Indians* (Cambridge, MA, 1929), p. 128.

7 C.G. Jung, *Psychology and Alchemy* (Collected Works, vol. 12; New York and London, 1953), pars. 71, 73. (Orig. 1935.)

8 Wilhelm Stekel, *Die Sprache des Traumes* (Wiesbaden: Verlag von J. F. Bergmann, 1911), p. 352. Dr. Stekel points out the relationship of the blood-red glow to the thought of the blood coughed up in consumption.

9 Reprinted by permission of the publishers from Henry Clarke Warren, *Buddhism in Translations* (Harvard Oriental Series 3) (Cambridge, MA: Harvard University Press, 1896), pp. 56–57.

10 Proverbs, 1:24–27, 32.

11 "Spiritual books occasionally quote [this] Latin saying which has terrified more than one soul" (Ernest Dimnet, *The Art of Thinking*, New York: Simon and Schuster, Inc., 1929, pp. 203–4).

12 Francis Thompson, *The Hound of Heaven* (Portland, ME: Thomas B. Mosher, 1908), opening lines.

13 *Ibid.*, conclusion.

14 Ovid, *Metamorphoses*, I, pp. 504–53 (translation by Frank Justus Miller, the Loeb Classical Library).

15 See pp. 2–3.

16 Jung, *Psychology and Alchemy*, pars. 58, 62.

17 *Grimm's Fairy Tales*, No. 50.

18 *The Thousand Nights and One Night*, Richard F. Burton translation (Bombay, 1885), vol. I, pp. 164–67.

19 Genesis, 19:26.

20 Werner Zirus, *Ahasverus, der ewige Jude* (Stoff- und Motivgeschichte der deutschen Literatur 6, Berlin and Leipzig, 1930), p. 1.

21 See p. 46.

22 See Otto Rank, *Art and Artist*, translated by Charles Francis Atkinson (New York: Alfred A. Knopf, Inc., 1943), pp. 40–41: "If we compare the neurotic with the productive type, it is evident that the former suffers from an excessive check on his impulsive life.... Both are distinguished fundamentally from the average type, who accepts himself as he is, by their tendency to exercise their volition in reshaping themselves. There is, however, this difference: that the neurotic, in this voluntary remaking of his ego, does not get beyond the destructive preliminary work and is therefore unable to detach the whole creative process from his own person and transfer it to an ideological abstraction. The productive artist also begins... with that re-creation of himself which results in an ideologically constructed ego; [but in his case] this ego is then in a position to shift the creative will-power from his own person to ideological representations of that person and thus render it objective. It must be admitted that this process is in a measure limited to within the individual himself, and that not only in its constructive, but also in its destructive aspects. This explains why hardly any productive work gets through without morbid crises of a 'neurotic' nature."

23 Abridged from Burton, *op. cit.*, vol. III, pp. 213–28.

24 Bruno Gutmann, *Volksbuch der Wadschagga* (Leipzig, 1914), p. 144.

25 Washington Matthews, *Navaho Legends* (Memoirs of the American Folklore Society, vol. V, New York, 1897), p. 109.

[For a discussion of the Navaho symbolism of the adventure of the hero, see Jeff King, Maud Oakes, and Joseph Campbell, *Where the Two Came to Their Father: A Navaho War Ceremonial*, Bollingen Series I, 2nd ed., (Princeton, NJ. Princeton University Press, 1969), pp. 33–49; Joseph Campbell, *The Inner Reaches of Outer Space: Myth as Metaphor and as Religion* (Novato, CA: New World Library, 2002), pp. 63–70; and Joseph Campbell, "The Spirit Land," *Mythos: The Shaping of Our Modern Tradition* (Silver Spring, MD: Acorn Media, 2007)—Ed.]

26 Dante, "Paradiso," XXXIII, 12–21 (translation by Charles Eliot Norton, *op. cit.*, vol. III, p. 252; quoted by permission of Houghton Mifflin Company, publishers).

27 See Oswald Spengler, *The Decline of the West*, translated by Charles Francis Atkinson (New York: Alfred A. Knopf, Inc., 1926–28), vol. I, p. 144. "Supposing," adds Spengler,

"that Napoleon himself, as 'empirical person,' had fallen at Marengo—then that which he *signified* would have been actualized in some other form." The hero, who in this sense and to this degree has become depersonalized, incarnates, during the period of his epochal action, the dynamism of the culture process; "between himself as a fact and the other facts there is a harmony of metaphysical rhythm" (*ibid.*, p. 142). This corresponds to Thomas Carlyle's idea of the Hero King, as "Ableman" (*On Heroes, Hero-Worship and the Heroic in History,* Lecture VI).

28 During Hellenistic times an amalgamation of Hermes and Thoth was effected in the figure of Hermes Trismegistus, "Hermes Thrice Greatest," who was regarded as the patron and teacher of all the arts, and especially of alchemy. The "hermetically" sealed retort, in which were placed the mystical metals, was regarded as a realm apart—a special region of heightened forces comparable to the mythological realm; and therein the metals underwent strange metamorphoses and transmutations, symbolical of the transfigurations of the soul under the tutelage of the supernatural. Hermes was the master of the ancient mysteries of initiation, and represented that coming-down of divine wisdom into the world which is represented also in the incarnations of divine saviors (see pp. 299–303). (See C. G. Jung, *Psychology and Alchemy,* part III, "Religious Ideas in Alchemy." [Orig. 1936.] For the retort, see par. 338. For Hermes Trismegistus, see par. 173 and index, *s.v.*)

29 Wilhelm Stekel, *Die Sprache des Traumes,* pp. 70–71.

30 *Ibid.*, p. 71.

31 Koran, 37:158.

32 Adapted from Burton, *op. cit.*, vol. III, pp. 223–30.

33 Compare the serpent of the dream; see p. 52.

34 Leonhard S. Schultze, *Aus Namaland und Kalahari* (Jena, 1907), p. 392.

35 *Ibid.*, pp. 404, 448.

36 David Clement Scott, *A Cyclopaedic Dictionary of the Mang'anja Language Spoken in British Central Africa* (Edinburgh, 1892), p. 97.

Compare the following dream of a twelve-year-old boy: "One night I dreamt of a foot. I thought it was lying down on the floor and I, not expecting such a thing, fell over it. It seemed to be the same shape as my own foot. The foot suddenly jumped up and started running after me; I thought I jumped right through the window, ran round the yard out into the street, running along as fast as my legs would carry me. I thought I ran to Woolwich, and then it suddenly caught me and shook me, and then I woke up. I have dreamt about this foot several times."

The boy had heard a report that his father, who was a sailor, had recently had an accident at sea in which he had broken his ankle (C. W. Kimmins, *Children's Dreams, An Unexplored Land,* London: George Allen and Unwin, Ltd., 1937, p. 107).

"The foot," writes Dr. Freud, "is an age-old sexual symbol which occurs even in mythology" (*Three Essays on the Theory of Sexuality,* p. 155). The name Oedipus, it should be noted, means "the swollen footed."

37 Compare V. J. Mansikka, in Hastings' *Encyclopaedia of Religion and Ethics,* vol. IV, p. 628; article "Demons and Spirits (Slavic)." The cluster of articles by a number of authorities, gathered together in this volume under the general heading "Demons and Spirits" (treating severally of the African, Oceanic, Assyro-Babylonian, Buddhist, Celtic, Chinese, Christian, Coptic, Egyptian, Greek, Hebrew, Indian, Jain, Japanese, Jewish, Moslem, Persian, Roman, Slavic, Teutonic, and Tibetan varieties), is an excellent introduction to the subject.

38 *Ibid.*, p. 629. Compare the Lorelei. Mansikka's discussion of the Slavic forest-, field-, and water-spirits is based on Hanus Máchal's comprehensive *Nákres slovanského bájeslovi* (Prague, 1891), an English abridgment of which will be found in Máchal's *Slavic Mythology* (*The Mythology of All Races*, vol. III, Boston, 1918).

39 Wilhelm Stekel, *Fortschritte und Technik der Traumdeutung* (Vienna-Leipzig-Bern: Verlag für Medizin, Weidmann und Cie., 1935), p. 37.

40 A.R. Radcliffe-Brown, *The Andaman Islanders* (2nd ed., Cambridge University Press, 1933), pp. 175–77.

41 R.H. Codrington, *The Melanesians, Their Anthropology and Folklore* (Oxford University Press, 1891), p. 189.

42 *Jataka,* 1:1. Abridged from translation by Eugene Watson Burlingame, *Buddhist Parables* (Yale University Press, 1922), pp. 32–34. Reprinted by permission of the publishers.

43 Coomaraswamy, *Journal of American Folklore* 57, 1944, p. 129.

44 *Jataka,* 55:1, 272–75. Adapted, with slight abridgment, from the translation of Eugene Watson Burlingame, *op. cit.*, pp. 41–44. Reprinted by permission of Yale University Press, publishers.

45 Nicholas of Cusa, *De visione Dei,* 9, 11; cited by Ananda K. Coomaraswamy, "On the One and Only Transmigrant" (*Supplement to the Journal of the American Oriental Society,* April–June, 1944), p. 25.

46 Ovid, *Metamorphoses,* VII, p. 62; XV, p. 338.

47 See p. 58.

48 Longfellow, *The Song of Hiawatha,* VIII. The adventures ascribed by Longfellow to the Iroquois chieftain Hiawatha belong properly to the Algonquin culture hero Manabozho. Hiawatha was an actual historical personage of the sixteenth century. See p. 256.

49 Leo Frobenius, *Das Zeitalter des Sonnengottes* (Berlin, 1904), p. 85.

50 Henry Callaway, *Nursery Tales and Traditions of the Zulus* (London: Trübner, 1868), p. 331.

51 Ananda K. Coomaraswamy, "Akimcanna: Self-Naughting" (*New Indian Antiquary,* vol. III, Bombay, 1940), p. 6, note 14, citing and discussing Thomas Aquinas, *Summa Theologica* I, p. 63, 3.

52 Sir James G. Frazer, *The Golden Bough* (one-volume edition), pp. 347–49. Copyright 1922 by the Macmillan Company and used with their permission.

53 *Ibid.*, p. 280.

54 Duarte Barbosa, *A Description of the Coasts of East Africa and Malabar in the Beginning of the Sixteenth Century* (London: Hakluyt Society, 1866), p. 172; cited by Frazer, *op. cit.*, pp. 274–75. Reprinted by permission of the Macmillan Company, publishers.

CHAPTER II: INITIATION

1 Apuleius, *The Golden Ass* (Modern Library edition), pp. 131–41.

2 Knud Leem, *Beskrivelse over Finmarkens Lapper* (Copenhagen, 1767), pp. 475–78. An English translation will be found in John Pinkerton, *A General Collection of the Best and Most Interesting Voyages and Travels in All Parts of the World* (London, 1808), vol. I, pp. 477–78.

3 E.J. Jessen, *Afhandling om de Norske Finners og Lappers Hedenske Religion,* p. 31. This work is included in Leem's volume, *op. cit.*, as an appendix with independent pagination.

4 Uno Harva, *Die religiösen Vorstellungen der altaischen Völker* ("Folklore Fellows Communications," No. 125, Helsinki, 1938), pp. 558–59; following G. N. Potanin, *Očerki ševero-zapodnoy Mongolii* (St. Petersburg, 1881), vol. IV, pp. 64–65.

5 Géza Róheim, *The Origin and Function of Culture* (Nervous and Mental Disease Monographs, No. 69), pp. 38–39.

6 *Ibid.*, p. 38.

7 *Ibid.*, p. 51.

8 Underhill, *op. cit.*, Part II, Chapter III. Compare p. 42, note 3.

9 Wilhelm Stekel, *Fortschritte und Technik der Traumdeutung*, p. 124.

10 *Svedenborgs Drömmar, 1774*, "Jemte andra hans anteckningar efter original-handskrifter meddelade af G. E. Klemming" (Stockholm, 1859), quoted in Ignaz Ježower, *Das Buch der Träume* (Berlin: Ernst Rowohlt Verlag, 1928), p. 97.

11 Ježower, *op. cit.*, p. 166.

12 Plutarch, *Themistocles*, 26; Ježower, *op. cit.*, p. 18.

13 Stekel, *Fortschritte und Technik der Traumdeutung*, p. 150.

14 *Ibid.*, p. 153.

15 *Ibid.*, p. 45.

16 *Ibid.*, p. 208.

17 *Ibid.*, p. 216.

18 *Ibid.*, p. 224.

19 *Ibid.*, p. 159.

20 *Ibid.*, p. 21.

21 Stekel, *Die Sprache des Traumes*, p. 200. See also Heinrich Zimmer, *The King and the Corpse*, ed. J. Campbell (New York: Bollingen Series, 1948), pp. 171–72; also D. L. Coomaraswamy, "The Perilous Bridge of Welfare," *Harvard Journal of Asiatic Studies* 8.

22 Stekel, *Die Sprache des Traumes*, p. 287.

23 *Ibid.*, p. 286.

24 Koran, 2:214.

25 S. N. Kramer, *Sumerian Mythology* (American Philosophical Society Memoirs, vol. XXI; Philadelphia, 1944), pp. 86–93. The mythology of Sumer is of especial importance to us of the West; for it was the source of the Babylonian, Assyrian, Phoenician, and Biblical traditions (the last giving rise to Mohammedanism and Christianity), as well as an important influence in the religions of the pagan Celts, Greeks, Romans, Slavs, and Germans.

26 Jeremiah Curtin, *Myths and Folk-Lore of Ireland* (Boston: Little, Brown and Company, 1890), pp. 101–6.

27 See pp. 52–53.

28 Ovid, *Metamorphoses*, III, 138–252.

29 Cf. J. C. Flügel, *The Psycho-Analytic Study of the Family* ("The International Psycho-Analytical Library," No. 3, 4th edition; London: The Hogarth Press, 1931), chapters 12 and 13.

"There exists," Professor Flügel observes, "a very general association on the one hand between the notion of mind, spirit or soul and the idea of the father or of masculinity; and on the other hand between the notion of the body or of matter (materia—that which belongs to the mother) and the idea of the mother or of the feminine principle. The repression of the emotions and feelings relating to the mother [in our Judeo-Christian monotheism] has, in virtue of this association, produced a tendency to adopt an attitude of distrust, contempt, disgust or hostility towards the human body, the Earth, and the whole material Universe, with a corresponding tendency to exalt and overemphasize the spiritual elements, whether in man or in the general scheme of things. It seems very probable that a good many of the more pronouncedly idealistic tendencies in philosophy may owe much of their attractiveness in many minds to a sublimation of this reaction against the mother, while the more dogmatic and narrow forms of materialism may perhaps in their turn represent a return of the repressed feelings originally connected with the mother" (*ibid.*, p. 145, note 2).

30 *The Gospel of Sri Ramakrishna,* translated into English with an introduction by Swami Nikhilananda (New York, 1942), p. 9.

31 *Ibid.*, pp. 21–22.

32 Standish H. O'Grady, *Silva Gadelica* (London: Williams and Norgate, 1892), vol. II, pp. 370–72. Variant versions will be found in Chaucer's *Canterbury Tales,* "The Tale of the Wyf of Bathe"; in Gower's *Tale of Florent;* in the mid-fifteenth-century poem, *The Weddynge of Sir Gawen and Dame Ragnell;* and in the seventeenth-century ballad, *The Marriage of Sir Gawaine.* See W.F. Bryan and Germaine Dempster, *Sources and Analogues of Chaucer's Canterbury Tales* (Chicago, 1941).

33 Guido Guinicelli di Magnano (1230–75?), "Of the Gentle Heart," translation by Dante Gabriel Rossetti, *Dante and His Circle* (London: Ellis and White, edition of 1874), p. 291.

34 Antiphons for the Feast of the Assumption of the Blessed Virgin Mary (August 15), at Vespers: from the Roman Missal.

35 *Hamlet,* Act I, scene ii, ll. 129–37.

36 Sophocles, *Oedipus Coloneus,* 1615–17.

37 Shankaracharya, *Vivekachudamani,* pp. 396 and 414, translated by Swami Madhavananda (Mayavati, 1932).

38 Jacobus de Voragine, *The Golden Legend,* LXXVI, "Saint Petronilla, Virgin." (Compare the tale of Daphne, pp. 50–51.) The later Church, unwilling to think of St. Peter as having begotten a child, speaks of Petronilla as his ward.

39 *Ibid.*, CXVII.

40 Gustave Flaubert, *La tentation de Saint Antoine (La reine de Saba).*

41 Cotton Mather, *Wonders of the Invisible World* (Boston, 1693), p. 63.

42 Jonathan Edwards, *Sinners in the Hands of an Angry God* (Boston, 1742).

43 Coomaraswamy, *The Dance of Siva* (New York, 1917), pp. 56–66.

44 Zimmer, *Myths and Symbols in Indian Art and Civilization,* pp. 151–75.

45 The brahminical thread is a cotton thread worn by the members of the three upper castes (the so-called twice-born) of India. It is passed over the head and right arm, so that it rests on the left shoulder and runs across the body (chest and back) to the right hip. This symbolizes the second birth of the twice-born, the thread itself representing the threshold, or sun door, so that the twice-born is dwelling at once in time and eternity.

46 For a discussion of this syllable, see p. 228.

47 Matthews, *op. cit.*, pp. 110–13.

48 Ovid, *Metamorphoses,* II (adapted from Miller: Loeb Library).

49 Kimmins, *op. cit.*, p. 22.

50 Wood, *op. cit.*, pp. 218–19.

51 W. Lloyd Warner, *A Black Civilization* (New York and London: Harper and Brothers, 1937), pp. 260–85.

52 Géza Róheim, *The Eternal Ones of the Dream,* pp. 72–73.

53 Koran, 4:116, 4:117.

54 Sir Baldwin Spencer and F. J. Gillen, *The Arunta* (London: Macmillan and Co., 1927), vol. I, pp. 201–3.

55 Róheim, *The Eternal Ones of the Dream,* pp. 49 ff.

56 *Ibid.*, p. 75.

57 *Ibid.*, p. 227, citing R. and C. Berndt, "A Preliminary Report of Field Work in the Ooldea Region, Western South Australia," *Oceania* XII (1942), p. 323.

58 Róheim, *The Eternal Ones of the Dream,* pp. 227–28, citing D. Bates, *The Passing of the Aborigines* (1939), pp. 41–43.

59 Róheim, *The Eternal Ones of the Dream,* p. 231.

60 R. H. Mathews, "The Walloonggura Ceremony," *Queensland Geographical Journal,* N. S., XV (1899–1900), p. 70; cited by Róheim, *The Eternal Ones of the Dream,* p. 232.

61 K. Langloh Parker, *The Euahlayi Tribe,* 1905, pp. 72–73; cited by Róheim, *The Eternal Ones of the Dream,* p. 232.

62 John Layard, *Stone Men of Malekula* (London: Chatto and Windus, 1942).

63 W. F. J. Knight, in his *Cumaean Gates* (Oxford: B. Blackwell, 1936).

64 W. J. Perry, *The Children of the Sun* (New York: E. P. Dutton and Co., 1923).

65 Jane Harrison, *Themis: A Study of the Social Origins of Greek Religion* (2nd revised edition; Cambridge University Press, 1927).

66 [This was a question to which Campbell would return a number of times, most notably in "Mythogenesis," an essay published in *The Flight of the Wild Gander* (third edition; Novato, CA: New World Library, 2001)—Ed.]

67 Euripides, *The Bacchae,* 526 f.

68 Aeschylus, Figure 57 (Nauck); cited by Jane Harrison (*Themis,* p. 61) in her discussion of the role of the bull-roarer in classical and Australian rites of initiation. For an introduction to the subject of the bull-roarer, see Andrew Lang, *Custom and Myth* (2nd revised edition; London: Longmans, Green, and Co., 1885), pp. 29–44.

69 All of these are described and discussed at length by Sir James G. Frazer in *The Golden Bough.*

70 Epistles to the Hebrews, 9:13–14.

71 Le P. A. Capus des Pères-Blancs, "Contes, chants et proverbes des Basumbwa dans l'Afrique Orientale," *Zeitschrift für afrikanische und oceanische Sprachen.* Vol. III (Berlin, 1897), pp. 363–64.

72 Koran, 10:31.

73 See p. 57.

74 See pp. 36–37. The Basumbwa (tale of the Great Chief, Death) and the Wachaga (tale of Kyazimba) are East African peoples; the Yoruba (tale of Edshu) inhabit the West Coast colony of Nigeria.

75 Koran, 6:59, 6:60.

76 Gospel According to Luke, 2:7.

77 Ovid, *Metamorphoses,* VIII, pp. 618–724.

78 Koran, 2:115.

79 Katha Upaniṣad, 3:12.

80 Gospel According to Thomas, 77.

81 Book of Job, 40:7–14.

82 *Ibid.*, 42:5–6.

83 *Ibid.*, 42:16–17.

84 Leon Stein, "Hassidic Music," *The Chicago Jewish Forum,* vol. II, No. 1 (Fall 1943), p. 16.

85 *Pranja-Paramita-Hridaya Sutra;* "Sacred Books of the East," vol. XLIX, Part II, p. 148; also, p. 154.

86 *Vajracchedika* ("The Diamond Cutter"), 17; *ibid.*, p. 134.

87 Compare p. 72.

88 *Amitayur-Dhyana Sutra,* 19; "Sacred Books of the East," vol. XLIX, Part II, pp. 182–83.

89 "To men I am Hermes; to women I appear as Aphrodite: I bear the emblems of both my parents" (*Anthologia Graeca ad Fidem Codices,* vol. II).

"One part of him is his sire's, all else he has of his mother" (Martial, *Epigrams,* 4, 174; Loeb Library, vol. II, p. 501).

Ovid's account of Hermaphroditos appears in the *Metamorphoses,* IV, pp. 288 ff.

Many classical images of Hermaphroditos have come down to us. See Hugh Hampton Young, *Genital Abnormalities, Hermaphroditism, and Related Adrenal Diseases* (Baltimore: Williams and Wilkins, 1937), Chapter I, "Hermaphroditism in Literature and Art."

90 Plato, *Symposium,* 178.

91 Book of Genesis, 1:27.

92 *Midrash*, commentary on Genesis, Rabbah 8:1.

93 See p. 73.

94 See pp. 238–240.

95 Compare James Joyce: "In the economy of heaven ... there are no more marriages, glorified man, an androgynous angel, being a wife unto himself" (*Ulysses,* Modern Library edition, p. 210).

96 Sophocles, *Oedipus Tyrannus.* See also Ovid, *Metamorphoses,* III, pp. 324 ff., 511, and 516. For other examples of the hermaphrodite as priest, god, or seer, see Herodotus, 4, 67 (Rawlinson edition, vol. III, pp. 46–47); Theophrastus, *Characteres,* 16.10–11; and J. Pinkerton's *Voyage and Travels,* Chapter 8, p. 427, "A New Account of the East Indies," by Alexander Hamilton. These are cited by Young, *op. cit.*, pp. 2 and 9.

97 See Zimmer, *Myths and Symbols in Indian Art and Civilization,* Figure 70.

98 See Figure 34.

99 See B. Spencer and F. J. Gillen, *Native Tribes of Central Australia* (London, 1899), p. 263; Róheim, *The Eternal Ones of the Dream,* pp. 164–65. The subincision produces artificially a hypospadias resembling that of a certain class of hermaphrodites. (See the portrait of the hermaphrodite Marie Angé, in Young, *op. cit.*, p. 20.)

100 Róheim, *The Eternal Ones of the Dream*, p. 94.

101 *Ibid.*, pp. 218–19.

102 Compare the following view of the Bodhisattva Dharmakāra: "Out of his mouth there breathed a sweet and more than heavenly smell of sandalwood. From all the pores of his hair there arose the smell of lotus, and he was pleasing to everybody, gracious and beautiful; endowed with the fulness of the best bright color. As his body was adorned with all the good signs and marks, there arose from the pores of his hair and from the palms of his hands all sorts of precious ornaments in the shape of all kinds of flowers, incense, scents, garlands, ointments, umbrellas, flags, and banners, and in the shape of all kinds of instrumental music. And there appeared also, streaming forth from the palms of his hands, all kinds of viands and drink, food, hard and soft, and sweetmeats, and all kinds of enjoyments and pleasures" (*The Larger Sukhavati-Vyuha*, 10, "Sacred Books of the East," vol. XLIX, Part II, pp. 26–27).

103 Róheim, *War, Crime, and the Covenant*, p. 57.

104 *Ibid.*, pp. 48–68.

105 First Book of Samuel, 17:26.

106 Koran, 4:104.

107 "For hatred does not cease by hatred at any time: hatred ceases by love, this is an old rule" (from the Buddhist *Dhammapada*, 1:5, "Sacred Books of the East," vol. X, Part I, p. 5; translation by F. Max Müller).

108 Gospel According to Luke, 6:27–36.

109 Reprinted by Professor Robert Phillips, *American Government and Its Problems*, Houghton Mifflin Company, 1941, and by Dr. Karl Menninger, *Love Against Hate*, Harcourt, Brace and Company, 1942, p. 211.

110 Gospel According to Matthew, 22:37–40; Mark, 12:28–34; Luke, 10:25–37. Jesus is also reported to have commissioned his apostles to "teach all nations" (Matthew, 28:19), but not to persecute and pillage, or turn over to the "secular arm" those who would not hear. "Behold, I send you forth as sheep in the midst of wolves: be ye therefore wise as serpents, and harmless as doves" (*ibid.*, 10:16).

111 Gospel According to Matthew, 7:1.

112 "And as troops of robbers wait for a man, so the company of priests murder in the way of consent. . . . They make the king glad with their wickedness, and the princes with their lies" (Hosea, 6:9; 7:3).

113 Menninger, *op. cit.*, pp. 195–196.

114 Swami Nikhilananda, *The Gospel of Sri Ramakrishna*, New York, 1941, p. 559.

115 Rumi, *Mathnawi*, 2. 2525.

116 "The Hymn of the Final Precepts of the Great Saint and Bodhisattva Milarepa" (c. A.D. 1051–1135), from the *Jetsün-Kahbum*, or Biographical History of Jetsün-Milarepa, according to Lama Kazi Dawa-Samdup's English rendering, edited by W.Y. Evans-Wentz, *Tibet's Great Yogi Milarepa* (Oxford University Press, 1928), p. 285.

117 "The Hymn of the Yogic Precepts of Milarepa," *ibid.*, p. 273.

118 Evans-Wentz, "Hymn of Milarepa in praise of his teacher," p. 137.

119 The same idea is frequently expressed in the Upaniṣads: viz., "This self gives itself to that self, that self gives itself to this self. Thus they gain each other. In this form he gains yonder world, in that form he experiences this world" (*Aitareya Aranyaka*, 2. 3. 7). It is known also to the mystics of Islam: "Thirty years the transcendent God was my mirror,

now I am my own mirror; i.e., that which I was I am no more, the transcendent God is his own mirror. I say that I am my own mirror; 'tis God that speaks with my tongue, and I have vanished" (Bayazid, as cited in *The Legacy of Islam,* T. W. Arnold and A. Guillaume, editors, Oxford Press, 1931, p. 216).

120 "I came forth from Bayazid-ness as a snake from its skin. Then I looked. I saw that lover, beloved, and love are one, for in the world of unity all can be one" (Bayazid, *loc. cit.*).

121 Book of Hosea, 6:1–3.

122 Bṛhadāranyaka Upaniṣad, 1. 4. 3. See p. 239.

123 Ananda K. Coomaraswamy, *Hinduism and Buddhism* (New York: The Philosophical Library, no date), p. 63.

124 Sigmund Freud, *Beyond the Pleasure Principle* (translated by James Strachey; Standard Edition, XVIII; London: The Hogarth Press, 1955). See also Karl Menninger, *Love against Hate,* p. 262.

125 Vajracchedikā Sūtra, 32; see "Sacred Books of the East," *op. cit.*, p. 144.

126 The smaller Prajñāpāramitā Hṛdāya Sūtra; *ibid.*, p. 153.

127 Nagarjuna, *Madhyamika Shastra.*

"What is immortal and what is mortal are harmoniously blended, for they are not one, nor are they separate" (Ashvaghosha).

"This view," writes Dr. Coomaraswamy, citing these texts, "is expressed with dramatic force in the aphorism *Yas klésas so bodhi, yas samsāras tat nirvānum,* 'That which is sin is also Wisdom, the realm of Becoming is also *Nirvana*'" (Ananda K. Coomaraswamy, *Buddha and the Gospel of Buddhism,* New York: G. P. Putnam's Sons, 1916, p. 245).

128 Bhagavad Gītā, 6:29, 6:31.

This represents the perfect fulfillment of what Evelyn Underhill termed "the goal of the Mystic Way: the True Unitive Life: the state of Divine Fecundity: Deification" (*op. cit., passim*). Underhill, however, like Professor Toynbee (see p. 15), makes the popular mistake of supposing that this ideal is peculiar to Christianity. "It is safe to say," writes Professor Salmony, "that Occidental judgment has been falsified, up to the present, by the need for self-assertion" (Alfred Salmony, "Die Rassenfrage in der Indienforschung," *Sozialistische Monatshefte,* 8, Berlin, 1926, p. 534).

129 Coomaraswamy, *Hinduism and Buddhism,* p. 74.

130 See E. T. C. Werner, *A Dictionary of Chinese Mythology* (Shanghai, 1932), p. 163.

131 See Okakura Kakuzo, *The Book of Tea* (New York, 1906). See also Daisetz Teitaro Suzuki, *Essays in Zen Buddhism* (London, 1927), and Lafcadio Hearn, *Japan* (New York, 1904). [See also Campbell's exploration of the symbolism of the tea ceremony in *Myths of Light: Eastern Metaphors of the Eternal,* edited by David Kudler (Novato, CA: New World Library, 2003), pp. 133–36.—Ed.]

132 Morris Edward Opler, *Myths and Tales of the Jicarilla Apache Indians* (Memoirs of the American Folklore Society, vol. XXXI, 1938), p. 110.

133 Compare p. 131.

134 See p. 96.

135 See p. 94.

136 See Zimmer, *Myths and Symbols in Indian Art and Civilization,* pp. 210–14

137 Compare the drum of creation in the hand of the Hindu Dancing Śiva, p. 108.

138 Curtin, *op. cit.*, pp. 106–7.

139 See Melanie Klein, *The Psycho-Analysis of Children,* The International Psycho-Analytical Library, No. 27 (1937).

140 Róheim, *War, Crime, and the Covenant,* pp. 137–38.

141 Róheim, *The Origin and Function of Culture,* p. 50.

142 *Ibid.*, pp. 48–50.

143 *Ibid.*, p. 50. Compare the indestructibility of the Siberian shaman (see p. 82), drawing coals out of the fire with his bare hands and beating his legs with an ax.

144 See Frazer's discussion of the external soul, *op. cit.*, pp. 667–91.

145 *Ibid.*, p. 671.

146 Pierce, *Dreams and Personality,* p. 298.

147 "The Descent of the Sun," in F. W. Bain, *A Digit of the Moon* (New York: G. P. Putnam's Sons, 1910), pp. 213–325.

148 Róheim, *The Eternal Ones of the Dream,* p. 237. This talisman is the so-called *tjurunga* (or *churinga*) of the young man's totem ancestor. The youth received another *tjurunga* at the time of his circumcision, representing his maternal totem ancestor. Still earlier, at the time of his birth, a protective *tjurunga* was placed in his cradle. The bull-roarer is a variety of *tjurunga.* "The tjurunga," writes Dr. Róheim, "is a material double, and certain supernatural beings most intimately connected with the tjurunga in Central Australian belief are invisible doubles of the natives.... Like the tjurunga, these supernaturals are called the *arpuna mborka* (other body) of the real human beings whom they protect" (*ibid.*, p. 98).

149 Book of Isaiah, 66:10–12.

150 Ginzberg, *op. cit.*, vol. I, pp. 20, 26–30. See the extensive notes on the Messianic banquet in Ginzberg, vol. V, pp. 43–46.

151 Dante, "Paradiso," II, 1–9. Translation by Norton, *op. cit.*, vol. III, p. 10; by permission of the Houghton Mifflin Company, publishers.

152 Ramāyāna, I, 45, Mahābhārata, I, 18, Matsya Purāṇa, 249–51, and many other texts. See Zimmer, *Myths and Symbols in Indian Art and Civilization,* pp. 105 ff.

153 Marco Pallis, *Peaks and Lamas* (4th edition; London: Cassell and Co., 1946), p. 324.

154 *Shri-Chakra-Sambhara Tantra,* translated from the Tibetan by Lama Kazi Dawa-Samdup, edited by Sir John Woodroffe (pseudonym Arthur Avalon), Volume VII of "Tantric Texts" (London, 1919), p. 41. "Should doubts arise as to the divinity of these visualized deities," the text continues, "one should say, 'This Goddess is only the recollection of the body,' and remember that the Deities constitute the Path" (*loc. cit.*). For a word about Tantra, see p. 95 and pp. 145–47 (Tantric Buddhism).

155 Compare, e.g., C. G. Jung, "Archetypes of the Collective Unconscious" (orig. 1934; Collected Works, vol. 9, part i; New York and London, 1959).

"There are perhaps many," writes Dr. J. C. Flügel, "who would still retain the notion of a quasi-anthropomorphic Father-God as an extra-mental reality, even though the purely mental origin of such a God has become apparent" (*The Psycho-Analytic Study of the Family,* p. 236).

156 "Paradiso," XXXIII, 82 ff.

157 See p. 147.

158 J. F. Stimson, *The Legends of Maui and Tahaki* (Bernice P. Bishop Museum Bulletin, No. 127; Honolulu, 1934), pp. 19–21.

159 Bruno Meissner, "Ein altbabylonisches Fragment des Gilgamosepos," *Mitteilungen der vorderasiatischen Gesellschaft,* VII, 1; Berlin, 1902, p. 9.

160 See, for instance, the Katha Upaniṣad, 1: 21, 23–25.

161 The above rendering is based on P. Jensen, *Assyrisch-babylonische Mythen und Epen* (Kellinschriftliche Bibliothek, VI, I; Berlin, 1900), pp. 116–273. The verses quoted appear on pp. 223, 251, 251–53. Jensen's version is a line-for-line translation of the principal extant text, an Assyrian version from King Ashurbanipal's library (668–626 B.C.). Fragments of the very much older Babylonian version (see p. 158) and still more ancient Sumerian original (third millennium B.C.) have also been discovered and deciphered.

162 Ko Hung (also known as Pao Pu Tzu), *Nei P'ien,* Chapter VII (translation quoted from Obed Simon Johnson, *A Study of Chinese Alchemy,* Shanghai, 1928, p. 63).

Ko Hung evolved several other very interesting receipts, one bestowing a body "buoyant and luxurious," another the ability to walk on water. For a discussion of the place of Ko Hung in Chinese philosophy, see Alfred Forke, "Ko Hung, der Philosoph und Alchimist," *Archiv für Geschichte der Philosophie,* XLI, 1–2 (Berlin, 1932), pp. 115–26.

163 Herbert A. Giles, *A Chinese Biographical Dictionary* (London and Shanghai, 1898), p. 372.

164 A Tantric aphorism.

165 Lao Tze, *Tao Teh Ching,* 16 (translation by Dwight Goddard, *Laotzu's Tao and Wu Wei,* New York, 1919, p. 18). Compare p. 131.

166 "Paradiso," XXXIII, 49–57 (translation by Norton, *op. cit.*, vol. III, pp. 253–54, by permission of Houghton Mifflin Company, publishers).

167 Kena Upaniṣad, 1:3 (translation by Swami Sharvananda; Sri Ramakrishna Math, Mylapore, Madras, 1932).

168 Poetic Edda, "Hovamol," 139 (translation by Henry Adams Bellows, The American-Scandinavian Foundation, New York, 1923).

169 *Jataka,* Introduction, i, 75 (reprinted by permission of the publishers from Henry Clarke Warren, *Buddhism in Translations* [Harvard Oriental Series 3], Cambridge, MA: Harvard University Press, 1896, pp. 82–83).

CHAPTER III: RETURN

1 *Viṣṇu Puraṇa,* 23; *Bhagavata Puraṇa,* 10:51; *Harìvansha,* 114. The above is based on the rendering by Heinrich Zimmer, *Maya, der indische Mythos* (Stuttgart and Berlin, 1936), pp. 89–99.

Compare with Kṛṣṇa, as the World Magician, the African Edshu (pp. 36–37). Compare, also, the Polynesian trickster, Maui.

2 "Taliesin," translated by Lady Charlotte Guest in *The Mabinogion* (Everyman's Library, No. 97, pp. 263–64).

3 See Gertrude Schoepperle, *Tristan and Isolt: A Study of the Sources of the Romance,* (London and Frankfurt-am-Main, 1913).

4 Harva, *op. cit.*, pp. 543–44; quoting "Pervyi buryatsii šaman Morgon-Kara," *Isvestiya Vostočno Siberskago Otdela Russkago Geografičeskago Obščestva,* XI, 1–2 (Irkutsk, 1880), pp. 87 ff.

5 John White, *The Ancient History of the Maori, His Mythology and Traditions* (Wellington, 1886–89), vol. II, pp. 167–71.

6 *Grimm's Fairy Tales*, No. 79.

7 C. G. Jung, *The Integration of the Personality* (New York, 1939), p. 59.

8 See Apollonios of Rhodes, *Argonautika:* the flight is recounted in Book IV.

9 *Ko-ji-ki*, "Records of Ancient Matters" (A.D. 712), adapted from the translation by C. H. Chamberlain, *Transactions of The Asiatic Society of Japan*, vol. X, Supplement (Yokohama, 1882), pp. 24–28.

10 Jaiminīya Upaniṣad Brāhmaṇa, 3.28.5.

11 Frobenius, *Das Zeitalter des Sonnengottes*, pp. 85–87.

12 Tomobe-no-Yasutaka, *Shintō-Shoden-Kuju.*

13 *Shintō-Gobusho.*

14 Izawa-Nagahide, *Shintō-Ameno-Nuboko-no-Ki.*

15 Ichijo-Kaneyoshi, *Nihonshoki-Sanso.*

16 Urabe-no-Kanekuni.

17 All of the quotations above will be found in Genchi Kato, *What Is Shintō?* (Tokyo: Maruzen Company Ltd., 1935); see also Lafcadio Hearn, *Japan, an Attempt at Interpretation* (New York: Grosset and Dunlap, 1904).

18 *Ko-ji-ki*, after Chamberlain, *op. cit.*, pp. 52–59.

19 Kramer, *op. cit.*, pp. 87, 95. The conclusion of the poem, this valuable document of the sources of the myths and the symbols of our civilization, is forever lost.

20 Gospel According to Matthew, 26:51; Gospel According to Mark, 14:47; Gospel According to John, 18:10.

21 Māṇḍūkya Upaniṣad, 5.

22 Washington Irving, *The Sketch Book*, "Rip van Winkle."

23 Book of Genesis, 5.

24 Curtin, *op. cit.*, pp. 332–33.

25 From Sir James G. Frazer, *The Golden Bough*, one-volume edition, pp. 593–94. Copyright 1922 by the Macmillan Company and used with their permission.

26 *Ibid.*, pp. 594–95. By permission of the Macmillan Company, publishers.

27 Adapted from Burton, *op. cit.*, III, pp. 231–56.

28 Gospel According to Matthew, 17:1–9.

29 A certain element of comic relief can be felt in Peter's immediate project (announced even while the vision was before his eyes) to convert the ineffable into a stone foundation. Only six days before, Jesus had said to him: "Thou art Peter; and upon this rock I will build my church," then a moment later: "Thou savorest not the things that be of God, but those that be of men" (Matthew, 16:18, 23).

30 Bhagavad Gītā, 11; 1:45–46; 2:9. From the translation by Swami Nikhilananda (New York, 1944).

31 Bṛhadāranyaka Upaniṣad, 1.1.1: translated by Swami Madhavananda (Mayavati, 1934).

32 Robinson Jeffers, *Cawdor*, p. 116. Copyright 1928 by Robinson Jeffers. Reprinted by permission of Random House, Inc.

33 *Summa contra Gentiles*, I, 5, par. 3.

34 Kena Upaniṣad, 2:3.

35 Bhagavad Gītā, 11: 53–55.

36 Gospel According to Matthew, 16:25.

37 Shankaracharya, *Vivekachudamani*, 542 and 555.

38 Bhagavad Gītā, 2:22–24.

39 *Ibid.*, 3:19 and 3:30.

40 "Taliesin," *op. cit.*, pp. 264–74.

41 Gospel According to John, 8:58.

42 Ovid, *Metamorphoses*, XV, 252–55.

43 *Grimm's Fairy Tales*, No. 50, "Little Briar-rose" (better known as "Sleeping Beauty"); conclusion.

CHAPTER IV: THE KEYS

1 For a discussion of this matter, see my Commentary to the Pantheon Books edition of *Grimm's Fairy Tales* (New York, 1944), pp. 846–56. [This commentary is also available as part of Campbell's collection of essays, *The Flight of the Wild Gander*, pp. 1–19.—Ed.]

2 Psalm XLI, 2–4; Douay.

3 See the Catholic Daily Missal under "Holy Saturday." The above is abridged from the English translation by Dom Gaspar Lefebvre, O.S.B., published in this country by the E. M. Lohmann Co., Saint Paul, MN. [At the time of the original publication of this volume, of course, the Catholic Mass would have been entirely spoken and sung in Latin.—Ed.]

4 In India the power (*Śakti*) of a god is personified in female form and represented as his consort; in the present ritual, grace is similarly symbolized.

5 Gospel According to John, 3:3–5.

PART II

CHAPTER I: EMANATIONS

1 See C. G. Jung, "On Psychic Energy" (orig. 1928, *Collected Works*, vol. 8), entitled in its earliest draft "The Theory of the Libido."

2 See Kant, *Critique of Pure Reason.*

3 Freud, *Moses and Monotheism*, translated by James Strachey (Standard Edition, XXIII, 1964). (Orig. 1939.)

4 Gospel According to Luke, 17:21.

5 See p. 164.

6 See p. 77.

7 See pp. 70–72.

8 See p. 73.

9 Fernando de Alva Ixtlilxochitl, *Historia de la Nación Chichimeca* (1608), Capítulo I (published in Lord Kingsborough's *Antiquities of Mexico*, London, 1830–48, vol. IX, p. 205; also by Alfredo Chavero, *Obras Históricas de Alva Ixtlilxochitl*, Mexico, 1891–92, vol. II, pp. 21–22).

10 Hastings' *Encyclopaedia of Religion and Ethics,* vol. V, p. 375.

11 See Mrs. Sinclair Stevenson, *The Heart of Jainism* (Oxford University Press, 1915), pp. 272–78.

12 See Māṇḍūkya Upaniṣad, 3–6.

13 Māṇḍūkya Upaniṣad, 8–12. [For Campbell's further thoughts on the sacred syllable *AUM,* see *Myths of Light,* pp. 33–35.—Ed.]

14 Māṇḍūkya Upaniṣad, 7.

15 *Ha idra zuta,* Zohar, iii, 288a. Compare p. 155.

16 *Ha idra rabba qadisha,* xi, 212–14 and 233, translation by S.L. MacGregor Mathers, *The Kabbalah Unveiled* (London: Kegan Paul, Trench, Trübner & Company, Ltd., 1887), pp. 134–35 and 137.

17 *Summa contra Gentiles,* I.i.

18 See pp. 19–22.

19 Johannes C. Anderson, *Maori Life in Ao-tea* (Christchurch [New Zealand], no date [1907?]), p. 127.

20 See *The Vedantasara of Sadananda,* translated with Introduction, Sanskrit Text, and Comments, by Swami Nikhilananda (Mayavati, 1931).

21 Translated from Richard Wilhelm, *Chinesische Märchen* (Jena: Eugen Diederichs Verlag, 1921), pp. 29–31.

22 Rev. Richard Taylor, *Te ika a Maui, or New Zealand and Its Inhabitants* (London, 1855), pp. 14–15.

23 The little circle underneath the main portion of Figure 59. Compare the Chinese Tao or *yin-yang;* see p. 131.

24 Kenneth P. Emory, "The Tuamotuan Creation Charts by Paiore," *Journal of the Polynesian Society,* vol. 48, no. 1 (March 1939), pp. 1–29.

25 *Ibid.,* p. 12.

26 Chāndogya Upaniṣad, 3.19.1–3.

27 A.S. Eddington, *The Nature of the Physical World,* p. 83. Copyright 1928 by the Macmillan Company and used with their permission. [The mythic image of the Cosmic Egg also resonates with that theory known by modern physicists as the Big Bang, first propounded by Georges Lemaître, a Belgian Roman Catholic priest.—Ed.]

28 "Entropy always increases." (See Eddington, pp. 63 ff.) [This is a restatement of what is known as the Second Law of Thermodynamics, first formulated in 1824 by French scientist Sadi Carnot.—Ed.]

29 Kenneth P. Emory, "The Tahitian Account of Creation by Mare," *Journal of the Polynesian Society,* vol. 47, No. 2 (June 1938), pp. 53–54.

30 E.A. Wallis Budge, *The Gods of the Egyptians* (London, 1904), vol. I, pp. 282–92.

31 *Kalika Puraṇa,* I (translated in Heinrich Zimmer, *The King and the Corpse,* edited by Joseph Campbell, The Bollingen Series XI, Pantheon Books, 1948, pp. 239 ff.).

32 Bṛhadāranyaka Upaniṣad, 1.4.1–5. Translated by Swami Madhavananda (Mayavati, 1934). Compare the folklore motif of the transformation flight, pp. 183–84. See also *Cypria* 8, where Nemesis "dislikes to lie in love with her father Zeus" and flies from him, assuming the forms of fish and animals (cited by Ananda K. Coomaraswamy, *Spiritual Power and Temporal Authority in the Indian Theory of Government,* American Oriental Society, 1942, p. 361).

33 Muṇḍaka Upaniṣad, 2.2.5.

34 Zohar, i, 91 b. Quoted by C.G. Ginsburg, *The Kabbalah: Its Doctrines, Development, and Literature* (London, 1920), p. 116.

35 Taittirīya Upaniṣad, 3.10.5.

36 The mythologies of the American Southwest describe such an emergence in great detail, so also the creation stories of the Kabyl Berbers of Algiers. See Morris Edward Opler, *Myths and Tales of the Jicarilla Apache Indians* (Memoirs of the American Folklore Society, vol. XXXI, 1938); and Leo Frobenius and Douglas C. Fox, *African Genesis* (New York, 1927), pp. 49–50.

37 George Grey, *Polynesian Mythology and Ancient Traditional History of the New Zealand Race, as Furnished by Their Priests and Chiefs* (London, 1855), pp. 1–3.

38 *Theogony,* 116 ff. In the Greek version, the mother is not reluctant; she herself supplies the sickle.

39 Compare the Maori polarity of Mahora-nui-a-rangi and Maki, p. 232.

40 S.N. Kramer, *op. cit.*, pp. 40–41.

41 Prose Edda, "Gylfaginning," IV–VIII (from the translation by Arthur Gilchrist Brodeur, The American-Scandinavian Foundation, New York, 1916; by permission of the publishers). See also Poetic Edda, "Voluspa."

42 "The Epic of Creation," Tablet IV, lines 35–143, adapted from the translation by L.W. King, *Babylonian Religion and Mythology* (London and New York: Kegan Paul, Trench, Trübner and Co. Ltd., 1899), pp. 72–78.

43 See Dante, "Paradiso," XXX–XXXII. This is the rose opened to mankind by the cross.

44 Book of Genesis, 3:7.

45 George Bird Grinnell, *Blackfoot Lodge Tales* (New York: Charles Scribner's Sons, 1892, 1916), pp. 137–38.

46 J.S. Polack, *Manners and Customs of the New Zealanders* (London, 1840), vol. I, p. 17. To regard such a tale as a cosmogonic myth would be as inept as to illustrate the doctrine of the Trinity with a paragraph from the nursery story "Marienkind" (*Grimm's Fairy Tales*, No. 3).

47 Harva, *op. cit.*, p. 109, citing S. Kraščeninnikov, *Opisanie Zemli Kamčatki* (St. Petersburg, 1819), vol. II, p. 101.

48 Harva, *op. cit.*, p. 109, citing Potanin, *op. cit.*, vol. II, p. 153.

49 P.J. Meier, *Mythen und Erzählungen der Küstenbewohner der Gazelle-Halbinsel (Neu-Pommern)* (Anthropos Bibliothek, Band I, Heft 1, Münster i. W., 1909), pp. 15–16.

50 *Ibid.*, pp. 59–61.

51 "The universe does not on the whole act as though it were under efficient personal supervision and control. When I hear some hymns, sermons, and prayers taking for granted or asserting with naïve simplicity that this vast, ruthless cosmos, with all the monstrous accidents which it involves, is a neatly planned and personally conducted tour, I recall the more reasonable hypothesis of an East African tribe. 'They say,' reports an observer, 'that although God is good and wishes good for everybody, unfortunately he has a half-witted brother who is always interfering with what he does.' That, at least, bears some resemblance to the facts. God's half-witted brother might explain some of life's sickening and insane tragedies which the idea of an omnipotent individual of boundless good will toward every soul most certainly does not explain" (Harry Emerson Fosdick, *As I See Religion,* New York: Harper and Brothers, 1932, pp. 53–54).

52 Harva, *op. cit.*, pp. 114–15, quoting W. Radloff, *Proben der Volksliteratur der türkischen Stämme Süd-Siberians* (St. Petersburg, 1866–70), vol. I, p. 285.

CHAPTER II: THE VIRGIN BIRTH

1 The version quoted here is from the translation by W.F. Kirby (Everyman's Library, Nos. 259–60).

2 *Kalevala*, Runo I, pp. 127–36.

3 *Ibid.*, pp. 263–80.

4 *Ibid.*, pp. 287–328.

5 *Ibid.*, pp. 329–44.

6 Leo Frobenius and Douglas C. Fox, *African Genesis* (New York, 1937), pp. 215–20.

7 The Gospel of Pseudo-Matthew, Ch. ix.

8 Kingsborough, *op. cit.*, vol. VIII, pp. 263–64.

9 Kalidasa, *Kumarasamibhavam* ("The Birth of the War God Kumara"). There is an English translation by R. Griffith (2nd ed., London: Trübner and Company, 1897).

10 E.E.V. Collocott, *Tales and Poems of Tonga* (Bernice P. Bishop Museum Bulletin, No. 46, Honolulu, 1928), pp. 32–33.

CHAPTER III: TRANSFORMATIONS OF THE HERO

1 Giles, *op. cit.*, pp. 233–34; Rev. J. MacGowan, *The Imperial History of China* (Shanghai, 1906), pp. 4–5; Friedrich Hirth, *The Ancient History of China* (Columbia University Press, 1908), pp. 8–9.

2 Giles, *op. cit.*, p. 656; MacGowan, *op. cit.*, pp. 5–6; Hirth, *op. cit.*, pp. 10–12.

3 Giles, *op. cit.*, p. 338; MacGowan, *op. cit.*, pp. 6–8; Edouard Chavannes, *Les mémoires historiques de Se-ma Ts'ien* (Paris, 1895–1905), vol. I, pp. 25–36. See also John C. Ferguson, *Chinese Mythology* ("The Mythology of All Races," vol. VIII, Boston, 1928), pp. 27–28, 29–31.

4 These three legends appear in the excellent psychological study by Dr. Otto Rank, *The Myth of the Birth of the Hero* (Nervous and Mental Disease Monographs; New York, 1910). A variant of the third appears in the *Gesta Romanorum,* Tale LXXXI.

5 The Charlemagne cycles are exhaustively discussed by Joseph Bédier, *Les légendes épiques* (3rd ed.; Paris, 1926).

6 Louis Ginzberg, *The Legends of the Jews* (Philadelphia: The Jewish Publication Society of America, 1911), vol. III, pp. 90–94.

7 George Bird Grinnell, *Blackfoot Lodge Tales* (New York: Charles Scribner's Sons, 1892, 1916), pp. 31–32.

8 Elsie Clews Parsons, *Tewa Tales* (Memoirs of the American Folklore Society, XIX, 1926), p. 193.

9 Adapted from Sister Nivedita and Ananda K. Coomaraswamy, *Myths of the Hindus and Buddhists* (New York: Henry Holt and Company, 1914), pp. 221–32.

10 Parsons, *op. cit.*, p. 193.

11 "Táin bó Cúalnge" (from the version in the *Book of Leinster,* 62 a–b): edited by Wh. Stokes and E. Windisch, *Irische Texte* (Extraband zu Serie I bis IV; Leipzig, 1905), pp. 106–17; English translation in Eleanor Hull's *The Cuchullin Saga in Irish Literature* (London, 1898), pp. 135–37.

12 *Book of Leinster*, 64b–67b (Stokes and Windisch, *op. cit.*, pp. 130–69); Hull, *op. cit.*, pp. 142–54.

13 From Eleanor Hull, *op. cit.*, p. 154; translated from the *Book of Leinster*, 68a (Stokes and Windisch, *op. cit.*, pp. 168–71).

14 Hull, *op. cit.*, pp. 174–76; from the *Book of Leinster*, 77 (Stokes and Windisch, *op. cit.*, pp. 368–77). Compare the transfiguration of Kṛṣṇa, pp. 198–201; see also Fig. 32.

15 Uno Holmberg (Uno Harva), *Der Baum des Lebens* (Annales Academiae Scientiarum Fennicae, Ser. B, Tom. XVI, No. 3; Helsinki, 1923), pp. 57–59; from N. Gorochov, "Yryn Uolan" (*Izvestia Vostočno-Siberskago Otdela I. Russkago Geografičeskago Obščestva,* XV), pp. 43 ff.

16 *Kalevala*, III, pp. 295–300.

17 Clark Wissler and D.C. Duvall, *Mythology of the Blackfeet Indians* (Anthropological Papers of the American Museum of Natural History, vol. II, Part I, New York, 1909), pp. 55–57. Quoted by Thompson, *op. cit.*, pp. 111–13.

18 Jacobus de Voragine, *op. cit.*, CIV, "Saint Martha, Virgin."

19 *The Wooing of Emer,* abstracted from the translation by Kuno Meyer in E. Hull, *op. cit.*, pp. 57–84.

20 Parsons, *op. cit.,* p. 194.

21 Firdausi, *Shah-Nameh,* translation by James Atkinson (London and New York, 1886), p. 7.

22 Opler, *op. cit.*, pp. 133–34.

23 Adapted from Nivedita and Coomaraswamy, *op. cit.,* pp. 236–37.

24 Coomaraswamy, *Hinduism and Buddhism,* pp. 6–7.

25 Gospel According to Matthew, 10:34–37.

26 Bhagavad Gītā, 18:51–53.

27 Antiphons of the nuns, at their consecration as Brides of Christ; from *The Roman Pontifical.* Reprinted in *The Soul Afire,* pp. 289–92.

28 Ginzberg, *op. cit.*, vol. I, pp. 305–6. By permission of the Jewish Publication Society of America.

29 Wilhelm Stekel, *Die Sprache des Traumes,* dream no. 421. Death here appears, observes Dr. Stekel, in four symbols: the Old Fiddler, the Squinting One, the Old Woman, and the Young Peasant (the Peasant is the Sower and the Reaper).

30 Bernardino de Sahagún, *Historia General de las Cosas de Nueva España* (Mexico, 1829), Lib. III, Cap. xii–xiv (condensed). The work has been republished by Pedro Robredo (Mexico, 1938), vol. I, pp. 278–82.

31 Thomas A. Joyce, *Mexican Archaeology* (London, 1914), p. 46.

32 "Taín bó Regamna," edited by Stokes and Windisch, *Irische Texte* (zweite Serie, Heft 2; Leipzig, 1887), pp. 241–54. The above is condensed from Hull, *op. cit.*, pp. 103–7.

33 Parsons, *op. cit.*, pp. 194–95.

34 Reprinted by permission of the publishers from Henry Clarke Warren, *Buddhism in Translations* (Harvard Oriental Series 3), Cambridge, MA: Harvard University Press, 1896, pp. 95–110.

Compare the stages of cosmic emanation, pp. 231–32.

CHAPTER IV: DISSOLUTIONS

1 Bhagavad Gītā, 10:20.

2 Bṛhadāranyaka Upaniṣad, 4. 3. 36–37.

3 James Henry Breasted, *Development of Religion and Thought in Egypt* (New York: Charles Scribner's Sons, 1912), p. 275. Reprinted by permission of the publishers.

Compare the poem of Taliesin, pp. 208–9.

4 Franz Boas, *Race, Language, and Culture* (New York, 1940), p. 514. See pp. 82–84.

5 Sahagún, *op. cit.*, Lib. I, Apéndice, Cap. i, ed. Robredo, vol. I, pp. 284–86.

6 Based on the translation by E. A. W. Budge: *The Book of the Dead, The Papyrus of Ani, Scribe and Treasurer of the Temples of Egypt, about* B.C. *1450* (New York, 1913).

7 Reprinted by permission of the Harvard University Press from Henry Clarke Warren, *Buddhism in Translations,* pp. 38–39.

8 Sylvanus G. Morley, *An Introduction to the Study of the Maya Hieroglyphics* (57th Bulletin, Bureau of American Ethnology, Washington, D.C., 1915). Plate 3 (facing p. 32).

9 *Ibid.*, p. 32.

10 The following account is based on the Poetic Edda, "Voluspa," pp. 42 ff. (the verses are quoted from the translation by Bellows, *op. cit.*, pp. 19–20, 24), and the Prose Edda, "Gylfaginning," LI (translation by Brodeur, *op. cit.*, pp. 77–81). By permission of the American-Scandinavian Foundation, publishers.

11 Gospel According to Matthew, 24:3–36.

EPILOGUE: MYTH AND SOCIETY

1 Odyssey, IV, 401, 417–18, translation by S. H. Butcher and Andrew Lang (London, 1879).

2 *Ibid.*, IV, 400–406.

3 Nietzsche, *Thus Spake Zarathustra,* 1.22.3. [The translation appears to be Campbell's own.—Ed.]

BIBLIOGRAPHY

Note on Method and Organization

THE PRIMARY PURPOSE of this list is to help readers find the sources that Campbell used to write this book. It also shows the remarkable breadth of reading—in mythology, ethnology, folklore, the modern and medieval literatures of Europe, psychology, philosophy, and religious scriptures of the Occident and Orient—that he incorporated into his first major independent work.

The book went through many revisions between the first draft in 1944, when it was known as *How to Read a Myth*, and its publication by the Bollingen Foundation in 1949. A letter in the Opus Archives written to Campbell's friend Henry Morton Robinson dated March 13, 1946, indicates that he had originally planned to cite fewer sources by relying heavily on the thirteen volume set *The Mythology of All Races*, published between 1916 and 1932 under the editorship of Louis Gray and John McCulloch. Unfortunately, the Macmillan Company had bought the republication rights to the set, and they refused to give him permission to make quotations while they considered putting out a new edition, forcing Campbell to track down new sources to illustrate his arguments.

The list comprises all of the citations in this third edition of *Hero*, except for a few minor ones. It includes those works from which a significant quotation is drawn, works that are cited more than once, and works that had a major effect on his thinking. Secondary citations (where Campbell cites a source "as quoted in" another work) were not included, although the works in which Campbell found them are included. When the second edition was published in 1968, Campbell made most of his citations from the writings of C.G. Jung as they appeared in *The Collected Works of C. G. Jung,* while he took his citations from Freud's writings from *The Standard Edition of the Collected Works of Sigmund Freud.*

The list is in four sections. The first includes those works cited by Campbell for which a particular edition is identified. Except as noted, these have been verified either from library catalogs or from books in Joseph Campbell's personal book collection, preserved at the Opus Archives.

The second section lists journal articles cited within the book. Most of these have not been verified.

Because of the difficulty in alphabetizing canonical works, these form the third section, arranged by religious tradition. This section contains works of religious scripture cited by Campbell. The works have been further broken down by faith or tradition. Since Campbell used sources available half a century ago, I have indicated the modern forms of the titles used in the Collected Works of Joseph Campbell, as well, when those vary, as those used by the Library of Congress, and noted when reprints or more recent translations are available.

With well-known literary works and religious canon, Campbell sometimes cited the work without giving an edition. I have listed these separately in the fourth section. My comments appear in brackets with the initials R. B.

—Richard Buchen, *Special Collections Librarian, Joseph Campbell Collection of the Opus Archives and Research Center on the campuses of Pacifica Graduate Institute, Santa Barbara, California*

Main Bibliographic List

Anderson, Johannes C. *Maori Life in Ao-Tea.* Christchurch, [N.Z.]: n.d.

Apuleius. *The Golden Ass of Apuleius.* Translated by W. Adlington. New York: The Modern Library, n.d.

Aristotle. *Aristotle on the Art of Poetry.* Translated by Ingram Bywater, with a Preface by Gilbert Murray. Oxford: Oxford University Press, 1920.

Arnold, Thomas Walker, and Alfred Guillaume, eds. *The Legacy of Islam.* Oxford: The Clarendon Press, 1931.

Bain, F. W. *A Digit of the Moon and Other Love Stories from the Hindoo.* New York and London: G.P. Putnam's Sons, 1910.

Bastian, Adolf. *Ethnische Elementargedanken in der Lehre vom Menschen.* Berlin: Weidmann, 1895.

Bédier, Joseph. *Les légendes épiques: Recherches sur la formation des chansons de geste.* 3rd ed. Paris: H. Champion, 1926.

Bellows, Henry Adams, ed. *The Poetic Edda,* Scandinavian Classics, 21/22. New York: The American-Scandinavian Foundation, 1923.

Bhagavad Gītā: *Bhagavad Gita: Translated from the Sanskrit with Notes, Comments, and Introduction by Swami Nikhilananda.* New York: Ramakrishna-Vivekananda Center, 1944.

Boas, Franz. *The Mind of Primitive Man.* New York: Macmillan, 1911.

———. *Race, Language and Culture.* New York: Macmillan, 1940.

Book of the Dead: *See* Budge, E.A. Wallis, *The Papyrus of Ani.*

Breasted, James Henry. *Development of Religion and Thought in Ancient Egypt.* New York: Charles Scribner's Sons, 1912.

Bṛhadāranyaka Upaniṣad: *The Brihadaranyaka Upanishad: With the Commentary of Shankaracharya. Translated by Swami Madhavananda, with an Introd. by S. Kuppuswami Shastri.* Translated by Madhavananda. Mayavati: Advaita Ashrama, [1934?].

Bryan, William Frank, and Germaine Dempster. *Sources and Analogues of Chaucer's "Canterbury Tales."* Chicago: University of Chicago Press, 1941.

Budge, E.A. Wallis, ed., *The Gods of the Egyptians.* London: Methuen, 1904.

———. *The Papyrus of Ani.* Translated by E.A. Wallis Budge. New York: Putnam, 1913.

Burlingame, Eugene Watson, ed. *Buddhist Parables.* New Haven: Yale University Press, 1922.

Burton, Richard Francis. *See* Thousand Nights and a Night.

Callaway, Henry. *Nursery Tales, Traditions, and Histories of the Zulus, in Their Own Words, with a Translation into English, and Notes, by Canon Callaway.* Springvale, Natal: J.A. Blair; London: Trübner, 1868.

Campbell, Joseph. "Folkloristic Commentary." *Grimm's Fairy Tales,* by Jacob and Wilhelm Grimm, pp. 833–64. New York: Pantheon, 1944.

Catholic Church. *Saint Andrew Daily Missal, by Dom Gaspar Lefebvre O.S.B. of the Abbey of S. André.* Bruges, Belgium: Abbey of St. André; St. Paul: E.M. Lohmann Co., [1943?].

Chavannes, Edouard. *Les mémoires historiques de Se-Ma-Ts'ien.* Translated by Edouard Chavannes. Paris: E. Leroux, 1895.

Codrington, R.H. *The Melanesians: Studies in Their Anthropology and Folk-Lore.* Oxford: Clarendon Press, 1891.

Collocott, E.E.V. *Tales and Poems of Tonga.* Bernice P. Bishop Museum Bulletin 46. Honolulu, HI: The Museum, 1928.

Coomaraswamy, Ananda Kentish. *Buddha and the Gospel of Buddhism.* New York: G.P. Putnam's Sons, 1916.

———. *The Dance of Siva: Fourteen Indian Essays.* New York: Sunwise Turn, 1924.

———. *Hinduism and Buddhism.* New York: Philosophical Library, n.d.

———. *Spiritual Authority and Temporal Power in the Indian Theory of Government.* American Oriental Series, V. 22. New Haven, CT: American Oriental Society, 1942.

Curtin, Jeremiah. *Myths and Folk-Lore of Ireland.* Boston: Little, Brown, 1890.

Dante Alighieri. *The Divine Comedy of Dante Alighieri.* Translated by Charles Eliot Norton. Rev. ed. 3 vols. Boston: Houghton Mifflin and Co., 1902.

Dimnet, Ernest. *The Art of Thinking.* New York: Simon and Schuster, 1929.

Edda, Poetic. *See* Bellows, Henry Adams.

Edda, Prose. *See* Sturluson, Snorri.

Eddington, Arthur Stanley. *The Nature of the Physical World.* Gifford Lectures, 1927. New York: Macmillan, 1928.

Edwards, Jonathan. *Sinners in the Hands of an Angry God: A Sermon Preached at Enfield, July 8th.* 2nd ed. Boston: n.p., 1742.

Eliot, T.S. "The Waste Land (1922)." In *Collected Poems, 1909–1935.* New York: Harcourt, Brace, [n.d.].

Evans-Wentz, W.Y., ed. *Tibetan Yoga and Secret Doctrines, or, Seven Books of Wisdom of the Great Path, According to the Late Lama Kazi Dawa-Samdup's English Rendering.* London: Oxford University Press, 1935.

———, ed. *Tibet's Great Yogi, Milarepa: A Biography from the Tibetan; Being the Jetsün-Kahbum or Biographical History of Jetsün-Milarepa According to the Late Lama Kazi Dawa-Samdup's English Rendering.* London: Oxford University Press, 1928.

Firdausi. *The Shah Nameh of the Persian Poet Firdausi.* Translated by James Atkinson. London, New York: F. Warne, 1886.

Fletcher, Alice C. *The Hako: A Pawnee Ceremony.* Bureau of American Ethnology Annual Report. Washington, DC: Government Printing Office, 1904.

Flügel, J.C. *The Psycho-Analytic Study of the Family.* 4th ed. The International Psycho-Analytical Library, no. 3. London: L. and Virginia Woolf, at the Hogarth Press and the Institute of Psycho-Analysis, 1931.

Fosdick, Harry Emerson. *As I See Religion.* New York, London: Harper & Brothers, 1932.

Frazer, James George. *The Golden Bough: A Study in Magic and Religion.* Abridged ed. New York: Macmillan, 1922.

Freud, Sigmund. *Beyond the Pleasure Principle.* In *The Standard Edition of the Collected Works of Sigmund Freud,* vol. 18, edited and translated by James Strachey et al. London: The Hogarth Press, 1955. Originally published 1920.

———. *The Future of an Illusion.* In *The Standard Edition of the Collected Works of Sigmund Freud,* vol. 21, edited and translated by James Strachey et al. London: Hogarth Press, 1961, pp. 1–56. Originally published 1927.

———. *The Interpretation of Dreams.* In *The Standard Edition of the Collected Works of Sigmund Freud.* Edited and translated by James Strachey et al. London: The Hogarth Press, 1953. Originally published 1900.

———. *The Interpretation of Dreams (second part).* In *The Standard Edition of the Collected Works of Sigmund Freud,* vol. 5, edited and translated by James Strachey et al. London: Hogarth Press, 1953. Originally published 1900–1901.

———. *Introductory Lectures on Psycho-analysis (part III)*. In *The Standard Edition of the Collected Works of Sigmund Freud*, vol. 16, edited and translated by James Strachey et al. London: Hogarth Press, 1963. Originally published 1916–1917.

———. *Moses and Monotheism*. In *The Standard Edition of the Collected Works of Sigmund Freud*, vol. 23, edited and translated by James Strachey et al., pp. 1–137. London: Hogarth Press, 1964. Originally published 1939.

———. *The Psychopathology of Everyday Life*. In *The Standard Edition of the Collected Works of Sigmund Freud*, vol. 6, edited and translated by James Strachey et al. London: Hogarth Press, 1960. Originally published 1901.

———. "Three Essays on the Theory of Sexuality." In *The Standard Edition of the Collected Works of Sigmund Freud*, vol. 7, edited and translated by James Strachey et al., pp. 123–245. London: Hogarth Press, 1953. Originally published 1905.

Frobenius, Leo. *Das unbekannte Afrika: Aufhellung der Schicksale eines Erdteils*. Veröffentlichung des Forschungsinstitutes für Kulturmorphologie. Munich: Oskar Beck, 1923.

———. *Und Afrika sprach*. Berlin: Vita, 1912.

———. *Das Zeitalter des Sonnengottes*. Berlin: G. Reimer, 1904.

Frobenius, Leo, and Douglas Claughton Fox. *African Genesis*. New York: Stackpole Sons, 1937.

Gennep, Arnold van. *Les rites de passage*. Paris: É. Nourry, 1909.

Giles, Herbert Allen. *A Chinese Biographical Dictionary*. London: B. Quaritch; Shanghai: Kelly & Walsh, 1898.

Ginsburg, Christian D. *The Kabbalah: Its Doctrines, Development, and Literature*. London: G. Routledge & Sons, 1920.

Ginzberg, Louis. *The Legends of the Jews*. Translated by Henrietta Szold and Paul Radin. 7 vols. Philadelphia: The Jewish Publication Society of America, 1911.

Gray, Louis H., and J.A. MacCulloch, eds. *The Mythology of All Races*. 13 vols. Boston: Archaeological Institute of America; Marshall Jones Company, 1916–1932. Contents:

I. Greek and Roman, by William Sherwood Fox. 1916.

II. Eddic, by J. A. MacCulloch. 1930.

III. Celtic, by J. A. MacCulloch; Slavic, by Jan Máchal. 1918.

IV. Finno-Ugric, Siberian, by Uno Holmberg. 1927.

V. Semitic, by S. H. Langdon. 1931.

VI. Indian, by A. B. Keith; Iranian, by A.J. Carnvy. 1917.

VII. Armenian, by M. H. Ananikian; African, by Alice Werner. 1925.

VIII. Chinese, by J. C. Ferguson; Japanese, by Masaharu Anesaki. 1928.

IX. Oceanic, by R. B. Dixon. 1916.

X. North American, by H. B. Alexander. 1916.

XI. Latin-American, by H. B. Alexander. 1920.

XII. Egyptian, by W. M. Müller; Indo-Chinese, by J. G. Scott. 1918.

XIII. Complete index to volumes I–XII. 1932.

Grey, George. *Polynesian Mythology and Ancient Traditional History of the New Zealand Race, as Furnished by Their Priests and Chiefs*. London: J. Murray, 1855.

Grimm, Jacob, and Wilhelm Grimm. *Grimm's Fairy Tales*. Unabridged edition. New York: Pantheon Books, 1944.

Grinnell, George Bird. *Blackfoot Lodge Tales: The Story of a Prairie People*. New York: Scribner, 1892.

Guest, Charlotte. *See* Mabinogion.

Gutmann, Bruno. *Volksbuch der Wadschagga: Sagen, Märchen, Fabeln und Schwänke den Dschagganegern nacherzählt*. Leipzig: Verlag der Evang.-Luth. Mission, 1914.

Harrison, Jane Ellen. *Prolegomena to the Study of Greek Religion*. 3rd ed. Cambridge: Cambridge University Press, 1922.

———. *Themis: A Study of the Social Origins of Greek Religion*. 2nd rev. ed. London: Cambridge University Press, 1927.

Harva, Uno. *Der Baum des Lebens*. Suomalaisen Tiedeakatemian Toimituksia, Annales, Sarja B, Nide 16, 3. Helsinki: Suomalainen Tiedeakatemia, 1923.

———. *Die religiösen Vorstellungen der altaischen Völker*. FF Communications no. 125. Helsinki: Suomalainen Tiedeakatemia, 1938.

Hastings, James, ed. *Encyclopaedia of Religion and Ethics.* 13 vols. New York: Charles Scribner's Sons, 1928.

Hearn, Lafcadio. *Japan, an Attempt at Interpretation.* New York: Grosset & Dunlap, 1904.

Hirth, Friedrich. *The Ancient History of China to the End of the Chou Dynasty.* New York: The Columbia University Press, 1908.

Holmberg, Uno. *See: Harva, Uno.*

Homer. *The Odyssey of Homer.* Translated by Samuel Henry Butcher and Andrew Lang. 2nd ed. London: Macmillan, 1879.

Hull, Eleanor. *The Cuchullin Saga in Irish Literature: Being a Collection of Stories Relating to the Hero Cuchullin.* London: D. Nutt, 1898.

Hume, Robert Ernest, ed. *The Thirteen Principal Upanishads, Translated from the Sanskrit with an Outline of the Philosophy of the Upanishads.* 2nd ed. London; New York: Oxford University Press, 1931.

Jeffers, Robinson. *The Roan Stallion... and Other Poems.* New York: Horace Liveright, 1925.

Jensen, Peter Christian Albrecht. *Assyrisch-babylonische Mythen und Epen.* Kellinschriftliche Bibliothek Bd. VI, I. Berlin: Reuther & Reichard, 1900.

Ježower, Ignaz. *Das Buch der Träume.* Berlin: E. Rowohlt, 1928.

Johnson, Obed Simon. *A Study of Chinese Alchemy.* Shanghai, China: n.p., 1928.

Joyce, James. *Finnegans Wake.* New York: The Viking Press, 1939.

———. *A Portrait of the Artist as a Young Man.* New York: Modern Library, [1928?].

———. *Ulysses.* New York: Modern Library, [n.d.].

Joyce, Thomas Athol. *Mexican Archaeology, an Introduction to the Archaeology of the Mexican and Mayan Civilizations of Pre-Spanish America.* London: P. L. Warner, 1914.

Jung, Carl Gustav. "Archetypes of the Collective Unconscious." In *The Collected Works of C. G. Jung,* vol. 9, part I, edited by Herbert Read et al., translated by R. F. C. Hull, pp. 3–41. Bollingen Series 20. New York: Pantheon, 1959. (Originally written 1934.)

———. *The Integration of the Personality.* New York, Toronto: Farrar and Rinehart, 1939. Republished, with revisions, in vol. 9, part i, of the *Collected Works.*

———. "On Psychic Energy." In *The Collected Works of C. G. Jung,* vol. 8, edited by Herbert Read et al., translated by R. F. C. Hull, 3–66.

Bollingen Series 20. New York: Pantheon, 1960. (Originally written 1928.)

———. *Psychological Types, or, the Psychology of Individuation,* translated by H. Godwin Baynes. London: K. Paul, Trench Trübner; New York: Harcourt Brace, [1946?]. Republished as vol. 6 of *The Collected Works of C. G. Jung.* Princeton, NJ: Princeton University Press, 1971. (Originally written 1921.)

———. *Psychology and Alchemy.* In *The Collected Works of C. G. Jung,* vol. 12, edited by Herbert Read et al., translated by R.F.C. Hull. Bollingen Series 20. New York: Pantheon, 1953. (Originally written 1935–1936.)

———. "Psychology and Religion." In *The Collected Works of C. G. Jung,* vol. 11, edited by Herbert Read et al., translated by R.F.C. Hull, 3–105. Bollingen Series 20. New York: Pantheon, 1958. (Originally written 1938.)

———. *Symbols of Transformation.* In *The Collected Works of C. G. Jung,* edited by Herbert Read et al., translated by R. F. C. Hull. 2nd ed., vol. 5, Bollingen Series 20. Princeton, NJ: Princeton University Press, 1967. (Originally written 1912.)

Kakuzo, Okakura. *See* Okakura, Kakuzo.

Kalevala. *Kalevala, the Land of Heroes.* Translated by William Forsell Kirby. Everyman's Library. London & Toronto: J. M. Dent & Sons, 1907.

Kalidasa. *The Birth of the War-God: A Poem.* Translated by Ralph T. H. Griffith. 2nd ed. London: Trübner, 1897. (Edition not verified. The quotation is possibly from the 1879 edition listed in the UCLA library catalog.)

Kato, Genchi. *What Is Shinto?* Tourist Library 8. Tokyo: Maruzen Co., Ltd., 1935.

Kena Upaniṣad. *Kena-Upanishad, with Sanskrit Text, Paraphrase with Word-for-Word Literal Translation, English Rendering, and Comments.* Translated by Sharvananda. Mylapore, Madras: Sri Ramakrishna Math, 1932.

Kimmins, Charles William. *Children's Dreams.* London: G. Allen & Unwin, 1937.

King, Jeff, Maud Oakes, and Joseph Campbell. *Where the Two Came to Their Father: A Navaho War Ceremonial.* 2nd ed. Bollingen Series, vol. I. Princeton, NJ: Princeton University Press, 1969. (Originally published 1943.)

King, L. W. *Babylonian Religion and Mythology.* Books on Egypt and Chaldaea, vol. 4. London: K. Paul, Trench, Trübner & Co., 1899.

Kingsborough, Edward King. *Antiquities of Mexico: Comprising Fac-Similes of Ancient Mexican Paintings and Hieroglyphics.* 9 vols. London: R. Havell [etc.], 1831–1848.

Klein, Melanie. *The Psycho-Analysis of Children.* International Psycho-Analytical Library, no. 22. London: L. & Virginia Woolf at the Hogarth Press and the Institute of Psycho-Analysis, 1932.

Knight, W. F. Jackson. *Cumaean Gates: A Reference of the Sixth Aeneid to the Initiation Pattern.* Oxford: B. Blackwell, 1936.

Koran. *The Holy Qur-An: Text, Translation and Commentary.* Translated by Abdullah Yusuf Ali. 2 vols. New York: Hafner Pub. Co., [1946].

Kramer, Samuel Noah. *Sumerian Mythology: A Study of Spiritual and Literary Achievement in the Third Millennium, B.C.* Memoirs of the American Philosophical Society, vol. XXI. Philadelphia: The American Philosophical Society, 1944.

Lang, Andrew. *Custom and Myth.* 2nd ed. London: Longmans, Green, and Co., 1885.

Lao Tse. *Laotzu's Tao and Wu Wei.* Translated by Dwight Goddard. New York: Brentano's, 1919.

Layard, John. *Stone Men of Malekula.* London: Chatto & Windus, 1942.

Loomis, Gertrude Schoepperle. *Tristan and Isolt: A Study of the Sources of the Romance.* Frankfurt a. M.: J. Baer & Co., 1913.

Mabinogion. *The Mabinogion.* Translated by Charlotte Elizabeth Guest Schreiber. Everyman's Library. New York: E. P. Dutton & Co., 1906.

MacGowan, J. *The Imperial History of China.* 2nd ed. Shanghai: American Presbyterian Mission Press, 1906.

Malory, Thomas. *Le Morte D'Arthur.* Everyman's Library. London, Toronto: J. M. Dent & Sons, 1919.

Mather, Cotton. *The Wonders of the Invisible World: Observations as Well Historical as Theological Upon the Nature, the Number, and the Operations of the Devils*... Boston, 1693.

Mathers, S. L. MacGregor. *Kabbala Denudata, the Kabbalah Unveiled, Containing the Following Books of the Zohar. 1. The Book of Concealed Mystery. 2. The Greater Holy Assembly. 3. The Lesser Holy Assembly.* London: Kegan Paul, Trench, Trübner & Co, [1887?].

Matthews, Washington. *Navaho Legends.* Boston, New York: Published for the American Folk-Lore Society by Houghton, Mifflin and Company, 1897.

Meier, Joseph. *Mythen und Erzählungen der Küstenbewohner der Gazelle-Halbinsel (Neu-Pommern).* Münster i. W.: Aschendorff, 1909.

Menninger, Karl A. *Love Against Hate.* New York: Harcourt, 1942.

Morley, Sylvanus Griswold. *An Introduction to the Study of the Maya Hieroglyphs.* Bureau of American Ethnology Bulletin 57. Washington: Government Printing Office, 1915.

Müller, F. Max, ed. *Buddhist Mahāyāna Texts, The Sacred Books of the East,* vol. 49. Oxford: Clarendon Press, 1894.

—pt. 1. The Buddha-karita of Asvaghosha, translated from the Sanskrit by E. B. Cowell.

—pt. 2. The larger Sukhāvatī-vyūha, the smaller Sukhāvatāi-vyūha, the Vagrakkedikā, the larger Pragñā-Pāramitā-Hridaya-Sūtra, the smaller Pragñā-Pāramitā-Hridaya-Sūtra, translated by F. Max Müller. The Amitāyur Dhyāna-Sūtra, translated by J. Takakusu.

———, ed. *The Dhammapada.* Translated by Max Müller. *The Sacred Books of the East,* vol. 10. Oxford: Clarendon Press, 1881.

Nelson, Ansgar. *See* Reinhold, Hans Ansgar.

Nivedita, and Ananda Kentish Coomaraswamy. *Myths of the Hindus & Buddhists.* New York: Henry Holt, 1914.

O'Grady, Standish Hayes, ed. and trans. *Silva Gadelica (I.–XXXI.): A Collection of Tales in Irish with Extracts Illustrating Persons and Places.* London: Williams and Norgate, 1892.

Okakura, Kakuzo. *The Book of Tea.* New York: Duffield, 1906.

Opler, Morris Edward. *Myths and Tales of the Jicarilla Apache Indians.* Memoirs of the American Folk-Lore Society, vol. XXXI. New York: American Folk-Lore Society, 1938.

Ovid. *Metamorphoses.* Translated by Frank Justus Miller. The Loeb Classical Library. London: W. Heinemann, 1933.

Pallis, Marco. *Peaks and Lamas.* 4th ed. London: Cassell, 1946.

Parsons, Elsie Clews. *Tewa Tales.* Memoirs of the American Folk-Lore Society, vol. XIX. New York: American Folk-Lore Society, 1926.

Peake, Harold, and H. J. Fleure. *Merchant Venturers in Bronze.* New Haven, CT: Yale University Press, 1931.

———. *The Way of the Sea.* New Haven, CT: Yale University Press, 1929.

Perry, W. J. *The Children of the Sun.* London: Methuen & Co., 1923.

Phillips, Robert. *American Government and Its Problems.* Rev. ed. Boston, New York: Houghton Mifflin Company, 1941.

Pierce, Frederick. *Dreams and Personality: A Study of Our Dual Lives.* New York, London: D. Appleton and Company, 1931.

Pinkerton, John. *A General Collection of the Best and Most Interesting Voyages and Travels in All Parts of the World.* 17 vols. London: Longman, Hurst, Rees, 1808. [An important source for the myths of Lappland and Siberia—R.B.].

Polack, J. S. *Manners and Customs of the New Zealanders: With Notes Corroborative of Their Habits, Usages, etc.* London: J. Madden, 1840.

Radcliffe-Brown, A. R. *The Adaman Islanders.* 2nd ed. Cambridge: University Press, 1933.

Ramakrishna. *The Gospel of Sri Ramakrishna.* Translated by Swami Nikhilananda. New York: Ramakrishna-Vivekananda Center, 1942.

Rank, Otto. *Art and Artist: Creative Urge and Personality Development.* Translated by Charles Francis Atkinson. New York: A. A. Knopf, 1943.

———. *The Myth of the Birth of the Hero: A Psychological Interpretation of Mythology.* Translated by F. Robbins and Smith Ely Jelliffe. Nervous and Mental Disease Monograph Series, no. 18. New York: The Journal of Nervous and Mental Disease Publishing Company, 1914.

Reinhold, Hans Ansgar, ed. *The Soul Afire: Revelations of the Mystics.* [New York]: Pantheon Books, 1944.

Róheim, Géza. *The Eternal Ones of the Dream: A Psychoanalytic Interpretation of Australian Myth and Ritual.* New York: International Universities Press, 1945.

———. *The Origin and Function of Culture.* New York: Nervous and Mental Disease Monographs, 1943. (Originally published in 1942.)

———. *War, Crime and the Covenant.* Journal of Clinical Psychopathology Monograph Series, no. 1. Monticello, NY: Medical Journal Press, 1945.

Rossetti, Dante Gabriel. *Dante and His Circle: With the Italian Poets Preceding Him (1100–1200–1300). A Collection of Lyrics, ed., and tr. in the Original Metres.* London: Ellis and White, 1874.

Sadananda. *Vedantasara of Sadananda with Introduction, Text, English Translation and Comments by Swami Nikhilananda.* Mayavati: Advaita Ashrama, 1931.

Sahagún, Bernardino de. *Historia general de las cosas de Nueva España.* México, D. F.: P. Robredo, 1938.

Sankaracarya. *Vivekachudamani, of Sri Sankaracharya: Text with English Translation, Notes and Index by Swami Madhavananda.* Mayavati: Advaita Ashrama, 1932.

Schoepperle, Gertrude. *See* Loomis, Gertrude Schoepperle.

Schultze, Leonhard. *Aus Namaland und Kalahari. Bericht an die Kgl. Preuss. Akademie der Wissenschaften zu Berlin über eine Forschungsreise im westlichen und zentralen Südafrika, ausgeführt in den Jahren 1903–1905.* Jena: G. Fischer, 1907.

Scott, David Clement Ruffelle. *A Cyclopaedic Dictionary of the Mang'anja Language Spoken in British Central Africa.* Edinburgh: The Foreign Mission Committee of the Church of Scotland, 1892.

Shrichakrasambhara Tantra: A Buddhist Tantra. Edited by John Woodroffe. Translated by Kazi Dawa-Samdup. *Tantrik Texts*, vol. 7. London: Luzac & Co., 1919.

Spencer, Baldwin, and Francis James Gillen. *The Arunta: A Study of a Stone Age People.* 2 vols. London: Macmillan, 1927.

———. *The Native Tribes of Central Australia.* London: Macmillan, 1899.

Spengler, Oswald. *The Decline of the West.* Translated by Charles Francis Atkinson. 2 vols. New York: A. A. Knopf, 1926–1928.

Stekel, Wilhelm. *Fortschritte und Technik der Traumdeutung.* Wien: n.p., 1935.

———. *Die Sprache des Traumes: Eine Darstellung der Symbolik und Deutung des Traumes in ihren Beziehungen zur kranken und gesunden Seele.* Wiesbaden: J. F. Bergmann, 1911.

Stevenson, (Mrs.) Sinclair. *The Heart of Jainism.* London, New York: Humphrey Milford, Oxford University Press, 1915.

Stimson, J. F., Edwin G. Burrows, and Kenneth Pike Emory. *The Legends of Maui and Tahaki.* Bernice P. Bishop Museum Bulletin 127. Honolulu, Hawaii: The Museum, 1934.

Sturluson, Snorri. *The Prose Edda.* Translated by Arthur Gilchrist Brodeur. New York: The American-Scandinavian Foundation, 1929.

Suzuki, Daisetz Teitaro. *Essays in Zen Buddhism.* London: Luzac and Company, 1927.

Taylor, Richard. *Te ika a Maui, or, New Zealand and its Inhabitants.* London: n.p., 1855.

Thompson, Stith. *Tales of the North American Indians.* Cambridge, MA: Harvard University Press, 1929.

Thousand Nights and a Night: *A Plain and Literal Translation of the Arabian Nights Entertainments, Now Entituled the Book of the Thousand Nights and a Night.* Translated by Richard Francis Burton. 10 vols. Benares: Printed by the Kamashastra Society for private subscribers only, 1885. (Probably the edition referred to as "Bombay, 1885.")

Toynbee, Arnold Joseph. *A Study of History.* London: Oxford University Press, 1934.

Underhill, Evelyn. *Mysticism: A Study in the Nature and Development of Man's Spiritual Consciousness.* New York: Dutton, 1911.

Warner, W. Lloyd. *A Black Civilization: A Social Study of an Australian Tribe.* New York, London: Harper & Brothers, 1937.

Warren, Henry Clarke, ed. *Buddhism in Translations.* Cambridge, MA: Harvard University, 1896.

Werner, Edward Theodore Chalmers. *A Dictionary of Chinese Mythology.* Shanghai: Kelly and Walsh, 1932.

White, John. *The Ancient History of the Maori, His Mythology and Traditions.* Wellington: G. Didsbury, 1887.

Wilhelm, Richard. *Chinesische Volksmärchen.* Jena: E. Diederichs, 1921.

Windisch, Wilhelm Oscar Ernst. *Die altirische Heldensage Táin bó Cúalnge. Nach dem Buch von Leinster...* Irische Texte, Extraband zu Serie I bis IV. Leipzig: n.p., 1905.

Wood, Clement. *Dreams: Their Meaning and Practical Application.* New York: Greenberg, 1931.

Woodroffe, John George. *Shakti and Shākta.* 3rd ed. Madras: Ganesh, 1929.

Young, Hugh. *Genital Abnormalities, Hermaphroditism & Related Adrenal Diseases.* Baltimore: Williams & Wilkins Company, 1937.

Zimmer, Heinrich Robert. *The King and the Corpse: Tales of the Soul's Conquest of Evil.* Edited by Joseph Campbell. Bollingen Series, vol. XI. [New York]: Pantheon Books, 1948.

———. *Maya: Der indische Mythos.* Stuttgart: Deutsche Verlags-Anstalt, 1936.

———. *Myths and Symbols in Indian Art and Civilization.* Edited by Joseph Campbell. Bollingen Series, vol VI. [New York]: Pantheon Books, 1946.

Zirus, Werner. *Ahasverus, der ewige Jude.* Stoff- und Motivgeschichte der deutschen Literatur, 6. Berlin and Leipzig: W. de Gruyter & Co., 1930.

Journal Articles

Capus, A. "Contes, chants et proverbes des Basumbua dans l'Afrique orientale." *Zeitschrift fur afrikanische und oceanische Sprachen,* vol. 3 (1897).

Chamberlain, B. H "Ko-ji-ki: Records of Ancient Matters." *Transactions of the Asiatic Society of Japan.* Vol. 10, Supplement (1883). (Copy in the Opus Archive is reprinted, with different pagination, by the Asiatic Society of Japan, 1906.)

Coomaraswamy, Ananda Kentish. "Akimcanna: Self Naughting." *New Indian Antiquary,* vol. 3 (1940). (Reprinted in *Coomaraswamy: Selected Papers,* Bollingen Series, LXXXIX. Princeton, NJ: Princeton University Press, 1977.)

———. "A Note on the Stick Fast Motif." *Journal of American Folklore,* vol. 57 (1944).

———. "On the One and Only Transmigrant." Supplement to the *Journal of the American Oriental Society* (April–June 1944). (Reprinted in *Coomaraswamy: Selected Papers, 2, Metaphysics.*)

———. "Symbolism of the Dome." *Indian Historical Quarterly,* vol. 14 (March 1938).

Coomaraswamy, L. "The Perilous Bridge of Welfare." *Harvard Journal of Asiatic Studies,* vol. 8 (1944). (By Doña Luisa Coomaraswamy, wife of Ananda Coomaraswamy, cited as D. L. Coomaraswamy.)

Emory, Kenneth. "The Tahitian Account of Creation by Mare." *Journal of the Polynesian Society,* vol. 47, no. 2 (June 1938).

———. "The Tuamotuan Creation Charts by Paiore." *Journal of the Polynesian Society,* vol. 48, no. 1 (March 1939): 1–29.

Espinosa, Aurelio. "A New Classification of the Fundamental Elements of the Tar-Baby Story on the Basis of Two Hundred and Sixty-seven Versions." *Journal of American Folklore,* vol. 56 (1943).

———. "Notes on the Origin and History of the Tar-Baby Story." *Journal of American Folklore,* vol. 43 (1930).

Forke, Alfred. "Ko Hung der Philosoph und Alchimist." *Archiv für Geschichte der Philosophie,* vol. 41, nos. 1–2 (1932): 115–126.

Meissner, Bruno. "Ein altbabylonisches Fragment des Gilgamosepos." *Mitteilungen der Vorderasiatischen Gesellschaft,* vol. 7, no. 1 (1902).

Salmony, Alfred. "Die Rassenfrage in der Indienforschung." *Sozialistische Monatshefte,* vol. 8 (1926).

Stein, Leon. "Hassidic Music." *Chicago Jewish Forum,* vol. 2, no. 1 (1943).

Canonical Works and Religious Scriptures

HINDU

[Campbell could not translate Sanskrit well, but he had worked closely with three scholars who did. At the time he was writing *The Hero with a Thousand Faces,* he was editing the unpublished works and lecture notes of the recently deceased Sanskrit scholar Heinrich Zimmer (died 1943), and he was also corresponding with Ananda Kentish Coomaraswamy, Curator of Asian Art at the Boston Museum of Fine Art. He was also helping with a translation of the Upaniṣads (including the commentary of the great Vedantist scholar Śaṅkaracharya, fl. c. A.D. 800) by Swami Nikhilananda of the Ramakrishna-Vivekananda Center in New York (New York: Harper, 1949–1959; reprinted by Dover Publications, 2003).

Other translations of the Upaniṣads include Robert Hume's *Thirteen Principal Upanishads* (revised edition 1931; reprinted 1983) and Sarvepalli Radhakrishnan's *The Principal Upanisads* (New York, 1953, reprinted Atlantic Highlands, NJ: Humanities Press, 1992)—R.B.]

Āranyakas

Aitareya Āranyaka (Aitareyāranyaka). The text quoted is found in a footnote attributed to Ananda Kentish Coomaraswamy on page 48 of Heinrich Zimmer, *The King and the Corpse.*

Brāhmaṇas

Jaiminīya Upaniṣad Brāhmaṇa (Jaiminīyabrāhmana Upanisadbrāhmana). This Brāhmaṇa is related to the Jaiminīyabrāhmana. Quotation from an unknown source. [A text and translation with different wording by Hanns Örtel, "The Jāiminīya or Talavakāra Upaniṣad Brāhmaṇa" (*Journal of the American Oriental Society,* vol. 16, no. 1, 1894), is in Campbell's book collection and was cited by Zimmer in a lecture delivered at the Eranos Conference of 1938.—R.B.]

Mahābhārata

Bhagavad Gītā (Bhagavadgītā). Quotations are from *The Bhagavad Gita.* Translated by Swami Nikhilananda (New York: Ramakrishna-Vivekananda Center, 1944).

Purāṇa

Most quotations are from Heinrich Zimmer's *Myths and Symbols in Indian Art and Civilization.*

Upaniṣads

Bṛhadāranyaka Upaniṣad (Brhadaranyakopanisad). Quotations are from *The Brihadaranyaka Upanishad.* Translated by Swami Madhavananda (Mayavati: Advaita Ashrama, [1934?]).

Chāndogya Upaniṣad (Chāndogyopanisad). Quotations are from Robert Ernest Hume (ed. and trans.), *Thirteen Principal Upanishads* (Oxford University Press, 1931).

Katha Upaniṣad (Kathopanisad). From Hume.

Kauṣītaki Upaniṣad (Kausītakibrāmanopanisad). From Hume. There are few other translations of this text.

Kena Upaniṣad (Kenopanisad). Quotations from *Kena Upanishad.* Translated by Swami Sharvananda. Mylapore, Madras: Sri Ramakrishna Math, 1932.

Māṇḍūkya Upaniṣad (Māndūkyopanisad), from Hume.

Mundaka Upaniṣad (Mundakopanisad), from Hume.

Taittirīya Upaniṣad (Taittirīyopanisad), from Hume.

BUDDHIST

Jātakas (Lives of the Buddha)

Quotations are from Henry Clarke Warren, ed., *Buddhism in Translations*; and Eugene Watson Burlingame, *Buddhist Parables.*

Sutras

[The Mahāyāna sūtras are translated from Sanskrit. Many translations are available, although most of these are translations from the Chinese versions, which often vary somewhat from the Sanskrit originals. The Dhammapada was translated from the Pāli language.—R.B.]

Amitāyur-dhyāna Sūtra (Amitāyurdhyānasūtra). In Max Müller, ed., *Buddhist Mahāyāna Texts.*

Dhammapada. In Max Müller, ed. and trans., *The Dhammapada.* Oxford: Clarendon Press, 1881. Reprinted with revisions, Woodstock, VT, 2002.

Larger Sukhāvatī-vyūha (Sukhāvatīvyūha [Larger]). In Max Müller, ed., *Buddhist Mahāyāna Texts.*

Prajñāpāramitā-hṛdaya Sūtra (Hrdaya, or Heart Sutra). In Max Müller, ed., *Buddhist Mahāyāna Texts.*

Smaller Prajñāpāramitā-hṛdaya Sūtra (Hrdaya). In Max Müller, ed., *Buddhist Mahāyāna Texts.*

Vajracchedikā ("The Diamond Cutter") (Vajracchedikā, also called the "Diamond Sūtra"). In Max Müller, ed., *Buddhist Mahāyāna Texts.* A more recent translation by Edward Conze was published in *Buddhist Wisdom: Containing the Diamond Sutra and the Heart Sutra* (New York, 2001).

Tantras

Cakrasamvāra Tantra (Cakrasamvāratantra). Quotations are from *Shrichakrasambhara Tantra: A Buddhist Tantra, Edited Kazi Dawa-Samdup* (London, 1919; reprinted New Delhi, 1987).

TAOIST

Tao Teh Ching (Tao Te Ching, sometimes known as the Lao Tzu or [in the Pinyin Romanization] the Laozi, after its author). Quotations attributed to *Laotzu's Tao and Wu Wei.* Translated by Dwight Goddard (New York, 1919).

JEWISH

Midrash Rabbah, commentary on Genesis (Midrash Rabbah, Genesis). Campbell's source is uncertain. There is a recent translation by Jacob Neusner, *Genesis Rabbah: The Judaic Commentary to the Book of Genesis* (Atlanta: Scholar Press for Brown Judaic Studies, 1985).

Zohar. Quotations from C.G. Ginsburg, *The Kabbalah: Its Doctrines, Development, and Literature* (London, 1920); also from MacGregor Mathers, *Kabbala Denudata, the Kabbalah Unveiled,* which uses a different versification from the standard one.

CHRISTIAN

Bible. The King James version is quoted.

Catholic Daily Missal. Probably *Saint Andrew Daily Missal, by Dom Gaspar Lefebvre O.S.B. of the Abbey of S. André* (Bruges, Belgium: Abbey of St. André; Saint Paul, MN: E.M. Lohmann Co., [1943?]).

Gospel of Pseudo-Matthew. Edition uncertain.

Roman Missal. Edition uncertain.

ISLAMIC

Koran. Quotations match the text of *The Holy Qur-An: Text, Translation and Commentary.* Translated by Abdullah Yusuf Ali (New York, [1946?]).

Works Cited Without Edition

Anthologia Graeca ad Fidem Codices, vol. II.

Apollonios of Rhodes (Apollonius Rhodius). *Argonautika.*

Blake, William. *The Marriage of Heaven and Hell.*

Carlyle, Thomas. *On Heroes, Hero Worship, and the Heroic in History.*

Epiphanius. *Adversus Heareses* (apocryphal Gospel of Eve quoted).

Euripides. *The Bacchae* (translated by Gilbert Murray).

Flaubert, Gustave. *La tentation de Saint Antoine.*

Gesta Romanorum.

Grimm's Fairy Tales. "The Frog King." [Campbell's quotations from this story do not match the text of the 1944 Pantheon edition, nor the older text of the Hunt translation. It is possible that he was translating from a German edition.—R.B.]

Heraclitus (fragments).

Hesiod. *Theogony.*

Irving, Washington. "Rip van Winkle." In *The Sketch Book.*

Jeffers, Robinson. *Cawdor.* Copyright 1928.

Kant, Immanuel. *Critique of Pure Reason.*

Longfellow, Henry Wadsworth. *The Song of Hiawatha.*

Martial. *Epigrams* (Loeb Library edition).

Nietzsche, Friedrich. *Thus Spake Zarathustra.*

Plato. *Symposium.*

Plutarch. "Themistocles."

Rumi. *Mathnawi.*

Shakespeare. *Hamlet.*

Sophocles. *Oedipus Coloneus.*

———. *Oedipus Tyrannus.*

Thomas Aquinas. *Summa Contra Gentiles.*

Thompson, Francis. *The Hound of Heaven.*

Virgil. *Aeneid.*

Voragine, Jacobus de. *The Golden Legend.* No edition is given for this influential medieval compilation of the lives of saints. Campbell owned a 1925 French edition entitled *La légende dorée, traduite du latin par Teodor de Wyzewa* (Paris: Perrin, 1925).

ILLUSTRATION LIST

PAGE xiv FIGURE 1. *Medusa* (carved marble, Roman, Italy, date uncertain). From the Rondanini Palace, Rome. Collection of the Glyptothek, Munich. Photo from H. Brunn and F. Bruckmann, *Denkmäler griechischer und römischer Sculptur*, Verlagsanstalt für Kunst und Wissenschaft, Munich, 1888–1932.

PAGE 3 FIGURE 2. *Viṣṇu Dreaming the Universe* (carved stone, India, c. A.D. 400–700). Dasavatara Temple (Temple of the Ten Avatars). Deogarh, Central India. Archeological Survey of India, courtesy of Mrs. A. K. Coomaraswamy.

PAGE 9 FIGURE 3. *Sileni and Maenads* (black-figure amphora, Hellenic, Sicily, c. 500–450 B.C.). Found in a grave at Gela, Sicily. *Monumenti Antichi, pubblicati per cura della Reale Accademia dei Lincei*, vol. XVII, Milan, 1907, plate XXXVII.

PAGE 14 FIGURE 4. *Minotauromachy* (red-figure krater, Greece, c. 470 B.C.). Here Theseus kills the Minotaur with a short sword; this is the usual version in the vase paintings. In the written accounts, the hero uses his bare hands. *Collection des vases grecs de M. le Comte de Lamberg, expliquée et publiée par Alexandre de la Borde*, Paris, 1813, plate XXX.

PAGE 17 FIGURE 5. *Shintō Fire Ritual* (photograph by Joseph Campbell, Japan, A.D. 1956). [On May 21, 1956, Campbell attended a ritual in Kyoto, Japan, conducted by a group of *Yamabushi* (mountain wizards). For more about this event, see Joseph Campbell, *Sake and Satori: Asian Journals—Japan*, Novato, CA: New World

Library, 2002, pp. 119–126.—Ed.] © Joseph Campbell Foundation (www.jcf.org).

PAGE 22 FIGURE 6. *The Monster Tamer* (inlaid shell and lapis lazuli, Sumerian, Iraq, c. 2650–2400 B.C.). The central figure is probably Gilgamesh. [This is the topmost register from the sounding-box plaque on an ornate lyre, found in the so-called Royal Tombs at Ur by Sir Leonard Woolley.—Ed.] Courtesy of the University of Pennsylvania Museum of Archaeology and Anthropology, Philadelphia.

PAGE 25 FIGURE 7. *Śakyamūni Buddha Beneath the Bodhi Tree* (carved schist, India, c. late ninth–early tenth century A.D.). Bihar, Gaya District. From the Nasli and Alice Heeramaneck Collection. Courtesy of the Los Angeles County Museum of Art.

PAGE 33 FIGURE 8. *Yggdrasil, the World Tree* (etching, Scandinavia, early nineteenth century A.D.). Richard Folkard, *Plant Lore, Legends and Lyrics* (c. 1844), after Finnur Magnusson, "The World Tree of the Edda," *Eddalàeren og dens Oprindelse, book III* (1825).

PAGE 36 FIGURE 9. *Omphalos* (gold phial, Thracian, Bulgaria, fourth–third century B.C.). Part of the so-called Panagyurishte Treasure. Archaeological Museum, Plovdiv, Bulgaria. © Erich Lessing/Art Resource, NY.

PAGE 40 FIGURE 10. *Psyche Entering Cupid's Garden* (oil on canvas, England, A.D. 1903). John William Waterhouse (1849–1917). © Harris Museum and Art Gallery, Preston, Lancashire, UK. The Bridgeman Art Library.

PAGE 43 FIGURE 11. *Apis in the Form of a Bull Transports the Deceased as Osiris to the Underworld* (carved wood, Egypt, c. 700–650 B.C.). From an Egyptian coffin in the British Museum. [In the original edition of this book, Campbell followed Budge in assigning the identity of the bull incorrectly to Osiris. Apis was the son of Hathor and protected the newly deceased on the journey to the afterlife. According to Diana Brown of the University of Edinburgh: "The images at the top symbolize the unification of the Two Lands—the lotus of Upper Egypt and the papyrus of Lower Egypt. The wavy lines at the bottom on which the bull is standing represent water. In ancient Egypt, the sky (Nut) was thought of as a watery expanse. Therefore the Apis bull is carrying the Osiris figure to the sky. The bull is identified with the creative, regenerative force through which the deceased is transfigured into Osiris, a supernatural being."—Ed.] E.A. Wallis Budge, *Osiris and the Egyptian Resurrection*, London: Philip Lee Warner; New York: G.P. Putnam's Sons, 1911, vol. I, p. 13.

INDEX

C

D

E

F

K

L

M

N

O

P

Q

R

S

T

U

V

ABOUT THE AUTHOR

Joseph Campbell was an American author and teacher best known for his work in the field of comparative mythology. He was born in New York City in 1904, and in early childhood became interested in mythology. He loved to read books about American Indian cultures and frequently visited the American Museum of Natural History in New York, where he was fascinated by the museum's collection of totem poles. Campbell was educated at Columbia University, where he specialized in medieval literature and, after earning a master's degree, continued his studies at universities in Paris and Munich. While abroad he was influenced by the art of Pablo Picasso and Henri Matisse, the novels of James Joyce and Thomas Mann, and the psychological studies of Sigmund Freud and Carl Jung. These encounters led to Campbell's theory that all myths and epics are linked in the human psyche, and that they are cultural manifestations of the universal need to explain social, cosmological, and spiritual realities.

After a period in California, where he encountered John Steinbeck and the biologist Ed Ricketts, Campbell taught at the Canterbury School, and then, in 1934, joined the literature department at Sarah Lawrence College, a post he retained for many years. During the 1940s and '50s, he helped Swami Nikhilananda to translate the Upaniṣads and *The Gospel of Sri Ramakrishna.* He also edited works by the German scholar Heinrich Zimmer on Indian art, myths, and philosophy.

In 1944, with Henry Morton Robinson, Campbell published *A Skeleton Key to Finnegans Wake.* His first original work, *The Hero with a Thousand Faces,* came out in 1949 and was immediately well received; in time, it became acclaimed as a classic. In this study of the "myth of the hero," Campbell asserted that there is a single pattern of heroic journey and that all cultures share this essential pattern in their various heroic myths. In his book he also outlined the basic conditions, stages, and results of the archetypal hero's journey.

Joseph Campbell died in 1987. In 1988 a series of television interviews with Bill Moyers, *The Power of Myth,* introduced Campbell's views to millions of people.

ABOUT THE JOSEPH CAMPBELL FOUNDATION

THE JOSEPH CAMPBELL FOUNDATION (JCF) is a nonprofit corporation that continues the work of Joseph Campbell, exploring the fields of mythology and comparative religion. The Foundation is guided by three principal goals:

First, the Foundation preserves, protects, and perpetuates Campbell's pioneering work. This includes cataloging and archiving his works, developing new publications based on his works, directing the sale and distribution of his published works, protecting copyrights to his works, and increasing awareness of his works by making them available in digital formats on JCF's Web site.

Second, the Foundation promotes the study of mythology and comparative religion. This involves implementing and/or supporting diverse mythological education programs, supporting and/or sponsoring events designed to increase public awareness, donating Campbell's archived works (principally to the Joseph Campbell and Marija Gimbutas Archive and Library), and utilizing JCF's Web site as a forum for relevant cross-cultural dialogue.

Third, the Foundation helps individuals enrich their lives by participating in a series of programs, including our global, Internet-based Associates program, our local international network of Mythological Roundtables, and our periodic Joseph Campbell related events and activities.

For more information on Joseph Campbell
and the Joseph Campbell Foundation, contact:

Joseph Campbell Foundation
www.jcf.org
1236 Waverly Place, #14D
New York, NY 10014-6823
info@jcf.org

For further details, contact:
Yogi Impressions LLP
1711, Centre 1, World Trade Centre,
Cuffe Parade, Mumbai 400 005, India.

Fill in the Mailing List form on our website and receive, via email, information on books, authors, events and more.
Visit: www.yogiimpressions.com

Telephone: (022) 22150207, 22155036
E-mail: yogi@yogiimpressions.com

Join us on Facebook:
www.facebook.com/yogiimpressions

Join us on Instagram:
www.instagram.com/yogi_impressions